CREATING AUSTRALIA

200 YEARS OF ART
1788-1988

Australia
1788-1988
arts

PRESENTED
by
THE AUSTRALIAN BICENTENNIAL AUTHORITY

Exhibition managed by International Cultural Corporation of Australia
Limited

Originated for ICCA and The Australian Bicentennial Authority by the
Art Gallery of South Australia

Sponsored by Boral Limited

Supported by Australian Airlines with assistance from the Seven Network

Indemnified by the Australian Government through the Department of
the Arts, Sport, the Environment, Tourism and Territories

CREATING AUSTRALIA

200 YEARS OF ART
1788-1988

by
THE ART GALLERY OF SOUTH AUSTRALIA

edited & introduced by
DANIEL THOMAS

selection co-ordinated by
RON RADFORD

with contributions by

Leigh Astbury, Murray Bail, Nicholas Baume, Tim Bonyhady,
Ian Burn, Roger Butler, Jane Clark, Robert Dixon, Christine Downer,
Mary Eagle, Helen Ennis, Julie Ewington, Renée Free, Anne Gray,
Jocelyn Gray, Grazia Gunn, Richard Haese, Noel Hutchison, Elizabeth Imashev,
Tim Johnson, John Jones, Joan Kerr, Hendrik Kolenberg, Frances Lindsay,
Robert Lindsay, Bettina & Desmond MacAulay, Joanna Mendelssohn,
Felicity St John Moore, Timothy Morrell, Gael Newton, Ian North,
Michael A. O'Ferrall, Barry Pearce, Ron Radford, Christopher Saines,
Linda Slutzkin, Terry Smith, Virginia Spate, John E. Stanton,
Luke Taylor, Daniel Thomas, Judith Thompson,
Margaret K.C. West

International Cultural Corporation of Australia Limited
Art Gallery Board of South Australia

Published on the occasion of *The Great Australian Art Exhibition 1788-1988*, originated by the Art Gallery of South Australia, managed by International Cultural Corporation of Australia and presented by The Australian Bicentennial Authority at: Queensland Art Gallery, Brisbane, 17 May – 17 July 1988; Art Gallery of Western Australia, Perth, 13 August – 25 September 1988; Art Gallery of New South Wales, Sydney, 21 October – 27 November 1988; Tasmanian Museum & Art Gallery, Hobart, 21 December 1988 – 5 February 1989; National Gallery of Victoria, Melbourne, 1 March-30 April 1989; Art Gallery of South Australia, Adelaide, 23 May-16 July 1989.

National Library of Australia Cataloguing-in-Publication data
Creating Australia, 200 years of art 1788-1988

Bibliography.
Includes index.
ISBN 0 642 13433 2
1. Art, Australian. I. Thomas, Daniel, 1931-. II. Radford, Ron, 1949-. III. International Cultural Corporation of Australia. IV. The Australian Bicentennial Authority. V. Art Gallery of South Australia. VI. Great Australian Art Exhibition 1788-1988 (1988-1989).

709'.94

Designed by John Nowland and Christopher Ball of John Nowland Design, Adelaide
Edited by Daniel Thomas
Typeset by Focusgraphics, Adelaide
Separations by Scanagraphix Pty Ltd
Printed by Owen King Printers Australia Pty Ltd, Melbourne

International Cultural Corporation of Australia Limited, P.O. Box N222, Grosvenor Place, The Rocks, Sydney, New South Wales 2000, Australia.
Telephone 02-241 1071

Art Gallery of South Australia, North Terrace, Adelaide, South Australia 5000, Australia.
Telephone 08-223 7200

Reprinted with corrections September 1988

Cover: Charles Conder, *A holiday at Mentone*, 1988 (detail of painting illustrated on p. 117), oil on canvas, Art Gallery of South Australia, Adelaide. State Government funds with assistance of Bond Corporation Holdings Ltd through the Art Gallery of South Australia Foundation to mark the Gallery's Centenary 1981

Collections Represented

Institutions: Alexander Library Building Art Collection, Perth; Allport Library & Museum of Fine Arts, State Library of Tasmania, Hobart; Anthropology Museum, University of Queensland, St Lucia, Brisbane; Art Gallery of New South Wales, Sydney; Art Gallery of South Australia, Adelaide; Art Gallery of Western Australia, Perth; The Australian Museum, Sydney; Australian National Gallery, Canberra; Australian War Memorial, Canberra; Bendigo Art Gallery, Victoria; City of Ballaarat Fine Art Gallery, Ballarat, Victoria; City of Portland, Victoria; Flinders University Art Museum, Bedford Park, Adelaide; La Trobe Collection, State Library of Victoria, Melbourne; Macleay Museum, University of Sydney; Mitchell Library and Dixson Galleries, State Library of New South Wales, Sydney; Monash University Collection, Clayton, Melbourne; Museum of Victoria, Melbourne; Museums & Art Galleries of the Northern Territory, Darwin; National Gallery of Victoria, Melbourne; National Library of Australia, Canberra; National Maritime Museum, Greenwich (on loan from The Admiralty, London); National Museum of Australia, Canberra; National Trust of Australia (New South Wales), Norman Lindsay Museum & Art Gallery, Springwood; Queensland Art Gallery, Brisbane; Royal Geographical Society, London; Royal Society of Victoria, Melbourne; Shepparton Art Gallery, Victoria; South Australian Museum, Adelaide; State Bank Victoria, Melbourne; Tasmanian Museum & Art Gallery, Hobart; University Art Museum, University of Queensland, St Lucia, Brisbane; Waite Institute, University of Adelaide

Private Collections: Mr & Mrs Colin Ballantyne, Alan Bond Collection, Arthur & Yvonne Boyd, Joseph Brown Collection, M.J.M. Carter Collection, Margaret Dodd, David Dridan, Robert Holmes à Court Collection, S.E. Coverdale, Dean Management Services Pty Ltd, James Fairfax Collection, Martin Gascoigne, Mr & Mrs Robin Gibson, William J. Hughes, Alan N. Jennings, Richard Larter, Dr & Mrs Colin Laverty, Ann Lewis, Mr & Mrs Howard Michell, Ian North, Mr & Mrs Lindsay Phillips, Ruth Simon, Clarice Thomas, Imants Tillers, Michael Tuckson, Lyn Williams, Mrs A.O. Worthington Wilmer, and seven lenders who wish to remain anonymous

Advisors to the Exhibition

James Mollison
Director,
Australian National Gallery

Hendrik Kolenberg
Curator of Art,
Tasmanian Museum & Art Gallery

Wally Caruana
Curator of Aboriginal Art,
Australian National Gallery

John Jones
Associate Director,
Deutscher Fine Art

Barry Pearce
Curator of Australian Art,
Art Gallery of New South Wales

Peter Sutton
Head of Anthropology,
South Australian Museum

Gaye Sculthorpe
Curator, Aboriginal Studies,
Museum of Victoria

Helen Ennis
Curator of Photography,
Australian National Gallery

FOREWORDS

The Australian Bicentennial Authority

It seems almost too obvious that one of the blockbuster exhibitions of the Bicentennial Arts program should be a survey of Australian art. Yet this will be the first time that the nation has brought together such a comprehensive range of art, combining well-known works and much-loved icons with unfamiliar works and little-known treasures. More important, The Great Australian Art Exhibition is much more than a large survey show; the distinctive themes developed by Daniel Thomas and his curatorial colleagues have transformed this survey into a powerful and seminal exhibition.

The Great Australian Art Exhibition offers a view of ourselves that is honest and moving as well as being stimulating, provocative and oddly reassuring. The power of the works of art to give an insight into what and who we are offers us a special form of understanding and knowledge of being Australian. It is something only the arts have the power to do.

To Daniel Thomas, Ron Radford and all at the Art Gallery of South Australia, to International Cultural Corporation of Australia, to the Australian National Gallery, the many museums, libraries, other institutions and private lenders, The Australian Bicentennial Authority pays tribute. Without this large number of organisations and individuals the making of the exhibition would not have been possible. Without the willingness of the six State Art Galleries to receive such an unusually large exhibition, the people of Australia would not have the opportunity of seeing their nation's experience embodied in art.

I have no doubt that The Great Australian Art Exhibition will not only be one of the most popular exhibitions ever mounted in Australia and a highlight of the Bicentenary, but also that the rich images and powerful memories we all take from this exhibition will be with us well beyond 1988.

Peter Sarah
Director, Arts & Entertainment, The Australian Bicentennial Authority, Sydney

International Cultural Corporation of Australia

The idea for a major Australian art exhibition was born in 1983 among a large and diverse group of proposals for the Bicentenary year brought together by International Cultural Corporation of Australia and the Council of Australian Art Gallery Directors for The Australian Bicentennial Authority.

The Great Australian Art Exhibition, as it came to be known, was always seen as an indispensable component of a Bicentenary celebration. It has turned out to be a truly great exhibition.

ICCA is proud to manage it, and deeply appreciative of the Australia-wide support it has had in its creation. Curators and scholars from all States have contributed to the debate on how to make this most daunting and ambitious project come to life. We thank them for their help. The State and regional galleries and libraries of Australia, other museums and institutions have lent with unprecedented generosity to this exhibition, as have many private owners. They have helped make this one of the most important exhibitions in our history, and we offer our sincere gratitude to them all. However, special thanks are due to the Australian National Gallery and the National Library of Australia for the special contribution of their loans to the exhibition's long tour.

The Australian Bicentennial Authority has contributed very substantially to the funding of the project, which ICCA is managing on the Authority's behalf. Boral Limited is the generous sponsor of the exhibition.

The Australian Government has indemnified this valuable presentation of our national heritage and ICCA acknowledges with gratitude the hard work and co-operation of the officers of the Department of the Arts, Sport, The Environment, Tourism and Territories who administer the indemnity scheme. It is particularly pleasing that through the active co-operation of all six State Art Galleries as receivers of this exhibition it will, in all probability, be viewed by a larger and wider audience than any previous art exhibition in this country.

For creating an exhibition of such historical sweep and scholarly flair, ICCA pays special tribute to Daniel Thomas, Director of the Art Gallery of South Australia, and his dedicated curatorial, registration, public programmes and administration team.

James B. Leslie, A.O., M.C.
Chairman, International Cultural Corporation of Australia, Sydney

Art Gallery of South Australia

The Art Gallery Board of South Australia was pleased to support this major project for the Australian Bicentenary by making many of its staff available for many months, first for research and development of the exhibition's content, then for conducting loan negotiations, assisting with preparation of objects for tour, providing documentation for the management by International Cultural Corporation of Australia and, finally, for preparing this book which has grown out of the exhibition.

In order to undertake the role of exhibition-producer for ICCA and The Australian Bicentennial Authority, the Art Gallery was provided with a special project team. We have enjoyed having Timothy Morrell, Exhibition Co-ordinator, and Lindsay Brookes, Registration Assistant, as temporary additions to our family for a year. The project manager for most of its span was Christopher Johnstone, the Gallery's then Manager Public Programmes; the Administrator James Schoff and Registrar Judith Hamilton-Shephard also made very substantial contributions.

The Art Gallery of South Australia's Director, Daniel Thomas, was Director of the exhibition and editor of this book and our Curator of Paintings & Sculptures, Ron Radford was the exhibition's Co-ordinating Curator.

Mr Thomas had been Senior Curator of Australian Art at the Australian National Gallery when the project was first proposed as an exhibition to be organized jointly from Canberra and Melbourne. He and Mr Radford were, I believe, an unrivalled team for supervising the curatorial development and artistic integrity of the project and then for persuading owners to lend to the exhibition and writers to contribute to the book.

I would like to think that the view from Adelaide, being somewhat distanced from the larger art-production centres of Melbourne, Sydney and the Northern Territory, is an especially objective and widely-sympathetic view of Australian art.

Heather Bonnin,
Chairman, Art Gallery Board of South Australia, Adelaide

CONTENTS

PREFACE

This is a book based on an exhibition of Australian art, an exhibition which was produced to tour all six Australian States as part of the Australian Bicentennial Authority's arts program for 1988-89. It differs from most previous accounts of Australian art.

First, there is the embrace of many visual-arts media: not only paintings and sculptures but also prints, drawings, photographs, ceramics, silver and furniture. However, the book is not an exact reflection of the exhibition; it includes illustrations of furniture and of some large sculptures which eventually, for reasons of transport costs, could not travel, and it illustrates some paintings and watercolours which, for reasons of fragility, must travel to fewer than all the six capital cities.

A book that was not related to an exhibition could have illustrated certain paintings whose condition was too fragile to tour at all, for example John Russell's friendship portrait of Dr William Moloney. It could have illustrated the visual art forms of film and video, which are not easily incorporated into an exhibition of objects. And it could have illustrated architecture, or monumental painting and sculpture, which are impossible to tour: ancient Aboriginal paintings and engravings on rock-faces in the Northern Territory and elsewhere, a 1930s triumph-of-technology mosaic mural by Napier Waller in Collins Street, Melbourne or futility-of-war statuary by Rayner Hoff in the Anzac Memorial, Sydney are great works of Australian art inevitably omitted from this selection made for a touring exhibition. No touring exhibition can be big enough to represent all aspects of our visual arts. The original selections included more fragile three-dimensional objects, eventually excluded on account of transport costs, and more works which illustrated the development of various art practices, eventually excluded when excessive numbers as well as clarification of the exhibition concept shifted the exhibition from art-history to the Australian experience.

Those works which were selected for the exhibition were all inspected and assessed during Australia-wide fieldwork by the Co-ordinating Curator, Ron Radford. They are all objects whose material presence and physical condition provide no let-down for viewers. That is the second difference between this and other accounts of Australian art. This is a selection of real objects, not of images. (Sometimes book-illustrations or lecture-slides are deceptively flattering.)

A third difference from past accounts is the embrace of many categories of art. Unfortunately, the study and assessment of Australian folk arts and commercial arts have not progressed sufficiently for more than the rather token inclusion of some folk furniture and carvings and a couple of advertising posters. However, there are colonial natural-history drawings and expedition sketches and 1970s/80s protest posters from outside the mainstream of art-market art.

Above all, Australian Aboriginal art is embraced. Since the 1940s, sophisticated art-lovers had appreciated it not as ethnography but as art. Now in the 1980s Aboriginal art is fully incorporated into the wider Australian consciousness as art. Initial planning for this exhibition assumed that separate exhibitions of Aboriginal art would be preferred by the Aboriginal people; only at a very late stage of planning did it become clear that exclusion of Aboriginal art from so broad a survey would be a continuation of art-as-ethnography attitudes. Although it is true that an exhibition of Australian art from 1788 to 1941 which toured north America in the 1940s included a dozen bark-paintings and that, since 1979, surveys of contemporary art have always included Aboriginal art, this is the first attempt to see it within the full continuity of Australian art, in both its traditional forms for Aboriginal people's use and its innovative forms for white collectors. Innovative work includes drawings by William Barak in the nineteenth century for a Melbourne public that had occupied his tribal lands, the toas for a science-minded missionary on the Birdsville Track, Jim Kite's carvings for travellers on the Overland Telegraph, Albert Namatjira's watercolours for mid-twentieth-century tourists to Alice Springs and the paintings first adapted from sand-drawings at Papunya in 1971.

The art of the first hundred years of European colonization has been poorly understood compared with the second hundred years, and this survey draws upon extensive recent research into colonial art; because watercolours and drawings cannot be displayed permanently in museums they remain too little known and in any case are often held in libraries not art museums. They are especially important in early colonial Australia. The strong presence of colonial art is a fourth significant aspect of this account.

Here we should point out that contemporary art in this survey of two hundred years can only be a token representation of the current art scene throughout Australia. No artist who has not had a substantial artistic career established ten years before the Bicentenary is included. We have favoured work by contemporary artists from regions outside Melbourne and Sydney and recent work outside the mainstream.

A fifth point is the Bicentennial Authority's policy concern for recognition of work by women and by artists from non-Anglo-Celtic cultural background. Most art exhibitions in Australia since the mid 1970s have accommodated feminist and 'multi-cultural' concern and so does this one. Women artists have a presence here from the 1830s with Theresa Walker, Martha Berkeley and Mary Morton Allport, the 1880s with Minnie Boyd and Alice Hambidge, and in the twentieth century works by women are numerous: Margaret Preston's, Grace Cossington Smith's and Bea Maddock's works are high points in Australian art. As for non-Anglo artists, the later colonial period is dominated by the work of Germans or Swiss; the twentieth century has an Italian, a Russian, more Germans and central Europeans, Scandinavians, a Latvian and many Aboriginal artists. Many more, including Italian, Greek, Middle Eastern, Chinese and Japanese Australians could have been represented if the art of the 1970s and 1980s had been allowed to overbalance the rest of the two hundred years. The exhibition was originally intended to be complemented in each State Gallery by surveys of contemporary Australian art.

However, it should also be pointed out that this is not a selection intended to characterize what artists have done or are doing in Australia. It is an exhibition not about art practice but about works of art. Peculiarly Australian images have been favoured. It is a Bicentenary exhibition whose purpose is to reclaim our past achievements for the widest possible audience, to show that the past can speak to the present, that it has complete continuity with the present, and that it will shape the future.

Before the 1960s, which saw the first widely accessible book, Bernard Smith's *Australian Painting 1788-1960*, there was scarcely any general awareness of Australian art. All that was well-known was the politically-useful 'national painting', the big pictures by McCubbin, Roberts and Streeton which coincided with the Centenary of 1888 and helped lead to federation of the colonies in 1901.

We now know that a rich and interesting achievement exists from all of the two hundred years, not only from the perhaps over-exposed 1880s. We now know that in the first of those two hundred years when there was little music, drama or literature of significance, it was art more than anything else which interpreted Australia to its people. More than an expression of society — although they are always partly that — works of art are a force which create a people's way of life, of feeling and thinking. Art, we contend, is the principal means by which 'Australia' has been invented and created.

From the first clear-eyed, amazed European observations of some of the 450 species of peculiarly Australian eucalyptus trees, notably that made by John Lewin with the aid of a camera lucida at Governor Bligh's farm on the Hawkesbury before 1810, to the delicate embrace of Aboriginal sensitivities in Tony Tuckson's abstract humanism of the 1960s and 1970s; from the scrutiny by Thomas Bock of Mathinna's specific individuality in 1842 to timeless dreams of inwardness or of otherness like Ian Fairweather's 1950s voyage to Asia or Justin O'Brien's homage to the Mediterranean, we have not only looked hard at nature, not only expressed the social and cultural structures of the day but we have also throughout two hundred years contributed to universal speculations about individual identity and the inner life. Such works of art help create and re-create not only Australia but also the world. Aboriginal works of art had always done just that for Aboriginal Australia and now they also do it for the world.

We hope this large exhibition and its book will do more than reclaim and reveal to a wide public the past two hundred years from the thousands of years of humankind's experience of a particular place which from 1817 was named Australia. We hope to demonstrate the power of works of art to shape us and our future.

Daniel Thomas

TRADITIONAL ABORIGINAL ART by DANIEL THOMAS

In the 1980s it has become a commonplace to say that Ubirr Rock is Australia's Parthenon. That is because Ubirr, being an accessible gallery of Aboriginal paintings on sheltered rock-faces in Kakadu National Park, an easy drive from Darwin, is the most likely of such sites to have been visited. Many other visually spectacular galleries of rock-paintings and rock-engravings throughout Australia may be of equal importance but are less easily reached by tourists. Nevertheless Ubirr, an outlier of the Arnhem Land escarpment on the East Alligator River near Oenpelli, can stand very well as an introduction to traditional Aboriginal art. The oldest paintings there may be 20,000 years old. Rock-engravings at Olary, South Australia, recently established by Margaret Nobbs and Ronald Dorn as being at least 32,000 years old, are among the most ancient works of art in human history and also relate to Central Australia's present-day paintings in acrylic on canvas. The most recent known paintings on rock in the Kakadu area were made in the 1960s, but the tradition continues strongly in paintings on eucalyptus bark.

These paintings on rock or bark, together with ceremonial songs and dances, embody the Aboriginal people's knowledge of their place in the world: stories of the creation of the land and the seasons, or of their relationships with nature and with each other. The paintings were made, and maintained, both to get what was needed from the Ancestral Beings and to pass on essential knowledge to future generations. They were not made as commodities for art-collectors' private houses or art museums throughout the world. They were made for their own people's very immediate social and religious purposes: they were made to maintain social life, and to push their world into the future. They are instruments of power and are most prized aesthetically if the images shimmer and glitter with a radiance of cross-hatching or dotting to match the shimmer of serpent-skin, of water, or of rainbows.

Rock-paintings and rock-engravings cannot be collected, let alone toured in art exhibitions. Monumental art is not portable. So Aboriginal decorative arts were collected before paintings and sculptures were available; that is, daily-use portable objects of fine craftsmanship and design; baskets, feather necklaces and shell necklaces made by women, shields and weapons made by men. Secret-sacred objects, rangga and tjurunga, a more contentious issue, were also collected as they were portable but they can no longer be publicly displayed in museums. In 1802 Captain Matthew Flinders, on North Island in the Sir Edward Pellew Group in the Gulf of Carpentaria off the McArthur River, observed with interest the painted and feather-decorated stones used in a totemic ceremony. They are depicted by the expedition artist William Westall in a painting on page 33.

Monumental arts seem to have been admired since Sir George Grey saw Wandjina paintings in 1838 in the west Kimberley region of Western Australia. A few portable paintings on bark, collected as ethnographic curiosities in the 1870s at Port Essington, not far from Ubirr and Oenpelli, included the *Lizard* which begins this picture survey. Then in 1912-13 an anthropologist, Baldwin Spencer, who had already collected McArthur River feathercraft in 1901-02 and who was also an art-collector (of works by Arthur Streeton and similar painters), collected for the Museum of Victoria in Melbourne fifty bark-paintings and clearly positioned them within the fine arts: "I commissioned two or three of the best artists to paint me a series of canvases, or rather 'barks' . . . the natives themselves very clearly distinguished between the ability of different artists. . . [These] first-rate examples of first-rate artists . . . were originally purchased in the Kakadu studios of Oenpelli." Is a commissioned work, made for a collector, of ethnography or of art, any longer a 'traditional' work? Not quite (as ethnography) and not really (as art).

Nevertheless, although categorizations are never perfect they are not entirely arbitrary, and the more than three hundred images in this book must be ordered somehow. So we have introduced Australian art with works by Aboriginal artists made in 'traditional' materials that were current, and made for uses that were current before European colonization. Even though Declan Apuatimi's sculpture was made for sale on the art market, it is made with the same materials and contains the same spirituality that resides in a pukamani burial-ceremony pole. On the other hand, recent art-market paintings from the Central Australian deserts, in the 'non-traditional' materials of acrylic paint on canvas, are placed elsewhere (with the visually similar twentieth-century art) despite the fact that their makers regard them as just as effective for maintaining the Dreaming as a 'traditional' drawing in the sand.

There are variations in attitude. Dr Stanton's essay on Charlie Numblar's Wandjina painting tells us that it, being a portable object made for sale, is only a depiction of a Wandjina spirit whereas a similar painting on a rock-face would *be* a Wandjina.

It should be clear enough from the illustrations and the essays that a great and ancient tradition of non-collectable art has in the past century entered the peculiar world of art-collecting. Its often extreme delicacy and refinement of technique, its crisp drawing, its subtle overlays, offer parallels with the delicate balance maintained by Australian Aboriginal people with Australian nature. Its human subject-matter is as rich and complex as the mythology and the metamorphoses of ancient Greece; it tells us about sex, politics, religion and nature.

Most important, Australian Aboriginal art, admired by the Euro-Australian art world as art throughout most of the twentieth century, is in the 1980s a very conspicuous reason for the white community's new respect for Aboriginal culture generally. The Aboriginal people are re-conquering the minds of their invaders, as the Greeks re-conquered the ancient Romans.

Port Essington, Cobourg Peninsula, Northern Territory. *Lizard*. Collected 1878. Ochres on eucalyptus bark, 28 x 109 cm.
Macleay Museum, University of Sydney

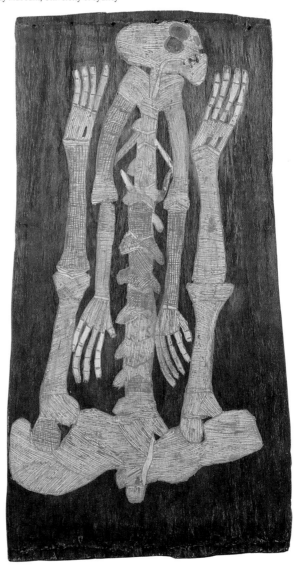

East Alligator River, Western Arnhem Land,
Northern Territory. *Spirit being called Yungwalia*.
Collected 1913. Ochres on eucalyptus bark,
126 x 37 cm. Museum of Victoria, Melbourne.
Gift of Professor W.B. Spencer, 1913
The fan-like object carried in one hand is a bunch
of feathers used in dancing, the club in the other
hand is for defence against hostile spirits from
other regions

Lofty NABARDAYAL NADJAMERREK, born 1926.
Dead man. c1968, Mann River Plateau, Western
Arnhem Land, Northern Territory. Ochres on euca-
lyptus bark, 59.7 x 28.4 cm. Art Gallery of South
Australia, Adelaide. State Government funds 1969
Although this position corresponds with the dispo-
sition of a corpse for burial, living people may be
depicted in the same posture

Melville Island, Northern Territory. *Grave post.* c1909. Ochres on wood, 231 x 19 cm. South Australian Museum, Adelaide. Gift of Mr Justice Herbert 1909

Melville Island, Northern Territory. *Grave post.* c1954, Ochres on wood, 223 x 28 cm. South Australian Museum, Adelaide. Collected for the Museum by Charles P. Mountford 1954

Melville Island, Northern Territory. *Grave post.* c1954, Ochres on wood, 231 x 22 cm. South Australian Museum, Adelaide. Collected for the Museum by Charles P. Mountford 1954

These posts are part of the elaborate *pukamani* funerary rituals on Bathurst and Melville islands.
They are erected over graves as gifts to please the dead. The carved and painted forms are symbolic of
a complex variety of people, landforms, animals, fish and objects

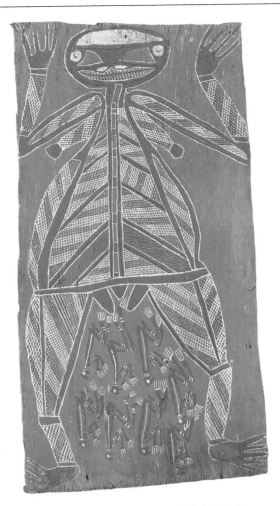

YIRAWALA, 1903-1976. *Maralaitj*. c1965, Croker Island,
Northern Territory. Ochres on eucalyptus bark, 62 x 31 cm.
Australian National Gallery, Canberra. Federal Government
funds 1976
This painting shows the creator ancestress Maralaitj giving
birth to the Northern tribes

MINIMINI MAMARIKA, 1904-1972. *The Malay prau*. c1948, Groote Eylandt, Northern Territory. Ochres on eucalyptus bark,
38 x 82.5 cm. Art Gallery of South Australia, Adelaide. Gift of Charles P. Mountford 1960
From the 17th century the Northern Territory was visited by Malay fishermen who came to catch and process *beche de mer*

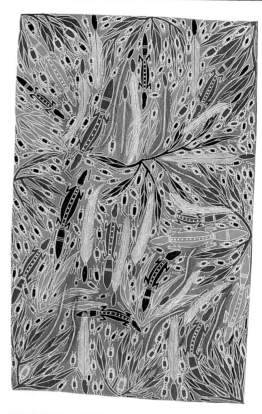

Robin NGANJMIRA, born 1951. *Brolga dance*. 1984, Oenpelli, Western Arnhem Land, Northern Territory. Ochres on eucalyptus bark, 77.5 x 51 cm. Australian National Gallery, Canberra. Founding Donors' Fund 1984
The painting depicts brolgas in the so-called "X-ray style", Mimi spirits, dilly bags, spears, spear-throwers and a butchered goanna. It probably refers to the ceremonial re-enactment of a hunt.

WANIMILIL, born 1949. *Mother totems*. c1981, Mulgurram, Central Arnhem Land, Northern Territory. Ochres on eucalyptus bark, 126 x 78 cm. Museums & Art Galleries of the Northern Territory, Darwin. Territory Government funds 1982

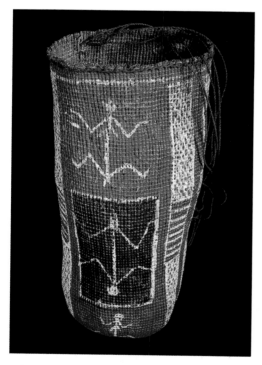

Gagadju group. *Basket*. c1912, Alligator Rivers area, Northern Territory. Ochre and clay on woven plant fibre, 30.5 cm. Museum of Victoria, Melbourne. Collected and presented by Professor W.B. Spencer 1912

Mara tribe. *Necklet of parrot feathers*. c1900, McArthur River, Northern Territory. Feathers of Trichoglossus sp., hair string; feathered segment 28.5 cm long. Museum of Victoria, Melbourne. Collected and presented by Spencer-Gillen Expedition 1901-2

Bob BALIR BALIR DIRDI, 1905-1977. *Mimi spirits*. c1968, Marrkolidjban, Western Arnhem Land, Northern Territory. Ochres on
eucalyptus bark, 82.5 x 48 cm. Art Gallery of South Australia,
Adelaide. State Government funds 1969
Mimis are the spindly, mischievous spirits who are believed to
have taught painting to the people of Western Arnhem Land.

Peter MARRALWANGA (DJAKKU), 1916-1987. *Daluk (spirit
woman)*. 1982, Marrkolidjban, Western Arnhem Land, Northern
Territory. Ochres on eucalyptus bark, 120 x 60 cm. The Robert
Holmes à Court Collection
A spirit woman from Kabolkdaykerreh on the floodplain of the
Tomkinson River. This site has a major dreaming significance for
the artist's mother's clan, Nakurulk.

George MILPURRURRU, born 1934. *The goose egg hunt*. 1983,
Mulgurram, Central Arnhem Land, Northern Territory. Ochres on
eucalyptus bark, 108.5 x 53 cm. Australian National Gallery,
Canberra. Federal Government funds 1984
The eggs of the magpie goose are a traditional food, gathered
from nests on the edges of the Arafura Swamp.

WAKUTHI MARAWILI, born 1921. *Crocodile and dog*. 1984,
North-east Arnhem Land, Northern Territory. Ochres on euca-
lyptus bark, 101.5 x 45 cm. Australian National Gallery, Canberra.
Founding Donors' Fund 1984
The ancestral crocodile Baru chases a dog across a river.
Diamond-shaped clan patterns were burned into Baru's back in
a legendary fire.

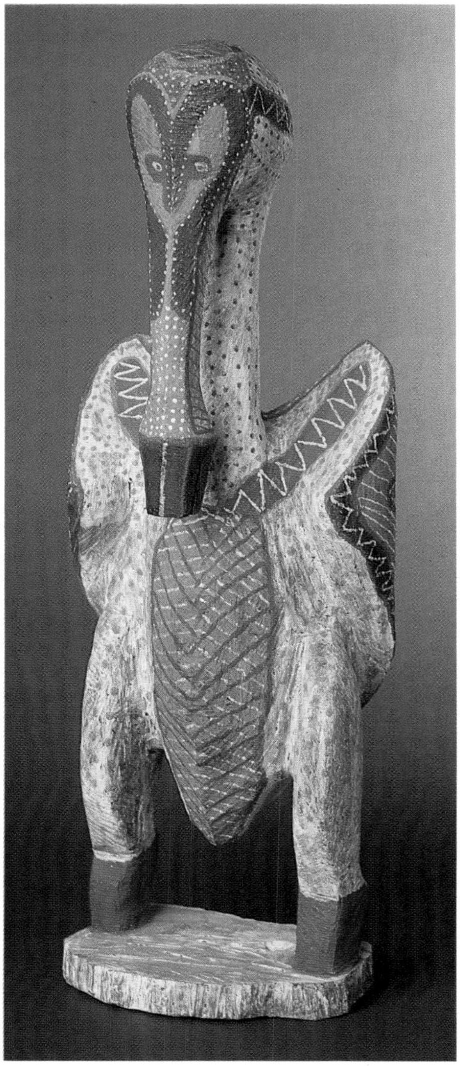

JUDE, *Pelican*. c1968, Bathurst Island, Northern Territory. Painted wood, 51.5 cm height. Art Gallery of South Australia, Adelaide. State Government funds 1968

Charlie RURRKULA, born c1935. *Narryan and Boloko* [Two snakes]. c1985, Korlobirrahola, Northern Territory. Ochres on wood, 216 x 27 cm. National Museum of Australia, Canberra. Federal Government funds 1985

Aurukun, North Queensland. *Crocodile*. 1958. Ochres on wood, 200 x 60 x 40 cm. Anthropology Museum, University of Queensland. Gift of the Rev. William MacKenzie 1958
Totemic representation used in Arplitch dance

Aurukun, North Queensland. *Echidna*. Collected 1962. Ochres on wood, 44.5 x 19.7 x 17.3 cm. National
Museum of Australia, Canberra. Transferred from the Australian Institute for Aboriginal Studies 1985
Made to be used in the ceremonial Echidna dance, in which the echidna dies after abducting the wife of
the ancestral Taipan, demonstrating the consequences of breaking marriage laws

North-east Queensland. *Bicornual basket*. c1870s/1880s. Red ochre on lawyer cane, 28 x 34 cm.
Museum of Victoria, Melbourne. Registered in the Museum Collection 1888
Probably brightly painted originally; made by a man, but used by a woman for gathering vegetable food

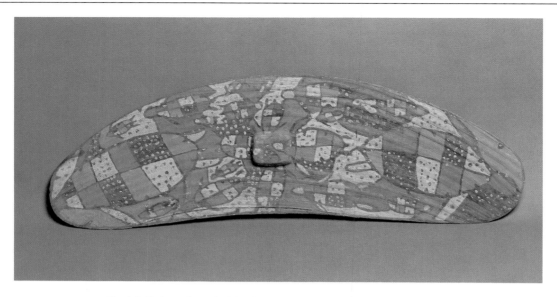

Yarrabah, North-east Queensland. *Rainforest shield*. c1938. Ochres on wood, 117 x 36 x 7 cm.
South Australian Museum, Adelaide. Gift of Miss U.H. McConnel 1953

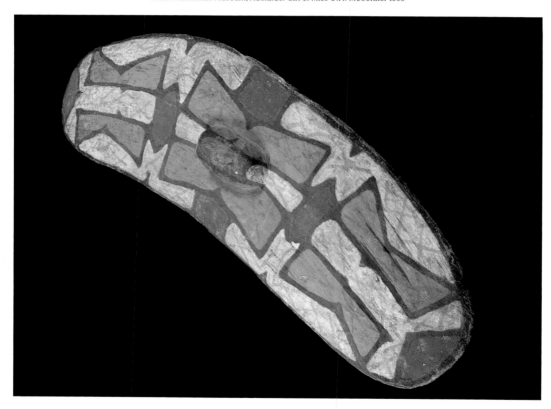

North-east Queensland. *Rainforest shield*. c1940. Ochres on wood, 97.5 x 28.5 cm. Museum of Victoria,
Melbourne. Gift of Mrs M. McKay 1942

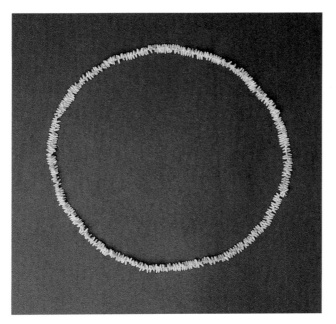

TRUCANINI, 1812?-1876. *Necklace*. c1860s/1870s, Tasmania. "Rishells" *(Acmaea Marginata)*, 60 cm circumference. South Australian Museum, Adelaide. Gift of Mrs W.A. Norman 1928

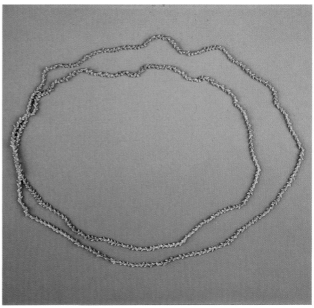

Tasmania. *Necklace*. Early 20th century, Bass Strait Islands. "Marriner" shells *(Phasianotrochus irisodontes)*, 182 cm total length. Tasmanian Museum & Art Gallery, Hobart. Unknown donor early 20th century

Fanny Cochrane SMITH, 1834-1905. *Basket*. Late 19th century, Tasmania. Plant fibre, probably Juncus, 13 cm diameter. Museum of Victoria, Melbourne. State Government funds 1952

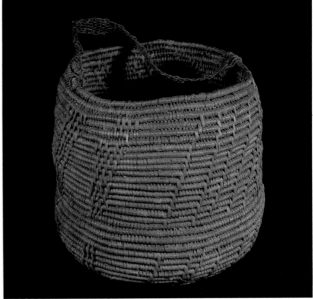

Lower Murray River, South Australia. *Coil basket*. c1870s/1880s. Plant fibres, 42 x 23 cm. Museum of Victoria, Melbourne. Registered in the Museum Collection 1888

Goulburn River, Victoria. *Broad shield*. c1900. Pipeclay, red ochre on wood, 103 x 27.8 cm. Museum of Victoria, Melbourne. Gift of A.C. LeSouef 1900

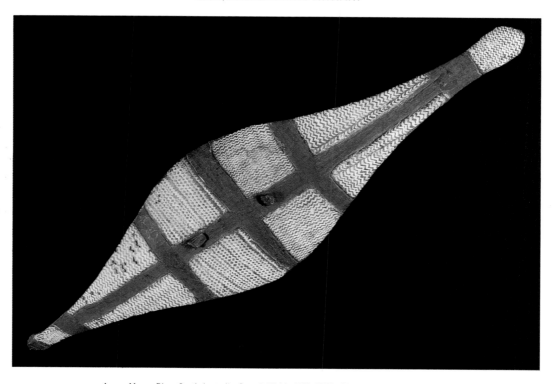

Lower Murray River, South Australia. *Broad shield*. c1870s/1880s. Pipeclay, red ochre on wood, 92.5 x 22.5 cm. Museum of Victoria, Melbourne. Registered in the Museum Collection 1888

Western Australia. *Pendant*. 1930s, collected on Sunday Island, WA. Pearl shell, ochre, human hair, 20 x 15.5 cm. South Australian Museum, Adelaide. Collected for the Museum by Charles P. Mountford, accessioned 1939 Pearl-shell pendants, rubbed with ochre to heighten the incised design, are precious ornaments which were used in trade. They were made to be suspended from a belt or from the neck on ceremonial or ritual occasions

Western Australia. *Broad shield*. Ochres on wood, 98 x 19.5 cm x 6.5 cm. South Australian Museum, Adelaide. State Government funds 1958

MONSOON by MICHAEL A. O'FERRALL

Mawalan Marika, *The Wawelag Sisters and Yulungurr the Rainbow Serpent,* 1959

The subject of this painting relates to one of the major ceremonial cycles of Arnhem Land. The imagery is drawn from the main characters of the several song cycles that deal with the travels of the Wawelag Sisters who, as two Ancestral Beings, travelled through the region creating sacred ceremonies and objects and naming places, plants and animals.

The mighty Rainbow Serpent Yulungurr is equally central to the painting's imagery and underlying theme. The physical powers of the northern monsoon rainy season in both its destructive and regenerative aspects are embodied in a cosmic idiom of the balance of life and death. The Rainbow Serpent as manifest in Yulungurr represents the tangible essence of these unseen forces, replete with all the additional oracular symbolism of sexuality, changeability and transformation.

Participation and management of the revelatory ceremonies focussing on Yulungurr and the Wawelag Sisters is shared by all Dhuwa moiety people in Arnhem Land. (Moiety means half, and is a semi-specialist term for a major social and spiritual division recognized by Arnhem Land Aborigines. People from the other moiety are known as Yirritja.) The rights to the related songs and dances, and to paintings, are shared between all the Dhuwa groups. Each landholding extended family owns special rights and relationships to sections of the cycles as they relate to its territory.

The main images in the painting depict a telescoped narrative of the final dramatic events described in the songs, culminating in the swallowing of the two sisters and their two children by the mighty Rainbow Serpent. The two sisters are shown at the top, dancing in a vain attempt to deter Yulungurr who has arisen from the sacred water-hole Mirraminna. His anger causes high winds and torrential rain to fall, depicted in the dotted lower-central panel. The left-hand snake represents one of the sisters already swallowed, whereas the right-hand snake, as a companion Ancestral Being, has eaten a fish, symbol of rebirth. Specific clans' cross-hatched designs surround the figures as formal idiomatic references to overflowing streams and rivers.

The importance of the painting's subject and the boldness of iconic representation denote the senior status of the artist who was for many years the leader of the Rirratjingu linguistic group in the Yirrkala region of north-east Arnhem Land. This painting, and many others by him in art museums and anthropology museums, was made at a particularly critical time when Aboriginal art began to emerge from its hitherto ethnographic cocoon. In the late 1950s and the 1960s several major exhibitions of Arnhem Land art resulted in a re-positioning of the works into an equivalent if uneasy rank with other Australian art practices and forms.[1]

The changing post-war economic conditions on mission settlements also saw organized efforts to build the production of Aboriginal art and crafts into commercially viable enterprises.[2] As custodians and practitioners of a hitherto largely secret-sacred art, Arnhem Land artists responded to the increased sympathetic interest and the financial opportunities, with both traditional and innovatory strategies. Traditional subjects and stylistic features were maintained but were often modified in individually re-interpreted imagery and compositions.

As an active participant in this widening process, the artist Mawalan not only provided an authoritative direction for future generations of artists at Yirrkala but also contributed many creative and innovative elements in the breadth of his work. His art is consciously designed to communicate the essence of his culture's traditions as he drew on the rich ceremonial and poetic base of his background. In his paintings he also strove to present these traditions in a contemporary and open form, acceptable to both Arnhem Land Aborigines and non-Aboriginal interpretation and understanding.

Relatively small by late-1980s Arnhem Land standards, Mawalan's paintings are a distillation of extensive painterly experience gained though initiation and practice, coupled with a closely observed living experience gained from his rich environment. The magic of this experience is evoked through the icon-like barks which he painted. The strength of his beliefs emanates with an authoritative tone from the same timeless dimension from which Yulungurr still speaks every wet season and sustains the people during the subsequent dry period.

MAWALAN MARIKA, 1908-1967. *The Wawelag Sisters and Yulungurr the Rainbow Serpent*. 1959, Yirrkala, North-east Arnhem Land, Northern Territory. Ochres on eucalyptus bark, 48 x 26 cm. Art Gallery of Western Australia, Perth. State Government funds 1959

FROM THE SKY, FOR THE LAND, TO THE ROCK by JOHN E. STANTON

Charlie Numblar, *Wandjina spirit*, c1973

The Wandjina art tradition dominates much of the west Kimberley region of Western Australia. This distinctive and relatively well-known style has always been directly associated with a living cultural tradition of rock art, where the cloud-like figures of mythological beings of the Dreaming are associated with fertility and the monsoonal rains.

Although this example is a more modern image on a sheet of bark, the design was traditionally applied in ochre to the walls of caves and other sheltered rock-faces, responsibility for maintaining each Wandjina painting residing with the ritual custodians of each particular site. According to local Aboriginal religious beliefs, each of these designs is a tangible manifestation of a specific mythological being; the large eyes, head-dress and neck-pendant (sometimes regarded as a breast bone) define the principal features of this design. Wandjina figures in general lack mouths, although one appears on this example. Many myths recall the activities of the Wandjina, who came out of the sky to live on the land; fishing, hunting and carrying out other activities similar to those subsequently practised by the Aboriginal inhabitants of the area. Although myths indicate that Wandjina were socially disruptive in some contexts, they also established a clear pattern for human activity. At one time, it is said, many Wandjina collaborated to fight against Aboriginal groups, whereas in other instances Wandjina were held responsible for bringing the thunder-head clouds of the monsoon, and controlled the fertility of the land and its occupants. It was only when the Wandjina had completed their time living on earth that they 'made themselves' into the land, leaving their images on the surfaces of the rock.

These sacred images were the responsibility of local Aboriginal groups, who regularly performed rituals beside the rock faces. These activities referred to the events of the mythic period of the Dreaming and from time to time the original image of the Wandjina was retouched or even repainted.[1] Continuing religious activity provided the context in which direct spiritual links were maintained between the living present and the eternal presence of the Dreaming. In return for this consideration and care, Wandjina would control the fertility of the land and its people, ensuring the regular arrival of the monsoons, sending out life-spirits for the newborn, and lending good fortune in everyday hunting and fishing activities.[2]

More recently, external influences have encouraged the spread of techniques for painting Wandjina-like figures on panels of bark — or sometimes even more alien media such as cardboard or Masonite composition board. Such figures are not Wandjina themselves, since Wandjina belong only to the specific place where he or she metamorphosed himself or herself. Rather, such bark paintings are *representations* of particular (or, more frequently, generalized) Wandjina and are essentially a response to external influences, both Aboriginal and non-Aboriginal. This piece is one such example.

The idea of painting Wandjina figures on bark appears to have emerged by the early 1930s, possibly as a result of Aboriginal trading links with mission stations further along the northern coastline. Although the market for bark-paintings developed at Port Keats (in the Northern Territory, immediately to the east of the Kimberley) only in the early 1950s, knowledge of this technique would have been present much earlier and was probably sustained through intermittent contact with people from Bathurst and Melville Islands and western Arnhem Land. These are all areas where a well-established bark-painting tradition could have influenced the cultural traditions of the Kimberley, despite the distance involved, since items such as carrying-containers and spear-throwers were already being decorated with designs primarily associated with water and fertility. Early paintings on bark sheets would have had little utility in the local setting; that is, other than as a response to external demands for such pieces.

Interest in the Wandjina tradition is well-established. George Grey's 1838 records of the art of the region created a great deal of controversy (published 1841),[3] and sporadic collecting of ethnographic materials continued until the 1930s, when a number of outstanding paintings on bark were obtained at Kunmunya Mission.[4] These were subsequently donated to the Western Australian Museum. In 1937 the Frobenius Institute at Frankfurt sponsored the first large-scale exploratory ethnological expedition to the Kimberley. H. Petri illustrated a Wandjina painting on bark[5] and obtained several more remarkable examples; other collectors followed suit.

The external influences which stimulated this development failed to contribute the technological expertise required for the production and long-term survival of the painted bark. Whereas Arnhem Land artists commonly used the juice of an orchid bulb to stabilize the ochres on the carefully prepared surface, this knowledge was lacking in the Kimberley. The bark was peeled from a different species of eucalypt and the flattening and treatment of the material was frequently inadequate: most earlier bark-paintings from the region have suffered substantial loss of surface pigments through lack of adhesion, and in some cases flaking has been accelerated as the bark dried and the sheet gradually resumed its former curvature.

Such problems have been largely circumvented in the modern period through the use of smaller pieces of bark (which are less susceptible to curling) and the use of commercial adhesives to stabilize the ochre pigments. The market for tourist arts and crafts has had a significant impact on the production of Wandjina images on bark, and in particular has created a demand for smaller paintings which are more easily transported. This has also encouraged the use of alternative media; for example, canvas and art board. In the interest of a perceived authenticity, stone slabs have also been painted for sale to collectors; these 'genuine' pieces have created little interest however, due to their weight and bulk.

The Wandjina has been 'borrowed' by commercial and arts organizations as a readily-recognized Western Australian symbol. Kimberley Aboriginal groups closely identified with this particular mythic constellation have not always approved of such an appropriation — if, indeed, they have been given an opportunity to comment. Although the superficial conjectures of science-fiction writers have added nothing to a greater public appreciation of this art style, such writings have engendered a

Charlie NUMBLAR, working 1970s. *Wandjina spirit*. c1973, Kimberley region, Western Australia. Ochres
on eucalyptus bark, 57.5 x 37.2 cm. Art Gallery of South Australia, Adelaide. State Government funds 1974

sense of familiarity with the image for members of the wider Australian community.

That this painting has been included in this survey of Australian art serves to remind the viewer of the profound religious basis for the world-view held by the First Australians; a perspective that has provided an enduring sense of continuity for people and place, and yet at the same time has been highly adaptive to the changing physical and social environment in which many Kimberley groups have found themselves.

Today these images may have a meaning rather different from that with which they were previously ascribed. Nevertheless, alien European images have long been present in conjunction with examples of Wandjina art, perhaps as early as the eighteenth century[6], and amply demonstrate the incorporative and experimental attributes of much Aboriginal Australian art.

From a cross-cultural perspective, then, some understanding of the socio-cultural context in which diverse art forms are produced and utilized is crucial in coming to some appreciation of the works of art themselves. This is just one such example; a demonstration that the production of commercial art has much to do with the assertion of a cultural identity that is constantly in the process of revision — as much as it has to do with the refinement of artistic and entrepreneurial skills relevant to the changing social order.

POLE PEOPLE by MARGARET K.C. WEST

Declan Apuatimi, *Male figure*, c1973

Declan Apuatimi was one of a new wave of Aboriginal artists who began to experiment with new forms of expression when the opportunity to do so was presented by a receptive European audience. After years of mission attitudes and assimilation policies, which were not always sympathetic to the pursuit of traditional practices, the growing appreciation of Aboriginal art among non-Aboriginal Australians was greeted with delight and often surprise by the artists. So when the Tiwi people's art and craft industry was formally established by the Aboriginal Arts Board of the Australia Council in 1972 at Nguiu, the one-time Catholic Mission on Bathurst Island, it gave artists like Declan the opportunity to pursue a more genial and traditionally-oriented way of making a living. Declan was middle-aged when his artistic career began to blossom; within a decade he became the best-known carver on his island and the first to be given a one-man touring exhibition.

One of the interesting aspects of Tiwi society on Bathurst and Melville Islands is the continual striving by the men to achieve power and status. In the past, an important man was one who could attract many wives. Since polygamy was abolished by the church, one of the remaining vehicles for obtaining status was through the arts. Here a man could achieve high prestige by being an exceptional songman, dancer or artist. Declan Apuatimi was considered by his countrymen and women to be such a man — someone who was gifted at all aspects of ceremonial performance which constitute the domain that we call the arts.

Declan could make a wide range of things, from delicately-woven armbands to bark canoes. However it was carving with wood in which he excelled. Usually he carved in ironwood which, true to its name, is a most difficult medium to penetrate with a bladed tool. It did however give a certain quality to Tiwi carving, a robustness and vitality often lacking in the more easily carved and surface-finished softwoods.

Declan, like other Tiwi, carved in a particular style that has cultural roots going back generations. However, his way of carving was highly personal and easily distinguishable from the work of other Tiwi carvers. Occasionally he carved birds, crocodiles and turtles, but it was figures that he preferred to make. The small figure-carving illustrated here is typical of his style and belongs to the period in the early 1970s when Declan began to produce carvings regularly. It is an interesting example of his formative period and shows that he had established already a mature new style of carving which remained consistent throughout the remainder of his life.

According to mood and available materials, Declan carved both large and small figures but, regardless of size, all his carvings, as this one illustrates, have a power which derives partly from his minimalizing technique, in which he delineates only the face and the base of the torso — teasing out only the essential features, which remain an elemental part of the wooden trunk. By way of contrast, the solidity of the figure is lightened by the lively decoration of white dots and panels of lines and hatching — decorations derived from those painted onto burial poles. The addition of the black cockatoo-feather top-knot, a typical Declan touch, also conforms to the head decoration worn during burial ceremonies. These decorations affiliate this carved figure with the culture hero Purukuparli, who long ago taught the Tiwi how to perform their burial ceremonies.

Here Declan, like other Aboriginal artists, has drawn for his inspiration upon the mythology of the creation era or the Dreaming. The Purukuparli story, concerning the mortality of man, is one of the most important myths as it provides the focus for the Tiwi's most important ceremony, the burial or pukamani ritual. It is during this ritual that the most elaborate body-decorations are worn, together with a variety of body-ornaments, to disguise the wearer from the deceased's ghost and thus to help it on its way to the land of the dead. Beautifully painted bark baskets and ceremonial barbed spears are also prepared. However the major works are the burial poles, carved in a variety of shapes and intricately painted with ochre patterns, which are erected around the deceased's grave at the completion of the ritual. These poles were the major form of carving that all Tiwi, such as Declan, began to learn during their initiation years and would be called upon to make from time to time throughout their adult lives.

The carving of figures or more naturalistic representations began in a limited way on Bathurst and Melville Islands in the pre-war 1930s, as a logical development of the embellishment of traditional burial poles which, although abstracted in shape, were themselves regarded as people, either ancestral beings like Purukuparli, or as representations of the deceased. This morphological analogy of poles with people was developed in the post-war period by artists such as Declan who liked to experiment with new forms and ideas while still conforming to the general principles of their artistic system.

This subtle mix of innovation and tradition, which is found in most late-twentieth-century Aboriginal art from the Northern Territory, vividly illustrates the ability of these cultures to absorb influences while maintaining their essential character. Appreciation of the vitality of Aboriginal art and its role in the Aboriginal people's contemporary world has been slow to evolve, due to conservative attitudes which preferred no changes to what was viewed as an enduring and unchanging tradition. After many years when such innovations were regarded with suspicion by an anthropology-minded market, modern Aboriginal works of art like Declan's sculptures are now accepted as mature cultural expressions of a people whose artists grow, develop, invent and experiment, just like artists from any other society. Such works of art are also considered by their makers to be important markers of their cultural identity and a medium which communicates something of their uniqueness to the outside world.

Declan APUATIMI, c1920-1985. *Male figure*. c1973, Nguiu, Bathurst Island, Northern Territory. Ochres on ironwood, cockatoo feathers, 39 x 11 cm. Art Gallery of South Australia, Adelaide. State Government funds 1974

NGALYOD, CREATOR OF THE COUNTRY by LUKE TAYLOR

Peter Marralwanga, *Ngalyod the Rainbow Serpent,* 1983

Peter Marralwanga was an Aboriginal artist who worked at his small family camp at Marrkolidjban between Oenpelli and Maningrida in western Arnhem Land.[1] The landscape of this region is now well-known for the spectacular ancient paintings in the caves of the Arnhem Land escarpment, some of which are accessible to visitors to Kakadu National Park. The people of the region are, in the 1980s, creating paintings which match or surpass the achievements of those earlier artists. Western Arnhem Land is home to one of the most profoundly spiritual arts being produced in Australia today.

Ngalyod the Rainbow Serpent is an Ancestral Being which the local people sometimes call the Rainbow or sometimes the Rainbow Snake. In this bark-painting Marralwanga depicts Ngalyod as a massive serpent-like figure with a crocodile's head and teeth. The figure wears a ceremonial feather headdress called *djaradjalina* and has fronds of a fern called *mankobin* (Dyrnaria quercifolia) attached to his back. The inclusion of ferns as part of the creature's body refers to features at a specific sacred site called Dilebang. At that site the ferns grow in profusion near a spring at the base of a tall rock pillar. The ferns are said to be attached to Ngalyod who lies under the ground at the site. In *Ngalyod the Rainbow Serpent*, Peter Marralwanga has given visible form to a figure of deep religious significance to Aboriginal people from western Arnhem Land. Ngalyod[2] is believed to be the creator of the western Arnhem Land landscape. Ngalyod maintains the cycle of the seasons, and is involved in all the major transformative stages of the contemporary human life-cycle, from birth, through ceremonial initiation and finally death which involves the journey of the human soul.

The style of representation in Marralwanga's painting is typical of western Arnhem Land art. This style is usually characterized by the way artists concentrate on capturing minute details of a particular species, either in the general proportions suggested by the outline shape of the figures or by emphasizing distinctive body-features which identify the species. For example, in relation to fish, the artist will be careful to show the correct fin position, or fin shape, of the species.

This painting of the Ancestral Being Ngalyod shows the figure as an amalgam of a number of distinct species. Western Arnhem Land artists represent the transformational potential of mythical figures in this way. Such figures possess the power to transform themselves into alternative manifestations in the natural world. Some of the primary manifestations of Ngalyod are the King Brown snake and the estuarine crocodile. In paintings of ordinary crocodiles, western Arnhem Land artists will show the broad snout and large teeth of the estuarine crocodile to differentiate it from the freshwater crocodile which has a long thin snout with many smaller teeth. Marralwanga has shown Ngalyod with the short snout and large teeth of the larger estuarine species. Paintings which combine numerous species within one figure provide a means of representing the very complex conceptual qualities of the Ancestral Beings in a directly perceivable form. Western Arnhem Land people gradually come to learn how diverse physical entities in their world are linked on the basis of the actions of the Ancestral Beings during the creation period. Artists such as

Marralwanga have a primary role in interpreting what they know of the Ancestral Beings and their paintings become a primary means by which such knowledge and insight about the spiritual world is transmitted to the younger generation.

The figure of Ngalyod is painted in a style that identifies the ceremonial importance of the subject. Marralwanga uses striking patterns of cross-hatching that infill the figurative form to suggest his power; generally in Arnhem Land the aesthetic force of a work is perceived as an emanation of the Ancestral creative power of the subjects. Such cross-hatching relates to designs called *rarrk* which are worn on the body during ceremonies. These designs are imbued with a measure of the power of the original Ancestral Beings who first created them. The colours consist of a limited palette of four earth-colours, red ochre, yellow ochre, charcoal and white, yet they are applied using a variety of different techniques to create the tensions within the work. The zig-zag pattern that runs down the body of the figure likens his power to flashes of lightning, and the shimmering optical effect created in some sections of cross-hatching suggests the iridescence of snakeskin. Marralwanga also uses the technique of adding brilliant white dots around the outline of the figure to give the form a sparkling appearance. While all the other colours employed are fairly easily procured, this brilliant white, or *delek* (naturally-occurring calcium magnesium carbonate), is mined at a very small number of sites in western Arnhem Land. Dilebang is such a site. The nodules of *delek* at this site are believed to be the faeces of Ngalyod, the transformed bones of Ancestral Beings swallowed by Ngalyod in the past. This substance is traded throughout the region for use in bark-painting and in ceremonial body-painting. Marralwanga's painting gains power partly as a result of the inherently powerful substances used in its construction.

Cool nooks such as the sacred site at Dilebang, with ferns or palms surrounding a spring or water-hole, are the home of Ngalyod during the dry season. They are lush pockets amid an otherwise harsh dry-season landscape characterized by savannah forest and the craggy sandstone outliers of the Arnhem Land plateau. Ngalyod created these sacred sites by tunnelling under the ground in a great journey which spans the length and breadth of western Arnhem Land. The association of Ngalyod with water, rain, and the creation of springs and water-holes, is a primary symbolic construction in western Arnhem Land Aboriginal belief. Ngalyod brings on the wet season by rising from his watery home into the sky to make the massive thunderclouds and torrential rain of the north Australian monsoon. The rainbow is a manifestation of Ngalyod's presence, hence the term Rainbow Snake, and the terrific natural forces displayed during the wet season indicate the great power of this Being. While Ngalyod slumbers coiled in water-holes during the dry season, he can be disturbed by humans who may damage the sacred site. Western Arnhem Land myths tell of numerous occasions where certain Ancestral Beings aroused the anger of Ngalyod by disturbances at these sites, whereupon the snake rose from the billabong and devoured the transgressors. Marralwanga himself was very serious in his desire to protect these sites from illicit activities and on one occasion he erected a barrier of flour drums across the Oenpelli-

Peter MARRALWANGA (DJAKKU), 1916-1987. *Ngalyod the Rainbow Serpent*. 1982, Marrkolidjban,
Western Arnhem Land, Northern Territory. Ochres on eucalpytus bark, 133 x 47 cm. The Robert Holmes
à Court Collection

Maningrida road to stop and check the activities of travellers.[3]

Marralwanga was a man of considerable ceremonial knowledge who during his lifetime took a major role in overseeing the correct performance of ceremonies, such as the Kunabibi, that symbolically recreate Ngalyod's journey. Participants gather from all over Arnhem Land to sing the songs that describe Ngalyod's journey and to perform the dances which relate to the specific sacred sites created by him. These ceremonial performances call on Ngalyod to release his power and maintain the fecundity of the land. People who attend such ceremonies say that it makes them feel healthy and strong and that they get 'more fat', an allusion to their improved well-being. They also say that the ceremony makes the 'fat' or sap run in the trees, and that Ngalyod will disgorge a multitude of food animals to replenish the world. In addition to this fertility aspect, the Kunabibi ceremony has an initiatory function. Children are removed from their parents for a period of several months to be taught the meaning of the ceremony. These initiates are described as having been 'swallowed' by the snake and as a finale to the ceremony they are 'disgorged' back into normal social life. In some mortuary ceremonies the souls of the dead are said to be 'swallowed' by the snake. However, Kunabibi is the occasion for the release of these souls back into the world where they may cause a

woman to conceive and so renew the cycle. The image of the Rainbow Serpent swallowing and later regurgitating things in a transformed state recurs in many different guises in western Arnhem Land myth and ceremony. Ngalyod is also said to swallow water during the dry season and regurgitate it in the wet. The image is apt in relation to many cycles of social and natural change.

Ngalyod the Rainbow Serpent is one of a set of paintings produced for a major exhibition of Marralwanga's work in the Aboriginal Traditional Arts gallery in Perth in 1983. The exhibition, and a previous one in 1981[4], allowed Marralwanga to display his considerable individual artistic talent and his knowledge of a broad range of the most important Ancestral subjects of the western Arnhem Land region.[5] Marralwanga was a man of considerable stature in ceremonial life and he used paintings such as this to share his beliefs both with his immediate family who observed the production of the paintings, and with the wider Australian audience who eventually bought them. He used the striking aesthetic qualities of his works to assert the power of the Ancestral Beings and to help maintain the continuing relevance of knowledge of the Ancestral realm in providing an understanding of the relationship between people and the land in his part of Australia.

COLONIAL ART : NATURE by DANIEL THOMAS

Throughout the Western world high art was more than usually interested in landscape during the century of Romanticism, 1760s-1860s, which roughly coincided with the first century of colonial Australia. And the European discovery and naming of Botany Bay in 1770 by Sir Joseph Banks and Captain James Cook were consequences of a European hey-day in the natural sciences.

Conrad Martens had been an expedition artist on board ship with Darwin in South America in 1834 and perhaps gained there some extra feeling for the tumult in nature's elements. Eugene von Guérard was similarly enthralled by Lake Gnotuk, a now-tranquil crater in a land of one-time volcanoes, and by a tormented Castle Rock released at tranquil sunset from the flayings of wind and ocean.

Waterfalls and mountain crags were conventional subjects for an age of romantic natural science, so conventional art-collectors, for example landowners in Victoria, bought paintings of waterfalls on the Wannon River, in the heart of their rich Western District, or Alexander Wilson, in the Wimmera District, commissioned a painting of Mount Arapiles, a spectacular specimen of geology which was his own property.

Outside the mainstream art-market there was a sharper sense of what was peculiarly Australian: small watercolour field-sketches of clear night skies or sand cliffs by Ludwig Becker, expedition artist with Burke and Wills on an 1860 journey to the desert interior; the thrill of salt-lake flatness and saltbush-country emptiness first depicted in the 1840s by the South Australian colonial surveyor-general and amateur artist Captain E.C. Frome, by a free-lance natural-history illustrator George French Angas and by S.T. Gill accompanying an expedition to the interior with the country's first imported camel.

Lewin was also for a time a farmer and so perhaps had more than a natural-history artist's feeling for the most ordinary and commonplace of Australian settlers' experiences: the ubiquitous eucalyptus trees (gum-trees), in hundreds of varieties, which were always present, always to be used for fuel or building, or to be cleared for agriculture or pastures. Alive or dead in 1805 gum-trees were already at the centre of everyday experience of nature in Australia. By 1833, aided by the high-art precedents of seventeenth-century Dutch paintings of ragged oak-forests, John Glover, another farmer-artist, produced the first great gum-tree in Australian art, not a natural-history specimen but a symbol of genial woodland landscape and golden grasses. Louis Buvelot from the 1860s would confirm that Australian nature provided a general sense of comfortable belonging in this non-European land; paintings of gum-trees reminded the European settlers in the great metropolis of Melbourne that these trees were fragrant, were beautiful, were ancient, were everywhere, and were theirs.

John Skinner Prout at South Yarra in December 1846 was perhaps the first to convey pleasure in the brilliance of Australian summer sunlight. Thomas Clark in the 1850s gave special attention to the rich herbage of Western District grasslands, the source of sheep-grazers' and cattlemen's wealth. However, the windy seacoasts near those grasslands were the scene of storms and shipwrecks, universally-experienced natural disasters indeed, but especially upsetting to colonists extremely dependent on their shipping links with the other side of the world.

The peculiarly Australian natural disaster, at least in the south-east of Australia, was fire — fire that could feed on those rich grasslands when they were ripened by summer and then storm through the combustible eucalyptus forests. William Strutt's *Black Thursday*, the largest painting from Australia's colonial period, is not about the beneficence of nature but about its peculiarly Australian terrors.

Nicholas CAIRE, 1837-1918. *Fairy scene at the Landslip, Black's Spur, Victoria.*
1878, from the album *Colonies* assembled 1890s. Albumen-silver
photograph, 27.4 x 22.5 cm. Australian National Gallery, Canberra.
Joseph Brown Fund 1981

Captain John HUNTER, 1737-1821. *"Go-mah. (Murry), 1/3 of the Nat.
Size"*, no. 33 from an album of 100 watercolour drawings of natural-
history subjects *Birds and flowers of New South Wales, drawn on the
spot in 1788, 1789 and 1790*. 1788/90, Sydney. Watercolour on paper, 22.6
x 18.5 cm. Rex Nan Kivell Collection, National Library of Australia,
Canberra. Presented 1959

William WESTALL, 1781-1850. *View in Sir Edward Pellew's group, Gulph of Carpentaria*. 1812, London, from sketches in Northern
Territory 1802, on Captain Matthew Flinders's 1801-3 voyage of exploration. Oil on canvas, 58.5 x 85 cm. National Maritime
Museum, Greenwich. On loan from The Admiralty, London

William WESTALL, 1781-1850. *Hawkesbury River (View no. 6)*. 1802, Hawkesbury River, NSW. Pencil on paper, 18.3 x 27.4 cm. National Library of Australia, Canberra. Federal Government funds 1959

John LEWIN, 1770-1819. *A View of the River Hawkesbury, N.S. Wales*. 1805, Sydney. Watercolour on paper, 46 x 58.5 cm. Dixson Galleries, State Library of New South Wales, Sydney. State Government funds 1955

John LEWIN, 1770-1819. *The Gigantic Lyllie of New South Wales.* 1810,
Sydney. Watercolour on paper, 54 x 43.2 cm. Art Gallery of New South
Wales, Sydney. State Government funds 1968

John LEWIN, 1770-1819. *View from Governor Bligh's Farm, Hawkesbury, New South Wales.* c1806-10,
Windsor, NSW. Watercolour on paper, 20 x 35.5 cm. Dean Management Services Pty Ltd, Melbourne

Augustus EARLE, 1793-1838. *Mosman's
Cave.* c1826-27, probably Sydney, from
sketches at the cave, Wellington, NSW,
1826. Watercolour on paper, 34 x 22.9 cm.
Rex Nan Kivell Collection, National Library
of Australia, Canberra. Presented 1959

John Skinner PROUT, 1805-1876. *Maria Island, from Little Swanport, Van Diemen's Land.* c1846, Hobart, from sketches, December 1845. Oil on canvas, 29 x 35.5 cm. M.J.M. Carter Collection, Art Gallery of South Australia, Adelaide

John Skinner PROUT, 1805-1876. *South Bank of the Yarra, near Melbourne.* December 1846, Melbourne. Watercolour on paper, 27.5 x 39.1 cm. Mitchell Library, State Library of New South Wales, Sydney

John GLOVER, 1767-1849. *A view of Mills Plains, Van Diemen's Land.* c1833, Deddington, Tasmania. Oil
on canvas, 76.2 x 114.6 cm. Art Gallery of South Australia, Adelaide. Morgan Thomas Bequest Fund 1951

Thomas CLARK, 1814-1883. *View on Muntham.* c1860, Melbourne, from sketches near Casterton,
Victoria. Oil on canvas, 71.6 x 122 cm. City of Portland, Victoria. Gift of James Trangmar 1880

Captain E.C. FROME, 1802-1890. *First view of salt desert, called Lake Torrens.* 1843, Lake Frome, South Australia. Watercolour on paper, 18 x 27.8 cm. Art Gallery of South Australia, Adelaide. State Government funds, Adelaide City Council funds and public donations 1970

George French ANGAS, 1822-1886. *Emus in a plain.* 1844/45, Adelaide? Watercolour on paper, 23 x 32.2 cm. Art Gallery of South Australia, Adelaide. Gift of Miss E.M. Johnson in memory of her father Arthur Lawrence Johnson, direct descendant of George Fife Angas, 1971

Ludwig BECKER, 1808-1861. *Mallee sand cliffs at the Darling.* 1860, River Darling, NSW. Watercolour on paper, 12.2 x 17 cm. La Trobe Collection, State Library of Victoria, Melbourne. Gift of the Royal Society of Victoria c1870

Ludwig BECKER, 1808-1861. *Meteor seen at the River Darling.* 1860, River Darling, NSW. Watercolour on paper, 12.3 x 17.2 cm. La Trobe Collection, State Library of Victoria, Melbourne. Gift of the Royal Society of Victoria c1870

Eugene von GUÉRARD, 1811-1901. *Lake Gnotuk*. 1857, Melbourne, from sketches near Camperdown, Victoria. Oil on canvas, 35.2 x 56.7 cm. City of Ballaarat Fine Art Gallery, Ballarat, Victoria. Gift of Lady Currie in memory of her husband Sir Alan Currie 1949

Louis BUVELOT, 1814-1888. *Upper Falls on the Wannon*. 1870s, Melbourne. Oil on canvas, 66.9 x 50.4 cm. M.J.M. Carter Collection, Art Gallery of South Australia, Adelaide

Eugene von GUÉRARD, 1811-1901. *Castle Rock, Cape Schanck*. 1865, Melbourne, from sketches at Cape Schanck, Victoria, 1863. Oil on canvas, 58.5 x 90 cm. M.J.M. Carter Collection, Art Gallery of South Australia, Adelaide

James SHAW, 1815-1881. *The Admella wrecked, Cape Banks, 6th August, 1859*. 1859, Adelaide.
Oil on canvas, 68.5 x 97.7 cm. Art Gallery of South Australia, Adelaide. Gift of Poppy Burgess and Gwen
Holland in memory of their grandfather Mortimer Burman 1967

Nicholas CHEVALIER, 1828-1902. *Mount Arapiles and the Mitre Rock*. 1863, Melbourne, from sketches at
Arapiles, near Horsham, Victoria, sunset 5 May 1862. Oil on canvas, 77.5 x 120.6 cm. Australian National
Gallery, Canberra. Federal Government funds 1979

"THOU SPIRIT OF AUSTRALIA" by ELIZABETH IMASHEV

John Lewin, *Kangaroos*, 1819

"Kangaroo, Kangaroo! Thou Spirit of Australia.
That redeems from utter failure, From perfect desolation,
And Warrants the creation Of this fifth part of the Earth"
Barron Field, "The Kangaroo" in *First Fruits of Australian Poetry*,
Sydney, 1819

This watercolour is an important symbolic statement as well as being one of the finest and last works of John William Lewin, Australia's first free-born professional artist. It was painted in 1819, some months before his death at the age of fifty.

The kangaroo was already a symbol of Australia. The first European drawing of a kangaroo, made in 1770 in north Queensland by Sydney Parkinson, the artist on Cook's first voyage, was followed by a painting in oils made in London by the animal-painter George Stubbs and exhibited in 1773 as *The Kongouro of New Holland, 1770*. By the end of the eighteenth century it had become a famous image, reproduced in prints and on pottery and silver.

The kangaroo soon also became a symbol of patriotism in New South Wales. The earliest surviving use of the kangaroo in this context is the 1806 Bowman Flag.[1] By the mid nineteenth century the kangaroo and accompanying emu had achieved acceptance as colonial emblems and were used as armorial bearers on official and unofficial coats of arms.[2]

In 1819, the year in which this watercolour was painted, the kangaroo also achieved recognition in another art form: a poem was dedicated to it by the literary-inclined Judge of the New South Wales Supreme Court, Barron Field, in his book *First Fruits of Australian Poetry*. It was only two years since Lachlan Macquarie, Governor of the colonies of New South Wales and Van Diemen's Land, had begun to use the name Australia in official documents in place of New Holland. The kangaroo, "Spirit of Australia . . . this fifth part of the Earth", is not only a zoological curiosity. It is also a companion for the bull, elephant, camel and buffalo which had long been conventional symbols for Europe, Asia, Africa and America.

Most works by natural-history artists like Lewin were intended to convey information; the aesthetic element was of secondary importance. Drawings and paintings done in New South Wales were sent to the Secretary of State for the Colonies in London. They were used in much the same way as photographs would be later in the century.

After nine years as Governor of New South Wales, Macquarie was feeling beseiged and threatened by the British Government's complaints about his administration. He sought to emphasize progress and development in the colony. Exploration and opening up of the rich inland plains west of the Blue Mountains was one of his major achievements.

Kangaroos is associated with the second inland expedition of the Surveyor-General, John Oxley, north-west in 1818 to the Macquarie Marshes and then east via the Liverpool Plains to the ocean at Port Macquarie. It relates to "Macropa Species, red kangaroo of the interior . . .", one of eight "drawings" by Lewin, copied from sketches of animals, birds and plants done on the expedition by George William Evans, and sent by Macquarie to London with a Government Despatch dated 25 March 1819.[3]

The landscape which forms the background of *Kangaroos* is virtually identical to the aquatint engraving entitled "Arbuthnot's Range, from the west", an illustration in John Oxley's *Journals of Two Expeditions into the Interior of New South Wales*, 1820. The subject was "Drawn by Major [James] Taylor after a sketch by Mr Evans." A monochrome composition of the same scene, probably by Major Taylor for the engraver for Oxley's *Journals*, is titled "Arbuthnot's Range the Acacia Pendula in the foreground . . ."[4]

Oxley on 6 August 1818 gave a description of the scene depicted in Lewin's *Kangaroos*: ". . . The hill was about three miles from our camp and from it a view of Arbuthnot's Range was obtained, distant nine or ten miles: its elevated points were extremely lofty . . . some hundreds [of kangaroos] were seen in the vicinity of this hill . . . it was consequently named Kangaroo Hill". Arbuthnot's Range is now known as the Warrumbungles and its distinctive peaks are familiar to travellers on the present-day Oxley Highway from Warren to Coonabarabran in New South Wales.[5]

Lewin's finished watercolour, the engraved illustration in Oxley's *Journals* and Taylor's monochrome sketch therefore all relate to the original sketch by Evans done on the Oxley Expedition. Such links between a single image in several contemporary versions are a common feature of early Australian art, especially if book illustration was intended.

In Lewin's composition a second tree and a figure group which appear on the right-hand side of the engraving have been replaced by two foreground kangaroos, one of which is copied from Evans's drawing as is one Acacia pendula (weeping wattle).[6]

Lewin had arrived in Sydney in January 1800.[7] From 1810, with Governor Macquarie's arrival, he received much vice-regal patronage. He accompanied the Governor's official tour when Macquarie first crossed the Blue Mountains in 1815. In 1817 Lewin was invited to join Oxley's first inland expedition, to the Lachlan and Macquarie Rivers, but declined because of ill health.

Perhaps Lewin's most important works are the large highly-finished watercolours of animals or birds and the botanical drawings which were done on commission for successive governors (King, Bligh and Macquarie) and for wealthy merchants. These watercolours have an insouciant grace and charm. In those of animals, Lewin painted their coats with masses of small, short brush-strokes in several layers, finely graded in tone to give the appearance of fur or skin, a tactile, three-dimensional effect. He perfected this technique early, in the Koalas, 1803, the Variegated Lizard, 1807, the Opossum, 1807, the Platypus, 1810,[8] and finally the Kangaroos, 1819.

Kangaroos is the only one of these works with a landscape background. The russet and golden grasses in the foreground are more typical of the settings in which he places his other animals, their habitat merely suggested by branches or foliage, not fully defined by landscape. Here the large standing animal is unmistakably Macropus Rufus or Red Kangaroo. The grazing kangaroo is perhaps the Eastern Grey Kangaroo, Macropus Giganteus, which would not be found together with the Red Kangaroo in reality; however, female Red Kangaroos are usually blue-grey[9].

John LEWIN, 1770-1819. *Kangaroos*. 1819, Sydney. Watercolour on paper, 39.5 x 56.5 cm. Rex Nan Kivell Collection, National Library of Australia, Canberra. Presented 1959

Kangaroos achieved immediate recognition as a major work. Copied by other artists,[10] it was perceived as very different from Lewin's many natural-history studies of insects, plants, birds and animals and from his fewer topographical landscapes from the settled districts near Sydney.

The animals grazing in Oxley's new-found inland plains inhabit an ancient land soon to be taken up by squatters with their flocks of sheep. The original home of the kangaroos was soon to become the Land of the Golden Fleece.

BUSHFIRE PANIC by CHRISTINE DOWNER

William Strutt, *Black Thursday, February 6th, 1851*, 1864

William Strutt's painting *Black Thursday* commemorates a day in the history of Victoria: 6 February 1851. "There was a Black Thursday in Port Phillip, so-called from the country being so overwhelmed with fire and smoke, as if a destroying angel had winged its way through the air, scattering firebrands far and wide; its wake lit up with flaming forests, the fire and smoke, as if waging a war with each other, spreading consternation and dismay throughout the length and breadth of the province". Edmund Finn, using the pseudonym of Garryowen, wrote this description of the events thirty-two years later, on the same day 6 February, but in the year 1883 when Strutt's picture based on these events was first seen in Australia.[1]

Both Garryowen and Strutt were in Melbourne on that day in 1851. It was the artist's first summer in Australia. Picture him at work in Thomas Ham's lithographic office, in the first year of the colony of Victoria's separation from New South Wales. He was preparing a lithograph for the Anti-Transportation League, in unbearable heat, continually brushing sand and dust off the stone while he worked. "We felt in town that something terrible (with the immense volumes of smoke) must be going on up country and sure enough messenger after messenger came flocking in with tales of distress and horror" he later wrote in his Australian diary.[2]

Strutt's picture, painted in London in 1864 from studies made before leaving Victoria in 1862, depicts the events of Black Thursday in terms of man's battle against the might of uncontrollable natural forces. By 1883 both Garryowen's account and Strutt's picture were being described as eyewitness accounts of the same event. They were not. Both men relied on the same kind of sources — reports from all over Victoria published in Melbourne's daily press, and stories at first remove.[3] Garryowen's reports were "historical, anecdotal and personal" and Strutt's were a form of visual reporting in general terms.

Black Thursday is a very large horizontal picture composed of groups of animals and people fleeing from an advancing fire which is not actually depicted except in terms of smoke and whirling dust. On the left of the canvas is a group of wild-eyed horses racing from the fire towards the picture's viewer. A black horse leaps over yoked bullocks fallen in an unsuccessful attempt to convey farmers and their property to safety. In front of the advancing line of horses, cattle and sheep are earlier casualties — sheep, birds, kangaroos and cattle, dead or dying. The skull of a horse and the rib-cage of a steer remind the viewer that this is not the first bushfire tragedy. The central group of figures is dominated by men on horseback, one of them bearing a rescued woman thrown across the withers of his white Arab. An Aboriginal stockman carries a European child behind the saddle of his bay, while another stockman on a white Arab cracks his whip in an attempt to urge his stock towards safety. The fleeing mass of animals is balanced on the right of the picture by men, women and children, on foot or in drays and carts, rushing away from the fire, some looking back fearfully to gauge their chances of safety. A collection of abandoned household goods is in the right foreground. It is a scene of terror and confusion, painted in the French Romantic/Orientalist tradition.

Although Strutt was English, his connections with France were predominant. His family had lived for some years on the island of Jersey, and eventually settled in Paris in 1837. Strutt's artistic training was French and he lived in Paris for eleven years. He was first enrolled in the atelier of Martin Drolling and in 1839 he was admitted to the École des Beaux-Arts.[4] There he was taught by Paul Delaroche and Horace Vernet. If a daily visit to the Louvre was part of Strutt's education[5], an occasional visit must also have been made to Versailles where Vernet's monumental work *Prise de la Smala d'Abd-el-Kadr*, 1845, was hung in a special gallery.[6] Sixty-six feet wide and sixteen feet high, it bore more than a fleeting resemblance to the popular panoramas which depicted other historical events and turned them into popular entertainment. It is the compositional basis for Strutt's *Black Thursday*.

Strutt based his subject-matter firmly on the fact of the fire, and made it a general statement of the terror and destruction which spread throughout Victoria on a specific day in February 1851. The elements of Romanticism and Orientalism, apart from use of Vernet's compositional model, are the result not so much of direct borrowing but of general influence. It was the artist's response to an upheaval of nature which overshadowed the political events of colonial Victoria, the separation from New South Wales. It is romantic because it is deeply felt, as Strutt's diary shows. And it soon began to be regarded as a documentary record by an eyewitness. But because it was painted in England, and its subject according to the critic James Smith "thoroughly Australian", the painting failed to find a purchaser even though it received favourable reviews when exhibited at the Scandinavian Gallery in the Haymarket in London in 1864.[7]

From 1864, the history of *Black Thursday* is that of an itinerant picture in search of a place in a public collection. Now recognized as a key work in the history of Australian art as well as in the artist's oeuvre, it found no permanent home for ninety years. Although for some time it graced the wall of the dining-room of the proprietor of the *Argus*, Edward Wilson, its size and subject-matter precluded its hanging comfortably in a domestic setting. Strutt always intended it for a public collection and had he been living in Victoria in 1864 he may have entered it in the competition for the purchase of a work by a local artist to be placed in the Museum of Art in Melbourne attached to the Public Library (now the National Gallery of Victoria). James Smith had fought long and hard to get the Trustees of Melbourne's Public Library to provide £200 for the prize. Chevalier's *Buffalo Ranges* — "the best of a very poor lot indeed" according to the Trustees' Chairman, Redmond Barry — was selected, reflecting the prevailing colonial interest in and taste for landscape.[8]

James Smith had tried, through the columns of the *Argus* in 1868, to get up a subscription to buy the picture for £200 to present to the Gallery in Melbourne, preferring it to the "two tawdry heads by Baxter" purchased on the advice of Sir Charles Eastlake.[9] Nothing came of this and so "I gave up the wish that had inspired me in painting 'Black Thursday' — that it should be hung in an Australian National Gallery" Strutt wrote in 1883[10], the year of its arrival in Australia. It had been seen in London by an agent of E.J. Wivell of Adelaide, who had arranged for its purchase and shipping to Adelaide for exhibition.[11] In the accompanying catalogue, *Black Thursday*

William STRUTT, 1825-1915. *Black Thursday, February 6th, 1851*. 1864, London, from sketches in Victoria. Oil on canvas, 106.5 x 343 cm. La Trobe Collection, State Library of Victoria, Melbourne. State Government funds 1954

is referred to as an historical record, summed up in the words of James Smith: "For it is, and must continue to be, the only authentic and accurate narrative on canvas of what was felt and suffered by thousands of our fellow colonists upon that calamitous Black Thursday; and its historical value, therefore, is likely to go on increasing year by year".[12] This emphasis on the work as a document was strengthened by the inclusion of Garryowen's account of the fires in the Wivell catalogue, indicating that in a post-photographic age, there was a new tendency to read paintings as if they were (and are) literal and accurate records of past events.

Victoria celebrated its Golden Jubilee in 1884, and *Black Thursday* was again exhibited as an ". . . episode in the History of Victoria".[13] Surrounded by paintings of the Australian landscape, its subject-matter placed it well outside the mainstream of local taste. Painting in Victoria in 1884 was at a low ebb, the Victorian Academy of Arts having failed to stimulate new talent and local critics making increasingly sarcastic and derogatory remarks on the merits of exhibited pictures. The appearance of works by von Guérard and Strutt in the 1884 Jubilee Loan Exhibition might have seemed like remainders of a golden age or else as reminders of Melbourne's outmodedness in the 1880s; the painting failed to find a buyer.

In 1890, *Black Thursday* was again exhibited with the Anglo-Australian Society of Artists in Sydney and Adelaide, and in 1901 it was for sale at £500 in the Victorian Gold Jubilee Exhibition held in Bendigo.[14] This provided yet another opportunity for its purchase for a public collection. But in the Federation year 1901, history-painting was the subject of an award, the Gilbee Bequest, which offered £1000 for a painting on the theme of Australian history.[15] In 1902 a further attempt to find a home for it failed

when a Fine Arts Committee advising the Art Gallery of South Australia decided that it was ". . . unfit to be associated with the 'Masterpieces and other considerable works of art at present in the Art Gallery'".[16] Shortly after this, it was acquired by a private collector and it remained there until 1954 when it was bought at auction for the La Trobe Library, for 150 guineas, as an historical record of an event in Victoria's history.[17]

The history of *Black Thursday* illustrates the difficulties experienced by artists in search of official patronage in Australia. As a literature of the history of Australian art developed, attitudes towards colonial painting changed. The teaching of the history of fine arts as an academic discipline in Australia produced a new group of writers and researchers on Australian art. Some, like Robert Hughes, continued to regard the colonial period as a wasteland of "elephantine academism",[18] an understandably popular view to generations of Australians reared on the myth of Roberts, McCubbin and Streeton as the 1880s basis of a truly Australian art. Strutt's importance as a colonial painter was recognized with a major exhibition of his work which travelled to four states in 1980 and the publication of a monograph on his life and work.[19] *Black Thursday*, however, was not included because of its fragile state. Having been acquired for a public collection, not because of its artistic merit but because of its subject-matter, it can nevertheless be recognized as a key work in the history of Australian art. And with the approach of each Australian summer, the event it commemorates — the powerlessness of man in the face of fire and natural forces out of control — is brought home to Australians who read of disastrous fires like those of Ash Wednesday in 1983, one hundred years after *Black Thursday* was first seen by Australians.

A NATIONAL LANDSCAPE by TIM BONYHADY

Eugene von Guérard, *North-east view from the northern top of Mount Kosciusko*, 1863

When he decided late in 1862 to accompany the German scientist Georg Neumayer on part of his magnetic survey of Victoria, Eugene von Guérard seems to have been particularly attracted by the prospect of visiting Mount Kosciusko, Australia's highest mountain, which is situated in New South Wales just across the Victorian border. As he was almost certainly aware, no professional artist had previously visited Mount Kosciusko, which von Guérard considered to be a subject of "Australian national interest". Presumably, he also expected that his paintings of the Kosciusko area would find a ready market because of the fame and significance of their subject.

In setting out in search of this national landscape, von Guérard was departing from his practice on his earlier sketching expeditions in Victoria. Previously he had combined the romantic with the prosaic. In part he had gone out in search of appropriate wilderness subjects for his paintings – especially waterfalls, fern gullies and grand vistas (such as he found at Mount Kosciusko). In part he had travelled in order to obtain commissions for homestead portraits, which guaranteed him some income on his return to Melbourne and meant that his expeditions were not purely speculative. However, on his 1862 trip, von Guérard appears to have had no interest in homesteads. He does not seem to have sketched any and certainly did not paint any following his return to Melbourne.

Von Guérard and Neumayer reached Mount Kosciusko on 18 November 1862 and spent the morning climbing the two peaks now known as the Ram's Head and Mount Kosciusko itself. On the Ram's Head, the artist had time to make a sketch of the view while Neumayer began, but then abandoned, his magnetic observations because the late spring weather was unsettled. The party then ascended the gentler grassy peak which they "supposed, and subsequently found to be, the highest point of Mt Kosciusko". However, probably to the disappointment of von Guérard, Neumayer decided that there was time for neither art nor science, even though they were on Australia's highest point. Amid strong wind and occasional rain, Neumayer hurried his companions "as much as possible" so that they might have time to climb the visually interesting rocky peak now known as Mount Townsend, Australia's second-highest mountain.

Having taken a short break for lunch and drunk von Guérard's health on learning that it was his fifty-first birthday, the men climbed Mount Townsend. Here there was time to make two sketches: one recording the view from the summit, the other forty feet lower down where Neumayer and his assistant took various scientific measurements. However, while engaged in this work the weather suddenly deteriorated. In attempting to return to their camp in a heavy gale and dense fog, two members of the party became separated from von Guérard and Neumayer. One of them suffered exposure and "became quite stiff and unable to move"; the other was lost for eighteen days.

On returning to Melbourne von Guérard began work almost immediately on a picture of the Mount Kosciusko region. Having no views from Mount Kosciusko itself, he chose to paint the view from Mount Townsend which he regarded as "the grandest, the loftiest, and the most imposing of all the Mountain Crags which constitute the Australian Alps". In choosing

this subject, von Guérard was probably also influenced by his incorrect belief that Neumayer's party "were the first men who had ever trodden" this peak "as the chief Guide stated that even he had never penetrated so far". Von Guérard did not think of Mount Townsend as a mountain distinct from Mount Kosciusko. Rather both he and Neumayer looked on it as one of three summits – "the northern top" – of Mount Kosciusko.

In working up his sketches into the finished painting, von Guérard adopted his standard technique, which in turn was common practice in mid-nineteenth-century view-making. In the middleground and background he reproduced one of his preparatory pen-and-ink-and-pencil sketches, providing an accurate record of the view from Mount Townsend across to Mount Jagungal, which looks deceptively high from Mount Townsend. In the foreground he invented, adding the rock pile at left in order to emphasize the physical insignificance of the men within the mountain landscape and to provide a link between foreground and background, foreground and sky. As well, he chose to show all members of the scientist's party, introducing not only the dramatic standing figure with windblown cloak – possibly a self-portrait – but also Neumayer's dog Hector, standing near his master who is taking scientific measurements with an assistant underneath the rocks at left.

The resulting painting, which was completed by April 1863, serves not only as an accurate view and a highly romantic image but also as a record of the day when Neumayer and von Guérard climbed Mount Townsend. Even the sky, with its transition from heavy rain to bright sunshine, an effect depicted by von Guérard in many of his landscapes, is particularly appropriate for this subject, given the gale which hit Neumayer's party. Rather than dating the picture "1863", when he had painted it, von Guérard chose instead to inscribe it with the particular date "18 Nov. 1862", his birthday and the day when the party had been on the mountain.

Von Guérard's audience in Victoria was, however, generally unreceptive to the drama of the painting which was "a complete rebuttal of the theory, if such a theory now be held by anyone, that Australian scenery possesses no elements of the sublime". Few appreciated "the chaos of old rocks, with ice and snow-covered slopes and peaks, and dark shadowy chasms reaching far down below the piled up columns of nature's masonry, . . . produced with wonderful effect". Instead most of his contemporaries appear to have found the picture too awe-inspiring, too sublime. As one critic wrote:

"Here we are high up among the clouds; rocks, rocks, rocks, on every side, huge shattered basaltic fragments; a deep crater-formed abyss at our feet, riven by subterranean fires; the whole under a cold mantle of snows lying in the wildest confusion, flung deep and thick in parts, with the black traprock showing through. Terribly true to nature, but most uncomfortable to look at."

Because of this unfavourable response, the painting remained unsold even though it was the first colonial picture of Australia's highest mountain region. Over a ten-year period von Guérard exhibited it without success at least three times in Melbourne and once in Ballarat. As he held the picture longer and the taste for Australian mountain views gradually disappeared,

Eugene von GUÉRARD, 1811-1901. *North-east view from the northern top of Mount Kosciusko.* 1863,
Melbourne, from sketches on Kosciusko 18 November 1862. Oil on canvas, 66.5 x 116.8 cm.
Australian National Gallery, Canberra. Federal Government funds 1973

Eugene von GUÉRARD. *Mountains from the north to the north-east seen from the peak of Mount
Kosciusko*. 18 November 1862, executed on the spot. Pen and ink and pencil on paper, 9 x 31.6 cm.
Dixson Galleries, State Library of New South Wales, Sydney

reviews of the painting grew increasingly negative. Finally, in 1873, he despaired and decided to include it in the Victorian Court at the Vienna Universal Exhibition. There, ignoring the picture's own history, it was said to demonstrate "that in our haste to get riches we do not altogether ignore the fine arts or those pursuits which have an educating and refining influence on the mind". There also — amidst fur skins and wines, meat and kangaroo tails, hams, cheeses and wool samples — the picture finally sold to a European buyer.

"PREVIOUSLY UNNOTICED BEAUTIES" by JOCELYN GRAY

Louis Buvelot, *Winter morning near Heidelberg*, 1866

Louis Buvelot's *Winter morning near Heidelberg* was one of a pair of views of Yarra Valley scenery which the artist painted for the third Melbourne Intercolonial Exhibition, October 1866 — February 1867. Altogether eleven paintings by Buvelot were shown in the art section of that industrial exhibition, but the artist seems to have regarded *Winter morning near Heidelberg* and *Summer afternoon, Templestowe* as the most significant of his exhibits.[1]

Some years later he referred to them in a letter to a friend in Switzerland: "Bit by bit my two large pictures made a name for themselves, and the Government bought them from me for the Melbourne National Gallery". He added, untruthfully in the light of the Government's acquisition of Nicholas Chevalier's 1864 prize-winning *Buffalo Ranges*, "I was the first Australian artist to have the honour of being hung there".[2] The paintings were bought from the artist in 1869 for the National Gallery of Victoria and he was paid £80 each for them. If not quite the first Australian paintings to enter that largely European collection, Buvelot's were the most conspicuous in its formative years and probably the most admired.

The very few pencil sketches from Buvelot's first twelvemonth in Melbourne following his arrival from Switzerland in February 1865 show us that he was already at work getting to know the prettier parts along the lower Yarra between Princes Bridge and the Hawthorn Bridge in the time that he had free from his portrait-photography studio in Bourke Street. After Buvelot's "year of sheer drudgery" as a photographer, he "made his exit". He and his wife Julie left 92 Bourke Street East and moved to 88 Latrobe Street East, and his occupation at this new address was given in the Melbourne Directory for 1867 as "Artist". From some time early in 1866 Buvelot, at the age of fifty-two and for the first time in his life, was free to give his whole attention to the business of being a landscape artist. The pencil sketches and the paintings in oils and watercolours that have come to us from 1866 indicate that his earliest foray beyond the city fringes was into the Yarra Valley.

He made his way there along the Heidelberg Road, pausing to take little pencil sketches of Northcote and of the Merri Creek. A traveller along the Heidelberg Road in 1848 had observed "The views are very pretty, — yes, very pretty; consisting of extensive undulations of thickly-wooded country, and ranges of blue hills in the distance: while the immediate road would be, were the grass green, a road through a park".[3] By 1866 the road to Heidelberg emerged from the slums and factories that had replaced the swamps of Collingwood, eventually crossing the Yarra at Heidelberg by the new Banksia Street bridge which linked the village north of the Yarra to the fruit-growing districts of Templestowe and Doncaster south of the Yarra. The Heidelberg Road here became the Templestowe Road. Buvelot's 1866 pair of paintings of a *Winter morning* and a *Summer afternoon* were paintings of places only three miles apart, both country destinations for city excursionists.

Upriver from the Johnston Street bridge at Collingwood as far as the Banksia Street bridge at Heidelberg the Yarra bends and twists between steep banks and is nowhere very wide. It is impossible now to locate the small stretch of the river and its banks that Buvelot has depicted in his *Winter morning* painting. The artist himself was probably not very much concerned with topographical exactitude since a large and highly-finished drawing[4] from 1866 of the same subject shows quite clearly on the right a hillside which is replaced in the painting by buildings and a cluster of trees.

Buvelot has nonetheless told us quite a lot about the general characteristics of this part of the Yarra Valley. He has shown us the pale straggly limbs of the peppermint gum with its sparse clusters of terminal foliage, and the yellow box, darker-stemmed and with heavier leafage, these varieties of eucalypt being the most commonly found in the area.[5] Two trees that have been killed by bushfire show the hollowed trunks that are a natural feature of bushland vegetation. We see a watercourse prone to heavy flooding, with the uprooting of large trees that is a common consequence of this flooding. The tumult of the last flood has passed and a huge tree-trunk lies prone, parallel to the bank with its great roots still bound by soil, a striking image meeting its reflection in the now tranquil waters of the river.

By the 1860s fewer and fewer sheep were stirring up the dust along the Templestowe (and Heidelberg) roads. The "thickly-wooded country" of which the 1848 traveller wrote was falling to the woodcutter's axe as the land was cleared and sheep-grazing in the Yarra Valley yielded to market-gardening and the establishment of orchards. The smoke of charcoal-burners' fires was replacing that of the drover's campfire, charcoal being in great demand for blacksmiths' forges until the 1880s (when coke from the gasworks began to replace it).[6] Does the little group of figures with their smoky fire on the Yarra's bank one wintry morning represent one of those bands of itinerant charcoal-burners?

In Buvelot's large oil painting *The Matterhorn from Zermatt Valley*, 1861,[7] a conifer, dislodged by mountain storms, trails its crown in the alpine stream that rushes through the valley. As with the *Winter morning near Heidelberg* from five years later and the other side of the world, the prospect is swathed in sunshine, the day calm and bright, and the indications of natural catastrophe subsumed into the tranquility of the present.

Some Swiss landscape-artist contemporaries of Buvelot made alpine hurricanes the principal subject of their paintings, and pictures of that kind were very popular. Buvelot instead allied himself with a group which preferred the play of sunshine and shadow on modest passages of commonplace landscape and on a sparse staffage of a few grazing farm-animals or one or two little figures going about some quiet (and universal) task of herding, carting wood, washing clothes or tending a fire. This gentle landscape mode eschewed both elemental drama and anecdotal business.

Buvelot was said, by contemporary critics, to have effected a poetical transformation of ingredients that were themselves unpleasing in aspect.[8] The view which reminded the critics of 'home' (Europe) was always kindly received. The *Argus* noted, on 27 March 1871, a number of views of Lilydale which Buvelot had just completed, and concluded the description of them with the comment that "While there is no sacrifice of truth, there is

Louis BUVELOT, 1814-1888. *Winter morning near Heidelberg*. 1866, Melbourne, from sketches near Heidelberg. Oil on canvas, 76 x 113 cm. National Gallery of Victoria, Melbourne. Colonial Government funds 1869

produced as the general result a picture as charming as an English green lane or woodland dell."

But then followed in the same article a hint that the process of weaning from the old standards of 'the beautiful' set by English landscapes had begun, for the reviewer continued: "Thanks to M Buvelot's poetical insight and picturesque interpretation Australian landscapes will begin to assume a new aspect in the eyes of those to whom they are most familiar."

In 1879, the *Argus* critic wrote cordially of a collection of watercolour views of Yarra River scenery painted by Julian Ashton. Ashton was said, by the critic, to have revealed the charms of the Yarra "Just as Buvelot has revealed all sorts of previously unnoticed beauties in our indigenous timber and foliage, and has caused us to look upon our sylvan scenery with something like a new sense of vision."[9]

The older "sense of vision" was that of the artists in the Australian colonies in the mid nineteenth century. Eugene von Guérard had come to Australia in 1852, Nicholas Chevalier in 1855, at a time when the majority of

settlers in Victoria had not been born in the colony. Von Guérard and Chevalier painted a nature that was alien to the settlers. Their romanticizing emphasis upon the antagonism of that nature towards human endeavour was in sympathy with the outlook of the majority of settlers. Less than a generation later, "By the beginning of the seventies, for the first time in Australia, the native-born outnumbered the immigrants . . . the immigrants might be oppressed by the 'weird melancholy' of the Australian bush, the strange still desolation into which they came as intruders. Their children, knowing no other land, accepted this one for their own . . . they did not feel themselves strangers."[10] Buvelot's *paysage intime* was an appropriate expression of the colonists' growing acceptance of their environment as no longer alien and antagonistic but their proper home, familiarly 'Australian' rather than discomfortingly 'non-European'. Buvelot's Australian landscape paintings acted as a catalyst in reconciling Victoria's settlers to their environment.

COLONIAL ART : CULTURE by DANIEL THOMAS

The Australian colonies of New South Wales, Van Diemen's land (later re-named Tasmania), Western Australia and South Australia were established in 1788, 1803, 1827 and 1836 respectively; Victoria and Queensland were separated from New South Wales in 1850 and 1859. The Northern Territory of South Australia, separated from New South Wales in 1863, was relinquished to the Federal Government in 1911.

Good professional artists were working in the small colonial capitals of Sydney, Hobart and Adelaide before the 1851 gold-rush in Victoria, but then Melbourne quickly became Australia's largest and richest city and the centre for colonial art.

The life of the colonies was expressed in art in many predictable self-images of progress: the growth of cities, the productive work of farming, whaling and mining, the riskier work of exploration, sport (and art itself), the accumulation of property and offspring, the presence of leisure and intellectual cultivation.

The Watling view of a ten-year-old Sydney is a naive expression of pride in surviving at the end of the world and getting something built. Major Taylor's panoramic view of 1823 adds to civic progress a political and social awareness of convicts and Aborigines. Jacob Janssen's and Conrad Martens's paintings of harbourside suburbs show the pleasantness of 1840s life in Sydney but Martens's later view of a large city in 1857/58 is a romantic image of the forces of nature, its skies and storms as important as its rich seaport. An image of progress in local life could also express universal concerns.

Conventional assertions of cultivation are the portraits of Miss Julia Johnston in fashionable neo-classical dress and ancient Roman hairstyle, aged twenty-one and performing filial devotion by her father's tomb in Sydney in 1824, Mrs Andrews playing a harp in Adelaide in 1840, Captain Cole a Melbourne merchant portrayed in 1853 in Roman medallion style. Augustus Earle's composition of the Emperor Trajan at the far limits of the ancient Roman Empire, possibly an allegory for Sydney's isolation in the 1820s at the furthest limits of the British Empire, strongly asserts the presence of neo-classical culture-symbols in colonial Sydney's painting. Neo-classical silver and lyre-shaped furniture were present in the colonies as well.

Agriculture, especially pastoralism, had a long-standing and dignified place in European high art and John Glover's 1835 paintings of his own flower garden and his own grain harvest receive blessings from Dutch painting; though not pastoral, their light and their mood are also blessed by Claude Lorrain's Roman paintings of Arcadian golden-age shepherds, for two hundred years the admired model for landscape art. Wheat, not wool, inspired the 1840s technological creativity of John Ridley's reaper which in turn inspired an extravagant silver testimonial.

For the Bicentenary years the two most interesting aspects of Australian colonial life are the British convicts dumped there and the Aboriginal people whose land it was. It is understandable that the convicts should have been suppressed from the art of their time; they are the invisible parents of new-money portrait subjects, Miss Julia Johnston or Mrs John Piper.

Aborigines on the other hand have a real presence in colonial art. A First Fleet artist in 1790, an amateur, drew a character-study of a painted warrior in a classical medallion format: "When angry and . . . intends to fight. . ." Perhaps the first large colonial oil painting was a cheerful corroboree painted in 1812 by John Lewin (now lost). But when John Glover in 1832 painted a corroboree in Tasmania he knew he was painting the past. He now occupied their land, and they were dispossessed. Many town views and landscapes, by Martens and Skinner Prout for example, use Aboriginal figures to confirm that the view is indeed Australian, even though Aborigines by then would have been less visible in reality.

The most ambitious figure subject from Australian colonial history was Benjamin Duterrau's *The Conciliation*, painted in 1840, when its Tasmanian Aboriginal subjects had all been relocated to an island well away from their own lands which were now the settlers' lands. Duterrau at least saw the coming together of the British and Aboriginal nations as an heroic moment, fit for a heroic history-painting, even if he failed to appreciate the misguidedness of the good intentions.

On the Australian mainland Augustus Earle in 1827 appears to have taken it for granted that Aborigines and settlers could share a cheerful breakfast after camping-out together. In 1850, Alexander Schramm, a German artist, depicted German settlers co-habiting kindly with Aborigines.

Eugene von Guérard in Victoria was less optimistic or sentimental, more fatalistic and clear-headed. He painted squatters' homesteads in Australia Felix, like Yalla-y-Poora, a tightly-curved and controlled composition which implies full possession and control of one-time Aboriginal land. At the Stony Rises, an island of bad land in the fertility of Australia Felix, he depicted a small Aboriginal family and in 1857 considered naming it *An Australian Sunset*. One child is at the centre, their tribal life might survive in this stony sanctuary, but on the other hand might not. It is one of the most beautiful and moving works of Australian art partly because it is ambiguous.

For the rest of the century, and longer, white Australians were prepared to believe that the Aboriginal people would not survive. The study of their ways, as in 1870s photographs by J.W. Lindt, would become a pastime, comparable with a geological outing from Melbourne to the Hanging Rock, a botanical outing to giant living-fossil tree-ferns at the Black's Spur, the acclimatization (and hunting) of European game. The full title of Darwin's 1859 book was *The Origin of Species by means of Natural Selection or the preservation of favoured races in the struggle for life*. Evolution and the survival of the fittest applied to people as well as plants and animals. Aboriginal life would certainly change and evolve. Burke and Wills perished in 1861 among well-nourished Aborigines from whom they could have learned to find bush tucker.

It is a paradox that the greatest heroes in Australian colonial life were inland explorers who failed. Melbourne's collective guilt for having instigated so ill-advised a project was displaced into works of art. A Michelangelesque monument by Charles Summers, the largest and finest statue ever made in Australia, was erected in their honour in the heart of the city.

Joseph LYCETT, 1775-1828. *Corroboree at Newcastle.* London?, mid 1820s, from sketches in Newcastle, NSW, 1815-1818. Oil on cedar panel, 71 x 122 cm. Mitchell Library, State Library of New South Wales, Sydney. Gift of Sir William Dixson c1937

Augustus EARLE, 1793-1838. *Bivouac of travellers in Australia in a cabbage tree forest, daybreak.* c1838, London, from sketches in Illawarra, NSW, 1827. Oil on canvas, 118 x 82 cm. Rex Nan Kivell Collection, National Library of Australia, Canberra. Presented 1959

THE PORT JACKSON PAINTER [? Henry BREWER, 1743-1796].
"When angry and (as I suppose) intends to fight at a future period".
c1790, Sydney. Gouache on paper, 30.5 x 24.3 cm. Rex Nan Kivell
Collection, National Library of Australia, Canberra. Presented 1959

After Thomas WATLING, 1762-after 1806. *View of the Town of Sydney.* c1801, London, probably commissioned by ex-Governor John
Hunter, from sketches by Watling in Sydney, 1800. Oil on canvas, 65 x 133 cm. Pair to a view looking across Sydney Cove from the
opposite side, 60 x 137 cm, sketched 1798-99. Private collection

Richard READ senior, 1778?-1828. *Governor Lachlan Macquarie, Mrs Lachlan Macquarie.* c1819, Sydney. Watercolours on ivory, each 9.2 x 7 cm. Tasmanian Museum & Art Gallery, Hobart. Gift of Dr W. Giblin 1898

John WEBSTER & William TEMPLE, working 1820-21. *Easy chair,* one of a pair made for Governor Macquarie. c1821, Sydney. Rose mahogany, casuarina, cedar, kangaroo-skin upholstery, 131 x 70.5 cm. Mint Museum, Museum of Applied Arts and Sciences, Sydney. Gift of the Vancouver Museum, Canada, 1961

W. B. GOULD, 1803-1853. *Still life with game*. c1840, Hobart.
Oil on canvas, 68.5 x 58.5 cm. Art Gallery of South Australia,
Adelaide. State Government funds 1981

Mary Morton ALLPORT, 1806-1895. *John Glover*. c1840, Hobart.
Watercolour on paper, 11.7 x 9.2 cm. Allport Library & Museum of
Fine Arts, Hobart. Allport Bequest funds 1967

Tasmania. *Console table*. c1825, Hobart. Cedar, 93 x 129 x 59 cm. Art Gallery of South Australia,
Adelaide. State Government funds 1984

John GLOVER, 1767-1849. *A corrobery of Natives in Mills Plains*.
c1832, Deddington, Tasmania. Oil on canvas, 56.5 x 71.4 cm.
Art Gallery of South Australia, Adelaide. Morgan Thomas Bequest
Fund 1951

Jacob JANSSEN, 1779-1856. *Sydney Harbour looking towards the
Heads.* 1848, Sydney. Pair to a view looking inland from the same
point. Oil on canvas, 73 x 98.5 cm. Mitchell Library, State Library of
New South Wales, Sydney. State Government funds 1932

Conrad MARTENS, 1801-1878. *View from Rosebank*, 1843, Sydney. Oil on canvas, 47 x 66 cm.
James Fairfax Collection

Thomas WOOLNER, 1825-1892. *Captain George Ward Cole*. 1853,
Melbourne. Plaster, 31 cm diameter; Huon pine frame. National
Gallery of Victoria, Melbourne. State Government funds 1964

Martha BERKELEY, 1813-1876. *Mrs Andrews with a harp*. c1840,
Adelaide. Watercolour on paper, 16.5 x 13.5 cm. Art Gallery of South
Australia, Adelaide. Gift of Barbara Rennie in memory of her parents
P.H. and F.A.B. Andrews 1987

Tasmania. *Sofa*. c1840, Hobart? Cedar, horsehair upholstery, 115 x 210 x 56 cm. Australian National
Gallery, Canberra. Federal Government funds 1981

Alexander SCHRAMM, c1814-1864. *A scene in South Australia*. c1850, Adelaide. Oil on canvas, 25.7 x 31.8 cm. Art Gallery of
South Australia, Adelaide. State Government funds 1981

South Australia. *Settee*. c1850s, Barossa Valley. Pine, red gum, 84 x 177 x 51 cm. Private collection. On loan to Art Gallery of
South Australia, Adelaide

John GLOVER, 1767-1849. *My Harvest Home*. 1835, Deddington, Tasmania. Oil on canvas, 76.2 x 113.9 cm. Tasmanian Museum & Art Gallery, Hobart. Gift of Mrs C. Allport 1935

William DUKE, 1815-1853. *Offshore whaling with the "Aladdin" and "Jane"*. 1849, Hobart. Oil on canvas, 86.8 x 113.5 cm. Tasmanian Museum & Art Gallery, Hobart. State Government funds 1978

Oswald BRIERLY, 1817-1894. *Amateur whaling, or A tale of the Pacific.* 1847, Sydney, based on an event off Twofold Bay, NSW.
Watercolour on paper, 47 X 95.7 cm. Dean Management Services Pty Ltd, Melbourne

Attributed to John WITHNELL, 1825-1898. *Garden chair.* c1865, Roeburne, WA.
Whalebone, 118 x 107 cm. National Trust of Western Australia, Stirling, WA

Thomas LYTTLETON, 1826-1876. *Adam Lindsay Gordon steeplechasing at Flemington, Saturday, 7 November 1868.* 1868, Melbourne. Oil on board, 37.2 x 61.2 cm. Private collection

S.T. GILL, 1818-1880. *"Might versus Right".* c1856, Melbourne? from earlier sketches on the goldfields of Victoria. Watercolour on paper, 26.9 x 36.6 cm. Mitchell Library, State Library of New South Wales, Sydney. State Government funds 1933

J.W. LINDT, 1845-1926. *An Aboriginal man and women*, from
the portfolio *Australian Aboriginals*. c1874, Grafton, NSW.
Albumen-silver photograph, 20.3 x 14.9 cm. Australian
National Gallery, Canberra. Federal Government funds 1982

Henry STEINER, 1835-1914. *Bracelet*. c1860, Adelaide. Gold, 6.1 cm. Art
Gallery of South Australia, Adelaide. Gift of Miss Jane Peacock 1945

Melbourne? *Mrs O'Mullane and her children*. c1852. Oil on canvas, 67.8 x 90.2 cm. National Gallery of
Victoria, Melbourne. State Government funds 1976
Possibly by Ludwig BECKER, 1808-1881, working in Melbourne from 1852

Eugene von GUÉRARD, 1811-1901. *Yalla-y-Poora homestead.* 1864, Melbourne, from sketches in the
Western District, May 1864, at the homestead near Beaufort. Oil on canvas, 69.9 x 121.9 cm. The Joseph
Brown Collection

Robert DOWLING, 1827-1886. *Jeremiah Ware's stock on Minjah Station.* 1856, near Warrnambool,
Victoria, Oil on canvas, 74.5 x 100.5 cm. Mr S. E. Coverdale, Hobart

William FORD, c1820-c1886. *At the Hanging Rock*. 1875, Melbourne. Oil on canvas, 78.9 x 117.3 cm.
National Gallery of Victoria, Melbourne. State Government funds 1950

William FORD, c1820-c1886. *The dairy herd, approaching storm*. 1877, Melbourne. Oil on canvas,
80 x 117.5 cm. M.J.M. Carter Collection, Art Gallery of South Australia, Adelaide

Augustus EARLE, 1793-1838. *Mrs John Piper with Thomas, Eliza, Anne and William Piper.* 1826, Sydney. Oil on canvas, 196.3 x
131.3 cm. Mitchell Library, State Library of New South Wales, Sydney. Gift of Mrs Bertha Dale (née Cox) and R.H. Cox Esq., 1921

A WOMAN OF SUBSTANCE by JOAN KERR

(Continued)

The indoor portrait of Mrs John Piper with four young children complements Earle's full-length outdoor portrait of her husband painted in the grand manner and similar in size and pretension to Augustus Earle's indoor portrait of Macquarie's successor, Sir Thomas Brisbane.[8] Piper, eighteen years older than his wife, is posed in front of his estate, dressed in the (unauthorised) Naval Officer uniform he had designed himself which combined — only too literally — signs that he was both an officer and a gentleman: "Admiral's epaulettes"[9] and top hat.

Piper had made a fortune as Naval Officer, being allowed to cream five per cent off all duties levied on goods imported into Sydney. He spent most of it on lavish living, as Deputy Assistant Commissary G.T.W.B. Boyes noted in 1824:

"Captain Piper is the Naval Officer here, a situation that has given him four or five thousand a year and I suspect he spends every farthing of it. He lives in a handsome house . . . and no expense whatever has been spared, I am told, to ornament this Fairy Palace. He keeps an immense establishment — they say he has upwards of a hundred men employed about him. He does the thing properly — for he sends carriages and four and boats for those who like the water, and returns his guests to their homes in the same manner. He keeps a band of Music and they have quadrilles every evening under the spacious verandahs that surround the house. At the table there is a vast profusion of every luxury that the *four* quarters of the globe can supply, for you must know this fifth or pickpocket quarter contributes nothing of itself.

"I was invited but declined. There is no honor in dining with Piper, for he invites everybody that comes here indiscriminately . . ."[10]

Nor would Boyes have had any desire to make the acquaintance of the mistress of the "Fairy Palace". Ann Piper was the daughter of two First Fleet convicts transported to Norfolk Island: James Sheers (or Shears) from Scarborough in Yorkshire and his wife Mary, née Smith. Children of convicts — especially of working-class convicts — were not admitted into the upper echelons of colonial society.[11] Piper could never marry Mary Ann Sheers while an officer of the New South Wales Corps, or without abandoning hopes of eventually returning home to Scotland. Their wedding did not take place until 10 February 1816;[12] she was twenty-four, their eldest child was nine, it was two years after Piper sold his military

commission and the year he began his Sydney home. All indicated a permanent commitment to the colony and to Ann. Unacknowledged when in Britain from 1811 to 1813, marriage and money would transform this Norfolk Island Cinderella into a suitable consort for "The Prince of Australia",[13] if not quite into a lady.

We are therefore looking at *nouveau riche* wealth in this painting: lavish spending to buy friends and social acceptability as much as a hedonistic lifestyle. Yet, after seven glittering years at Henrietta Villa, Captain Piper committed the unforgiveable sin; he lost his money. In March 1826 the house and other properties were mortgaged for £20,000; in June 1827 they sold at auction for £5,170.11s.[14] The Pipers retired inland to Alloway Bank, a rural retreat near Bathurst, where Ann produced three more children: Mary Andrewina (born 30 November 1827), Jane Adelaide (born 25 June 1831) and Henry James, their thirteenth and last child, born 5 May 1834. John spent his time farming, entertaining and again going bankrupt. He died in 1851. Ann lived for another twenty years, dying of "apoplexy" on 28 July 1872, aged almost eighty-one.

Most of the contents of Henrietta Villa had been sold off in June 1827, although the Pipers apparently retained two small oil heads of husband and wife, also attributed to Earle, along with the silver and other possessions.[15] Frederick Garling, the solicitor father of the painter of the same name and a long-standing friend, is likely to have bought the large portraits at the 1827 auction.[16]

Earle travelled the world out of interest in exotic scenery and customs but since colonial patrons paid real money only for flattering images of themselves, he willingly provided them (sometimes tongue-in-cheek). Technical limitations may partially explain Ann Piper's lack of individuality.[17] She is closer to the smooth-faced provincial dolls which Earle's uncle, the American portraitist Ralph Earl painted than to Reynolds's or Lawrence's idealized aristocrats. Nevertheless, Mary Ann, the convicts' daughter, metamorphosed into Ann, the grandest woman in Sydney, only through suppressing her past and her personality.[18] Within the illusory world created so precariously by her amiable, improvident husband she had to appear just a polyphiloprogenitive possession. It is arguable whether Earle was being subtly sardonic, professionally inept, or merely male in depicting that passive state so literally.

Augustus EARLE, 1793-1838. *Boy with sulphur-crested cockatoo* [probably Alexander Septimus Piper in
mourning for his brother Frederick Octavius Piper]. 1826, Sydney. Oil on canvas, 90 x 68.8 cm.
M.J.M. Carter Collection, Art Gallery of South Australia, Adelaide

CONVICT COLONY: MAKING IT IN STYLE by JOHN JONES

Richard Read, *Miss Julia Johnston,* 1824

Richard Read arrived in Sydney from London, aged in his mid thirties, in October 1813. He had been convicted of forging currency notes, as had a number of the other professional artists in New South Wales during the colony's earliest years. In Sydney he supported himself by running a drawing school, the first in Australia, and quickly gained a reputation for portrait work in watercolour and on ivory in the Georgian miniature tradition.[1]

Notable founders of the colony of New South Wales sat for him. Many of these portraits by Read are in the Mitchell Library, Sydney, though the best-known are the exquisite miniatures of Governor Lachlan and Mrs Macquarie in the Tasmanian Museum & Art Gallery, Hobart, and the portrait of Miss Elizabeth Broughton, 1814, in the Rex Nan Kivell Collection, Canberra. Read for over ten years was the sought-after portraitist of colonial society. Augustus Earle (from 1825) and another Richard Read (from 1819)[2] became his only rivals. In 1826 he received an absolute pardon. Some time in the following year he returned, via New Zealand and Tahiti, to England, where he died.[3]

Richard Read executed this mourning picture in 1824. As a Regency-style memento of death and a portrait of an elegant young woman it is much more sophisticated than the usual straightforward portraits of Australian colonists.

The family of the girl represented is of considerable historical significance in New South Wales. Miss Julia Johnston was the eldest daughter of Major George Johnston and his convict wife Esther whose portraits Read had painted. Johnston was reputedly the first colonist to set foot on the shores of Sydney Cove on 26 January 1788, the date now designated as "Australia Day", a national day for annual celebration. Born at Annandale, Scotland, in 1764, he saw action with the British forces in the American War of Independence, then sailed in the First Fleet to Australia with the detachment of marines. In Sydney he had positions of authority under Governors Phillip and Hunter, but quarrelled with Governors King and Bligh. In 1800 he was sent home to England under arrest for rum-running; not brought to trial, he returned to Sydney in 1801. He was turbulent but indispensable. He brutally quelled the uprising of Irish convicts in 1804. Then in 1808 he arrested the colony's Governor, William Bligh and assumed the Lieutenant-Governorship; this time, at his subsequent court martial in England, Johnston was found guilty of rebellion and was cashiered but a favourable appeal and powerful friends brought him back to Sydney in 1813. He settled to quieter pastoral pursuits on his large suburban estates at Annandale, Bankstown and Cabramatta and on the south coast at Lake Illawarra.

George Johnston's liaison with the beautiful convict Jewess, Esther Abrahams, whom he had met in 1787 on board ship for Botany Bay, was regularized, at Governor Macquarie's urging, in 1814. She had presented Johnston with three sons and four daughters. He had not lost face with the colonial government; Macquarie was a frequent visitor at Annandale Farm and Johnston had adopted milder pleasures one of which was an interest in local flora and fauna. At Annandale he planted the first Norfolk Island pines in the colony.[4]

The painting belongs to a then new and fashionable genre of neo-classical mourning pictures. These were a celebration of antique Roman virtues in modern life which, though stemming from a long tradition of funerary art, first became a popular category at this time, not only in England but more particularly in the recently-federated former colonies of the United States.[5] Angelica Kauffmann's composition *Fame decorating the Tomb of Shakespeare*, disseminated by Francesco Bartolozzi's print of 1782, was the model for numerous mourning images. The type popularly adopted usually showed a woman with a classical hairstyle and in classical garb, beside a tomb and within a garden rich in allegorical symbols. A tree, predominant in the image — weeping willow, laurel, oak, yew, cypress — was an expression of life, of knowledge, and of death. Ivy, forget-me-not, lily and rose all held particular associations. Richard Read, who patronized Sydney's colonial neo-classical poets[6] and produced classical subjects in his own art, probably included the mourning-picture genre in his classes for ladies, where he supplied embroidery-designs and taught watercolour drawing.

In the background of the Johnston painting there is a tomb. George Johnston died in 1823 and was buried at Annandale in the family vault designed three years earlier by the architect Francis Greenway. There the father joined his eldest son George, killed in a riding accident at Camden Park in 1820 and thus the cause of the tomb's erection. In 1824 this painting was executed by Richard Read to show the grave in its enclosure and, standing before it, Johnston's eldest daughter Julia.

It was painted in summer, an anniversary commission, her father having died on 5 January 1823. The tree behind her is now well established and the roses that were also planted around the new grave some years earlier are blooming. Julia, whose name is Roman, wears a fashionable neo-classical columnar-style dress of blue summer muslin and a hairstyle found in antique Roman portrait-busts. She carries an ostrich-plumed hat and a green parasol. Her stole is embroidered with roses and her slippers are of satin. A gold cross on a chain is pinned above her heart. A white spaniel sits at her feet. Beyond the garden and the classical white tomb designed by Greenway stretches a recognizably Australian gum-tree land-scape; the rural countryside is now an inner western suburb of Sydney.

This, the loveliest of Richard Read's known paintings, brings together many threads in Australia's founding history. It tells us of the Georgian architect Greenway and his patron the cultured Governor Macquarie, who together stand for the first high style in the colony. It commemorates the man who arrested Governor Bligh, who claimed to be the first colonist to tread on Sydney's shores and whose life mirrors the careers of other military adventurers who became substantial landowners and farmers in New South Wales. And his daughter's stylishness surely comes from Esther Abrahams, the one-time milliner, sentenced at the age of about fifteen to seven years transportation from London to "Botany Bay" for trying to steal twenty-four yards of silk lace.[7]

So this picture of filial devotion to a dead father (and sisterly devotion to an eldest brother) also honours a still-living, spirited, ex-convict mother, who had become an excellent property manager during Mr Johnston's

Richard READ, c1778-1828. *Miss Julia Johnston.* 1824, Sydney. Watercolour, gouache, on paper on stretched canvas,
34.5 x 25.5 cm. Private collection

absences from thirty years of farming at Annandale. In the elegant Julia, the illegitimate issue of a typical colonial union of convict and soldier, we have a striking demonstration of the opportunities for betterment at the far side of the world in what had begun as a British colony of thieves and forgers. No wonder she brought out the best in a convict artist.

A COLONIAL AUGUSTAN AGE by RON RADFORD

Augustus Earle, *Trajan inconsolable after the Battle of Ctesiphon*, c1827

Augustus Earle painted ambitious and impressive life-size pictures of classical statues of Apollo, Minerva and Melpomene as decorations for a series of Sydney concerts. These Greco-Roman figures were respectively of the civilizing god and goddess of the arts and wisdom and the muse of the art of tragedy.[1] Young Augustus had been trained as a painter in the classical manner of Benjamin West (1738-1820), a pioneer in European art of neo-classical figure compositions. His name Augustus, given him by his artist father, was a name derived from Augustus Caesar, the first Roman Emperor, under whose long and relatively stable rule (27 B.C. – A.D. 14), the arts and agriculture flourished. The Augustan age produced the great classical writers Ovid, Horace and Virgil. The eighteenth century in Britain was regarded as a new Augustan age. When Australia was being colonized by Britain all educated Europeans were fully grounded in the history and literature of Greece and Rome, the great colonizers of the past.

By the 1820s, New South Wales colonial society was producing classical odes written in the Virgilian manner, to expound the imperial destiny of an emerging civilization in a newly-invented "Australia", for by then the neo-classical word Australia, derived from the Latin *Terra Australis* (South Land), had displaced New Holland as a name for the continent. In the programme for the musical concert for which Earle in July 1826 provided decorations of a muse and the gods of the arts, the glee *Hark Apollo strikes the Lyre* was followed by a stirring locally-written nationalistic song *The Trumpet sounds Australia's Fame*. Neo-classical villas were being carved out of local sandstone; neo-classical furniture was being carved out of local cedar; 'imperial' roads were being carved out of the Blue Mountains, Sydney's 'Alps' that had previously barred the way inland to recently-discovered fertile Virgilian plains beyond, a New South Wales counterpart to the Roman Campagna.

This was the atmosphere in which Augustus Earle produced the colony's first large portraits in the grand manner, with backgrounds of classical drapes, Roman columns or classical villas. More significantly, Earle also created the first painting in Australia of an elevated European subject, *Trajan inconsolable after the Battle of Ctesiphon*.[2] In European cultures classical or biblical subjects had been regarded always as the highest form of art. Before Augustus Earle, Australian colonial artists had been concerned with making visual and scientific records of the unknown land, its native inhabitants, the new colonists' settlements, the new citizens, the flora and the fauna. It was Earle, Australia's first important non-Aboriginal artist, who introduced European high art and noble themes.

Born in London, Augustus Earle was the son of an American loyalist. Both his father, James Earl, and his uncle, the better-known Ralph Earl, were American colonial portrait painters who had completed their training in London at the Royal Academy under the guidance of yet another American colonial artist, Benjamin West. West had left Philadelphia to study in Rome and later settled in London where he became a painter to King George III. He helped establish the Royal Academy of which he became President after the death of Sir Joshua Reynolds in 1792. It was a post West held for almost three decades until his death. Young Augustus

Earle, like so many American and British artists, inevitably came under the influence of Benjamin West and the classical tradition. Earle exhibited classical and historical subjects at the Royal Academy such as *The Judgement of Midas*, 1806, *The Battle of Poitiers*, 1808, and *Cassius taking possession of the City of Corioli*, 1811.

The energetic Earle had a restless and adventurous spirit and became an unusually well-travelled artist. He journeyed first to the Mediterranean where he sketched, among other things, classical ruins. Then in 1818 he left London for New York and later worked in Philadelphia where Benjamin West had begun his career. From 1820 to 1824 Earle worked in Peru and Brazil and was bound for Calcutta when he was accidentally stranded on the tiny South Atlantic island of Tristan da Cunha. The next vessel took him to Hobart in Van Diemen's Land where he stayed almost four months before sailing on to Sydney, arriving there in May 1825. He left Australia permanently at the end of 1828.

Earle's American colonial experiences and artistic connections and his classical art-training fitted him to help establish a substantial fine-art tradition in the Australian colonies. In Australian art he was a pioneer, producing the first Australian genre subjects (the most notable being bushranging), and the first lithographs as well as the first grand portraits in oil and the first elevated subject picture: *Trajan inconsolable after the Battle of Ctesiphon*. This subject surely appealed to educated colonists, attempting to raise the colony above the status of a gaol and to re-create a classically-educated English Georgian society in the South Pacific.

Earle, commissioned in 1825 to decorate the dining-room of Sydney's Government House for a farewell banquet in honour of Governor Brisbane, had made a large transparency on gauze which represented the Greek philosopher Diogenes, lantern in hand, searching for an honest man and finding him in the person of Sir Thomas Brisbane. This banquet transparency, the figure decorations of Apollo, Minerva and Melpomene at the concert theatre and the painting of the Roman Emperor Trajan, were poignant images to the colonists involved in conquering and civilizing the 'wilderness' and its Aboriginal inhabitants, the latter viewed at best as primitive but noble savages.

Such subjects would have appealed particularly to the colonists' notions of the Course of Empire. During the two or three generations of neo-classical culture in Australia, from the beginning of British settlement to about 1860, the Course of Empire[3] was a dominant theme in literature and the visual arts; it provided poets, painters and explorers with a rhetoric which would announce the imperial destiny of a young nation. Throughout history empires had risen and fallen successively in Egypt, Persia, Greece, Carthage, Rome, Britain and, recently, America. Could not this westward Course of Empire mean that the young colony of New South Wales was currently the newest extension to the continuing pattern?

How relevant then was this subject of Trajan? He had been the first emperor for a century to attempt to extend the Roman Empire, waging a ten-year war against the Parthians on the furthest eastern borders of the Empire. The war culminated in a Roman victory at the Battle of Ctesiphon in A.D. 115. It was said that Trajan wept, despite his triumph, because he

Augustus EARLE, 1793-1838. *Trajan inconsolable after the Battle of Ctesiphon.* c1827, Sydney. Oil on canvas, 76.5 x 92 cm. Art
Gallery of South Australia, Adelaide. Gift of the Art Gallery of South Australia Foundation 1987

was too old to continue even further east beyond the River Tigris and repeat the conquests made by Alexander the Great in India. The painting shows that moment of self-recognition, with the battle-sated Trajan on the right, collapsed on a rock. He has laid down his sword and with a weary gesture discourages the young enthusiastic officer who is urging him on towards a turbanned warrior on horseback in the distance.

Does the exhausted Trajan at the far-flung eastern edge of his empire here symbolize the world-weary empires of the past, and the enthusiastic upright young officer the new empire of the future in the South Seas?[4] Could the theme also be more personal to Earle? The artist had been marooned on Tristan da Cunha and was now struggling to make a living in Sydney as an artist on the eastern edge of the British Empire's most remote colony, the other side of the world from Europe. It is possible that Augustus Earle painted *Trajan inconsolable after the Battle of Ctesiphon* in the second half of 1827 when a broken leg curtailed his travels in search of exotic new scenery and hampered his portrait commissions. During this period of confinement he may well have seen a comparison between himself, confined by infirmity, and Trajan, denied further conquests by age. Certainly, Earle exhibited in his studio gallery at 10 George Street, Sydney, a lithographic print on the subject of Trajan which was noted in a list of Earle's works seen by the Reverend John McGarvie in October 1826 and later referred to as "A fine engraving, in a superior style, of the celebrated Roman Emperor, Trajan".[5] This print is in all likelihood the basis for the painting.

The figure subject is very much after the manner of Benjamin West and his American students such as Samuel Morse, John Trumbull and Washington Allston[6] with all of whom Earle, his father and uncle associated. The composition is stagey, with carefully posed 'actors' in a frozen tableau. Trajan's dismissive hand is at the exact centre of the composition. The figures are based loosely on classical sculptures widely known from plaster casts and from books and old-master engravings.[7] The figure of Trajan resembles both the Hellenistic Greek sculpture of the suffering Laocoon and the Belvedere Torso; the standing soldier is based on the Apollo Belvedere. Casts of all three sculptures were available to art students in the cast-room of the Royal Academy, London. The partially-hidden horse is more closely based on George Stubbs's painting *Horse frightened by a lion*, 1763, which was also a popular engraving.

It is not known whether Earle painted any other classical subjects while in the Australian colonies. He did not sign his work, and other of his Australian works may be lost as was this painting until the end of 1986. However, they are unlikely to have escaped critical attention in their day and there would have been little time to execute more oils and watercolours than those which are already known to have been made during the short time he spent in Australia.

It is believed that the painting came into the possession of the aristocratic Sir Charles Augustus FitzRoy, Governor of New South Wales from 1846 to 1855, and that just prior to his return to Britain, FitzRoy gave it to a servant in whose family the work descended until 1986. Augustus Earle's painting *Trajan inconsolable after the Battle of Ctesiphon* is a newfound key to Australian early-colonial neo-classical culture, a key to a colonial Augustan age.

"TO QUIT BARBAROUS FOR CIVILIZED LIFE" by TIM BONYHADY

Benjamin Duterrau, *The Conciliation*, 1840

Benjamin Duterrau was one of the few Australian colonial artists so committed to particular subjects that he painted them regardless of whether they would sell. A minor English painter of portraits and genre subjects, Duterrau continued to paint such pictures when he emigrated to Tasmania in 1832. His main interest in Hobart, however, became the Tasmanian Aborigines whom he depicted in near-life-size portraits, large ethnographic paintings of the Aborigines' traditional "occupations and amusements" and history paintings recording the "conciliation" of the Tasmanians by the Methodist bricklayer, George Augustus Robinson. Because of both their subject matter and the awkwardness of their execution, Duterrau seems to have found no purchasers for these paintings, apart from his first four portraits of the Aborigines and possibly two later works. Nevertheless, he continued to paint them, sometimes on canvases of vast dimensions. On his death in 1851, he had thirteen such paintings in his possession as well as two of Aborigines from Victoria and two of Tahitians. Auctioned in Hobart, "the pictures were thought very little of, and were sold at but trifling prices".

Duterrau's interest in the Aborigines was triggered by the success of George Augustus Robinson in rounding up the remaining "wild" Tasmanian Aborigines and bringing them into captivity. Robinson's success — achieved with the aid of a group of "domesticated" blacks between 1830 and 1834 on a series of expeditions through Tasmania — meant that rural colonists were freed of the fear of Aboriginal attack which had overshadowed their lives for more than a decade. For ensuring by peaceful means that colonization could proceed unimpeded, Robinson came to be regarded by many settlers as a hero. The Aborigines also came to be seen in a new light. No longer were they feared and hated. Instead they engendered curiosity, if not pity, as representatives of what was thought incorrectly to be a 'dying' race.

Duterrau's first paintings of the Tasmanians were portraits of Robinson's four most famous "domesticated" followers: Woureddy, Trucanini, Manalargenna and Tanlebouyer. Painted in 1833 but dated 1834, these portraits are — like all of Duterrau's work — unsuccessful as records of the Aborigines' clothing, physiognomy or skin colour (though they do provide useful information relating to the way they wore their hair). Nevertheless, three years later 113 citizens petitioned the Governor of the colony to acquire the paintings for "some public place" because "The Aborigines . . . as a race may be said to have become extinct from the civilization they are daily acquiring at their present settlement." Consequently, it was "desirable for the sake of future generations of Van Diemen's Land to preserve four likenesses painted by Mr Duterrau in their native state". In response to this petition, the Governor in 1837 purchased the portraits from Duterrau for eighty guineas, and ordered that they be hung in the Chamber of the Legislative Council of Van Diemen's Land — a remarkable parallel to the acquisition by the Canadian Legislature in 1856 of twelve paintings of Indian life by Paul Kane and George Catlin's unsuccessful attempt in 1839 to persuade the United States Congress to purchase his Indian Gallery.

Even before this purchase, Duterrau had begun working on his most ambitious and important Tasmanian work — an elaborate figure composition he called the "National Picture" in which he drew heavily on Renaissance and classical prototypes in terms of both the overall composition and the poses of individual figures. As described by Duterrau, this picture was intended to be "in commemoration of the Aborigines of this Island, and of the benefits received through their conciliation to the colony of Van Diemen's Land, by the exertions of Mr G.A. Robinson, who is the principal figure in this picture, conversing in a friendly manner with the wild natives, which induced them to quite barbarous for civilized life". By "National Picture", Duterrau seems to have meant that the painting would record the meeting of the Aboriginal and British nations, rather than that the event was one of national significance for Australia.

Duterrau's picture shows Robinson in his bush clothing standing unarmed — and hence with great bravery — among a group of "wild" armed Aborigines. His left hand is raised in an oratorial gesture as he informs the Aborigines of the benefits of submitting to his authority; in his right hand he holds (rather than shakes) the hand of the Aboriginal chief. The surrounding "wild" Aborigines view Robinson with a variety of attitudes, described by Duterrau, as ranging from "Anger", "Suspicion" and "Incredulity" to "Cheerfulness" and "Credulity". Though not strictly relevant to the scene, Duterrau included two ethnographic vignettes of Aborigines making and straightening spears in the very front of the picture to increase its interest. Peeking over the rise in the background at right are four of Robinson's domesticated followers — Manalargenna and Tanlebouyer at left and Woureddy and Trucanini at right.

Whereas Duterrau's own description of this subject does not indicate whether it was intended to represent a specific group of Aborigines, one near-contemporary source indicates that it represents the conciliation of the Big River and Oyster Bay tribes in December 1831. The capture of those two tribes had been the primary object of the unsuccessful Black Line — a cordon made up of both military men and civilians, which had swept across Tasmania in October 1830, attempting to drive all the Aborigines into the Forestier Peninsula. Robinson's subsequent conciliation of those tribes not only firmly established his reputation but was also the pinnacle of his career. By the time Duterrau arrived in Tasmania, the members of both tribes, numbering twenty-six in all, had been transported to Flinders Island. Duterrau consequently found all his models among the "domesticated" Aborigines who, in accompanying Robinson, had been partly responsible for the surrender of the Big River and Oyster Bay Aborigines.

Duterrau worked on *The Conciliation* for about five years before painting this canvas. In 1834 he made a series of preliminary sketches. Then in 1835, in an endeavour to create interest in his proposed painting, he published an etching of the subject and an accompanying description of it, and also executed a plaster bas-relief of the entire composition as well as thirteen small plaster relief portraits based on individual figures within it. Around the same time, an editorial in the *Hobart Town Courier* attempted to promote Duterrau's project, suggesting unsuccessfully that a subscription should be established to support him in his work. Two years later, Duterrau again unsuccessfully sought support for his work when he placed an advertisement in the *Courier* informing the public that

Benjamin DUTERRAU, 1767-1851. *The Conciliation*. 1840, Hobart, from sketches of 1834, composition of
1835. Oil on canvas, 119.5 x 167.5 cm. Tasmanian Museum & Art Gallery, Hobart. Friends of the Museum
Fund, the General Fund and State Government funds 1946

"A work of such magnitude as the national picture, requires invention, composition, expression and strong general effect, all of which is
completely arranged, the black people have stood for every attitude in the
picture, together with Mr Robinson, consequently may be computed as
more than half the work already done. A little encouragement would put
the parts together . . ."

Finally, in the early 1840s when he was already more than seventy
years old, Duterrau recognized that he would not obtain public patronage
for his "National Picture" and decided that he nonetheless would execute a
series of paintings on this theme. In 1840 he painted *The Conciliation*
which at three feet and eleven inches high by five feet and six inches wide
(119 x 168 centimetres) was to Duterrau no more than "a sketch" for the
"National Picture". In the same year he appears to have completed another
large work, *Mr Robinson's first interview with Timmy,* now in the Australian
National Gallery, which depicts the central group within *The Conciliation*.
Probably in 1843 he painted the *National Picture,* present whereabouts
unknown, which was ten feet high, fourteen feet wide and came on a
stretcher "with hinges in the centre to fold up".

In accordance with the canons of history painting, Duterrau intended
The Conciliation not only as a celebration of Robinson's achievement in
inducing the Aborigines "to quit barbarous for civilized life" but also as "a
moral lesson for the present and succeeding generations". The lesson,
according to the *Hobart Town Courier* in 1835, was "to shew the advantage

of mild and gentle treatment, and its final superiority over force and
bloodshed". Duterrau and his supporters hoped the painting "would help
to strengthen and extend feelings of universal philanthropy, instead of
national contentions which too frequently break out in cruelty and
diabolical massacre, under the cloak of war and martial tactics – it would
in a measure cause a respect for the life of man whether black or white".

This lesson is plausible if Robinson's conciliation of the Aborigines is
simply contrasted with the Europeans' previous attempts to subjugate the
Aborigines. However, the picture's celebration of Robinson is indefensible
if his later work with the Aborigines is considered. By the early 1840s, when
Duterrau finally came to execute his paintings, about half of the Tasmanians who had been removed to Flinders Island as a result of the
Conciliation had died, at least partly due to Robinson's ineptitude as
commandant of the settlement.

Duterrau, however, continued to look on Robinson with great admiration – probably because he regarded the deaths of the Aborigines on
Flinders Island as an unfortunate but unavoidable consequence of Christian efforts to civilize them. According to one visitor to his studio in 1841,
the artist pointed to a portrait of Robinson and exclaimed: "There is a real
hero, though not one of your world's heroes." "With glowing face" Duterrau
turned again and again towards Robinson's portrait "and once more
rehearsed his noble deeds".

ET IN ARCADIA EGO (I too once lived in Arcady) by RON RADFORD

John Glover, *A View of the Artist's House and Garden, in Mills Plains, Van Diemen's Land*, 1835

John Glover, the artist who had earlier gone south from England to the warmer Mediterranean in search of the Arcadian rural felicity created in painting by Claude Lorrain in Italy, as an old man in 1830 ventured much further south — to an island in the South Seas. There he created his own real Arcadia where his bones were finally laid to rest.[1] The painting of his own house and garden in Tasmania[2] expresses not only the artist's joy in this new Arcadian paradise but also his firm sense of possession of his own land in a new country and his rapid transformation of it to his European ideals. It emphasizes the colonist's feeling for nature tamed in the benign Australian wilderness. But although the depiction of the sun and the general mood is comparable with Claude's paintings, its style is not; it is not an idealized landscape, it is realistic.

The painting depicts in loving detail the artist's new shingle-roofed stone farmhouse and wooden studio-gallery (both erected two years earlier) and his flourishing new garden as they appeared in the summer of 1834-35. The studio, with two skylight windows and vine-decked verandah with strange ski-jump skillion roof, is situated within the garden. The verandah, which was possibly used for outdoor painting in the warmer months, is elaborately constructed to maximize the light, otherwise an ordinary lean-to roof would have sufficed. The house faces north-east; the studio faces north-west, the southern hemisphere's sunniest aspect. A small low hot-house with glass panes similar to the studio skylights can be seen at the side of the studio.

The artist has exaggerated the sharpness of the conical hill and the flatness of the plain, thereby making a slightly artificial stage to display a garden in bloom. However, the flowering plants would have been well advanced after three good seasons and the garden's luxuriance is probably not exaggerated.[3]

The Glovers had reached their new northern Tasmanian property in March 1832, having travelled overland from Hobart. John Glover named the farm Patterdale after a village on Ullswater in the picturesque Lake District in England. At the English Patterdale, Glover had owned Blowick Farm which he used as a retreat from London and where he once planned to retire. The gabled roof and general appearance of Glover's Tasmanian farmhouse have more in common with the basic architecture of many Lake District cottages than with other typical hip-roofed Tasmanian Georgian buildings. Glover's Patterdale is thus a nostalgic transplant from northern England to the warmer Mills Plains near the village of Deddington, about forty kilometres south-east of Launceston.

Glover's contemporary, the romantic poet William Wordsworth, constantly eulogized his beloved Lake District in terms of a nostalgic microcosm, a self-sufficient paradise of childhood dreams and memories. In his *Home at Grasmere* (written at the beginning of the nineteenth century when Glover was first capturing in watercolour the magic of the Lake District) Wordsworth praises the region as ". . . all Arcadian dreams, All golden fantasies of the golden age, . . ." And elsewhere, a "Paradise, and groves/ Elysian Fortunate Fields — like those of old/ Sought in the Atlantic Main — why should they be/ A history only of departed things". Wordsworth's writing here evokes the romantic pastoral mood associated with both the ancient Roman poetry of Virgil and the seventeenth-century Italian landscape paintings of Claude Lorrain.[4]

Glover was a farmer's son and never outgrew a passion for pastoral landscape. He bought a Lake District farm then sold it for an imaginary agricultural golden age in a painting by Claude Lorrain.[5] Finally in the far south he achieved an Arcadia of his own. Like Wordsworth's *Home at Grasmere*, Glover's *A View of the Artist's House and Garden, in Mills Plains, Van Diemen's Land* records the fulfilment of a childhood dream. The painting has a straightforward childlike innocence. It is a very direct presentation of the simple triangles and rectangles of buildings and hill, set in a pretty flower garden under a beaming sun.

This simplicity had its precedents, earlier than Glover and Wordsworth. An extension of the romantic view of a golden age in an innocent distant past was the admiration of simple peasant existence in the natural countryside of one's own time and place. In painting, the shift owed much to the influence of the Dutch seventeenth-century masters, the more naturalistic contemporaries of Claude Lorrain. So it became fashionable to romanticize not only ancient ruins or neo-classical country houses but also rustic peasant cottages and their informal gardens, as in Wordsworth's own Dove Cottage and garden at Grasmere. Glover's house and garden picture is, to some extent, derived from this early-nineteenth-century cult of nature and its cottage aesthetic.[6]

His large cottage-garden is laid out in the fashion of a formal square or parterre. The straight paths lead the eye to the front door and its flanking windows. The plots are bordered by paths leading to focal points such as the large Tasmanian tree-fern and the creek-filled pond. In the centre, below the large tree-fern, there appears to be a sizeable vegetable plot. Glover was a keen gardener and had experimented with acclimatization of many species of plants.[7] In 1830, the family transported large quantities of seeds, seedlings and potted plants and although many of the plants died from lack of fresh water, some survived the journey from London to Hobart. John Glover junior who, it appears, did much of the gardening, wrote in a letter from Patterdale to his sister Mary that in the summer of early 1833 ". . . I had the long job of gathering and clearing garden seeds as they ripened . . ." Some of the flowering annuals depicted in the painting were presumably cultivated from those seeds.

Magnificent clumps of pink roses occupy the foreground of the painting. John Glover proudly wrote in his London exhibition catalogue of 1835 of another of his paintings, *Hobart Town taken from the Garden where I lived*, 1832, probably the last painting executed in Hobart before he moved to northern Tasmania, ". . . The Geraniums, Roses &c., will give some idea to what perfection Gardens may be brought to in this country . . ." The 1832 painting of the garden in Hobart is a forerunner to the Patterdale painting and, since the Glover family left Hobart on 12 March 1832, the earlier painting would probably have been completed in January or February of that year, three years before the Patterdale painting. Other imported species of plants which appear prominently in the Patterdale painting are hollyhocks, mullein, rosemary, chinese hibiscus, heather, broom, lilies and laurustinus.

John GLOVER, 1767-1849. *A View of the Artist's House and Garden, in Mills Plains, Van Diemen's Land.* 1835, Deddington,
Tasmania. Oil on canvas, 76.5 x 114.3 cm. Art Gallery of South Australia, Adelaide. Morgan Thomas Bequest Fund 1951

Glover took the opportunity to represent accurately the Australian bush on the small hill (now called Pinners Pine) in the background of the painting. The afternoon sun which back-lights the scene rings the distant native trees with golden haloes. The artist, who often portrayed English and Italian scenes according to the formulae and mannerisms of seventeenth-century landscape painting, portrayed Tasmania more naturalistically. In his depiction of the local bush, as seen on this hill covered with snow gums and manna gums (sometimes known as ribbon gums), there is no stylization or generalization of the indigenous vegetation as is the case with most colonial artists. The open ground is visible through the trees.[8] He was struck by this and in his 1835 exhibition catalogue noted of his painting *Launceston and the River Tamar*, which was based on his first drawing executed in Tasmania in 1831, "There is a remarkable peculiarity in the Trees in this Country; however numerous, they rarely prevent your tracing, through them, the whole distant Country". He also noted that ". . . it is possible, almost everywhere, to drive a carriage as easily as in a park in England."

Australian landscape's resemblance to English park scenery had been constantly remarked upon since the 1790s. Whether or not Glover saw the hills surrounding his farm as a gentleman's park, he certainly distinguished them from his highly-cultivated plain in the foreground. The junction between the natural wilderness of the hills and the productive irrigated plain is distinctly marked by the road which provides access to the farm.

The painting's date can be established from three small preliminary drawings in a sketchbook which was commenced on 19 December 1834. Glover was a swift and prolific painter and his elaborate garden picture would have been made between that date and early January 1835. The final date can be deduced from the fact that sixty-eight paintings (including this one) for his London exhibition (of which sixty-one had been executed in

Tasmania) were shipped by the sixtyeight-year-old Glover on the *Protector* which departed Launceston on 15 January 1835.[9]

The artist's final painting to be completed for his first London exhibition since leaving England in 1830, it seems a deliberate attempt not only to assert his elaborate new realist style but, more significantly, to display his new Antipodean Arcadia to the London art-world which had never fully accepted him despite his financial success, and perhaps also to a wider public. His exhibition, in one of the most fashionable streets of the wealthy West End of the capital of the British Empire, was presented as being ". . . descriptive of the scenery and customs of Van Diemen's Land". In this painting Glover is proclaiming that here are "*my* new house and studio, *my* new garden and *my* new country". His next important work, painted two months later, was *My Harvest Home* which depicts a golden autumn harvest of grain in his new land of plenty. Glover's summer garden painting is an assertive statement of a successful cultural transplant.

Here above an unwalled paradise garden the declining sun-god radiates from behind the pyramid-like hill. Immediately below is a centrally-placed tree-fern looking like an exotic oasis palm. The pyramid hill and the flat, fertile cultivated plain with its 'palms' adjoin the flooding valley of a small Tasmanian river which had been named the Nile. We can reflect on this scene of repleteness and repose, its nature-worship, its Christian and Egyptian associations: a Garden of Eden; a setting for a Rest on the Flight into Egypt — the country where pyramid tombs claimed immortality for the dead and were placed in the setting sun above the irrigated lands on the western side of the Nile. Suggestions of both Biblical and Virgilian associations of tranquility and hope are here brought together to bear on the establishment of a new civilization. This was Glover's recording of what he knew would be his final place of rest, his final Paradise: Et in Arcadia Ego.[10]

EDEN BEFORE THE WHITE SERPENT by RON RADFORD

Eugene von Guérard, *Stony Rises, Lake Corangamite*, 1857

When Eugene von Guérard first exhibited this his most dramatically symbolic and poetic painting at the Victorian Society of Fine Arts, Melbourne in December 1857 its title was *Stony Rises, Lake Corangamite*. The geological phenomenon of undulating rocky land still gives its name, the Stony Rises, to a place between Camperdown and Colac in the Western District of Victoria. The painting's more appropriate title, supplied when the work was illustrated a month earlier on the cover of the *News Letter of Australasia* was the non-geographically-specific *An Australian Sunset*. Although von Guérard, like other mid-nineteenth-century artists, was keenly interested in accurately recording geological wonders he was also interested in romantic association. However, one searches in vain for a specific site at the Stony Rises which could have been used for this painting; landscape features have been exaggerated and changed for the artist's symbolic and poetic purposes. The place-name title was perhaps intended to assist a sale among the wealthy landowners of the Western District; in the year after it was painted the work was bought by Frederick Dalgety, founder of the large pastoral firm of Dalgety & Company and soon the artist's most generous patron. Von Guérard probably preferred his first title *An Australian Sunset*. The painting's setting sun becomes a symbol for the decline of Australia's Aboriginal people.

When von Guérard visited the area in April 1857 there were only sixteen survivors of the local Colac tribe (ten men, five women and one child), all of whom worked on local sheep or cattle stations and some of whom were already degraded by the destructive ways of the white man.[1] Von Guérard, acutely aware of the degradation, had written in his Ballarat goldfields diary in 1854 of "... a miserable group of eight Aborigines, clad in the most ludicrous odds-and-ends of European wearing apparel, and nearly all in a drunken condition. It is sad to see how the poor creatures are demoralized by the white man's influence."[2]

Von Guérard in his *Stony Rises, Lake Corangamite* deliberately chose to show the Aborigines in the conditions of their immediate past — their natural state before the fall. At first glance the Aboriginal camp seems like an ideal Arcadian seclusion: a safe and bountiful site. Around the camp the native trees and giant boulders form a natural protective wall. The protective stones may also be intended to suggest an ancient sacred enclosure, a Stonehenge. There is a natural abundance of food. A man carries a freshly-caught wallaby, another wallaby has been deposited near the Aboriginal shelters, or wurns, and three Aborigines and their dogs are drinking from a well-supplied creek or pond. In the immediate centre foreground, surrounded in the picture by six adults, is one jubilant child welcoming his father's return from a successful hunt. The centrally-placed child can be seen as the future of the Aboriginal race. Perhaps von Guérard also had in mind an allusion to the continuity of his own ancient lineage. Himself an only descendant of a distinguished family, the fortysix-year-old artist painted the survival of the Aboriginal race when he and his wife were expecting their first child. Victoria von Guérard, their only child, was born on 4 December 1857, the day *Stony Rises, Lake Corangamite* was first exhibited.

But is this really a scene of well-being? Is not the white serpent about to strike in this Aboriginal Eden? The glorious sunset has not produced an atmosphere of warm optimism. On the contrary the mood is brooding and melancholic and the Aboriginal camp is cast in dark shadow. Are not the two wisps of smoke, visible on the wooded plain below, reminders of European encroachment? In the left-hand foreground of the picture the growth of the prickly blackberry[3] amongst the native grasses is surely a European intrusion into the camp. The young blackwood trees are evocative of vertical Roman pines, the trees of European graveyards, trees associated with death. The tallest native tree has already begun to die. The sinking sun in the exact centre of the composition has already descended behind a boulder. Only its rays can be seen.[4]

The local Aborigines had retreated from European settlement to the protective security at the Stony Rises, not useful as grazing property for the voracious run-holders in this region which in 1836 had been named *Australia Felix*, "the better to distinguish it from the parched deserts of the interior country". The Stony Rises remains relatively unproductive, a deeply undulating island in the surrounding sea of rich grazing-land of Australia Felix. It was claimed as part of the large holdings of the Manifold family which in the 1980s still owns a small part of it. Ironically it was the Aborigines in the late 1830s who first guided the Manifold brothers and their stock safely through the barrier of the Stony Rises.[5] Aboriginal archaeological remains have been found there and like many striking geological formations,[6] parts of the Stony Rises may have been sacred ground for the Aborigines. Von Guérard has put the naturally weird atmosphere of the place to his evocative purpose. Within a month or so of von Guérard's visit, the geologist, author and school-inspector James Bonwick, toured the same region and commented, "The Rises are a remarkable gelogical [*sic*] feature. The basalt, instead of being spread out, as on the plains, or massive, as in mountains, is here reared up as waves petrified in their rise. . . . Once in the Rises it is no easy matter to get out again from the Victorian Labyrinth. In some parts the chasms are deep and the bold fronts of the Barriers in the dim evening twilight have a most unearthly appearance; especially when frowning upon some yawning cavern, from whose dismal recesses one hears the mysterious flitting of bats, and the repulsive growls of wild cats."[7]

True to the romantic attitude to science in his time, the artist has taken great pains to specify the rocks and the vegetation: the blackwoods, the eucalypts, the grass-trees,[8] the various native grasses and what could be a blackberry vine. According to ideas dominant in early-nineteenth-century European culture, all God's creations in all their detail are worthy of recording as part of the spirituality of the earth's living forces. However, this is not a geologically or geographically accurate painting of the Stony Rises. It is not even a composite picture, made up from several drawings, as are some other works by von Guérard. Three on-the-spot landscape drawings[9] of 3 April 1857 (none of which includes Aborigines) are in an artist's sketchbook but none of them relates directly to the finished painting. The commentary in the *News Letter of Australasia* where the

Eugene von GUÉRARD, 1811-1901. *Stony Rises, Lake Corangamite*. 1857, Melbourne. Oil on canvas, 71.2 x 86.4 cm. Art Gallery of
South Australia, Adelaide. Utah Foundation through the Art Gallery of South Australia Foundation and State Government funds 1981

painting was first illustrated notes ". . . some slight adaptation to the exigencies of art . . .".

Von Guérard has given drama to the composition by vastly increasing the scale of the rocks. Judging from the size of the adult Aborigines, the large boulders would be approximately seven metres in height. However, the largest boulders in the area are no more than two or three metres, and there are other geological and geographical anomalies in the picture. The painting is a caprice and probably the artist's least topographically-accurate work. He has used the idea of the kind of rocky land around the Stony Rises, derived from his sketches, as a dramatic setting for a valedictory to the Aboriginal race: a gloomy monument to their displacement.

Von Guérard was not unique in concerning himself with this theme. By the 1850s, the earlier animated night-time paintings of Aboriginal corroborees by John Lewin, Joseph Lycett, Augustus Earle, John Glover, J.M. Skipper and S.T. Gill gave way to a more melancholy use of twilight. Alexander Schramm and Charles Hill painted the Aborigines of South Australia in dark settings. Robert Dowling in the mid 1850s did paintings of the displaced Western District Aborigines and Tasmanian Aborigines in dark landscapes. H.J. Johnstone's much-copied painting, *Evening Shadows*, 1880, is the last major painting of this kind.

Like most other German Romantic painters von Guérard had had a long training in Italy as well as Germany and he was a mature artist in his early forties when he arrived in Victoria in 1852. This painting shows the artist's perfectly-balanced absorption of both the southern landscape tradition, of which Claude Lorrain in Rome was the greatest exponent, and the northern tradition of which Jacob van Ruisdael in Holland was the finest exponent. In the painting, one can see that from the Claudean tradition von Guérard takes the classical balance of composition, the structure of the landscape (the boulders could be Roman ruins), the figures perfectly at home in their environment (the Aborigines could be Arcadian shepherds), the dissolving distant vista, the foreground water, the tranquil mood and warm twilit sky. In contrast to Claudean calm, the wild and romantic rocky landscapes of Salvator Rosa were an important alternative within this Italian seventeenth-century landscape tradition. The Stony Rises was described by Bonwick as "the wildest of Victoria's Wilds". In the painting the rugged irregularity of rocks and other forms, and the powerful contrasts of light and dark, are part of the heritage of Rosa. (Von Guérard went to a fancy-dress ball in Melbourne dressed as Rosa.)

The sombre, melancholic northern qualities, essentially Dutch, which can be seen in *Stony Rises, Lake Corangamite* are the symbolic theme, the dark brooding mood, the meticulous rendering of detail and the symbolic dying tree. However, von Guérard was a characteristic nine-teenth-century romantic landscape painter. The dark gothic shapes silhouetted against the lurid sky take him into the religious realm of the great German Romantic artist Caspar David Friedrich, whose work would have been familiar during training in Düsseldorf. But it is the naturalistic care devoted to geology, botany and, above all, ecology which make him a major artist of his time, the time when Charles Darwin was formulating the theory of evolution, finally published in 1859 in his *The Origin of Species by means of Natural Selection, or the preservation of favoured races in the struggle for life*.

This painting is the human counterpart to two others by von Guérard, both also of 1857, which similarly suggest an Australian Eden threatened by European intrusion. In *Mount William from Mount Dryden* kangaroos grazing within the protection of a natural stone circle are stalked by a European fox. In *Ferntree Gully in the Dandenong Ranges* [10] lyrebirds are depicted in a natural sanctuary formed by a "cloister" of tree ferns. *Stony Rises, Lake Corangamite* is one of Australia's most strikingly romantic images, an apparently naturalistic landscape of a specific place and time of day, yet dense with adjustment for broad symbolic significance. It suggests the poignant moment in an Aboriginal Eden immediately prior to the fall brought about by the white serpent.

GROWTH OF POWER by JOCELYN GRAY

Conrad Martens, *View from the crags above Neutral Bay,* 1857/58

Conrad Martens's watercolour View from the crags above Neutral Bay, 1857/58, is surely one of the finest and most arresting of all his Sydney Harbour depictions. It is unusual in the context of his total oeuvre in that it shows the harbour during the breaking of a storm. We sense the sudden drop in temperature, and know that in a very short space of time vast curtains of squally rain will sweep in and obliterate from view the townscape and opposing harbour. Two large vessels have furled their sails and streams of smoke from a steamer and from activities on land indicate the force and direction of the coming gale. We may suppose that the white goat in the centre foreground has been introduced as a pictorial accent of sharp tonal contrast among the prevailing darks. The goat is also the creature of Pan, alert to the coming tumult in nature. This tumult may well be the Sydney 'southerly buster' with its preface of dust-laden cloud, sweeping in from the south-east and striking at shipping from all directions at once as wind and rain are deflected from the complex confines of the harbour. A smiling haven has suddenly become the locus of destruction.

Such purposeful evocation of a disturbing mood is rare in Martens's landscapes. His prospects are most often genial and sunny. His views were usually commissioned by patrons whose wish was to perpetuate the ideal or the reality of peace and prosperity attained in their new home with its amazingly beautiful harbour and remarkable skies. Martens most often composed such views to a formula grounded in the tradition of the 'Picturesque', with a foreground devised from botanical and geological features proper to the Harbour environment to give a natural-seeming framework for the prospect beyond, including Martens's typically wide and deep skies with their finely observed cloud-structures. Such views were, however, characteristically lacking in any suggestion to the viewer of sensible temperature. The terms 'cool' and 'warm' relate in such pictures to Martens's systems of colour harmonies in the pictorial environments he was composing. Inspecting them, Fuseli would make no call for parasol or umbrella, as — perhaps apocryphally but all the same aptly — he was supposed to have reacted to the weatheriness of John Constable's landscapes.

View from the crags above Neutral Bay is, however, one of a small number of 'breaking of the storm' watercolours which Martens produced during the late 1850s and at no other period of his artistic career, and for which Fuseli might well have called for oilskins as well as an umbrella. These are, in particular, *Watson's Bay and the Gap*, dated 1856 (private collection, Sydney), the undated *Sydney from South Head Road* (Rex Nan Kivell Collection) and another *View of Sydney from Neutral Bay,*[1] *1857/58* (Australian National Gallery) . Few in number, Martens may have elected to restrict his output of these 'bad weather' pictures as a consequence of heeding an observation made by John Ruskin in *Modern Painters* I (which Martens had read in 1848 and re-read in the mid 1850s, and from which he transcribed a good number of passages into his commonplace book) concerning the "rainclouds" painted by the watercolour artist who had taught both Martens and Ruskin — Anthony Van Dyck Copley Fielding. Ruskin concluded his remarks in praise of Fielding's cloudy skies with the comment "Had he painted five instead of five hundred such, and gone on

to other sources of beauty, he might . . . have been one of our greatest artists".

Although atypical in featuring harbour views modified by the effect of stormy skies, these paintings are all the same typical of Martens's marvellous gift for subsuming a wealth of intelligent observation of particular effects of nature into precepts of the art of landscape-painting which were significant for him.

During 1834 while journeying from Montevideo to Valparaiso on board HMS *Beagle* as artist-topographer with Captain Robert FitzRoy's admiralty survey expedition, Martens had applied himself to mastering principles of geology, botany and meteorology, this last relatively-new science a specialty of FitzRoy. At the conclusion of his *Beagle* experience, Martens was using his sketchbook to include entries that were like extracts from a ship's log, regularly noting daily weather conditions and distance run. He jotted down the names of cloud-forms and the colours of the tropical sky, recording the way in which squally weather and sunset affected the appearance of the sea. These intelligent perceptions thereafter informed the appearance of the magnificent skyscapes which characterize his New South Wales art.

Martens, though, did not make his views with a weatherman's eye alone. Throughout his painting life he was in the habit of transcribing into his sketchbooks and commonplace books, notes on the artistic practice of landscape painters past and present. From C.R. Leslie's *The life of John Constable* he transcribed a passage about Constable's cloud studies, ". . . all dated, with the time of day, the direction of the wind, and other memoranda on their backs." Ruskin's *Modern Painters* I & II seems to have been a godsend to Martens, judging from the many passages he transcribed from Ruskin, in particular those concerning Turner. It is surely no accident that, leafing through the etched plates of Turner's *Liber Studiorum*, a work highly recommended by Martens to his audience on the occasion of his *Lecture upon Landscape Painting* of 1856, we are constantly reminded of similarities of composition, effects of light and shade and spaciousness between Turner's pictures and those of Martens. *View from the crags above Neutral Bay* is a tour de force of composition in light and shade and a culmination of Martens's study of the art of contriving a particular atmospheric effect in terms of what he had studied in Ruskin's pronouncements on Turner's use of chiaroscuro. Whereas the intelligent observation of natural phenomena is self-evident in the *Neutral Bay* view just as much as in Martens's beautiful little watercolour studies of *Moonlight, Dawn, Sunset* (all in the Dixson Collection, Sydney), we should be mindful of the contribution of artifice to this 'breaking of the storm' view as to all Martens's finished paintings, and of his own "perfect conviction", as he put it in his 1856 lecture — "of the many and great disadvantages under which all labour who aspire to art in this distant country for it is through the *medium* of *art only* that we *learn* to *see nature correctly*".

If Martens was stimulated to this outstanding work by re-reading Ruskin's *Modern Painters* and generally ruminating in preparation for his own mid-winter *Lecture upon Landscape Painting*, delivered to the Sydney Sketching Club at the Australian Library on 21 July 1856, he also drew upon

Conrad MARTENS, 1801-1878. *View from the crags above Neutral Bay.* 1857/58, Sydney. Watercolour on paper, 45.8 x 65.8 cm.
The Alan Bond Collection

familiar experience. He had lived in Sydney since 1835, since 1844 in his own romantic Gothic home in an elevated position at North Sydney, watching the year's succession of winter squalls, summer thunderstorms and sub-tropical downpours, as well as the city's peculiar 'southerly busters'. And the crags above Neutral Bay were an easy, familiar walk from home, doubtless often gazed from; this view, though presumably painted from one of his usual pencil sketches, was less dependant on the sketch than were the views of more distant places visited, and sketched, only once.

Finally, the unusual sombre grandeur of the work might be due to a vice-regal commission and nationalistic stirrings. The watercolour was completed in June 1858 for "Alf Denison Esq", a one-year-old son of Sir William Denison. Sir William had been Governor of Van Diemen's Land, where in 1854 he secured Australia's first new constitution with fully responsible government. From December 1854 to January 1861 he was Governor-General of Australia and Governor of New South Wales; in November 1855 he proclaimed a Constitution Act which gave responsible government to New South Wales and he also became Governor of Norfolk Island. The breaking storm lights a growing seaport metropolis but it particularly spotlights Denison's Government House residence at the centre of the picture and at the left Fort Denison, built on Pinchgut Island in 1855 as a precaution against Russian invasion. At centre middleground the waters of Neutral Bay are also lit to silhouette two Norfolk Island pines, exotics from Denison's "little autocracy".[2]

This picture is first of all, and obviously, a cosmic study of weather, a panorama of earth, air (wind), fire (shafts of sunlight), water. It is also, and obviously to those who know and care for art, a sophisticated artistic construct, following Martens's precept that ". . . it is through the medium of art only [e.g. Claude, Turner, Constable] that we learn to *see nature correctly* [i.e. the familiar weather, the sandstone crags of Sydney]". Not at all obvious, but nevertheless significant, are the private souvenirs of a Governor-General's term in the colony, a term which saw a steady increase in the colony's own independence and strength. The highly visible power of nature is also an image for a perceptible shift in political and mercantile power from Britain to New South Wales.

REAPING THE REWARDS by JUDITH THOMPSON

Julius Schomburgk, *The John Ridley Testimonial candelabrum,* 1860

Julius Schomburgk's candelabrum was made as a testimonial to John Ridley, the inventor of a wheat-harvesting machine which greatly assisted the survival and prosperity of the young colony of South Australia. It also stands as testimony to the young country and to the era in which it was made. And besides its symbolic motifs of Australia and South Australia and their colonial achievements it also represents mid-nineteenth-century customs and style, as manifested in Britain and her colonies, in the United States and in continental Europe.

Silver sculptures and centrepieces, which were ornaments for the centre of a banqueting table, were the period's usual presentations and testimonials. The world's first international exhibition, The Great Exhibition of the Works of Industry of all Nations held in the Crystal Palace in London in 1851, displayed many of these flamboyant silver objects. Reflecting the current fashion for the natural sciences, trees, ferns and sculptural groups of exotic anthropology abounded in the exhibited silver.

There was a particular tendency for exotic tropical plant-forms to be used for naturalistic ornamentation. For example, in the Great Exhibition there were several objects based on the forms of the giant waterlily Victoria Regia (Victoria amazonica) which had been discovered in 1837 in British Guiana by Robert Schomburgk and classified as a lily by Richard Schomburgk, scientist elder brothers of the silversmith Julius. They had been students of and were friendly with Alexander von Humboldt, the Prussian geographer and naturalist who was the most influential scientist-celebrity of the early nineteenth century. Botanical naturalism in the decorative arts reached the height of its popularity in the 1850s; the greatest efforts were made to ensure realism, following the example of Humboldt.

Artists and designers were also influenced by the European notion of pride in overseas Empire, in the exotic as European property. Palm trees were popular motifs and were often used to support glass dishes or to shelter groups of Arabs and camels. Besides these exotic Moorish scenes, Indian scenes were used and so were Australian,[1] each with native flora, fauna, 'noble savages', subject races, or other characteristic inhabitants, such as gold-diggers or sheep-shearers. Sculptural groups also depicted colonial figures playing British games such as cricket.[2]

Silver trophies, presentation pieces and testimonials were popular in Britain but they were the mainstay of the silversmith in Australia.[3] In the United States, too, silver which was intended for special and decorative purposes also carried the most extreme styles and fanciful designs mingled with allusions to local history or parochial achievements. Considering the popularity of such presentations it was only to be expected that when in 1858 the Legislative Council of South Australia agreed to provide the funds for a suitable testimonial to John Ridley for his services to the Colony, an elaborate silver centrepiece would result. The person chosen to make it was Julius Schomburgk, a goldsmith who had emigrated to Adelaide from Prussia in 1850 following his brother Richard, the botanist, and a group of German intellectuals.[4] Other German silversmiths emigrated later.[5] Germans dominated the trade of silversmithing in South Australia in the nineteenth century and produced some of the best silver and gold work in colonial Australia.

In 1841-42 the young colony of South Australia[6] was in dire financial straits. Large numbers were driven from the city onto the land and into primary production. So successful was this shift and so large the South Australian wheat crop which followed in 1842, that there was a drastic shortage of labour for harvesting. John Ridley, a British miller who had arrived in the colony in 1840, produced a reaping machine peculiarly adapted to extensive open plains and a warm climate. By his invention, standing crops were reaped mechanically: combs and beaters swept off the heads of wheat and the labour-intensive and time-consuming operations of binding, carrying and stacking were avoided. Ridley refused to take out a patent on this labour-saving device, thereby allowing the colony to reap its full benefits and to prosper. By 1844 Ridley's reaper had been largely instrumental in saving the colony. The removal of British corn duties in 1847 led to further prosperity, as South Australia initiated Australian wheat exports to England. South Australians held Mr Ridley in very high esteem but, still refusing any government reward for his invention, he returned to England with his family in 1853, wealthy from his flour-mill, his landholdings and his shares in the copper mine at Burra.

In September 1860 the Adelaide *Observer*[7] reported that Mr Julius Schomburgk, after some six months' work, had completed the Ridley testimonial. It was sent to London and in February 1861 a number of South Australian colonists met there and formally presented Ridley with the testimonial, a large silver candelabrum in which the wood, gold, silver and malachite were all native to South Australia.[8] In all likelihood this was the first sculptural centrepiece with Australian motifs to have been made in Australia.

The form of the candelabrum was entirely in keeping with the current styles for silver centrepieces and testimonials. A tree-fern, which had become a useful and popular emblem for Australia, provides the central support. An opossum, a lizard and a platypus are featured on the silver mount of the blackwood (Acacia melanoxylon) base. The base is itself heavily ornamented, being decorated with malachite panels, cast-silver foliage and figures of an emu, a kangaroo and an Aborigine, upon whose shield is engraved the inscription:

> Testimonial by the colonists of South Australia to John Ridley Esq. for the great boon which he has conferred upon the Province by his invention of the Reaping Machine.

Aboriginal figures are also placed by the tree-fern: a man is climbing it; seated at its foot is a woman partly covered with an opossum-skin rug; their dingo is nearby. On each of the three candle-holders are reliefs of bearded Aboriginal faces. A further Aboriginal figure sits on top of the tree-fern, supporting in his raised arms a sheaf of wheat atop which is a polished block of malachite surmounted finally by a gold model of Ridley's reaper. Sprouting from the top of the tree-fern are sprays of Sturt's Desert Pea (Clianthus formosus), later to become the floral emblem of South Australia.

The candelabrum remained in England until John Ridley's daughter donated it to the University of Adelaide in 1930. It is now housed at the Waite Agricultural Research Institute of the University, a testimonial to John Ridley for his public spirit and his creativity and also to the progressive colony in which he lived for thirteen years.

Julius SCHOMBURGK, c1812-1893. *The John Ridley Testimonial candelabrum*. 1860, Adelaide. Silver, gold, malachite, blackwood,
66 cm high. University of Adelaide, Waite Agricultural Research Institute. Gift of Miss J.T. Ridley 1930

HEROIC FAILURE by CHRISTINE DOWNER

Charles Summers, *Maquette for the Burke and Wills Monument,* 1862

The Victorian Exploring Expedition, under the leadership of Richard O'Hara Burke, set out from Melbourne's Royal Park on 20 August 1860. It had been charged by the Committee responsible ". . . to explore the country intervening between [Cooper's Creek] and Leichhardt's track, south of the Gulf of Carpentaria, avoiding, as far as practicable, Sturt's route to the west, and Gregory's down the Victoria (or Cooper) on the east".[1] When news of the fate of Burke and his second-in-comand Jack Wills and the survival of John King reached Melbourne on 2 November 1861, the process of myth-making began. The expedition was spoken of in terms of a battle lost against the forces of nature and Burke in terms of a chivalrous soldier who died a hero and martyr.[2] "No conqueror dying on a field of battle could earn a fame more pure or glorious" it was said, and almost immediately there began a movement to have the explorers commemorated in a fitting manner.[3] Failure was to be transformed into victory by presenting the deaths of Burke and Wills as heroic deeds, a more comfortable process than public castigation and lamentation.

Almost from the first, it was assumed that any monument would be the work of the colony's most eminent sculptor, Charles Summers.

As nothing had been heard of Burke and Wills since March 1861, rescue missions were despatched to search for them.[4] When Summers's studio exhibition of local artists' work opened in October 1861, he showed nine works, including two designs for a memorial to Sir John Franklin.[5] Franklin, a former Governor of Tasmania, disappeared while exploring the Arctic in 1847. Lady Franklin mounted a search mission and news reached the world in 1859 that his remains had been found and his exploration had been a success. The parallels between the disappearances of Franklin and of Burke and Wills would have been evident to anyone visiting the exhibition. Monumental commissions were obviously on Summers's mind.

"How shall we do enough to mark our sorrow, our gratitude, and our pride?" asked the *Argus*, when the fate of the explorers was known. A public monument was the accepted European tradition of honouring heroes. Summers immediately began a number of works which would remind any committee charged with making a choice of artist for such a monument of his suitability. By 22 November, his medallion portraits of Burke and Wills, executed in wax by "a lady" who was probably his pupil Margaret Thomas, were on view.[6] By 29 November, his first design for a monument was inspected by the Governor of Victoria. The terracotta model, a quarter the size of the proposed statue, depicted Burke standing beside a seated Wills, his right hand shading his eyes as he looked into the distance, while to his left was a resting camel.[7] Each corner of the supporting plinth was cut away to accommodate full-length figures of Australian Aborigines or other members of the expedition.

Summers's first design for a public monument was conceived in the heroic tradition. But the fate of the explorers captured public imagination as well, and popular culture required its monuments in other terms. Summers obliged by modelling a group of three figures for Kreitmeyer's waxworks in Bourke Street.[8]

In July 1862, Summers again wrote to the Chief Secretary saying that he was ". . . now engaged in preparing another [design] which I shall be happy to submit to your approval in the course of a short time".[9] Although £4000 had been included in the government's estimates for the monument as early as February 1862, it was not until November that a Board of Design was appointed and the competition announced.[10] No competition had been held for a public memorial in Australia before this — memorial sculptures for British colonies were usually supplied by British sculptors working at 'home'.

A public memorial to Burke and Wills was ". . . to do honor to the dead by setting up a Memorial which would keep alive the remembrance of their triumph and their fate, and being ever before us, should stimulate us to follow the example of their courage, endurance, and self-devotion".[11] The competition maquette which Summers submitted is the one shown here, owned by the Royal Society of Victoria, the sponsor of the Victorian Exploring Expedition. Wills is seated on Burke's right, as in the first design. The figure of Burke is still placed standing, but his right arm rests on Wills's shoulder, while his left hand holds a scroll. A cloak falling from his shoulders is draped across his right arm, linking the two figures. The figure of Wills is directly based upon Michelangelo's Giuliano de Medici in Florence and the contrappostal twist of the body is very successful in drawing the eye of the viewer to the front of the monument and the dominant figure of Burke. Summers acknowledged his debt to Michelangelo by appearing regularly at fancy-dress balls in that guise.[12]

A second maquette for the work was made, in order to comply with the wishes of the Board of Design, who expressed some anxiety over the ability of the sculptor to execute a colossal group in bronze from a model one-sixth the final size. That maquette, 118 cm high, is now in the collection of the Warrnambool Art Gallery, Victoria, and is far more realistic in its portrayal, although this may be due to the repairs which it has undergone.

The first casting of the final work took place on 16 September 1864. But Summers, ever the perfectionist, decided to re-cast the figure of Burke in one piece and to increase its height to thirteen feet. This was done in the ". . . presence of about 130 ladies and gentlemen" at his studio on 1 February 1865. Initial apprehension for the success of this second casting was allayed when the figures were removed from his studio and raised on the granite pedestal on 30 March. The City Council finally having given in to public pressure, the group was placed at the intersection of Russell and Collins Streets where it remained until the advent of cable trams caused its removal in 1886. The composition was particularly effective on this site, the figure of Burke looking west across the vista from the crest of Collins Street hill, and that of Wills drawing the eye of those approaching along Russell Street. At its unveiling, in April 1865, the *Argus* reported that Burke " . . . is surveying the country to the left, and is calling the attention of Wills to some particular features, and Wills, with pencil in hand, is making a note of them. Both men are in ordinary bush costume."[13] Four low-relief panels, erected during September 1866, completed the monument.

The present location, its fourth, on the edge of Melbourne's city square, is unsympathetic to the monument's artistic integrity.[14] Burke and

Charles SUMMERS. *Robert O'Hara Burke and William John Wills, leaders of the Victorian Exploring Expedition.* 1865, Melbourne. Bronze statue, 390cm; granite pedestal, 460cm. Melbourne City Council. Charles Nettleton photo, c1875

Charles SUMMERS, 1825-1878. *Maquette for the Burke and Wills Monument.* 1862, Melbourne. Plaster, 72.5 x 35.5 x 29.2 cm. Royal Society of Victoria, Melbourne

Wills's life and death have been the subject of film and television — the equivalent today of the waxworks and panoramas of the 1860s. Yet with each report today of those who go missing or die in the centre of Australia we are reminded of the fate of Burke and Wills. The individual today is no closer to conquering this land than they, and those who survive, like the Aborigines who sustained King, know how to live in harmony with the land and its seasons.

In 1866, after the models for the panels were placed on display, an anonymous writer summed up conditions governing exploration in Australia[15]: "The explorer reckons upon pasturage and water, which he may find, or may not. He has no series of savage villages or villagers to reckon upon. Human life and animal life are at a standstill. Above are the bright blue sky and raging sun; below, the burnt-up earth. Men and women there are none to aid — life is all but extinct; and — if his provisions fail him, he has nothing to do but lie down and die".

COLONIAL ART: THE INDIVIDUAL by DANIEL THOMAS

The inner life of individuals is not necessarily found in portraits, the most numerous of paintings in early-colonial Australian art. (They dwindled in number after photography was invented.) Portraits of public figures are usually symbols. Robert O'Hara Burke was a desert-conqueror, not an individual. An anonymous body-painted Aborigine was presented as a warrior type. Mrs Andrews with her harp was a symbol of cultivation in colonial domestic life; John Glover with his palette and brush, posing before the gum-trees which he had depicted in art, was a symbol of a particular professional occupation. And Mrs Piper and Mrs O'Mullane with their many children, well-dressed, well-behaved and well-supplied with toys, are symbols of their husbands' success in 1820s Sydney and 1850s Melbourne.

On the other hand many portraits made for private family ownership are individual and emotional. The artist can conduct a psychological transaction simply by scrutinizing the subject for some hours. However, T.G. Wainewright already knew the Cutmear twins and was presumably fond of them when he drew them: they were the Gatekeeper's daughters at the Prisoners' Barracks in Hobart where Wainewright, a convicted forger transported from London, was an inmate. The portrait could have been a gift, not a commission.

Widows, and portrait subjects in old age, often seem to escape conventionality. There is genuine grief to be expressed if the spouse's death was recent, there are a lifetime's memories, and there is the atmosphere created by the surviving family. William Nicholas in 1845 at Camden Park near Sydney, with Elizabeth Macarthur in her seventies and more than ten years a widow, would have known that she had been since 1790 the chaotic convict colony's principal example of harmonious family life. She had educated her many children, managed her husband's merino flocks during his eight year's absence from the colony and established the reputation of New South Wales as a centre for wool-growing; later she saw the amazing success of Australian wool exports in the mid 1830s. She was a lady of taste, ability and dignity and although she was, in a sense, a mother-figure for the whole young Australian nation, she and her conservative, gentlemanly children expected the artist to make only this modest miniature portrait. It is an image of mutual love and respect within a family, and of an old woman's memories — memories that would have included Elizabeth Farm at Parramatta, the simple house which since 1794 had been her principal home and which she might have preferred to the later mansion at Camden Park.

Mrs Adolphus Sceales, another widow but a young one, has dressed in mourning for an 1856 portrait group painted by Robert Dowling; her late husband's Aboriginal groom, Black Jimmie, stands by his former master's chestnut gelding. The departed rider's presence is palpable in the memories not only of the widow but also of the black servant, the horses and the dogs. Mrs Sceales must have shared a love for riding with her husband over these sparsely-timbered grasslands in the characteristic Warrnambool weather of squalls and showers, shadows and sunshine. The painting is a powerful image of absence, of loss of a beloved partner.

The inner life is not likely to be a matter for much speculation in a colonial society, busy creating its material infrastructure. However, the Aboriginal people clearly provoked serious thought. The same artists that were commissioned to portray public figures also drew or painted or modelled Aboriginal portraits.

Especially in Tasmania, where the race was seen to be "nearly extinguished", they attained a kind of celebrity, famous for being perhaps the last of their race. Thomas Bock's *Jimmy, native of the Hampshire Hills, Van Diemen's Land*, was drawn when the Hampshire Hills were cleared of Aboriginal people; *Mathinna* had been born in 1834/35 on Flinders Island in Bass Strait, at Wybalenna where all the Tasmanian Aborigines were being re-settled. Benjamin Law's pair of portrait busts of Woureddy, 1835, and Trucanini, 1836, show the two most famous of those who had helped a missionary "conciliate" the remaining Aboriginal people and persuade them to leave their own tribal lands for Flinders Island. Law might have known that Trucanini had seen her mother killed by a white settler and her first husband murdered by sealers; he certainly knew her crucial role in the "Conciliation" process. Her portrait is highly emotional. It is not a mourning-tribute to a beloved husband such as Mrs Sceales was to commission. It shows instead an embittered woman, mourning not only the unnatural deaths in her own family but also her race. It may also show self-doubt concerning her own actions.

Mathinna also speaks clearly to us across the centuries. Thomas Bock's portrait session with the lively, if confused, seven-or-eight-year-old girl must have been an intimate and troubling occasion for the artist. Taken in to live at Government House, conscious of her "sore feet & shoes & stockings", attached obsessively to a red dress which "she always wears", Mathinna's "training" was not complete when Lady Franklin departed Hobart a year later. Bock shows us most vividly that the future, if any, indeed lies with sore feet and red dresses, not with the old-time dignity of kangaroo-skin mantles. Social change might be painful but it might produce a solution.

In South Australia there were further artists sensitive to the Aboriginal people's individuality. Theresa Walker's 1830s pair of wax portrait-medallions imply the comfortable state of husband and wife. Also from South Australia is another portrait of a young person in western clothing, this time a substantial oil painting, *Nannultera, a young cricketer of the Natives' Training Institution*, 1854, by J.M. Crossland. Here there is an awareness that the boy himself is participating in the social changes. We and the artist see not only innocence but also a compact to take a leap into the future.

Of course, it is not only portraits and symbolist mythologies which take us inside ourselves. The major artists do it surreptitiously; at-first-sight straightforward subjects slowly reveal themselves as mythologies. Von Guérard's Aboriginal family at the Stony Rises shows us a way of life but was also *An Australian Sunset*, touching our hearts about the future; Glover's house-and-garden painting, as well as an expression of pride in the cultivation of the 'wilderness', was also an old man's summing up of a lifetime and a tranquil assumption that his own death in this Arcadia would be fulfilled and thankful.

Joseph LYCETT, 1775-1828. *The residence of John McArthur* [sic] *Esq. near Parramatta, New South Wales.* c1823, London, for an 1825 engraving from sketches in Sydney, 1820-22. Watercolour on paper, 20.8 x 28.6 cm. M.J.M. Carter Collection, Art Gallery of South Australia, Adelaide
Elizabeth Farm, named after Mrs Macarthur, occupied 1794

William NICHOLAS,1809-1854. *Elizabeth Macarthur.* 1845, Camden Park, NSW. Watercolour on paper, 27.9 x 20.9 cm. Private collection
Mrs John Macarthur, manager of Australia's first merino flocks during her husband's long absence from the colony, here a widow in her seventies

Robert DOWLING, 1827-1886. *Mrs Adolphus Sceales on Merrang Station with Black Jimmie.* 1856, near Warrnambool, Victoria. Oil on canvas, 76 x 101.5 cm. Australian National Gallery, Canberra. Founding Donors' Fund 1984
Jane Sceales, a widow with her late husband's Aboriginal groom Black Jimmie and his chestnut hunter

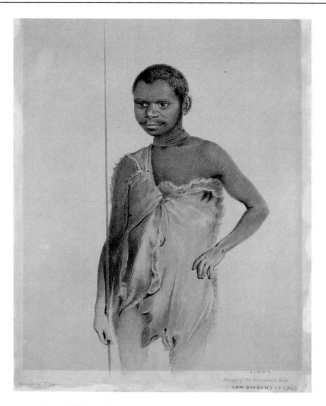

Thomas BOCK, 1790-1855. *Jimmy, native of the Hampshire Hills, Van Diemen's Land.* 1837, Hobart. Watercolour on paper, 29.3 x 22 cm. Tasmanian Museum & Art Gallery, Hobart. Gift of the Tasmanian Government 1889

T.G. WAINEWRIGHT, 1794-1847. *The Reverend William Bedford.* c1846, Hobart. Pencil and watercolour on paper, 38.6 x 33.8 cm. Tasmanian Museum & Art Gallery, Hobart. Bequest of Miss Ruth Bedford 1963

T.G. WAINEWRIGHT, 1794-1847. *The Cutmear twins.* c1842, Hobart.
Watercolour and pencil on paper, 32.4 x 30 cm. Australian National
Gallery, Canberra. Federal Government special grant 1969
The Gatekeeper's daughters at the Prisoners' Barracks, where the
artist was an inmate

Theresa WALKER, 1807-1876. *The Aboriginal Encounter Bay Bob.*
1838, Adelaide. Wax, 10.6 cm diameter. Australian National
Gallery, Canberra. Federal Government funds 1979

Theresa WALKER, 1807-1876. *Aboriginal woman.* 1838, Adelaide.
Wax, 10.25 cm diameter. Australian National Gallery, Canberra.
Federal Government funds 1979

ABORIGINAL CELEBRITIES by TIM BONYHADY
Benjamin Law, *Woureddy, an Aboriginal chief of Van Diemen's Land,* 1835
Trucaninny, wife of Woureddy, 1836

For most of the early nineteenth century, the Tasmanian Aborigines had virtually no place in the art of the island's European colonists. After being depicted by a series of maritime expeditions ending with the Baudin expedition which visited Tasmania in 1802, virtually no Europeans painted the Aborigines for almost three decades. This failure to depict the Aborigines, which provides a striking contrast to considerable artistic interest in Aborigines in New South Wales, was partly due to the relative dearth of European artists in Tasmania in this period. However, it also came about because of the much greater resistance to European settlement provided by the Aboriginal Tasmanians. The colonists, it seems, did not want to know their enemies through art.

All this changed in the early 1830s as a result of crucial changes in the relationship between colonists and Aborigines, which coincided with the arrival of a number of new artists in Tasmania. Most significantly, the Methodist bricklayer, George Augustus Robinson, began his "friendly mission" to the Aborigines. Assisted by a group of "domesticated" Aborigines, Robinson succeeded in conciliating the remaining "wild" Aborigines whereas the settlers had failed in their attempts to subjugate the blacks by force. Consequently, the Aborigines no longer constituted a threat to the colonists. They were also thought incorrectly to be dying out and therefore, because they were racially distinct from the mainland Australian Aborigines, "interesting indeed to the philosopher", that is to the scientist. Moreover, some of Robinson's "domesticated" blacks had achieved minor celebrity status among the Europeans on account of their role in assisting his work. Primarily through Robinson, these Aborigines were readily available as sitters for the growing number of local colonial artists.

The result was a dramatic upsurge in colonial portraits of the Tasmanian Aborigines. Beginning in the late 1820s, Thomas Bock painted a number of sets of portraits of them in watercolours, while Benjamin Duterrau painted them in oils from the early 1830s. More remarkably, Robinson's "domesticated" Aborigines provided the subjects for several sculptures. Previously the colonial artists in both New South Wales and Tasmania had executed almost no sculptures and the limited demand for such art had been met by imported works; colonial portraits had on the whole been restricted to paintings and drawings which required less time, material and financial commitment than sculpture. However, in 1835 Duterrau attempted a number of relatively crude plaster relief sculptures which were all related to his planned "National Picture" of an Aboriginal conciliation subject. Around the same time, Benjamin Law executed the earliest major pieces of Australian sculpture — plaster busts of Robinson's two most famous companions, Woureddy and Trucanini.

Law embarked on his first sculpture of Woureddy within five weeks of arriving in Hobart in February 1835 as an assisted agricultural emigrant. This quick venture into art — and equally rapid abandonment of agriculture — is not altogether surprising. Law came from a family of artists and arrived in Hobart as a sculptor of considerable accomplishment. He also seems to have been encouraged to attempt a bust by Robinson, whom the sculptor probably met through their common religion; both men were devout Wesleyans. Just as Robinson had previously given Bock his first commissions to paint the Tasmanians, so he arranged for Woureddy to sit for Law and then assisted the sculptor to sell his work. By April 1835 the bust was finished and on display at the conciliator's house where Robinson was happy to "permit any visitors to inspect it, and compare its very close and beautiful resemblance to the original".

Whereas Law did not attempt to live solely off his art — working in addition as master of the Hobart Infant School — his bust of Woureddy was so popular that he continued to practise as a sculptor for about another three years, though without repeating the success of his first Australian work. In addition to portraits of Robinson, John Pascoe Fawkner and two Aborigines who visited Tasmania from Victoria — none of which seems to have survived — he executed a bust of Woureddy's wife Trucanini. Already in July 1835 it was reported that Law was "about to commence modelling" a bust of Trucanini, who probably sat for him around this time. However, it was only in October 1836 that he advertised that he had "completed his model of the female, Trucaninny" (spelt thus at the time; today Trucanini or Truganini is preferred) and had "several duplicates ready for delivery, either in Bronze or Stone colour".

To his contemporaries, Law's busts of Woureddy and Trucanini were principally valuable as ethnographic records — a function they appear to serve quite well (though, in accordance with the current European vogue for the neo-classical, Law converted the Aborigines' kangaroo skins, which they wore only as mantles, into toga-like garments strongly suggestive of the antique). As if Woureddy were no more than a model for an extraordinary hairstyle and peculiar jewellery, Robinson wrote in 1835 that "The drapery is an imitation of the Kangaroo skin worn by the Aborigines in their primitive state. The necklace is also Aboriginal and is made of the sinews of the Kangaroo tail. The VDL Abo are wooley headed. The ringlets on Woureddy's head is twisted and spun out at which time in dressing they use a mixture of ochre and grease." A few years later, the Polish scientist John Lhotsky noted that the busts were "of full size, perfect likenesses . . . As the race of the natives of this island is nearly extinguished, these casts will retain a constant historical value". Consistent with this attitude, most examples of the sculptures were eventually acquired by natural-history museums both in Australia and overseas.

Law's busts were, however, also recognized as accomplished works of art. Law gained considerable praise for his work and both portraits were included in the first Tasmanian art exhibition held in Hobart in 1837. Conscious of the difficulties faced by sculptors in gaining patronage, local critics pointed to Law's busts as evidence of the cultural progress of the colony. As its significant event for March 1835, the *Hobart Town Almanack* recorded (not quite accurately) that Law's casts were "the first attempt at sculpture in the colony". The *Morning Star* was proud to note "that neither the sister colony [of New South Wales], nor even India can yet boast of any gentleman, who pursues the peculiar line of art which Mr Law has chosen".

Though generally found now in pairs, it may be significant that Law's bust of Woureddy received a much more favourable response than that of Trucanini. Perhaps it was simply the novelty of his first sculpture which led to its better reception. Perhaps it was also that the colonists had greater

Benjamin LAW, 1807-1890. *Woureddy, an Aboriginal chief of Van Diemen's Land*. 1835, Hobart.
Trucaninny, wife of Woureddy. 1836, Hobart. Bronze-painted plaster, pair, 75 x 48.3 x 27 cm, 66 x 42.5 x
25.7 cm. Australian National Gallery, Canberra. Federal Government funds 1981

interest in the Aborigines in 1835, when some of Robinson's companions still remained in Hobart, than they did the following year when they all had been shipped to Flinders Island. However, the different response to the busts may have also resulted from Law's very different characterization of the two sitters. Law's bust of Woureddy, which was clearly done under Robinson's influence, gives no hint of the decimation of the Tasmanians. As noted by Mary Mackay, it shows Woureddy "as hunter, warrior and man-

in-command, a Greek hero in kangaroo skin". A year later, Law seems to have developed his own appreciation of what had happened to the Aborigines and executed by far the most emotional colonial portrait of an Aborigine. Trucanini, who saw her mother killed by a white settler and her first husband brutally murdered by two sealers, is "sorrowing, mourning the slain members of her family and race".

UNCONQUERABLE SPIRIT by HENDRIK KOLENBERG

Thomas Bock, *Mathinna*, 1842

The circumstances of Mathinna's life[1] and sorry death highlight the tragic plight of Tasmanian Aborigines following British settlement in the early nineteenth century. Thomas Bock's portrait stands as a poignant record of her people.[2]

Mathinna was born on Flinders Island, off north-eastern Tasmania, in Bass Strait. She was the second daughter of Wongerneep and Towterer,[3] a Chief of an Aboriginal tribe (the Lowreenne) from Low Rocky Point near Port Davey, in south-western Tasmania.

Mathinna's parents were victims of a social experiment which forced Aboriginal people from their tribal lands and sent them to live at Wyba-lenna, a station established for them on Flinders Island. Towterer and his followers were coerced to leave their lands in 1833 by George Augustus Robinson who had been specially appointed by the Lieutenant-Governor of the colony to collect the Tasmanian Aboriginal people. Half of them died within two weeks of their re-location.

On Flinders Island most of the survivors were given European names; Towterer became Romeo and Wongerneep became Eveline. They were forced to wear European clothes and eat European food, prevented from cutting their hair according to their Aboriginal custom and obliged to co-exist with other tribes regardless of traditional differences or hostilities. Towterer and Wongerneep's first daughter, "Mr Robinson's Duke" was not allowed to live with them and was placed in the Queen's Orphan School, Hobart. She died soon after.

Mathinna was born some time between July 1834 and June 1835 and named Mary (she received the name Mathinna at Government House); she was taken from her parents when she was quite young, and put to live with the family of Robert Clark, the catechist and teacher at Wybalenna.

Towterer died on Flinders Island in 1837 at about thirty-seven years of age. Wongerneep remarried an Aboriginal man named Parlin or Hannibal also from a south-west Tasmanian tribe; she died in 1840.

It is not known exactly when Mathinna went to live at Government House, but according to a letter from Mathinna to her stepfather she was living there in September 1841. The Governor, Sir John Franklin brought several Aboriginal children to live at Government House after he first visited Flinders Island in 1838. Mathinna was taught by the same governess employed for Sir John Franklin's daughter Eleanor, and was described by the Reverend G.P. Gell as "a very nice intelligent child".

When the Franklins left Tasmania in 1843 Mathinna was sent to the Queen's Orphan School. In that year fifty-six children at the school died of scarlet fever. In 1844 she was returned to Flinders Island, where her stepfather Parlin died in 1846. In 1847 the remaining Aboriginal people on Flinders Island were moved permanently to Oyster Cove near Hobart and Mathinna was again returned to the Queen's Orphan School.

Mathinna left the Orphan School in 1851 when she was sixteen and went to live at Oyster Cove. By that time only about thirty people were still living there. Five years later she was dead, aged twenty-one, ". . . intoxi-cated . . . in mud and water on the road . . . choked, suffocated and stifled . . .".[4]

Thomas Bock, who was transported to Tasmania in 1824 with a fourteen-year sentence, had practised as an engraver in Birmingham.[5] He was listed in Andrew Bent's *Tasmanian Almanacks* from 1825 to 1829 as a portrait-painter and engraver, and was at first involved in the production of a bank-note, and letterheads and illustrations for other Almanacks. Following his full pardon in 1833 he soon established himself as a leading Tasmanian portraitist.

Bock excelled in miniatures. His portraits of the Aborigines, including several in profile in blue monochrome watercolour, reveal sharp powers of observation and a real ability to render life-like portraits with great attention to detail on a small scale. He must also have had a lively curiosity since he was one of the first to take up the making of daguerreo-types and photographs, in which his stepson Alfred followed him.

Bock painted one portrait of Mathinna in 1842, judging from letters which Lady Franklin wrote to her sister describing the portrait and Mathinna. He had previously painted for Lady Franklin, in 1837, a set of watercolour portraits of Tasmanian Aborigines. Three versions of these portraits are known – in the Art Gallery of South Australia, Adelaide (formerly in the Royal Anthropological Institute, London), the Pitt Rivers Museum, Oxford and the Tasmanian Museum & Art Gallery, Hobart. Hobart's collection consists of fourteen portraits, which Bock was commissioned by Henry Dowling to copy from the set he had painted for Lady Franklin.

It is not known whether the portrait of Mathinna which Bock painted for Lady Franklin is this portrait now in the collection of the Tasmanian Museum & Art Gallery, to which it was given in 1951 by Mrs J.H. Clark, Thomas Bock's granddaughter. A second version might have been made.[6]

This watercolour portrait has been presented as an oval since the nineteenth century despite the fact that it is fully rectangular in format and should show Mathinna's feet. In spite of modern restoration techniques, the oval stains caused by the use of a poor-quality cardboard mount remain obtrusive, so presentation as an oval remains the best option. The oval or cameo-like mount, common to portrait miniatures, was probably adopted initially to sentimentalize the subject.

Lady Franklin was not a sentimentalist but an intelligent, energetic do-gooder, a childless second wife of a naval explorer who was also an amateur of the natural sciences. Education was her "hobby of hobbies".[7] Anthropology was not a special interest. Yet she did commission Bock to produce his Aboriginal portraits in 1837, Mathinna in 1842 and she accepted from James Wilson, during a visit in 1839 to New South Wales, ". . . a present of an oil painting, representing a pretty aboriginal girl".[8]

Great houses of the time were generous as a matter of course in their accommodation of visitors, poor relations, and orphans. The orphan Mathinna, fatherless from 1837, motherless from 1840, was one of many charitable and educational projects in Lady Franklin's Government House, a child appreciated for her prettiness no doubt, but more because of her intelligence and potential for development.

The six-or-seven-year-old Mathinna's letter of 14 September 1841 from Government House to her stepfather on Flinders Island told him "I am a good little girl, I have pen & ink cause I am good little girl. I do love my

Thomas BOCK, 1790/93-1855. *Mathinna*. 1842, Hobart. Watercolour on paper, 30.1 x 24.6 cm. Tasmanian
Museum & Art Gallery, Hobart. Gift of Mrs J.H. Clark, granddaughter of the artist, 1951

father. I have got a doll & shift & a petticoat. I read. . . . I have got a red
frock like my father. Come here to see my father. I have got sore feet &
shoes & stockings & am very glad . . ."[9]

In February 1843, Lady Franklin wrote to her sister Mrs Simpkinson in
England enclosing a copy of Bock's Mathinna portrait: " . . . the portraits of
two Tasmanian natives . . ., they were quite savages. Mathinna's will show
the influence of some degree of civilization upon a child of as pure a race
as they, and who in spite of every endeavour, and though entirely apart
from her own people, retains much of the unconquerable spirit of the
savage; extreme uncertainty of will and temper, little if any self-control, and
great acuteness of the senses and felicity of imitation . . . The attitude is
exactly hers, and she always wears the dress you see her in — when she
goes out, she wears red stockings and black shoes."[10]

A drawing of Mathinna, back at Flinders Island in February 1845, was
later inscribed "This girl was trained (or attempted to be trained) by Lady
Franklin as a servant."[11]

"RECLAIMED FROM BARBARISM" by JOHN JONES

J.M. Crossland, *Nannultera, a young cricketer of the Natives' Training Institution, Poonindie,* 1854

Nannultera, a young cricketer of the Natives' Training Institution, Poonindie is one of the most evocative images of an Australian Aborigine in European-Australian art. For one thing we are touched by its vivid display of the innocence of youth. We are touched by the fact that we know so little of so individual a presence. We find it hard to reconcile the long tradition of white admiration for black achievement in sports and entertainment, but so often withheld from the higher achievements of their rich cultures.

The young cricketer represented in this portrait is a South Australian Aboriginal boy, Nannultera, who was converted to Christianity and who joined the new Natives' Training Institution at Poonindie, near Port Lincoln, in September 1851.

We know only little about him. He was apparently taken up by Mr and Mrs William Elder and then committed to the care of the Institution's founder, Mathew Hale, the Archdeacon of Adelaide.[1] As well as being an excellent cricketer, Nannultera was a gentle, well-mannered boy and the youngest of the Aborigines at Poonindie. In 1854 he was taken back to Adelaide where he stayed with William Elder's brother George. Matthew Moorhouse, the South Australian Protector of Aborigines and a friend and supporter of Hale, arranged for Crossland to paint this portrait while the boy was in Adelaide.[2]

Working in the fluent traditions of late-Georgian and early-Victorian painting, J.M. Crossland was the most accomplished portrait-painter working in colonial South Australia and after Ludwig Becker and William Strutt he was the best portraitist working in the Australian colonies in the mid nineteenth century. Ill health may have prompted him in his fifties to emigrate in 1851 from London to the colony of South Australia.[3]

He seems to have made his name in 1853 with the first of a series of portraits of Charles Sturt, an earlier hero of inland exploration, retiring that year from colonial government service.[4] Prominent members of official society sat to him including the Governor of the colony, Sir Henry Young and Lady Young; the Chief Justice, Charles Cooper; the Mayor of Adelaide, James Hurtle Fisher, M.L.C. and the Anglican Dean of Adelaide, James Farrell. A year before his death Crossland contributed to the First Exhibition of the South Australian Society of Arts, held in Adelaide at the Council Chambers, North Terrace, in 1857. The scale and accomplishment of Crossland's full-length and half-length oil portraits were novel to the colony and suited the new confidence of a growing community, reflecting its ambitions. They are also unusual in their frequent evocation of intelligence and sensitivity in the colony's businessmen and officials.

Nannultera, a young cricketer of the Natives' Training Institution, Poonindie is one of a pair of portraits commissioned by Archdeacon Hale from Crossland in 1854. Its companion painting, *Samuel Conwillan, a catechist of the Natives' Training Institution, Poonindie*, is not a sporting image. In contrast it represents one of the older Aboriginal leaders of the Institution, holding a Bible.[5] Archdeacon Hale paid only six pounds and five shillings for Conwillan's portrait, perhaps a special price for a churchman; a full-length portrait of Adelaide's Mayor earned Crossland seventy guineas.

The Natives' Training Institution at Poonindie had been founded by Mathew Hale in 1850. Unlike most Christian missions to the Australian Aborigines, Poonindie stands out for the degree of permanence it achieved, the enlightened insights brought to bear on its foundation and the support which Hale's personal commitment and generosity evoked from the Church and government of the day.[6]

Hale's aim at Poonindie was to found "... a Christian village of Australian natives, reclaimed from barbarism and trained to the duties of social Christian life".[7] The whole direction of his work was to 'civilize' the Aborigines committed to his care. If this intention showed a lack of understanding of their traditional culture, it expressed, for the mid nineteenth century, the practical necessities required if Aboriginal and European people were to live and work together. Towards this aim, in the preparatory isolation of Poonindie the emphasis was on formal education, industrial occupation (sheep-station work, cropping, building) and Christian piety.

In the sense of Juvenal's *Orandum est ut sit mens sana in corpore sano* (Your prayer must be for a sound mind in a sound body), Samuel Conwillan's grave portrait commemorates the achievement of the mind, whereas Nannultera's displays the qualities of bodily recreation. Cricket had been deliberately introduced at Poonindie by Archdeacon Hale. On a visit there in 1853 (during which he baptised Samuel Conwillan), Augustus Short, the Bishop of Adelaide noted that "... I was pleased at watching ... two Australian Native 'elevens' thus enjoying themselves and remarked, not only on their neatness in 'fielding and batting' but ... the perfect humour which prevailed throughout the game: no ill temper shown, or angry appeals to the Umpire as is generally the case in a match of *Whites*".[8]

Cricket continued to play a role in the life of the Institution. Later an Aboriginal team would play against the boys from St Peter's Collegiate School in Adelaide and vice versa at Poonindie.[9] Despite early difficulties and setbacks the Institution flourished and by the 1870s had become self-supporting. When, as Bishop of Perth, Hale revisited his beloved Poonindie in 1872 he found some eighty-six Aborigines living there, some 200 acres under profitable cultivation and a production rate of 100 bales of wool per year. More significantly, he found seventy-five per cent of the Aborigines were attending daily church service and the entire population in excellent health.[10]

Not until shortly before his death in Bristol in 1895 (and still in possession of the portraits of Samuel Conwillan and Nannultera) did Hale learn of the final failure and break-up of his enterprise of 1850. Ever the saint, the Bishop wrote his last letter to "his dear people lately belonging to the Poonindie Mission" exhorting them to let it be seen by the holiness of their lives, what they had shared together.[11]

The paintings of Nannultera and Conwillan are important as documents of hope, despite our difficulty in coming to terms with the paternalism of nineteenth-century Christian missionary endeavour. If Mathew Hale (and others like him) had faults, they were the faults of the age, not the man. He was a friend of the Aborigines and a selfless champion of their cause. His work at Poonindie was a very real attempt to bridge the social and cultural differences between the conquering Europeans and the indigenous people of this land.

J.M. CROSSLAND, 1800-1858. *Nannultera, a young cricketer of the Natives' Training Institution, Poonindie*. 1854, Adelaide. Oil on canvas, 99 x 78.8 cm. Rex Nan Kivell Collection, National Library of Australia, Canberra. Presented 1959

J.M. CROSSLAND. *Samuel Conwillan, a catechist of the Natives' Training Institution, Poonindie*. 1854, Adelaide. Oil on canvas, 99 x 79.7 cm. Rex Nan Kivell Collection, National Library of Australia, Canberra

CENTENARY ART: NATURE by DANIEL THOMAS

One hundred years after the First Fleet delivered its convicts and soldiers to Botany Bay and Sydney Cove, Australian colonists no longer felt like colonists. By 1888 a majority had been born in Australia and they were native Australians.

Art in the Centenary years, the 1880s and the 1890s, withdrew from the colonial task of interesting the world in exotica and instead looked inwards to its own most familiar, commonplace or characteristic aspects.

The comfortably commonplace was already present in colonial art in Lewin's, Glover's and Buvelot's gum-tree landscapes. Suburban farmlands near Melbourne or Sydney now grew European weeds and fruit-trees, and the commonplace was no longer uniquely Australian. Buvelot's Yarra Valley of eucalyptus trees at Heidelberg was infested with golden-blossoming gorse, a noxious weed. Lewin's Hawkesbury River gum-trees on Governor Bligh's farm had given way to poplars and pink-and-white apple-blossom.

Henceforth, if peculiarly Australian nature was emphasized in art then the work was likely to be intended as a National Symbol. Frederick McCubbin's *Lost*, 1886, at first sight a study of the subtle beauties in eucalyptus bush vegetation, is even more than a National Symbol and is ultimately a Symbolist painting; invisible nature-spirits have enchanted a child with the beauty of wildflowers, warmth and fragrance.

In the early spring of 1889 the young artists of Centenary Melbourne held a manifesto-exhibition of Australia's first consciously avant-garde paintings. They were small nine-by-five-inch "Impressions", most of them directly painted from suburban nature or from city life. Some were Symbolist. There was a wax relief by C. Douglas Richardson of a nude female spirit of the *Wind*. Blossom studies were given titles referring to Herrick's poetry, and many of these "Impressions" of transient effects were consciously symbolic of the transience of youth and beauty and love.

The 9 by 5 Impression Exhibition was appreciated by the fashionable art-collecting world of Melbourne, "lovers of the beautiful" well able to admire the "clever little sketches" and the Aesthetic display arrangements: "Scarves and draperies of soft clinging silk, of the reds that Millais has made popular, and the greens beloved of the aesthetic. The great blue and green vases . . . were filled on the opening day with japonica and roses, violets and jonquils, and the air was sweet with the perfume of daphne . . . The main idea of the impressionist movement is a revolt against conventionality . . ."[1] Besides the calculated provocation of their small size and their sketchiness (". . . splashes of colour . . . slap-dash brushwork . . .[not] pictures [but] palettes") the Impressions' picture-frames had abandoned conventional mouldings and gold finish for flat timbers with touches of painted decoration. The source of this provocative aestheticism was James McNeill Whistler, then London's most famous contemporary artist, and behind him and many other European Impressionists at the time was the art of Japan.

The eccentric emptiness of Arthur Streeton's *Early summer — Gorse in bloom* was 'Japanese', and this was a good-sized exhibition-painting not a special-event provocation like the 9 by 5s. Charles Conder's blossom

trees on a Hawkesbury River farm had many models in Japanese art.

To point out that work which claimed to attack convention had in fact made use of unfamiliar Japanese conventions is not to deny that the young artists had also succeeded in their aim "To render truthfully, and thus obtain first records of effects widely differing and often of very fleeting character". That meant "effects" of colour, light and tone; unusual violets, pinks and greens found not only in the small Impressions but also in passages within large paintings like Streeton's *Golden summer, Eaglemont*.

A large, slowly-developed painting from "long contemplative brooding over the subdued effects of quiet light", David Davies's *Moonrise* is a masterpiece of "truthful rendering" of an effect, but nevertheless very Japanese in its composition and only vaguely indicated as being Yarra Valley Australian in minor details of gum-tree silhouette and post-and-rail fencing.

The colonial period's more traditional concern for expressing the great tumultuous forces in nature continued and was climaxed in 1891 by Arthur Streeton's *"Fire's on"*. As in Strutt's vast bushfire subject and James Shaw's shipwreck, there is death in this painting. But nature's participation in this death is metaphoric, not literal; explosives, set off for excavation of a railway tunnel, were the cause of the death. Yet the upright format of this landscape-painting, like that of McCubbin's *Lost*, is a suggestion that a spirit of the land has risen from its usual horizontality to torment intruders.

"Fire's on" is also by far the most impressive of the few Australian paintings which take as their subject the "effect" of noon-day glare, a time of day which can be dangerous in itself, with blinding light and dehydrating, burning heat.

W.C. Piguenit's *The Flood in the Darling 1890* is another peculiarly Australian natural disaster. Streeton saw a biblical "Burning Fiery Furnace" in his *"Fire's on"* subject and no one would have missed, in the 1890s, a parallel between a real flood in the New South Wales outback and the biblical Deluge, visited on a sinful world. Nature attacks remorsely, slowly and in silence.

A final traditional strand in the Australian Centenary's uses of nature in art is also provided by Streeton. Only partially a truthful rendering for the sake of modernity, not at all a propitiation of the dangerous forces in nature, *Golden Summer, Eaglemont*, painted in the summer of 1888/89, is a Centenary hymn of praise to an Australian's native land. It expresses blissful, personal happiness in the look and feel of a generalized "Australia" more than in the particular place it depicts (though truthfully-rendered Yarra Valley Impressionist effects are in it). But it also, like some of Glover's and von Guérard's earlier paintings, claims continuity with the great tradition in poetry and painting of the Pastoral, the art which from Virgil's ancient Roman poetry to Claude's and Turner's paintings paid homage to the nymphs and shepherds who attend to flocks and herds. The homage was usually to a past Golden Age, in an imaginary Arcadia. Streeton's *Golden Summer* was a Golden Age in the present, and in a real Australia rich from wool-growing.

Arthur STREETON, 1867-1943. *Early summer — Gorse in bloom.* October 1888, Heidelberg (?) near Melbourne. Oil on canvas, 56.2 x 100.6 cm. Art Gallery of South Australia, Adelaide. Gift of the Art Gallery of South Australia Foundation 1982

Charles CONDER, 1868-1909. *The farm, Richmond, New South Wales.* August 1888, Richmond near Sydney. Oil on canvas, 45.6 x 51.3 cm. National Gallery of Victoria, Melbourne. State Government special grant 1979

"THE SCENT OF THE EUCALYPTUS" by JANE CLARK

Frederick McCubbin, *Lost,* 1886

"In everything Mr McCubbin paints there is that spirit of truth which wins the sympathy of the heart. He tells us everyday stories, and we feel they are true. With an innate love for bush subjects, and with the scent of the eucalyptus in his being, he can depict with sympathetic feeling scenes which appeal to Australian hearts."
The Studio, London, September 1909, p. 69

Frederick McCubbin was born in 1855 in Melbourne and was therefore part of the first native-born generation of Australian colonial painters. He commenced his professional training in Melbourne, first at an Artisans' School of Design, then from 1871 at the National Gallery of Victoria's recently-opened drawing school. He was proudly Australian. "There used to be a sort of legend about that time that Australia would do great things in Art", he later recalled. "Where it sprang from or how goodness only knows".[1] He was a voracious reader, affectionately known as "The Prof" to his friends and fellow students. At a young age he was captivated by the idea of painting "stupendous historical pictures — *The Battle of Waterloo, Raleigh, Queen Elizabeth* — long-forgotten events from the history book at school."[2] But he also joined Tom Roberts on outdoor sketching expeditions around the suburbs of Melbourne: along the Yarra River at Studley Park, for example, where "for the first time [he] got awakened to the beauties of Australian landscape". Both young men were influenced by the *intimiste* landscape style of the senior Melbourne painter Louis Buvelot. As McCubbin recalled, "Most of us owe it to him that slowly we were able to see the paintable qualities of that which lay immediately around us".[3]

In 1885 McCubbin and Roberts, together with Louis Abrahams, pitched camp at Box Hill to paint out in the open — *en plein air* — at weekends and over the summer months. It was there in 1886 that McCubbin painted *Lost* in the suburban bush of Houston's Paddock, about fourteen kilometres east of Melbourne, easily reached by suburban railway.[4] A little girl is standing alone in thick bushland: a careful study of one "familiar corner of nature".

McCubbin's intimate close-up view of the native vegetation and the absence of any panoramic vista are in marked contrast to most earlier colonial Australian landscape-painting conventions. As described by a contemporary journalist, this is simply "a scene in the bush, with a lost child, who constitutes the forlorn centre of a grove of saplings, and an undergrowth of withered grass and scrub".[5] A pathway of yellowing bush grasses guides the viewer's eye towards the solitary figure. The soft blue-green of eucalyptus leaves in the foreground links up with the colour of her dress; and yet she is enclosed in the stillness of her setting by a barrier of delicate, sharply focused twiggy shrubs and saplings (the boxwood or red gum native to Box Hill).

The effects of soft, even, outdoor lighting and the shallow space cut off by a hazy, broadly-painted background screen of trees led contemporary critics to label this and similar works "impressionist". "How curious it is by the way", commented a writer in *Table Talk*, "that some of our best artists, Messrs Tom Roberts, McCubbin and Streeton are all a little touched with the mania which afflicts the French impressionists, looking at nature as though through a glass darkly, neither recognising her definition of form nor her positive colour . . . I do not write this in disparagement of the work of the three gentlemen . . . I admire their landscapes in spite of what I regard as their incompleteness . . .".[6] In fact McCubbin and his friends knew little if anything of progressive French impressionist painting. They particularly admired and emulated the *juste milieu* (middle-of-the-road) open-air realism of the contemporary French painter Jules Bastien-Lepage and his European followers.[7] McCubbin has left a description of the difficulties of working *en plein air* on such a large scale: setting up the canvas securely and then carrying home the wet oil painting — especially difficult if the weather happened to turn windy.

In *Lost*, McCubbin combines his love of local landscape and history with the sentiments of popular Victorian narrative art. He suggests a storyline — with events before and after the episode depicted — but his painting is not burdened with specific anecdotal details. The girl's apron appears to be filled with wildflowers, so we can assume that her absorption in a search for beauty and fragrance has led her to a strange part of otherwise familiar bushland near her home. We do not know whether this 'lost child' story ends happily ever after or not. However, it is summer and she will not suffer cold. And although the child is crying there is a clear indication, in the extreme foreground, that she will not remain lost: at the centre of the viewer's entry into the painting is a conspicuously broken twig, presumably the last of several which will trace the wildflower-gatherer's path for searchers or re-trace it if the child collects herself. The vertical format, not the usual convention for landscape, is in itself a reminder that this painting is a figure subject; the vertical canvas stands for the partially-concealed standing child. It also suggests, subtly, the possibility of a nature spirit, an invisible figure half-sensed by the child as well as the viewer. (McCubbin, twenty years later, did paint fairies, seen in the bush by children.)[8]

The theme of children lost in the Australian bush was longstanding in both art and literature by 1886. Marcus Clarke's story *Pretty Dick* and Henry Kingsley's three-volume novel *Recollections of Geoffry Hamlyn* (London, 1859) were well-known examples, the latter's chapter "The Lost Child" being reprinted as late as 1871.[9] Distressing accounts of the three Duff children, rescued after nine days in the bush in 1864, had received extensive local media coverage; Nicholas Chevalier drew "Lost in the Bush" for *The Illustrated Melbourne Post*, 22 September 1864. William Strutt exhibited *The Little Wanderers, or The Lost Track* at the Royal Academy in London; and S.T. Gill's 1865 lithograph of the Duff children was still widely circulated later in the nineteenth century. In addition, McCubbin may well have been inspired by an almost contemporary news item: the finding of little Clara Crosbie alive "after Three Weeks Lost in the Bush". *The Australasian Sketcher*'s description of this timely rescue near Lilydale in June 1885 included a black-and-white wood-engraving typical of popular press illustrations of the day,[10] and Lilydale is a short distance beyond Box Hill, on the same suburban railway line.

However, McCubbin's presentation of the theme transcends historical records and newspaper illustrations alike. *Lost* was the first of his

Frederick McCUBBIN, 1855-1917. *Lost.* 1886, Box Hill near Melbourne. Oil on canvas, 115.8 x 73.7 cm.
National Gallery of Victoria, Melbourne. Felton Bequest Fund 1940

ambitious, large-scale bush genre paintings dramatizing the hardships and stoic perseverance of Australia's pioneers, in "that union of landscape and bush episode which", as one contemporary observed, "he has somewhat made his own."[11] Although the prospect of missing children had been an ever-present nightmare for the early settlers, by the 1880s history and mythmaking were beginning to blur in romantic accounts of a heroic pioneering past — especially in the imagination of city dwellers. Boomtime Melbourne was then riding high on an optimistic wave of pride in that Centennial decade, similar to but less self-examining than our several years of Bicentennial celebrations.

An intense relationship with his native land is the foundation of McCubbin's art. He left Australia only once — on a brief visit to Europe in 1907 — and his paintings held an immediate appeal for the community in which he lived and worked. "Nature under our Australian sky seems to me like a shy reserved person", he once explained, ". . . but you have only to wait and watch her varying moods, and you will find all the beauty you can desire."[12]

This painting invites its viewer to participate in the discovery of a lost child; but even more McCubbin, one of the first major Australian-born colonial painters, encourages us, by close-up, low-level scrutiny of warm, scented, subtly-coloured leaves, bark and grasses, to participate in an Australian-born child's intense, entranced absorption in "all the beauty you can desire".

PASTORAL by TERRY SMITH

Arthur Streeton, *Golden Summer, Eaglemont,* 1889

"Fancy if you could grasp all you feel and condense your thoughts into a scheme which would embrace sweet sound, great colour and all the slow soft movement".
Arthur Streeton to Tom Roberts, 1890[1]

A young Australian artist joyously invokes the ultimate dream of all Romantics: to experience nature's essences and appearances so intensely that a work of art spontaneously creates itself, drawing together all the heightened human senses into a harmony indistinguishable from nature itself. Arthur Streeton writes from Sydney to his mentor, friend and fellow-painter, Tom Roberts, reminiscing about the enchantment of the two past summers in Melbourne, where on a hill above the suburban village of Heidelberg they had worked with Charles Conder and others at outdoor landscape painting. (A previous outdoor painting camp established at Box Hill had been especially favoured by the older artists, Roberts and Frederick McCubbin.) Streeton's fantasy was both specifically national yet something more: to create a total work of art. His posing this as a future hope was properly, if perhaps unduly, modest: he had come, two summers earlier, closer than any of his contemporaries to achieving such a goal — in *Golden Summer, Eaglemont,* 1889, painted when he was twenty-one.

The broad blaze of sunlight across the middle, running left and right, highly-keyed yellow-and-white hatching on top of heavy underpainting . . . over the foreground shadow we leap, as it were, straight into this bold hill-crest, dazzling but also absorbing to the eye: white patches everywhere disturb an easy diagonal reading of the whole — how can this density of paint effect such weightlessness? There are two different speeds at work here, evident at first glance, a push and pull of contraries that seem typical of every level of Streeton's approach to painting. He wants the instant "grasp all you feel", but he also wants a condensing, embracing "scheme". Freely felt, unmediated first impressions vie with the considered schemata of academic composition. Look beyond and before the sunblasted crest: in the valley are speeding slivers of opulent darker hues; in the right foreground is placed a staid vignette of a boy watching sheep, a sheep eyeing off a magpie.

The twisting, tumbling deep blues and greens of the distant valley have all the fluidity and immediacy of an oil-sketch painted directly from observation. This narrow band would have not been out of place in The 9 by 5 Impression Exhibition of oil-sketch "impressions", mostly on 9-by-5-inch panels or boards, held in Melbourne in August 1889, some four months after the first display of *Golden Summer, Eaglemont.* Many views of this favourite Yarra Valley vista were included in that famous showing of 182 works, most by Streeton, Conder and Roberts: among them Conder's *Dandenong from Heidelberg,* Roberts's *Across the Dandenongs.* But the most striking was Streeton's *Impression for "Golden Summer".* It was larger, painted before the idea of a group show of uniform 9 by 5s, and probably one of the first works to announce, at the end of 1888, that a "Heidelberg School" might displace the "Box Hill School" which had existed across the valley since the end of 1885. Streeton's *Impression* seems to have become a kind of talisman of artistic possibility for the group; it appears on the wall of a room in Conder's 9 by 5 *Impressionists' camp,* a loving meditation in which his friends Roberts and Streeton wait in their Eaglemont 'camp' for winter Sunday rain to stop.[2] Conder also tells us that wine was called "Golden Summer" by Streeton.[3]

Impression for "Golden Summer" exemplifies the manifesto provided by the artists in their catalogue of The 9 by 5 Impression Exhibition:

"An Effect is only momentary: so an impressionist tries to find his place. Two half-hours are never alike, and he who tries to paint a sunset on two successive evenings, must be more or less painting from memory. So, in these works, it has been the object of the artists to render faithfully, and thus obtain first records of effects widely differing, and often of very fleeting character."[4]

Impression for "Golden Summer" embodies the moment before nightfall, as shadows race across the moving sheep and as the blazing sun, setting behind us, casts its pink glow everywhere. Twists of coral colour becoming dancing trees, a blur of black a hurtling dog, turnings of white the sides of a sheep and a shouting man caught in the light; a battle between sunlight and shadow is joined, all hanging on the quickly flickering square brush. The big painting, *Golden Summer, Eaglemont,* entraps this kind of energy in two of the key areas: the sunlit crest and the liquid valley beyond. But it is less specific about the time of day: it offers a memory of midday in the high sunlight, late afternoon in the encroaching shadows, sunset in the touches of pink, even darkness in the deeper hues in the valley.

Streeton in both paintings may well be paying homage to Louis Buvelot, who died in May 1888, the month the railway was opened to Heidelberg, and whose *Summer afternoon, Templestowe,* 1866, one of the principal Australian paintings in the National Gallery of Victoria, Melbourne, during Streeton's formative years, is a sheep-dominated landscape in the Yarra Valley. Streeton later said that Buvelot's painting had inspired his first visit to Heidelberg, for a day's painting at Templestowe. At the railway station a chance meeting with a friend produced the offer of the semi-derelict house on the nearby Mount Eagle estate, which became a young artists' resort for two years.[5] Heidelberg, twelve kilometres from Melbourne, was a pretty, supposedly English-looking farming district which had attracted excursionists and honeymooners for twenty years. In 1865 the view of the Yarra from Mount Eagle was being compared with that of the Thames from Richmond Hill outside London.[6] The view from Richmond Hill was titled *England* in one of J.M.W. Turner's largest paintings; Eaglemont became Streeton's specially favoured painting ground and in *Golden Summer* he made it stand for Australia.

Streeton's sketch and painting, to those not privileged to know this particular landscape, both look as if they are set in real sheep country, in rolling hills on the slopes of the Great Dividing Range, anywhere from the Western District of Victoria to Queensland, from Australia Felix to the Darling Downs. The farm buildings in the *Impression* exist only as a white flash on a distant hill but for the big painting the artist has invented a large, high-roofed woolshed (with profile more common to cowsheds and an unusual, if not entirely functionless, chimney), a small outhouse among the trees, and some containing-yards suggested with breathtaking brevity.

Arthur STREETON, 1867-1943. *Golden Summer, Eaglemont*. 1889, Heidelberg near Melbourne. Oil on canvas;
81.3 x 152.6 cm. William J. Hughes, Perth

The few outer-suburban sheep have multiplied into a station-owner's mob. Streeton turned an impression of a particular place into an image which is also symbolic of Australian scenery in general.

This brings into play two other "slow soft movements". The basic rhythms of human toil, of work on the land, are evident in this depiction of sheep-farming, at the end of a day's labour. And rural industry is shown as part of the earth's natural cycles, as a gentle covering over a larger geological inevitability that may — if the shattered, windblown trees are any indication — be more relentlessly brutal.

The bold inscriptions made by Streeton across the lower portions of the painting are the final clues to his intentions, and tie together the disparate visual logics within the painting. His large signature is a clear sign of both authorship and witness, "1889" says when, "Eaglemont" declares where. "I saw this, I felt this, I became this, and here it is" — the artist/painting seems to be saying. This is a clear affirmation of what has been called the fundamental postulate of Romanticism, that "sentiment and natural appearance are necessarily coherent".[7]

Streeton also wrote, as the first word on the left, in somewhat smaller script: "Pastoral". This refers to the industry he had painted, as well as to the poetic mood he wished to evoke. Explaining the inspiration of his famous *Shearing the rams*, Tom Roberts wrote:

> "It seems to me that one of the best words spoken to an artist is, 'Paint what you love, and love what you paint', and on that I have worked; and so it came that being in the bush and feeling the delight and fascination of the great pastoral life and work I have tried to express it."[8]

The rest of Roberts's letter, describing the golden-fleece activity of the shearing shed, is a lyric reverie as intense as that felt by Streeton before a sweeping vista. Streeton, in the summer of *Golden Summer*, had written to Roberts from Eaglemont: "Yes, I sit here in the upper circle surrounded by copper and gold, and smile joy . . . as all the light, glory and quivering brightness passes slowly and freely before my eyes."[9]

These words describe exactly what we are seeing when we look at this painting, but they would apply equally well to a seventeenth-century pastoral by Claude Lorrain, the master of Mediterranean light and the first great landscape painter in European art. Claude embodied the calm stillness of the classical dream of Arcadia or Eden but also opened the way for the Romantic sense of immersing oneself in Nature. Streeton sits, two hundred and fifty years later, overlooking a place inconceivable to Claude (or to Turner, his greatest follower), but sees it, partly, through the same eyes. This shows just how powerfully persistent was this pastoral tradition in art and literature. It also shows the beginnings of traditions persisting as a presence even in the moment of their ending.

The artist-prized immediacy of the "impression", the oil-sketch made on the spot seeking the essentials of a scene, triumphantly survives Streeton's enlargement and ennoblement as *Golden Summer, Eaglemont* and is then framed with some of the narrative characteristics of genre painting, so popular in Victorian England, to create a mixture of pure landscape and subject painting unusual for its time, exceptional for its place.[10] These features, added to the exotic nature of its subject, caused it, in 1891, to become the first painting by an Australian-born artist to be exhibited at the Royal Academy, London — but with the generalized title *Golden Summer, Australia*.[11]

Golden Summer, Eaglemont/Australia was the first of the broad-vista landscapes which Streeton was to make his own. Vital, free brushing, intuitively inventive ways of representing unfamiliar phenomena, delight in the unusual beauties of the bush, a youthful zest for the pleasures of good living and evident optimism about the future of this new land continued in many subsequent paintings, and were projected as images of Australian life. Streeton did this so often and so well that such interpretations became conventional for virtually all Australian landscape painting, spreading to influence — first as a liberation, then as a limitation — the way we have come to see our sunblessed country.

DELUGE OF PITILESS SILENCE by BARRY PEARCE

W.C. Piguenit, *The Flood in the Darling 1890*, 1895

W.C. Piguenit's masterpiece *The Flood in the Darling 1890*, completed in 1895, tells us much about the importance of landscape painting in the nineteenth-century European romantic movement, and of the long legacy which that movement produced in Australia. The picture's breadth and air of solitude combine with the elemental presence of sky and water to evoke a mood. That mood is nature eternal, and it provides the first impression, before thoughts of place or subject. Piguenit expressed the infinite mystery of nature's stillness more compellingly in the grand-scale *The Flood in the Darling 1890* than did any other nineteenth-century Australian painter.

Given his isolated beginnings as an artist, it is remarkable that Piguenit was able to tap into the sense of a far-distant art movement and to develop such a commanding and universal feeling in his painting. Unlike John Glover, Conrad Martens, Eugene von Guérard, Nicholas Chevalier and Louis Buvelot[1], all important colonial painters who shared his fascination for the Australian wilderness, Piguenit was born in Australia (in Hobart) and was largely self-taught. The others had come from Europe already mature and professionally equipped with artistic conventions to impose upon the new world. Piguenit, who like Frederick McCubbin travelled abroad only very late in life[2], is the first significant artist to resolve his necessarily indirect knowledge of his European cultural inheritance with direct experience of the Australian environment into which he was native-born.

Perhaps *The Flood in the Darling 1890* had its stylistic germination in those early years in Hobart when Piguenit worked at the Survey Office of the Lands Department. He had started there at the age of fourteen and later was encouraged in his painting by a Scottish artist Frank Dunnett, who arrived in Tasmania about 1859. Dunnett was said to have "received lessons in painting from J.M.W. Turner"[3], who had died only a few years earlier and whose reputation was at a peak. It may be that Piguenit saw engravings of Turner's paintings, monochromatic images of the great English artist's visions, which could have encouraged Piguenit in his interest towards the dramatic blending of water, land and sky and underlined for him the power of nature's elements as symbols.

Later, after he had moved in 1880 to Sydney from Hobart, having resigned from the Survey Office in 1872, contemporary critics compared Piguenit's work with the Scottish school. In particular they pointed out its similarity to that of the successful romantic painter Peter Graham.[4] Piguenit would have been able to see in the Art Gallery of New South Wales, Sydney a number of British landscape paintings whose breadth and drama may have inspired him: paintings by William Wyllie, John Mogford and George Cole, all bought between 1877 and 1884, and especially a work by Graham called *Rising mists*, bought in 1888, whose handling of cloud and mountain has an uncanny resemblance to Piguenit's own method of painting.[5]

The prevailing taste which influenced the purchase of such works in Sydney encouraged this kind of painting locally, and led to the acquisition of a number of Piguenit's works for the Gallery during his lifetime.[6]

Art-historical considerations aside, *The Flood in the Darling 1890* is above all a landscape of fact. Piguenit loved nothing more than to see the dominance of nature over all else. When floods occurred in western New South Wales during March and April 1890, the Darling River reportedly bloating to forty miles wide, swallowing vast tracts of land[7], he travelled to the river to capture not its dreadful devastation at Bourke, where the entire population was left homeless and cut off, but rather the miraculous effect of a seemingly endless plain of water mirroring a vast outback sky.

Newspapers of the day reported the desperate struggles for survival, food shortages, the losses of property, drownings, people fleeing in terror to the rapidly shrinking patches of dry land as the waters rose about them. None of this was of interest to Piguenit as a painter. He was not a social realist or an illustrator. He could not make figure compositions, as did the Melbourne artist Aby Altson who, in response to the headlines about the floods at Bourke, painted a large subject-picture, *Flood sufferings*, 1890.[8] Piguenit saw not suffering, death and destruction but rather, above it all, the eternal, pitiless beauty of nature's pattern.

A pencil sketch[9] for the painting records his observations of the nuances of tone and colour in his subject: "delicate purplish grey clouds"; "warm yellow band of clear sky"; "pinkish glow round sun"; "sun almost rose colour"; "edges of clouds golden near sun"; and so on. In that sketch the orb of the sun is placed in the centre, just above the horizon; it is not shown in the painting. There it remains hidden behind the clouds, its presence felt mainly through a silvery strip of light on the horizon, perhaps symbolizing hope of recovery.

The length of Piguenit's stay in the west is not known. A diary from his Tasmanian years records his experiences both as a bushman of considerable ruggedness and an observer of sensitivity.[10] Other reports describe his intrepid trudges through scrub, river valleys and across cloud-enshrouded mountains with a heavy sack, photographing and sketching as an unpaid member of exploring expeditions.[11] Therefore it can be assumed that he was well equipped for survival in the flood regions. The water as depicted in the painting comes down to the bottom edge of the composition, with sparse indication of solid land. Boats in the Bourke area were in extremely short supply and it was necessary to travel by the more dangerous means of the horse, prone to stumble in holes created by the flood waters.[12] As trains were cut off, Piguenit presumably used horses to get to the area and to seek out his motif.

How he went about making his painting once he came back to Sydney is not known. Piguenit carried a wet-plate camera on at least one Tasmanian expedition and the technique of his paintings of that period suggests a basis in his photographs (although no photographs by him have yet been found or identified). But it is unlikely that his work from the flood trip derives from photography, rather to his drawings and to his memory.

At the bottom of the sketch for *The Flood in the Darling 1890* are other thumbnail images of the subject. Piguenit exhibited in 1890 two other flood paintings from his trip: *"Out West" during the Flood of 1890, Gunda Booka Range* and *"Out West" during the Flood of 1890, Mt Oxley*.[13] There is also a painting on the subject of drought on the Darling in a private collection.[14] Piguenit was awarded the Wynne Prize for landscape in 1901

W.C. PIGUENIT, 1836-1914. *The Flood in the Darling 1890*. 1895, Sydney, from sketches on the Darling. Oil on canvas, 122.5 x 199.3 cm. Art Gallery of New South Wales, Sydney. Colonial Government funds 1895

for a painting, present whereabouts unknown, entitled *Thunderstorm on the Darling*. However there is no doubt that *The Flood in the Darling 1890* was consciously worked on over a period of years as his *magnum opus*, not only of his work from the area, but also of his career to that moment.

The Flood in the Darling 1890 is, then, a climactic painting in more ways than one. As well as recording a catclysmic event of nature, it closes a chapter of romantic colonial painting in Australian art. Piguenit was to continue to receive patronage for ambitious wilderness subjects, such as *Kosciusko* commissioned at the artist's request in 1902 by the trustees of the Art Gallery of New South Wales following the recent occasion of Australian Federation. But a bold new spirit of painting was in the air. Australian Impressionism, based largely on a sunlit and more openly comfortable aspect of Australian landscape, was well established by 1895 and at its peak in Sydney under the inspiration of Tom Roberts and Arthur Streeton.[15] Piguenit had little regard for this new movement, in spite of his unusually high-keyed palette in *The Flood in the Darling 1890*. Indeed the

Art Gallery of New South Wales's purchase of this picture in 1895 reflected a schism in the Sydney art world; 1895 was the year that the Society of Artists was established in Sydney as a breakaway group from Art Society of New South Wales[16] and the Gallery hedged its bets by acquiring simultaneously Piguenit's painting from the Art Society and Streeton's *Cremorne Pastoral* from the Society of Artists.

For today's viewer, *The Flood in the Darling 1890* reflects Piguenit's response to an event that remains part of Australia's present. The cycles of bushfire, drought and flood go back beyond memory and have remained unaffected by two hundred years of European civilization. Nature and the land often shrug off Australia's human inhabitants with tragic consequences. Yet most Australians would admit, as Piguenit found, and other artists such as Russell Drysdale, Sidney Nolan and Lloyd Rees have found since, that in these events there is a strange, fascinating beauty that is part of the tragedy and an indelible part of being Australian.

AT THE DRAGON'S MOUTH by BARRY PEARCE

Arthur Streeton, *"Fire's on"*, 1891

Fire's on depicts the blasting in 1891 of a railway tunnel through the eastern face of the Blue Mountains at Lapstone, sixty kilometres inland from Sydney, immediately above the coastal plain. The tunnel was an improvement to the main western line inland across the Great Dividing Range, a greater confrontation with the terrain than the previously existing zig-zags. Few visitors to the Australian Impressionist collection at the Art Gallery of New South Wales, Sydney, fail to be impressed by the impact of this vertical composition and its glaring light.[1] Yet *"Fire's on"* does not conform to the usual comfortable subject-matter of Australian Impressionism. It is not the image of an idyllic place. There is indeed a sense that if one shared the position of the painter it would be a precarious one: perched on a rocky cliff, dust drifting up from the spectacle of human labour, explosions shattering the air and, high above, a zenith sky of searing blue in concert with the sun-heated rocks below. Streeton himself, in one of the most evocative letters ever written by an Australian artist, spoke of the danger, the difficulty, the light, heat and fumes, in his attempt to paint the scene. His letter to Frederick McCubbin was written in exhilaration during the spring of 1891:

"The sun is beautiful in the morning . . . march off at 9.30 to my work . . . through a canyon where big brown men are toiling all the hot day . . . I've past the west mouth and now am arrived at my subject, the other mouth, which gapes like a great dragon's mouth at the perfect flood of hot sunlight. There is a cutting through the vast hill of bright sandstone; the walls of rock run high up and are crowned by gums bronze green, and they look quite small, being so high up, and behind is the deep blue azure heaven, where a crow sails along like a dot with its melancholy, hopeless cry — long drawn, like the breath of a dying sheep. Right below me the men work, some with shovels, others drilling for a blast. I work on the W. Colour drying too quickly and the ganger cries 'Fire', 'Fire's on', all the men drop their tools and scatter and I nimbly skip off my perch and hide behind a big safe rock. A deep hush is everywhere — then, 'Holy Smoke!', what a boom of thunder shakes the rock and me. It echoes through the hills and dies away 'mid the crashing of tons of rock; some lumps fly hundreds of feet sometimes and fall and fly everywhere among the trees; and then a thick cloud laden with fumes of the blasting powder. All at work once more — more drills; the rock is a perfect blazing glory of white, orange, cream and blue streaks here and there where the blast has worked its force. Work awhile, then again 'Fire', 'Fire's on!' — and off we go, and then work again . . .'Tis like painting in the 'Burning Fiery Furnace'; so beautiful and bright and yet so difficult to attain."[2]

Later he wrote to Tom Roberts describing the death at noon of one of the workers, which is the subject of the group of figures at the bottom of the painting:

"This morning, hot, windy and warm, as I travel down the line, and the mirage sizzling and jiggering over the railway track. I arrive at my cutting, 'the fatal cutting', and inwardly rejoice at the prosperous warmth all glowing before me as I descend and re-ascend the opposite side up to my shady, shelving sandstone rock, perched high up . . . I look up and down at my subject; is it worth painting? Why, of course, damn it all! That is providing I'm capable of translating my impression to the canvas. All is serene as I work and peg away, retiring under the rock a bit when they light any shots . . . 12 o'clock . . . and now I hear 'Fire, fire's on', from the gang close by; rest my billy on the rock, take out my pipe, and listen for the shots, with my eye watching the bright redgum yonder. BOOM! and then rumbling of rock, the navvy under the rock with me, and watching says, 'Man killed'. He runs down the sheltered side, and cries, 'Man killed!'. Another takes it up and now it has run through the camp. More shots and crashing rock, and we peep over; he lies all hidden bar his legs — and now men, nippers and two women hurry down, a woman with a bottle and rags. All the shots are gone but one and all wait and dare not go near. Then someone says the last hole was not lit, and they raise the rock and lift him on to the stretcher, fold his arms over his chest, and slowly six of them carry him past me."[3]

Critics of the time commented that this subject was not in accord with the traditional idea of the picturesque.[4] Contrary to creating an atmosphere of harmony and repose, it projected a confrontation with the landscape by men, machines and progress. Why did Streeton, always steeped in poetic thoughts and references, and whose descriptions of the sublime effects and moods of nature linked him to a romantic tradition, suddenly turn to such a harshly realistic theme? Even though he associated a dragon, and Holy Smoke, and a biblical notion of the Burning Fiery Furnace to the subject of *"Fire's on"*, the reportage or descriptive aspect of the painting is more than equal to its poetic ideas.[5]

"Fire's on" signifies a vigorous new charge of ambition that took hold of Streeton once he had moved to Sydney from Melbourne in the middle of 1890. Tom Roberts was already painting large-scale genre subjects in *Shearing the rams*, 1890, and *A break away!* 1891,[6] and no doubt Streeton, under the strong nationalistic impulse that was in the air of Australia at that time, was impelled to match his achievement. Not a gifted figure draughtsman, Streeton channelled his ambition into heroic landscape. When he got to the Blue Mountains, he wrote to Roberts of the new possibilities that had been opened up, and of the numerous watercolours he was making in preparation for his big picture.

"Fire's on" is a unique painting in many ways, but it is not entirely without parallels in the rest of Streeton's work. There are his war paintings of 1918 which show the destructive effect of man on the French landscape, although they do not operate at the same level of pictorial energy.[7] There is certainly an alliance between the composition of *"Fire's on"* and Streeton's upright japoniste paintings of the early 1890s. Just as it is difficult to sense a firm foothold in *"Fire's on"* — his description of working from a sandstone rock shelf "perched high up" is hardly reassuring — so it is in many of those narrow panels painted around Sydney Harbour which are decorations without gravity, tantalizing fragments of rock, tree and water seen from unlikely angles. The artist's more characteristic *Golden Summer, Eaglemont*, 1889, *"Still glides the stream and shall forever glide"*, 1890, and *Cremorne Pastoral*, 1895[8], are evocations of places where we would like to be, to sit easily and dream; the japoniste verticals are not.

However, *"Fire's on"* is not decorative either. It tells us something far more relevant about Streeton's character than his tendencies toward the Aesthetic Movement, his poetic associations, or even about his powers of reportage. *"Fire's on"* is about the palpable, living energy of a prodigiously ambitious talent.

Streeton was a largely self-made artist. He was discovered painting on the beach at Beaumaris in Victoria by his much older colleagues

Arthur STREETON, 1867-1943. *"Fire's on"*. 1891, Lapstone near Sydney. Oil on canvas, 183.8 x 122.5 cm.
Art Gallery of New South Wales, Sydney. Colonial Government funds 1893

McCubbin and Roberts and although naturally loquacious and widely read he had not received the benefit of their long and rigorous academic training.[9] Therefore *"Fire's on"* represents the first real proving of his ability to equal them in painting the 'big' picture, as he gave himself the challenge of a subject that others less tenacious would have found impossible.

His intentions to startle are written all over the picture. Amongst many directional forces there are only two significant vertical elements in the picture, in the gum-trees at the top; the main horizontal is in the large boulder at the base. The rest is action. From the bottom of the left side the eyes travel up through the rocks, trees and shadows in a series of short, zig-zagging diagonals imaging the sound of explosives and visually echoing the softer movements of the other side of the picture, through the dazzling cream and ochre passages of earth and rock at the entrance of the tunnel, to the spillage from a rail cart, and the drift of figures into the distant heat-haze. There is no structure or stability in this painting. Yet somehow, through the sheer force of his talent and the boundless energy of his youth — he was only twenty-four years old when he painted it — Streeton has electrified with light and movement the entire surface of the canvas into a vibrant living whole. He was still to paint works of great poetry, but never again would he achieve the special synthesis that is in *"Fire's on"*. Sadly, the programme of painting that his three-month period above Lapstone apparently inspired, with his eyes turned to "the gates of the west", did not

eventuate. In the short term he was drawn back east to the lights and comfort of the city on the plain.

There is little information about how Streeton went about painting *"Fire's on"*. His letter to Roberts on 6 November 1891 describes the stretching of his six-by-four-feet canvas on a rock "like an eagle's eyrie".[10] In that letter he describes the death of a man a few days earlier, but the later death referred to in the letter to Roberts of 17 December, quoted above, is the subject of the painting. Therefore it can be assumed that Streeton had worked on this large canvas in the field for about six to eight weeks before he returned to Sydney at the end of December.

It is instructive also to compare *"Fire's on"* with the same subject in watercolour.[11] The watercolour is a more prosaic work and, presumably, more accurate as a document. Rocks and tree-trunks appear in the left side of the oil painting which are not in the watercolour, indicating Streeton's conscious manipulation of the design of the oil, and improvement of its sense of movement and vibrancy. It is likely that he made such additions later in the studio.

However, Streeton's love of the outdoors, of the sun on his skin, and his admiration for the "roaring camp" and the strong bronzed characters that he met there, indicates that in spite of any studio refinement, the painting of *"Fire's on"*, was essentially a *plein air* event. It was a part of Streeton's identification with Australian life.

THE ENCHANTED MOONRISE by RON RADFORD

David Davies, *Moonrise*, 1894

David Davies's masterpiece, *Moonrise* is one of the most breathtakingly beautiful landscapes in Australian art. Ever since its first appearance in 1894, its evocative mood, subtle sombre tones and "exquisite simplicity" have enjoyed adulation from artists and the Australian art world.[1] It has been very much a painters' painting.

Moonrise characterizes perfectly Melbourne painting of the 1890s; its shift from the brilliantly sunny 1880s paintings by Tom Roberts, Arthur Streeton, Charles Conder and others is a shift from Australian nationalism to international aestheticism. Conder had left Melbourne for Europe in 1890, Streeton and Roberts departed for Sydney in 1890 and 1891 and Melbourne landscape-painting soon turned to subdued grey days and moonlit subjects. It was as if Roberts and Streeton took the sun with them to Sydney. Davies too had painted hot, sunny works[2] before three years study overseas, but after his return to Australia in 1893 most of his new-style landscapes were nocturnes. The display of the large and successful *Moonrise*, first at the Victorian Artists' Society and then from 1895 in the permanent collection of the National Gallery of Victoria, itself helped to create in Melbourne a vogue for evening subjects and paintings of grey days. From the mid 1890s Walter Withers, John Ford Paterson, E. Phillips Fox, Tudor St George Tucker, Clara Southern, Jane Sutherland, Jane Price, Frederick McCubbin and others almost consistently painted poetic and quiet sunless landscapes.

The darker grey days and nights and introspective mood of some of Melbourne's landscape paintings of the 1890s was not merely a response to the weather of that city. Nor can it be explained by the economic depression of the 1890s which hit Melbourne more severely than it did other cities. Nor is it significant in this context that the National Gallery of Victoria was much less committed to patronizing local artists than were the Art Gallery of New South Wales and (from the end of the 1890s) the Art Gallery of South Australia. It was the general mood of the times, not so much melancholy or depressed as wistful, although sometimes also gloomy.

In 1901 the Sydney critic A.G. Stephens wrote in his preface to the *Bulletin Story Book*, "Verlaine's cult of faded things, extolling the hinted hue before the gross colour, finds a natural home in Australia — in many aspects a Land of Faded Things — of delicate purples, delicious greys, and dull dreamy olives and ochres". Paul Verlaine was an influential French Symbolist poet of the *fin de siècle* and the filtered influences of European Symbolist painting and poetry, James McNeill Whistler's aesthetic painting, and Art Nouveau design, all had a modifying influence on the naturalism and freshness of the Melbourne landscape painters who had first come together in the late 1880s as "Impressionists". The interest in the dying day became for many artists a significant preoccupation. To some it became an obsession.

For Davies the interest in the dying day became such an obsession. Born in 1864 of Welsh parents in a Welsh community in Ballarat, Victoria, his biographer, James MacDonald, suggests that ". . . perhaps his Celtic parentage may be taken to account for his persistent endeavour to get at the inner meaning of nature, and so to present it that in his work apparent

matter-of-fact statements of reality always have, inherent in them, the mystery that pervades life. In character, he was dreamy and retiring, but industrious, . . .".[3]

Davies began his training in Ballarat under a Welshman, James Price,[4] and even at this early date when his crisp style demonstrated the influence of John Mather[5] he showed some predilection for early morning and evening scenes. In 1886 Davies began his studies at the National Gallery School in Melbourne under George Folingsby, and there made a copy from a reproduction of a portrait by Rembrandt. It is possible that when he reached Paris in 1890 he studied and savoured the painterly textures and shadowy tonal subtleties of Rembrandt, to use them later in his dusky tonal landscapes such as *Moonrise*. After Paris, where he studied at the Académie Julian, he moved to England and at St Ives, Cornwall, worked with a *plein air* (outdoor) painting colony before returning to Melbourne.

Templestowe, where he settled, is now a Melbourne suburb but in the 1890s it would have reminded Davies of the gentle undulating hills of his Ballarat birthplace; the treeless hills and slopes behind the Sebastopol Welsh church where he was baptized is a similar terrain to that around Templestowe. A farming district in the valley of the Yarra, Templestowe is adjacent to Heidelberg where fellow-artist Walter Withers lived throughout the nineties. Heidelberg and other parts of the Yarra Valley had since the 1860s attracted artists and excursionists because it seemed domesticated and 'English'. When Frederick McCubbin's "Some remarks on the history of Australian art" was published in 1916[6] he took four paintings as character-istic examples of a national art. One was of brilliant Sydney sunshine, a Hawkesbury River landscape by Streeton, *The Purple Noon's Transparent Might*, 1896; the other three were subdued paintings of the Yarra Valley: Louis Buvelot's *Summer afternoon, Templestowe*, 1866, Walter Withers's *Tranquil winter*, 1895 — and David Davies's *Moonrise*, 1894. Davies had chosen to live in countryside traditionally favoured by artists, and where his wife's family also owned land.

Davies returned to Australia with a subtle and refined technique; he had seen the results of *plein air* painting and participated in its practice in Paris and St Ives. He would also have seen first-hand the nocturnes of James McNeill Whistler and others,[7] confirming his love of evening light. Whistler's near-abstract landscapes titled as *Notes*, *Harmonies*, and *Nocturnes* showed admiration for Japanese prints and screens. The Japanese-inspired Aesthetic Movement in Europe was a deliberate break with the European tradition of landscape-painting, a tradition of classical balance and controlled gradation of distant vistas. Lessons learnt from Japanese art were the simplification of the composition and subject and the flattening or compression of depth by a raised horizon-line and an open foreground. David Davies's *Moonrise*, with its long foreground of dried-up grasses and weeds, high horizon and prominent low moon, is similar in composition to a Japanese screen. Such screens conventionally include long grasses and a low moon, and represent one of the four seasons, most usually autumn.

However, summer is not only more convenient for outdoor sketching

David DAVIES, 1864-1939. *Moonrise*. 1894, Templestowe near Melbourne. Oil on canvas, 119.2 x 150 cm. National Gallery of Victoria, Melbourne. Colonial Government funds 1895

or painting, for "long contemplative brooding over the subdued effects of quiet light"[8] on this hill close to the artist's studio; summer with its warm fragrances is also more an Australian preference, more evocative of sensuous childhood reverie for Australian-born colonials like Davies. *Moonrise* expresses universal experiences, the seasons, the end of day, tranquility and rest. It does so in a highly artistic, fully Japanese manner, with a suggestion of a path winding to the moon. But it locates the experience in a land of eucalyptus-tree silhouettes and post-and-rail fences for the few who wish to recognize such details. The style is that of a Japanese screen but the experience is an Australian summer night.

One of Davies's first Templestowe landscapes, and the one which is closest in appearance to *Moonrise*, 1894, is a small painting now also entitled *Moonrise*, c1893, in the collection of the Art Gallery of South Australia. Both are simple compositions: a grassy slope is dissected by sheep tracks flanked by a few weeds and bushes, there is a distant fence and the white moon. The smaller painting has, particularly in the sky, some of the underlying and modulated broken colour we associate with French Impressionism. The handling of the paint is also more direct. In the larger *Moonrise*, however, Davies has lifted the horizon and muted the colour; it

is a tonal harmony of innumerable greys and olives with a slight blush of rose in part of the sky. The paint application is thick and dry yet descriptive. It is not difficult to imagine reaching down and picking the dry overgrown thistles, or stepping into the landscape, hearing the crackle of dry grass underfoot. The space in the painting has been carefully graded and one can sense the subtle swell and curve of the disappearing hill.

Moonrise, 1894, shows Davies's careful observation of nature, although it would not have been painted on the spot. The composition is the result of intense study of the local landscape and recording a series of close observations over a long period. But it is a new kind of landscape in that it is not specific about place or time. The painting's intensely convincing naturalism only heightens its mystery and its evocative mood. Davies has described an apparently ordinary Australian rural scene and yet its features are only hinted at and barely perceptible. One's imagination is invited to enter and complete this timeless, placeless painting. The magical power of *Moonrise* is its universality and its depiction of the Yarra Valley near Melbourne is only incidental. It expresses an age-old mood of reverie and bewitchment.

Charles CONDER, 1868-1909. *How we lost poor Flossie.*
1889, Melbourne. Oil on wood panel, 25 x 9.2 cm. Art Gallery
of South Australia, Adelaide. Elder Bequest Fund 1941
In the 9 by 5 Impression Exhibition, 1889

Charles CONDER, 1868-1909. *Dandenong from Heidelberg.* 1889, Heidelberg near Melbourne. Oil on cardboard, 11.5 x 23.5 cm; in
artist's painted pine frame. M.J.M. Carter Collection, Art Gallery of South Australia, Adelaide
In the 9 by 5 Impression Exhibition, 1889

Arthur STREETON, 1867-1943. *The national game.* 1889, Melbourne. Oil on cardboard, 11.8 x 22.9 cm.
Art Gallery of New South Wales, Sydney. State Government funds 1963
In the 9 by 5 Impression Exhibition, 1889

Tom ROBERTS, 1856-1931. *Saplings.* c1889, Melbourne. Oil on wood
panel, 23.2 x 13.3 cm. Art Gallery of South Australia, Adelaide.
Morgan Thomas Bequest Fund 1927

CENTENARY ART: CULTURE by DANIEL THOMAS

The six Australian capital cities held a much greater population than the bush but the city-dwellers knew they depended on the wheat, the gold and, above all, the wool produced in the bush for export. Australian society since the growth of an illustrated press in the 1850s had been especially interested in bush life. For the 1870 "Centenary of Australia" (being the Centenary of Captain James Cook's charting of the east coast of New Holland) an *Australia Illustrated* was planned for publication in London. It was delayed but was a precursor to several lavish picture-books for the 1888 Centenary, the best being the locally-published *Picturesque Atlas of Australasia*.

The illustrative images of city progress and bush life in these books and in the press were joined by a remarkable outbreak of similar subjects in ambitious paintings, now the most popular and famous of all Australian works of art.

Tom Roberts's *Allegro con brio, Bourke Street west*, 1886, a smaller picture of big-city bustle, might not have received its musical title before its first public appearance, with additional notes of colour and movement, in 1890. It was the summer of 1885/86, the artist's first summer back in Melbourne after nearly five years' study in Europe. He was "primed with whatever was latest in art" but such boulevard views were conventional images of urban progress and it is not the subject but its "effect", the characteristically Australian sunlit glare, which would have interested Roberts. He was perhaps the first artist to be startled by the look of an Australian summer after time overseas. (In 1956, Fred Williams would be another.) By the time it was exhibited in 1890 the picture was an historical document; Melbourne was still busy with hansom cabs and Bourke Street Hill was still no doubt the horse-centre of the city, selling saddlery, horses, carriages and carts, but since October 1886 cable-trams had displaced cabs at the centre of the street.

The big pictures, mostly of bush life, were 'historical' from the beginning. They were conscious attempts to give nobility and dignity to high moments in characteristically Australian working life: shearing the year's growth of wool from the sheep which produced Australia's wealth; mustering cattle after their annual spell in mountain country; stages in a pioneer family's life; a bush burial; or less predictably cyclic human-interest subjects: a gold-digger down on his luck; an out-of-work family "on the wallaby track"; a family's flood sufferings; breaking the news of a husband's death in the gold-mines; a family cart on the road in a dreadful hot wind; a mob of thirsty sheep on the road, stampeding at the smell of water.

Such pictures were partly stimulated by nationalistic self-analysis at the time of the Australian Centenary. However, pictures of regional life were also an international fashion, at its height in the 1870s and early 1880s. Jules Bastien-Lepage was then its most famous protagonist, a specialist in the potato-harvests of the Meuse region of France, but it was well-established in the 1850s with J.F. Millet's and Jules Breton's harvesters and gleaners. Fishermen at Newlyn or Whitby, grape-harvesters in Provence, the fellahin of Egypt, factory-workers in London or Paris, regional pilgrimages, baptisms, weddings and funerals populated European painting at the time.

International regionalism was naturalistic in style and its intentions were partly political, to give a remote region or a poorly-honoured type of labour the dignity of a presence in high art; but the intentions were also partly historical, to record regional customs or obsolescent craft skills before they disappeared.

"Thoroughly Australian" became a recurring form of praise from Australian critics when these set-pieces of naturalistic nationalism appeared. Those same critics recognized that they were being shown the past. Bushrangers were nearly twenty years in the past when Tom Roberts painted them in 1895, Roberts's *Shearing the rams* was recognized in 1890 as "representative of a style of shearing [i.e. hand-shears] which in pastoral history will soon be a thing of the past"[1] and his *A break away!* in 1891 as an unlikely event when long-distance droving had given way to rail transport of stock.

The city artists took care to generalize the big pictures. The bit of suburban bush used for McCubbin's *Down on his luck* could have been anywhere in Australia. Although *A break away!* and *Shearing the rams* were subjects from the New South Wales border country near Albury (a political plus in itself during intercolonial rivalries) they too could have been anywhere in the bush. Streeton's heat-drenched *The selector's hut (Whelan on the log)*, was painted at suburban Heidelberg but no selectors would have been found so close in. His *Golden summer* was shifted inland from Heidelberg by the additions of a large mob of sheep and a large woolshed.

If Australian men and women at work were the principal concern of Australian art in the Centenary years, Australian leisure produced the brilliant tour de force of young Conder's *A holiday at Mentone*, 1888, a japoniste adaptation of Whistler to the pleasures of the mid-day sun enjoyed by young city-dwellers at a Melbourne beach.

Blamire Young's art poster, a new aspect of commercial graphic design, advertises bicycles to ride for leisure. Excursionists' destinations near Melbourne included an Aboriginal settlement, Coranderrk at Healesville, and there Billy Barak produced non-traditional drawings which were collected with interest. Bridget Darmody, photographed by Captain Sweet at the railhead at Parachilna may not be heading into the Flinders Ranges on an excursion, but even going home to a sheep station is an adventure if it's by camel-transport. Streeton's *The national game* shows Melbournians watching Australian Rules football at winter dusk in 1889.

One of the loveliest images of Centenary leisure is Tom Roberts's *The Sunny South*. It is an outdoor painting at an artists' camp at Mentone in the summer of 1886/87 so perhaps the "bathers, about to emerge from the shadows of the ti-tree to plunge into the sunshine and the sea"[1] are his fellow-artists. Their sturdy nakedness exactly matches the colour and the bulk of the pink tree-trunks and we may be sure that Roberts intended a visual suggestion that these men are not only naturalistic naked bathers but also nude nature-spirits, Australians now entirely at home in a land only recently settled by their kind. These European nudes in an Australian landscape-painting are the first to be so totally at one with their new land.

Captain Samuel SWEET, 1825-1886. *Camel and Miss Bridget Darmody.* c1885, Parachilna, Flinders Ranges, South Australia. Albumen-silver photograph, 15.6 x 20.5 cm. Australian National Gallery, Canberra. Federal Government funds 1986

Blamire YOUNG, 1862-1935. *Swift's bicycle poster.* c1898, Melbourne. Colour lithograph, 69 x 46 cm (irregular). La Trobe Collection, State Library of Victoria, Melbourne. Gift of Troedel & Cooper Ltd 1968

William BARAK, c1824-1903. *Dancing scene.* c1880s, Coranderrk, Healesville, Victoria. Gouache on cardboard, 73.4 x 55.7 cm. La Trobe Collection, State Library of Victoria, Melbourne. Accessioned 1918

Tom ROBERTS, 1856-1931. *The Sunny South.* Summer 1886/87, Mentone near Melbourne. Oil on canvas,
30.8 x 61.2 cm. National Gallery of Victoria, Melbourne. Felton Bequest Fund 1940

Arthur STREETON, 1867-1943. *The selector's hut (Whelan on the log).* 1890,
Heidelberg near Melbourne. Oil on canvas, 76.7 x 51.2 cm. Australian National
Gallery, Canberra. Federal Government funds 1961

Jane SUTHERLAND, 1855-1928. *The harvest field.* 1897, Melbourne. Oil on canvas, 69 x 102 cm.
Private collection

Walter WITHERS, 1854-1913. *Early morning, Heidelberg.* 1898, Heidelberg near Melbourne. Oil on
canvas, 45 x 91.7 cm. Art Gallery of South Australia, Adelaide. Elder Bequest Fund 1899

CELEBRATION by RON RADFORD

Charles Conder, *A holiday at Mentone*, 1888

Charles Conder's masterpiece *A holiday at Mentone* is an Australian image of celebration. It is a celebration of Australian light, leisure and the beach. It is a celebration, painted by a youth, of the pleasures of the good life for young people. On a personal level it marks the young Conder's celebration of his arrival in big-city Melbourne from old-fashioned Sydney to join his new friend and mentor Tom Roberts and to meet Arthur Streeton and, above all, to work in a lively, advanced art scene; it is a celebration of vital new art-professional friendships and of progressive art. On a national level it happens to have been painted in the year 1888, when Australia's Centenary was celebrated; Conder was living in Sydney during the Centennial celebrations of January 1888, then in Melbourne he found a spirit of optimism in Australia's largest and richest city at the height of a financial boom. The scene is appropriately bathed in the brightest light hitherto captured in Australian landscape art.

The most elaborate of all Conder's pictures, it was presumably calculated to impress; the young artist chose it to launch himself on the Melbourne art-world, in the annual exhibition of the Victorian Artists' Society in November 1888. Painted at the Melbourne bayside beach of Mentone in October's fresh spring sunlight, a month after his arrival from Sydney, it therefore coincided with the celebration of Conder's twentieth birthday. The shadowless light of high noon was painted on the spot but the picture would have been completed in the artist's city studio and its foreground figures then added; there exists a study for the woman reading in the foreground, a study which was later exhibited in The 9 by 5 Impression Exhibition of August 1889 under the title *The sun and I*.

The complex composition of *A holiday at Mentone* is a striking and very deliberate arrangement. The painting is not merely a spontaneous impression. The most obvious feature of the picture is the placement of the wooden footbridge. The cream-painted bridge cuts across the upper half of the painting and its mauve shadow divides the painting evenly in half. The compositional device of a narrow bridge set high in the painting had been used by Tom Roberts in his *Winter morning after rain, the old bridge, Gardiner's Creek*, 1885,[1] a work of subdued, close tones painted shortly after his return to Melbourne from Europe. In London, Roberts would have been aware of James McNeill Whistler's Battersea Bridge paintings, which in turn were influenced by Japanese woodcut prints by Hokusai and Hiroshige. Conder of course knew from magazines and his Sydney friends of the works of Whistler and the Japanese-inspired Aesthetic Movement before he met Roberts; Whistler was London's most famous contemporary artist. Conder abandoned the aesthetics of Tokyo rain or London fog or Melbourne overcast to do a Whistler in the mid-day sun.

Japanese influence is found in other aspects of the painting besides the dramatic compositional device of the footbridge. Jane Clark has pointed out that "The strands of seaweed are almost calligraphically treated. And Conder's ever-ready wit is epitomized by his placement of the open Japanese umbrella: blown unobserved by the sea breeze from its rightful place besides its owner's feet — for all the world like a Japanese printer's seal gone astray from beneath its line of characters."[2] The outer wall of the baths would not have retained its boldly-lettered cropped place-name MENT. . . without the permission given to such eccentricities by Japanese art. Or was this also the influence of photography?

The simple colour-scheme divides the work into two horizontal sections, the upper third a clear blue and the lower two-thirds a bright creamy white. Against this colour-scheme Conder has animated the surface with marks of black (three figures seen through the bridge, the hat and shoes of the standing man on the right), and of red (the hat and Japanese parasol of the woman, the *Bulletin* magazine by the hand of the sleeping man at the centre, the ribbons and parasols of the women on the bridge). The composition could well be titled in full Whistlerian fashion *Harmony in Blue and Cream* (although there are of course supplementary colours like red and mauve). The young Conder sparkles as a natural virtuoso of colour orchestration.

The arrangement is so self-conscious, especially the placement of the figures, that the composition is like a stage set. One might expect witty dialogue between the three foreground figures posed against the well-lit beach backdrop. The stiffly horizontal man in the centre is comical as an image of holiday relaxation, the seated woman on the left 'pretends' to read her *Bulletin* while the standing man on the right 'deliberately' turns his back on her.

Conder, however, is less concerned with a particular anecdote here than with the abstract, decorative structure of the painting, the brilliant Australian light and the general mood of holiday. Although the subjects of Australian colonial art include romantic coastal views and even occasional remote beaches, it was not until the mid 1880s that the beach became a constant and important subject in Australian art, as it had earlier become an important subject in European art with the French impressionists. It is a subject which today epitomizes Australians' love of the sun and their beach-worship. It has become part of Australia's national self-image, distinguishing us from a mother-country in northern Europe. John Mather, Tom Roberts, Frederick McCubbin, Charles Conder and Arthur Streeton (in that order) established the beach subject as part of Australia's significant iconography in the second half of the 1880s.

In the beach paintings of the 1880s we see men, women and children, both middle-class and white-collar city workers, promenading formally by the water's edge, which they may have reached by suburban railway or tramway. Besides Mentone, other Mediterranean seaside place-names, Sorrento and San Remo, had been given to holiday places near Melbourne; the English seaside also provided the names Brighton, Cowes and Torquay. Here at Mentone on their day out of the city, excursionists partake of the fresh sea breeze; it is not summer and they are dressed up in good clothes. Bathing was naked and took place out of public view. If it was a busy city beach, sea-bathing, with an admission charge, was available in the segregation of enclosed baths like the one to the right of *A holiday at Mentone*. Not till the turn of the century did recreational bathing occupy the public beaches in daylight.

Probably the first beach subject by Conder is *Coogee Bay*,[3] painted during Easter 1888 in the company of Roberts who was visiting Sydney and had only just met the nineteen-year-old, sent out from London four years

Charles CONDER, 1868-1909. *A holiday at Mentone*. October 1888, Mentone near Melbourne; Melbourne. Oil on canvas, 46.2 x 60.8 cm.
Art Gallery of South Australia, Adelaide. Bond Corporation Holdings Ltd through the Art Gallery of South Australia Foundation
and State Government funds, to mark the Gallery's Centenary 1981

earlier to prevent him becoming an artist. The title of the painting which Roberts painted on the outing with Conder is inscribed on the canvas *Holiday sketch at Coogee*. Conder could have had this in mind when he titled *A holiday at Mentone*. Conder had painted further Sydney beach scenes before he left for Melbourne to join Roberts in September 1888. One of these beach scenes, *All on a Summer's Day*,[4] includes a tiny distant image of Roberts painting in the open on top of a cliff. This relatively simple Sydney beach painting (despite its title, executed not in summer but autumn, April 1888) is a forerunner to the more complex Melbourne beach painting *A holiday at Mentone* painted six months later, before the next summer became too hot for outdoor painting. The prominent placement in the composition of a reading woman with a parasol off-centre on the open foreground beach is a Japanese compositional device used in both paintings. But there the similarity ends. The contrast of the two paintings shows how quickly the precocious Conder developed with Streeton under Roberts's encouragement when he arrived in Melbourne. Conder's Sydney beach paintings (more than his other New South Wales subjects) demonstrate his greater concern for flat decorative and illustrative mannerisms over impressionistic naturalism. Despite the fairly high key of *All on a Summer's Day* one is not conscious of the sparkling light evoked and aerial perspective. (Both these qualities of distance and light are aggressively captured in Roberts's and Streeton's Sydney beach paintings a few years later.) However, after Conder's arrival in Melbourne, under the spell of Roberts and Streeton, he combines his decorative placement with greater *plein-air* realism, as indeed Streeton's paintings thereafter showed a greater tendency for decorative effects.[5]

A holiday at Mentone clearly demonstrates Conder's new interest in distance and radiant light. The footbridge pillars frame a series of four delightful coastal views. The view below the section of the footbridge

second from the left is a remarkably complete beachscape composition in itself. Conder has accurately portrayed the dunes vanishing in the distance. The glowing pearly colours of the beach promenaders on the right of this enclosed little view contrast with the black staccato mark of the woman with the child on the left. Even when the painting was first exhibited a reviewer of the exhibition commented in *Table Talk* magazine that it ". . . has all the best work in the dreamy background . . .".[6] It is one of the most beautiful passages of Australian impressionist painting. Conder was good at such intimate touches and crammed many of them onto this modest-sized canvas. He nearly always worked on an intimate scale and this small painting was the second-largest canvas he completed in Australia.[7]

Conder, Streeton and Roberts often worked closely together in Melbourne. Streeton and Conder, over ten years junior to Roberts, competed for his attention. They inspired one another to great heights of aesthetic feeling. All three were very much in love with life, their art and each other. During their fleeting time together they created works, like *A holiday at Mentone*, of poetic magic. It is surprising to realise that these central figures of the so-called Heidelberg School worked together in Melbourne for little more than a year and a half. This was a short time in their lives and a very short time in the history of Australian art, but nevertheless in that time they produced the nation's finest impressionist paintings — paintings which have captured the nationalistic imagination of succeeding generations of Australians. In Australia's Bicentennial year, exactly one hundred years after Conder's masterpiece *A holiday at Mentone* was executed, perhaps the nation's most charming impressionist picture can be seen as an innocent and youthful celebration: it evokes a spirit of optimism in the colonists' social and economic life, nationalism in its sunny outdoor leisure, and internationalism in its up-to-date Japanese stylishness.

INDEPENDENCE: "THOROUGHLY AUSTRALIAN IN SPIRIT" by LEIGH ASTBURY

Frederick McCubbin, *Down on his luck,* 1889

Frederick McCubbin's *Down on his luck* portrays the melancholy meditation of the unsuccessful gold-prospector considering his fate. Ostensibly an image of failure and defeat, the painting immediately struck a responsive chord in contemporary audiences and it continues to appeal today. To city people what seemed so attractive in bush types such as McCubbin's prospector was a life lived close to the soil, a life that would be somehow 'truer' to their whole being. There was a powerful psychological appeal in the idea that independence could be attained by being in close touch with nature and the land. If one were to experience poverty or failure, then such experiences seemed somehow simpler and nobler in the bush. There were deemed to be psychological compensations in the experience of rural as opposed to urban poverty. This was evident in the contemporary response to *Down on his luck*, which applauded the "hard fare" but "independence" of the bushman's life on the wallaby track and found consolation in the lyrical beauty of the secluded landscape.

Whereas Arthur Streeton responded to the summer drought of 1888-89 by painting his hilltop vision of a sunlit landscape, *Golden summer, Eaglemont*, McCubbin chose to return early in 1889 to the site of the artists' former bush camp at Box Hill in order to paint *Down on his luck*, a subject for an autumnal setting. There in 1886 he had painted *Lost*, one of his first images of Australian national life, a picture of a lost child, and he no doubt considered the intimate, enclosed bush at Box Hill more appropriate for the melancholic, introspective nature of his subject than the open vistas of the Yarra Valley landscape.[1] However, unlike the earlier *Lost*, dense bush does not enclose and envelop the figure, denying access. In the open glade portrayed in *Down on his luck*, the highlight following the downward slope of the land in the mid-distance provides a hint of a bush track, suggesting the freedom of the bushman simply to move on, should he choose. The patch of bushland near a Melbourne suburban railway station served well enough as the setting for a subject from rural bush life.

The landscape was mostly painted on the spot, following the principles and dictates of the open-air realism of the then-famous French painter, Jules Bastien-Lepage, whom McCubbin greatly admired. He conveyed his observation of time and place through details such as the familiar motif of the tracery of gum saplings and grasses in the foreground, the effect of the slight breeze gently wafting the smoke from the campfire into the surrounding bush, and the "evening shadows gradually stealing over the trees, and causing them, as they recede into the forest, to be enshrouded in a faint grey mist".[2]

Yet beyond the concern to record a moment of nature, McCubbin's aim to imbue the scene with a pervasive mood and atmosphere, evocative of the noble melancholy subject, can be felt in the subtly-related tonal values of the landscape and the subdued grey sky above. The figure of the bushman, reminiscent of the sturdy peasant type favoured by Bastien-Lepage and his followers, was modelled by a fellow-artist, Louis Abrahams. The closer treatment of the figure suggests careful work in McCubbin's city studio, though he strove for a union of figure and landscape, consciously relating the colours of the bushman's clothing to

those of the bush. The *Argus* critic of 4 May 1889 saw such an affinity between bushman and landscape that the two seemed almost incapable of separate existence:

"The lonely figure and all its sylvan surroundings are rendered with a true feeling for nature and with a fitting appreciation of that harmony which the poet and painter would alike conceive as existing between the stillness and the seclusion of the sequestered bit of woodland scenery . . . and the melancholy meditativeness of the solitary human being who is sadly ruminating on the perversity of his ill fortune?"

McCubbin was familiar with the local tradition in painting and illustration of portraying itinerant bush workers, swagmen and sundowners eking out an existence 'on the wallaby track'.[3] In contemporary usage, the term may have suggested a degree of poverty and hardship, but it also carried with it more optimistic connotations of a democratic lifestyle 'tied to no man' and of a land of plenty which would provide. *Down on his luck* is inevitably selective in its presentation of bush life: the lone bushman is seen as independent of the master-and-servant relationship which was in fact an essential part of Australian pastoral life in the 1880s. The decade had also seen the organization of widely dispersed rural workers into large and powerful industrial unions and the divisions between rural labour and capital had become increasingly apparent. Part of the popularity of the 'wallaby track' theme in art was due to the fact that it allowed urban dwellers to project their aspirations for independence onto a fixed romantic image of the bushman, excluding awareness of changing social conditions in the rural scene. Nevertheless, by the late 1880s, when McCubbin painted his picture, the waning of the boom had caused growing rural unemployment and saw an increasing number of men wandering the countryside in search of work.[4]

A nostalgic attitude towards the passing of the individual gold-prospector from the contemporary scene informs McCubbin's choice of subject. From the 1860s onwards, most gold-miners were not individual prospectors but instead worked for large mining companies in a traditional employer-employee relationship.[5] However, as the figure of the individual gold-prospector passed from view it acquired by the late 1880s a symbolic status in art and literature. The gold-prospector came to symbolize the freedom and independence of a past age, a time when egalitarian ideals and individual initiative were not in conflict and could be equally rewarded by a democratic society.[6]

Ultimately the subject of *Down on his luck* stems from the goldfields illustrations of artists such as S.T. Gill. Gill's anecdotal watercolour *Bad results* presents an early version of the theme in showing a dejected digger being comforted by his companion.[7] In 1888 J. Davis appears to have adapted Gill's image in his drawing of "The Gold-Digger: Down on his luck" for *Victoria and its Metropolis*; the accompanying text described how "the early diggings are full of tales of the silent, solitary stranger [whose] golden dreams dwindled down to the mere hope of finding enough to keep the spark of life [within him]".[8] Both artists portray the despondent digger with his bowed head supported by his hand — a traditional melancholia pose — which anticipates McCubbin's later treatment of the motif.

Frederick McCUBBIN, 1855-1917. *Down on his luck.* 1889. Box Hill near Melbourne; Melbourne. Oil on canvas, 114.5 x 152.8 cm. Art
Gallery of Western Australia, Perth. Colonial Government funds 1896

In *Down on his luck* McCubbin thus pays tribute to the rapidly passing phenomenon of the individual gold-prospector; he celebrates the 'lone hand' — the independent prospector who, scorning to accept wages from any man, endures a solitary life in the bush, turning the fact of endurance itself into a victory over fate. McCubbin simultaneously omits specific details of the prospector's occupation and limits the role of anecdote to present a more universal image of the itinerant bush worker: seated on a fallen log; a small campfire his companion for the moment; a billy-can lying empty on its side, recently used to boil water for making tea; a swag of worldly goods in a grey blanket lying on the ground, awaiting use for a night's sleep. For contemporaries the pessimistic implications of the picture were mitigated by ideas of the hard fare but freedom of life 'on the wallaby'. The writer in *Table Talk* of 26 April 1889 saw that:

"The face tells of hardships, keen and blighting in their influence, but there is a nonchalant and slightly cynical expression, which proclaims the absence of all self-pity . . . and the misty atmosphere around which is so dreamily subduing the leaves and branches of the trees into a general neutrality of colour seems to leave the lonely figure of the wanderer untouched as he sits brooding over what might have been. Mr McCubbin's picture is thoroughly Australian in spirit, and yet so poetic that it is a veritable bush idyll . . ."

"AN AUSTRALIAN INCIDENT": EXPLOSIVE ACTION, STILL HEAT
by LEIGH ASTBURY

Tom Roberts, *A break away!* 1891

A break away! presents an image of Australian pastoral life which is striking in its visual immediacy and concentrated action: a horseman valiantly strives to thwart the death-rush of sheep to a water-hole in a sleepy, drought-stricken land. "Looking at the large canvas", enthused a critic in *Table Talk* on 17 July 1891, "one feels the story; its impression is conveyed to the eye by the painting." The picture was painted early in 1891 in the shearing shed at Brocklesby near Corowa in New South Wales, where Roberts had painted *Shearing the rams* the previous year.

The desolate outback landscape in *A break away!* suggests that Roberts's imagination had turned further inland than Corowa in order to pay tribute to the heroic "workmen of the Eastern Interior".[1] The image of the bushman struggling to overcome the forces of nature marks a turning away from the broad social issues implicit in *Shearing the rams*.[2] The 1890 Maritime Strike, which saw violent clashes on the waterfronts of Sydney and Melbourne, and the first signs of the oncoming economic depression, had begun to undermine confidence in labour relations and the future of society. Artists and writers increasingly sought to locate the 'real Australia' in the outer pastoral regions, far away from the corrupting influences of cities and towns. The horseman in *A break away!* seizes the opportunity for heroic action denied to city dwellers; his enemy is the harshness of the land, not society and its machinations.

"An Australian incident – tragic, realistic, picturesque", declared the *Table Talk* writer of *A break away!* and he praised Roberts's evocation of the hot, barren landscape, essential to the meaning of his subject: "A bit of arid country, with ragged gum trees and stunted box positively frizzling in the heat of a January day". The readiness with which the critics embraced the image of Australia as an essentially arid land, characterized by intense heat and light, was partly due to a succession of droughts during the 1880s. The 1888 Centennial Year culminated in one of the worst ever recorded, at a time when artists and writers were seeking to identify a typical Australian landscape in their work. By the end of the decade there was also a growing awareness amongst meteorologists that the normal climatic cycle of the Australian inland included dry seasons.[3] Yet the capacity of the land to withstand the effects of drought was being adversely affected by man's exploitation of it; the landscape in *A break away!* bears the imprint of customary farming methods employed in the the Riverina District of New South Wales. Most of the natural Murray pine and box timber (seen on the left of the picture) was traditionally cleared by the practice of ring-barking in order to promote natural grass growth; but years of overstocking had already caused the disappearance of native grasses and changes in pasture types. The resistance of the land was further weakened by the rabbit invasion of the early 1880s.[4] *Unlike Shearing the rams*, which emphasized the provident and generative powers of nature, in *A break away!* Roberts suggests the imperviousness of the land to the efforts of man to 'improve' it.

Roberts's most immediate inspiration for *A break away!* may have stemmed from his first-hand experience of the Riverina in 1888-89 when the severe drought forced large numbers of sheep and cattle onto the road in search of feed. A newspaper article written at the same time as Roberts was painting his picture records that "Time was, and indeed it is not yet very remote when poor brutes were very often a week on the roads with very scant picking of sere grass and scrub, and no water whatever".[5] Yet by 1891 the scene portrayed in Roberts's picture was no longer characteristic of the Riverina. The pastoral industry had been rapidly transformed in the 1880s through the widespread introduction of wire fencing, the extension of the railway network to more isolated areas and the growth of small selection holdings.[6]

A break away! therefore pays homage to an anonymous but heroic incident from the vanished past of the pastoral industry. A detail such as the outdated chock-and-log fence reveals Roberts's nostalgia for that past era. But although he looked to a more romantic past for inspiration, Roberts did so with the discerning eye of a realist artist and expressed his admiration of the "newer men" of historical painting who "insist that any subject painted, must be done true to the conditions under which it is supposed to have existed".[7] The theme of a breakaway by cattle was frequently treated in illustrations in newspapers and magazines in the 1870s and 1880s and the intense action of *A break away!* was prefigured in Frank Mahony's large canvas, *Rounding up a straggler*, of 1889.[8] Many of these images were modelled on readily available illustrations of the American cowboy portrayed in vigorous action. In contrast, it was Roberts's commitment to historical accuracy that governed his decision to portray a breakaway of sheep rather than of cattle: "In the Riverina, as a rule, only sheep are now depastured. Hence the artist has also chosen to depict sheep rather than cattle – for consistency's sake".[9] Roberts's choice of subject in *A break away!* was thus a critical one: it entailed a rejection of the American frontier imagery popularized by artists and illustrators like Mahony, as well as a desire to lend historical veracity to the developing mythology associated with the Australian bushman.

In 1890 Roberts had written of his desire to express "the meaning and spirit" of Australia's "great pastoral life and work", but in communicating this general ideal in a single painting, he maintained that "it was only possible to take one view, to give one portion of all this".[10] He sought to typify his pastoral subjects through a specificity of treatment and effect in the finished painting. Despite the dynamic nature of the subject, *A break away!* had evolved through a process of careful, even painstaking, preparation and the final picture was composed and painted in the shearing shed at Brocklesby. However, in order to capture the effect of searing heat and light, Roberts made preliminary oil sketches in the open air, including a sketch of the chock-and-log fence with effects so strongly marked as to suggest fierce overhead sunlight – a dazzling glare.[11] Two drawings from his sketchbook contain the first seeds of the final composition, and demonstrate that Roberts's initial conception had envisaged the powerful diagonal thrust of the mob of sheep countered by the insweeping movement of horse and rider.[12] In the finished picture, this confrontation is echoed in the criss-crossing of a streak of cirrus cloud with a dust-spiral rising in the distant sky; in turn, these elements emphasize the still heat of the day in contrast to the explosive action in the foreground.

To Roberts, the structural ambiguity of *A break away!* (observable in

Tom ROBERTS, 1856-1931. *A break away!* 1891, Corowa, NSW; Melbourne. Oil on canvas, 137 x 168 cm.
Art Gallery of South Australia, Adelaide. Elder Bequest Fund 1899

the contradictory spatial relationships) may have seemed essential to the meaning and overwhelming visual impact of the scene. His disregard for conventional artistic effects becomes clear in an article he wrote about the Art Gallery of New South Wales in 1891. He reserved his highest praise for works which produced "a marvellous seeming reality" and argued that the "apparently haphazard arrangement" of Etienne Dinet's north African *Snake Charmer*, 1889, in fact contributed to its "sense of freshness and healthfulness".[13] A contemporary writer acknowledged similar qualities underlying Roberts's vision of *A break away!*: "In the picture extremes meet, and the artist has dared to blend a fierce swirl of excitement with a perfect trance of repose".[14]

In an interview with A. G. Stephens in 1899, Roberts still maintained that a painting "fixes one thing for you — one scene, one mood, one idea" and he prized *A break away!* "as the work in which his art had so far most nearly realized his idea".[15]

NO SWEAT by VIRGINIA SPATE

Tom Roberts, *Shearing the rams*, 1888-90

A shadowy interior pervaded by dusky light; a huge shed built of rough-hewn trees; the rhythmic bend and turn of men at work: at left a boy gathers a fleece, a man drags in a great unshorn merino ram; at the centre are four shearers, behind them a man sharpens his shears, another tosses back his head to drink; at right an older man watches; others, almost undifferentiated, just capture the light in the depths of the warm shadows of the shed. Encountered more times than one can remember — in faded classroom reproductions, on fly-blown office calendars, on matchbox covers, jigsaw puzzles, *Shearing the rams* has long been the obligatory illustration in every book on the 'authentic' Australia, so familiar to us that we scarcely need look at it any more.[1]

Roberts conceived *Shearing the rams* as "most really and absolutely Australian", a view shared by those who saw it when it was exhibited in his studio in Collins Street, Melbourne in May 1890.[2] From the first, the painting attracted comment; an editorial in *The Argus* claimed that it was not "artistic" because it was not "beautiful or elevating or instructive . . . A thing may be altogether perfectly depicted and yet altogether unworthy of depiction". Roberts replied,

> ". . . being in the bush and feeling the delight and fascination of the great pastoral life and work, I have tried to express it . . . lying on piled-up wool-bales, and hearing and seeing the troops come pattering into their pens . . . the quick running of the wool-carriers, the screwing of the presses, subdued hum of hard, fast working, and the rhythmic click of the shears, the whole lit warm with the reflection of Australian sunlight, it seemed that I had there the best expression of my subject, **a subject noble enough and worthy enough** [emphasis added] if I could express the meaning and spirit — of strong masculine labour, the patience of the animals . . . and the strong human interest of the whole scene."[3]

The painting was addressed, not to the shearers, but to Roberts's artist colleagues and to the well-dressed ladies and gentlemen who came to his studio, the middle-class professionals, businessmen, politicians and their wives who were his first patrons. He probably intended it for similar audiences in Europe for he and his friends had decided to submit paintings "with a decided leaning towards nationality" to the Royal Academy in London and to the Paris Salon.[4]

It was generally accepted that Australian art should use Australian subjects — even the conservative *Argus* objected less to the Australian subject than to the failure of Roberts's painting to be "beautiful or elevating or instructive". Such qualities were found in, for example, Frederick McCubbin's *Down on his luck* or Roberts's own painting of an old scrub cutter, *End to a career*, both of which represent the melancholy acceptance of misfortune over which a few sentimental tears could be shed.[5] They suggest that for the city audience the best rural workers were humble — passive survivors rather than active shapers of their society. Roberts's work was different — in Australia as in Europe — in its depiction of "strong masculine labour": the shearers are bowed over their work, but the elasticity of their poses suggests (at first sight), that at the end of the day they can stand straight.

The masculine imagery is reinforced by the expensive rams, depicted as the climax of the shearing season and as symbol of Australia's chief source of wealth; they were hand-shorn whereas the more numerous ewes had to submit to the fast, recently-introduced machine-shears, and hence to cuts and bleeding.

Why could not the *Argus* critic see a painting so full of detail about the processes of shearing as "instructive"? Why was the hard but noble work of producing what Roberts called "the accumulated wealth and growth of the year" not seen as "elevating"? Why did part of Roberts's city audience refuse to see this dimension of meaning? Recent writers have approached such questions by locating the painting in its very specific conditions of production — in contemporary labour history and the relationship between squatters, selectors and shearers — and in its address to specific Melbourne audiences.[6] In this context the work should be seen not so much as the description of something real, but as an act of faith, an expression of the belief that through initiative, will-power and hard work any "strong masculine" person could struggle out of poverty, triumph over adversity and make his way in the world.

The painting's message was to those who had similarly triumphed or who shared the belief that they could do so. This had been Roberts's own experience and he may have felt it confirmed by those he painted, for selectors often worked as shearers in their own or other sheds, and Brocklesby station in the Riverina District of New South Wales, where the painting was executed, was of the modest size in which this could have occurred. That this was so is suggested by the fact that the owner of the station is seen only indistinctly at the far end of the shed sharing the work, whereas in other representations of such subjects the owner or overseer is generally represented in a dominant position.[7] *Shearing the Rams* presents Roberts's view of a dream, the dream of owning one's own property, controlling the fruits of one's labours; a dream to which the economic crisis of the 1890s put an end.

The picture shows shearing as hard, but almost enjoyable ('no sweat' to use the vernacular literally). This kind of painting had no way of showing that most shearers were itinerants who might work an eleven-or twelve-hour day in appalling conditions, as recounted in 1893:

> "It was hugger-mugger of food on dirty boards, just one step removed from the well-filled troughs of swash and potatoes round which I have seen pigs crowd at home . . . They are readers of George and Hyndham; Bellamy's 'Looking Backward' is to be found in every shed . . .
> "Men hardly count upon getting more than four or five months employment in the year . . . the roughness of the existence in the intervals of work is unknown and probably unimagined by anyone who has not endured it . . . ninety percent of the wandering population is unmarried, and they may die hungry, thirsty, and homeless in the bush without greatly affecting any other human lives . . ."[8]

This passage describes conditions in Queensland which may have been worse than in the Riverina, but Roberts aimed to speak "to all times and all places", and even in this "one place" all was not harmonious. The men in his picture would have been Union men in an industry in which strikes were rife — and severely repressed — in the period leading to the General Strike of 1890. That the painting's appeal was to those who had a vested interest in enforced harmony in the shearing industry is suggested

Tom ROBERTS, 1856-1931. *Shearing the rams.* 1888-90, Corowa, NSW; Melbourne. Oil on canvas, 121.9 x
182.6 cm. National Gallery of Victoria, Melbourne. Felton Bequest Fund 1932

NO SWEAT by VIRGINIA SPATE

(Continued)

by the fact that it was purchased, not by the Labor politicians who were Roberts's friends, or by the National Gallery of Victoria but by a Melbourne stock-and-station agent.[9]

Whether Roberts intended to produce a socially harmonious image is of less significance than what the painting itself conveys. Let us look a little closer. Where was the artist standing in relation to the shearers? Where do the viewers — those of the 1890s or the 1980s — stand? In some indeterminate space, hovering above the floor, looking down on the figures in the foreground who display the different phases of removal of the fleece in an almost cinematic way;[10] we are observers of their work, disembodied eyes, with no visual means of participating in it. Nor can we identify with the individual men: the faces of some are turned towards us, but their features are hidden; the others are in profile, and only the tar-boy in the mid-ground looks outwards, grinning at us, as if to break the illusion of a self-contained 'moment' of reality, and to suggest that instead we are watching a *tableau*, a carefully composed enactment by artfully posed figures — whom Roberts did, indeed, pay handsomely as models.

The "strong masculine labour" was here that of the artist. It was he who controlled the image, and shaped what we can see. Roberts gave a journalist a straightforward account of his work in creating his image of "the great pastoral life and work":

> "He fixed himself on a station and all one spring [1888] he studied and made studies of the light, the atmosphere, the shed, the sheep, the men and the work . . . The artist returned to town, worked at portrait-painting through the autumn and winter and in the next spring [1889] went out again. He set up his canvas in the shed this time. He worked all through the shearing . . . returned to town . . . and began the long work of finishing a great picture."[11]

He made it one of the most highly controlled paintings of its period. Look, for example, at the inexorable diagonals of the perspective lines of floorboards pulling the eye into depth, away from its scrutiny of the fleece peeling off the body of the ram; look at how the shed-divisions and roof-beams focus on the tar-boy; look how each individualized figure in the

group of working men is locked into position by the heavy verticals created by the rough-hewn pillars or by the distant fragment of light and forearm of the second man; look at how the bodies of the stooped men are locked together by linkage of arms and legs, and repetition of arching backs. Thus, despite their seemingly individual features — which we struggle to see — these are not individual men working, but a single labouring machine.

Roberts wrote that, unlike a poet who could enumerate the many aspects of pastoral life, the painter's medium meant that "it was only possible to take one view".[12] And although the 'tar-boy' was modelled by a ten-year-old girl, his "one view" of "strong masculine labour" necessarily excluded the role of women in the work of the pastoral station. Roberts's view also excluded Aborigines, despite the fact that an illustration in a book which probably inspired Roberts's composition showed an Aborigine dragging in a ram in the same pose as the figure in the painting. Roberts did paint an Aborigine at this time, inscribing his portrait "Gubbie Wellington, one of the last blacks of Corowa", but in the first years of Australia's second century it was generally assumed that the Aborigines were a dying race, and there was no place for them in the high arts.[13]

Shearing the rams was "the perfect expression of one time and one place" — the view of the bush from Collins Street. Its style, however, promises to tell us the truth about a form of work which has assumed mythic status in our society; and even though it represents the 'truth' of an Anglo-Australian male painter living in Melbourne a century ago, its promise of truth still lures us into a fascinated scrutiny, convinced that nothing is withheld, seeking harder and harder for the moment when we can feel we have penetrated to its reality. Because this "perfect expression of one time and one place" seeking to become "art for all times and all places", is so loaded with ambiguous messages of freedom and constraint, individuality and anonymity, power and powerlessness, candour and artifice, sincerity and play-acting, it can, if we engage with it, continue to speak to us today.

Tom ROBERTS, 1856-1931. *Allegro con brio, Bourke Street west.* c1886, Melbourne, figures left foreground added 1890. Oil on canvas, 51.2 x 76.7 cm. National Library of Australia, Canberra. Federal Government funds 1918

CENTENARY ART: THE INDIVIDUAL by DANIEL THOMAS

Consciously public 'national painting' of national life dominated Australian art in the 1880s and 1890s but we have seen nevertheless that Tom Roberts's painting of seashore bathers implied by juxtaposition that those naked men at leisure were also nature-spirits in private communion with trees. David Davies's uninhabited *Moonrise* invites its viewers to melt into nature, tempted by a cold moon-goddess as old as Babylon. Streeton's *"Fire's on"* and McCubbin's *Lost* implied the loss of self to nature, one by violent, crackling, sun-heated rocks, the other by the gentle allure of warmth and leafy fragrance. Piguenit's *The Flood in the Darling 1890* was a silent, creeping Deluge, a reminder to the viewer of Biblical punishment for secret sins. So nature could often be a vehicle for inwardness.

The mythic qualities in, say, *"Fire's on"*, *Lost* and *Moonrise* are powerful and they align these paintings with Symbolism, the newest (late 1880s) art movement of the time and a reaction from the supposed objective truthfulness of Impressionism to subjective expression of ideas, moods and emotions.

Young Australians working in Paris moved promptly into the new wave of art and Rupert Bunny's *Sea idyll*, a large painting of merfolk frolicking and music-making by the surf, was from 1892 the most conspicuous showpiece of modern Australian art displayed in Melbourne's National Gallery of Victoria. Equally famous was Bertram Mackennal's *Circe*, first exhibited in Paris in 1893, a confrontational, erotic temptation to base behaviour — for which one will suffer by transformation into swine. As often in Australian art, Circe is a masterpiece by a young man, twenty-nine

when he produced this statue of imperious sexuality, a young man moved by the lasting power of Homer's archaic Greek myths.

E. Phillips Fox's *Eighty-five years* is an especially beautiful example of the many studies of old age made at the time; Emma Minnie Boyd's *The letter* was also a traditional subject. Even so they both stand for sensitive introspection and thoughts of change: the old woman to dust and bones; the young letter-reading woman to a world outside the house in whose doorway she stands — perhaps if it is a love-letter to another life, another name.

The very moment of metamorphosis from woman to tree, in order to avoid rape, is the subject of Mackennal's *Daphne*, another ancient Greco-Roman myth, and C. Douglas Richardson's *The cloud* is a dematerialized woman who provides the nourishment of moisture to thirsty flowers (she illustrates a poem by Shelley). Sydney Long's *The Spirit of the Plains* is probably a woman, possibly Aboriginal, in any case androgynous, and certainly absorbed more by music in the air than by material or fleshly things.

All these images are of women and several are by women artists. Perhaps because women can undergo change much more radically than men, can give birth to part of themselves in another person, they are more likely to dominate the art of the inner life.

Alice Hambidge's *By the candle light* is of a young woman abstractedly combing her hair, gazing at herself before sleep, dreaming herself into the next day and the more distant future. Who am I? She probably knows the answers can be different every time the question is asked of the mirror.

Alice HAMBIDGE, 1869-1947. *By the candle light.* 1899, Adelaide. Watercolour on paper, 33.5 x 51.6 cm.
Art Gallery of South Australia, Adelaide. Elder Bequest Fund 1899

Bertram MACKENNAL, 1863-1931. *Daphne.* 1897, London. Bronze, 50 x 15 cm. Queensland Art Gallery, Brisbane. State Government funds 1974

C. Douglas RICHARDSON, 1853-1932. *The cloud.* c1900, Melbourne. Bronze, 46.2 x 15.7 cm. Australian National Gallery, Canberra. Joseph Brown Fund 1979

Emma Minnie BOYD, 1858-1936. *The letter.* 1889, Melbourne. Oil on canvas, 45.8 x 30.7 cm. M.J.M. Carter Collection, Art Gallery of South Australia, Adelaide

E. Phillips FOX, 1865-1915. *Eighty-five years.* 1891, St Ives, Cornwall. Oil on canvas, 35.4 x 29.3 cm. Art Gallery of South Australia, Adelaide. M.J.M. Carter Collection 1987

TEMPTRESS IMPERIOUS by NOEL HUTCHISON

Bertram Mackennal, *Circe*, 1892

"Circe of the lovely tresses, human though she was in speech, proved her powers as a goddess . . ." Homer

The young Australian sculptor Bertram Mackennal produced his controversial masterpiece *Circe* in 1892. The finished bronze-painted life-size plaster version was first exhibited at the Palais des Champs-Élysées in Paris at the 1893 Salon Exhibition that opened in May.[1] The sculpture gained recognition for the artist by the award of a *mention honorable* and much praise. This was the first of many distinctions and honours that the eventual Sir Bertram Mackennal, K.C.V.O., R.A. would obtain during his illustrious life as an Australian expatriate, largely in England.

Mackennal was born in Fitzroy, Melbourne, in 1863, of Scottish-born parents. His father, John Simpson Mackennal, was a sculptor and the architectural modeller of the ornate plaster ceilings found in many of Melbourne's public buildings.[2] The son became apprenticed to his father and, although from 1878 he attended the National Gallery School in Melbourne to learn drawing, most of his skills in sculptural modelling were learnt from J.S. Mackennal. By the time he left Australia for the first time, in 1882, in order to study abroad, he had acquired sufficient training not only to gain entry to the Royal Academy Schools in London but also to find that they were useless for his further studies. He left London and went to Paris where he learnt about art by visiting artists' studios, including those of the great contemporary French sculptor Auguste Rodin.

In 1886 he was appointed head of modelling and design at the Coalport Potteries in Shropshire and from there sent to the 1886 Royal Academy of Arts Summer Exhibition his relief *The Five Foolish Virgins*.[3] Then, having gained a commission to design the relief panels on the facade of Parliament House, Melbourne, Mackennal returned to Australia in 1888. While there, a competition for a monumental group to be placed in front of the National Gallery of Victoria was announced by its trustees and Mackennal submitted an entry, *The Triumph of the Truth*. Making a controversial decision, the trustees decided not to award the first prize at all and gave the second prize to Mackennal. Disillusioned, and advised by local supporters and the French actress (and amateur sculptor) Sarah Bernhardt, then on tour in Australia, Mackennal left Melbourne and returned to Paris in 1891.[4] In 1892 he exhibited two smaller sculptures at the Salon but it was after he had placed "much time, money and thought into my *Circe*" that he reaped the reward of artistic acclaim.[5]

Who was Circe? What were her attributes that the twentynine-year-old Australian was stirred to make such a dramatically convincing and powerful work?

Circe is one of the key figures in Greek mythology. She links the great voyage sagas of both the Argonauts and Odysseus (Ulysses), as well as other epic stories that have disappeared.[6]

As a divine being with great powers for good and evil, the ability to foretell the future, the capability of coupling with males who take her fancy, and also the capacity to act as a redemptive intermediary with Zeus, the lord of the gods, she is capable of both great cruelty and deep compassion. The ancient Greek epic poets Homer and Apollonius (the author of *The Voyage of the Argo*) indicate her crucial role. Her father is Helios (The Sun). She is the sister of the king of fabled Colchis, the city where the Golden Fleece was kept before Jason and his Argonauts stole it with the help of the king's daughter, the priestess and witch Medea. As the intercessory for Medea and Jason to Zeus, angry after they had treacherously murdered Medea's brother, Circe is to be seen as the point of connection between the divine and the earthly.[7]

In Homer's great epic *The Odyssey*, Circe is a more ambivalent being. There she is a beguiling sorceress who has the power to turn humans into animals. After she has intoxicated his crew, turned them into swine and locked them in a sty, the Greek hero Odysseus overcomes the wiles of Circe and makes her his mistress and adviser. Yet all the foreknowledge that Circe provides to Odysseus helps him little; his crew continue as uncontrollable specimens of the base side of human nature.[8]

Mackennal depicts Circe as an imperious sorceress in the act of casting her spell. She stands erect, arms out-stretched and fingers flexed. She gazes straight towards the viewer. Her full-breasted nude body is taut with controlled and directed energy. The coiled long tresses of her hair, mentioned by Homer, are encircled by a cord-and-leather headpiece that suggests writhing snakes — an indication of her sorceress's powers and divine attributes. Divine status is further reinforced by the twin snakes of lust and death rising at her feet and encircling her standpoint. They are a transition to the bronze-relief scene on the base below.[9]

The base's band of *bas-relief* figures depicts frenzied bacchanalic couplings that suggest the animalism of human passions. The winged figure of Eros (Love) crouches head on knees at the front; true love is perhaps deploring vice.

Mackennal's format of a single life-size figure with an integrated base bearing a scene related to the action of the major figure was unusual in French sculpture of the late nineteenth century. It owed more to Italian Mannerist sculpture of the sixteenth century, as well as to the devices used by the major British sculptor of the late nineteenth century, Sir Alfred Gilbert, R.A.[10]

On the other hand the sexuality of Mackennal's bold female figure, footnoted with an elaborating relief, had few parallels in the 'New Sculpture' movement that had arisen in Britain at that time.[11] Mackennal's approach owed much to his knowledge of the reliefs and studies of the French master, Auguste Rodin. Such an approach was decidedly un-British. The overt sexual acts depicted on the base were too much for the Hanging Committee for the 1894 Royal Academy of Arts Summer Exhibition in London. Mackennal was requested to cover the base in red woollen baize so that the public would not be infected by its noxious images; yet even then it was reported that the sculpture "drew wandering and admiring eyes".[12] Subsequently, *Circe* was fully revealed by the illustration in the annual *Royal Academy Illustrated* for 1894. Before this incident the Director of the National Gallery of Victoria, the painter Bernard Hall, had already tried to interest his trustees in buying Mackennal's sculpture. He wrote on 22 January 1894: "It seems to me to be a genuine work of genius — very remarkable and impressive — without doubt I should say Young Australia's

Bertram MACKENNAL. *Circe.* 1902/1904, Paris, from an 1892 model. Bronze
statuette, 57 cm high. The Joseph Brown Collection

Bertram MACKENNAL, 1863-1931. *Circe.* 1982, Paris; cast in bronze c1902.
Bronze statue, 204.6 cm high. National Gallery of Victoria, Melbourne
Felton Bequest Fund 1910

chef d'ouvre [sic]",[13] but the recommendation was rejected. When Mackennal brought *Circe* with him on a visit to Australia in late 1900 the Gallery
made an offer of £800 for the full-size unique bronze cast[14] but he instead
took up an offer by the Austrian Consul in Melbourne, Carl Pinschof, to buy
Circe for £1000. The bronze-founder, E. Gruet jeune, Paris, not only cast the
full-size statue but in 1902-04 also produced an edition of about eight
statuette-size casts.[15]

It was not until 1910 that the Trustees of the National Gallery of
Victoria were able to buy, for £1200 from the estate of the deceased Carl
Pinschof, the most significant sculpture that Bertram Mackennal ever
produced.[16] "Young Australia's masterpiece", nearly a century after her
making, still stands for the seductive fascination exerted by the experience
and antiquity of Europe, be it the archaic power of Homeric Greece or the
legend in her lifetime that was Bernhardt.

NATIVE COMPANIONS by JOANNA MENDELSSOHN

Sydney Long, *The Spirit of the Plains,* 1897

The image is haunting; once seen it remains at the edges of the viewer's memory, like a dream from long ago.

For a work of its time, painted by a man steeped in popular Victorian imagery, *The Spirit of the Plains* is surprisingly simple in composition. There is the girl piper — a slim, straight-backed bush-spirit — leading her birds in a dance. The moon in front of her head is not quite a halo, although in later versions it was to become one. The concept of sainthood is irrelevant to this ethereal pagan. Her presence is emphasized pictorially by a gap in the frieze of gum-trees that forms the flattened background to the procession.

These gums, placed in receding groupings, encourage a theatrical reading of the painting. It is almost as though they form a stage-setting for the performance of a new antipodean production. The concept of landscape as backdrop was one that Long would have seen in Tom Roberts's *Bailed up* and *In a corner on the Macintyre*, both first exhibited at the Society of Artists' inaugural exhibition in Sydney two years earlier. But whereas Roberts painted myth-making nationalism related to specific bushranging incidents in the then-recent past, Long concentrates here on the decorative qualities of his nature-myth and leaves the details of a possible story to the viewer's imagination.

As well as the theatrical reference of the trees, the very shallowness of the picture space has another implication. This painting was seen by the artist as a decoration rather like Pierre Puvis de Chavannes's self-consciously archaic panels. The carefully planned pattern-like structure of Puvis's work appealed to Long's decorative sense and he is one of the few non-Australian painters Long admitted admiring.

A rhythmic decorative composition in harmonies of blues, greens and greys. A girl leading her flock of brolgas in a dance so that they make one gloriously complex curve in which their dark heads read like a piece of music notation. A music score surges in the air, behind the piper. This is the most formally perfect piece Long ever made, relying on the purely abstract qualities of line and tone, while at the same time playing on our recognition of music and our yearning to understand the mystery of the girl and her flock.

Its gently harmonized decorative qualities combined with subtle myth-making give *The Spirit of the Plains* an unusual place in the history of Australian art in that it is a painting which is Art Nouveau in style. This makes it a bridge between the high-prestige medium of painting and the artisan skills of wood-carving, metalwork and other design forms.

The essentially decorative nature of the work was commented on by the critics of the time, as well as another quality. The *Sydney Mail* critic called it "queer" and the *Daily Telegraph* noted the birds "weirdly capering to the sloughing of the winds".[1] The critics' use of language seems almost as though they were faced with a painting outside their experience of art, so they grasped for words in an attempt to describe the quality of other-worldliness that is essential to its appeal. The idea of faerie and fantasy was very much a part of the literary scene that most closely sympathized with European Symbolism and Art Nouveau, so it is hardly surprising to find Long using the forms of Art Nouveau to create a new myth for the Australian bush.

Long's aim to create a genuine Australian mythology, which was to be expressed in images and not words, is central to his only major piece of writing, published eight years after *The Spirit of the Plains* was first exhibited. Long was not an accomplished writer and he probably had considerable editorial help in presenting this elegantly worded argument for nationalism.

After rejecting the validity of foreign-born artists' visions of Australia, and of the imagery of the old world, he wrote:

". . . the Australian artist will never be able to people the bush with nymphs, or the rivers with naiades, unless he invents a special Australian brand, or forgets his native landscape. They will never look convincing among the gum-trees, and men in armour even be more ridiculous. This lack of any tradition has to a certain extent curbed the imagination of the figure painter. He is brought face to face with the elements that suggested to the Greeks their beautiful traditions, and as he cannot use their symbols, he will have the joy of making new ones suitable to his surroundings. The drover, the shearer, the bullock driver, and even the bush-ranger, to the utilitarian person, seem to be all that is needed as a keynote for Australian landscape, but yet to me the background calls for something that will better express the lonely and primitive feeling of this country. A feeling more suggestive of some melancholy pastoral to be rendered in music, and perhaps rather beyond the limits of painting, yet given the artist with imagination and a complete knowledge of his materials, he should produce work of the most imaginative kind from his surroundings."[2]

Not that Sydney Long was averse to painting European myth-making. In 1898, only a year after *The Spirit of the Plains*, he exhibited *Pan*, which for all its Art Nouveau detail and moodily nocturnal tones was a literal interpretation of *A Musical Instrument*, a poem by Elizabeth Barrett Browning. A Victorian English poem was interpreted in the decorative forms of *fin de siècle* art — which is one of the contradictions of Sydney Long. With the notable exception of his illustrations to Christopher Brennan's poetry, Long's iconography relates to popular rather than esoteric sources. And from comments Long made at the time it seems clear that he regarded his Brennan illustrations simply as a piece of commissioned work for which he was paid.

That is one of the reasons why *The Spirit of the Plains* is so intriguing. Another is that Sydney Long does not appear to have been a likely candidate to have painted such an enticing work.

The youngest child of a large and not especially affluent country-town family in Goulburn, New South Wales, he first attracted the patronage in Sydney of Julian Ashton with a piece of Victorian kitsch — a nocturne of Circular Quay. His first public success was *By Tranquil Waters*, 1894, a deliberate exercise in the then-radical style of Impressionism, but nevertheless with the decorative overtones favoured by the widely available English art magazine *The Studio*. Presumably it was this deliberately fashionable avant-gardism that caused the writer of the *Bulletin's* review to

Sydney LONG, 1871-1955. *The Spirit of the Plains*. 1897, Sydney. Oil on canvas, 62.8 x 134 cm. Queensland Art Gallery, Brisbane.
Gift of William Howard Smith in memory of Ormond Charles Smith 1940

say that his earlier works "might have been art; but they looked like arguments to prove that a cockroach has an immortal soul with bone knobs on the end like a Cape York Woomera."[3]

The *Bulletin* writer was, perhaps unknowingly, poking fun at a continuing theme in Long's art: the assumption of close communion between humankind and the natural world, and a further suggestion that animals might share an aesthetic sense with us (especially for music). Long's paintings with farmers' women feeding poultry and calves, or sharing mid-day shade with cattle and sheep, would not have been provocative. Naked female bathers receiving a flock of red flamingoes were. The naturalistic boy bathers in *By Tranquil Waters* disturbed some viewers, perhaps because the principal boy becomes a budding pagan faun by his projection of pan-pipe music along the sunlit river-banks.

Our interdependence with animals, and the power of music over them, had been part of Western mental furnishing since ancient Greek times. The Symbolist spirit of the times in the 1890s encouraged the re-entry of such subjects into European art. It is probable however that Sydney Long was especially receptive to peculiarly Australian influences.

His one literary effort, *The Trend of Australian Art . . .*, already quoted, goes on to say that the Australian artist, "Instead of Pans and Centaurs . . . will bid the Aboriginal blossom out in all the graceful proportions of manly vigour; . . ." And in the previous year, 1904, Long had painted *The Music Lesson* in which an Aboriginal woman plays a flute,

surrounded by magpies. (Who is giving the lesson, who receiving, is left ambiguous.)

Closer in time to *The Spirit of the Plains* we find that natural heritage interested the art world of Sydney. In 1894, Ku-ring-gai Chase was dedicated as a national park, instigated by the same man who had already instigated the Art Gallery of New South Wales as an art museum.[4] The same man's music-teacher friend Ethel Pedley wrote the best-selling storybook *Dot and the Kangaroo*[5] for " . . . the children of Australia, in the hope of enlisting their sympathies for the many beautiful, amiable and frolicsome creatures of their fair land, whose extinction through ruthless destruction is being surely accomplished". The book's 1898 illustrations, by Frank Mahony, include *Dot dances with the Native Companions*, a sunset dance by water at the edge of a grassy plain. ("'It's a Human', said the Kangaroo apologetically [to the birds]; 'It's quite a little harmless one. Let me introduce you.'")

Today we call these graceful birds brolgas and in northern Australia they can still be seen sinuously dancing at dusk, most accessibly for tourists at the Townsville Common. In the nineteenth century they were invariably called Native Companions. So Sydney Long's ambiguously rendered human in *The Spirit of the Plains* is, if not Aboriginal, then a 'White Aborigine', a European who has gone native in order to receive companionship from the birds.

TWENTIETH-CENTURY ART: NATURE by DANIEL THOMAS

The twentieth century coincided in 1901 with the official birth of Australia. The six British colonies federated to become a new nation, the Commonwealth of Australia. Australian nature was by now more a tradition than a discovery. It decorated daily life or symbolized nationhood.

Australia was part of the British Empire and a distinctly imperial note was struck by Hans Heysen's *Red Gold*, 1913, a large painting of large and ancient gum-trees, a grandiose display of maturity and power; an affirmation that this was an ancient land and one which understands the maintenance of nature's cycles, that men and cattle will complete a day's work, the seasons will turn, the centuries will see the great trees come and go. Max Meldrum's *Four o'clock* poplars, painted in France a few years earlier, are less baroque, more a formalist abstraction from clear observation of dark flaming verticals rising from a dense green horizontal slab of meadow, past small old houses and a little chateau, into a hot copper-coloured sky.

The intimate counterpart to public grandeur in oil painting was an outbreak of luxurious craftsmanship. Watercolour painting, etching and wood-engraving were as much a part of this early-twentieth-century taste as were silver, porcelain and fine furniture.

J.J. Hilder's opalescent *The dry lagoon* was used in 1918 to illustrate Dorothea Mackellar's colour-luxuriating poem *My Country* : "I love a sunburnt country,/ . . . I love her jewel sea/ . . . The sapphire-misted mountains/ The hot gold rush of noon/ . . . An opal-hearted country . . .". Its stylized formula for melaleuca trees was hugely appreciated by Chinese artists when it toured to Beijing and Nanjing in 1975. Blamire Young's *Pastoral Symphony* shows a more usual cultural exchange in its Chinese styling of Australian eucalyptus boughs as does Lionel Lindsay's fine wood-engraving *Syrian goat and rhododendrons*, 1925, in its use of a traditional Chinese animal-and-flower formula.

Less oriental but equally refined were the period's characteristic crafts of wood-carving and china-painting, often with Australian motifs, though Robert Prenzel's fireplace-surround is decorated with non-Australian water-lilies and Floy Hubble's china plate with proteas. Klytie Pate's earthenware vase carries Australian flora in relief and Elizabeth Soderberg's copper bowl the flying-fox or fruit bat which feeds on Sydney's fig-trees. Evan Jones's dessert dish is formed from nature unmodified, a pearl-oyster shell supported by naturalistic silver leaves and flowers.

Such extreme refinement had already produced in European art a reaction in favour of the 'primitive'. Gauguin had gone to the peasants of Brittany and to Polynesia, the wild Fauves had emerged in Paris, followed in 1907 by Picasso's African/Oceanic Cubism. In the British decorative arts the Omega Workshops took up this taste for naive directness and influenced the art-pottery of Gladys Reynell, whose emu beaker was made in London. Merric Boyd's sinuous gum-tree bowl is more a product of the earlier aesthetic Arts and Crafts Movement but nevertheless shares directness and rough simplicity with the new 'primitivism'.

Jim Kite, an Aborigine, was himself a real 'primitive', apparently inventing his own naive art-form of carving in soft stone for his own pleasure and as collectors' items for South Australians travelling the desert along the Overland Telegraph. Today we wonder whether his frog carving might have had personal totemic significance at Charlotte Waters.

In the 1930s the railway reached Alice Springs and a small tourist industry began to develop in Central Australia. Albert Namatjira's watercolour views of that beautiful desert country then began and from them grew a whole school of tourist-market art. Now, however, its conventional repetitiveness can be read as an affirmation of tribal ownership of the land and as the development of a new code of symbols. Trees and rocks conceal nature-spirits; wrinkled, veined branches and trunks can be read as arms and bodies, faces appear in rocks. Because of the European watercolour medium the work was perceived in its day as white art by black men, a peculiar variation on Hans Heysen's gum-trees; now it is re-Aboriginalized and we see it as a creative variation on traditional Aboriginal art.

Margaret Preston's *Aboriginal landscape*, 1941, an oil painting which imitates the look of Arnhem Land bark-paintings to represent bush landscape on the outskirts of Sydney, is one of the first works of Euro-Australian high art frankly to express admiration for Aboriginal art. (Decorative and commercial art had already been appropriating Aboriginal symbolic designs.) Weaver Hawkins's 1949 *Bushscape*, similarly of suburban Sydney sandstone bush, is closer to the spirit of Aboriginal art in its choice of an angophora tree with pink fleshy bark and a suggestion of a human skull emerging from its trunk; man and nature are interchangeable, as in Aboriginal Dreamings.

Kenneth Macqueen's kangaroos have been alarmed while grazing among dead trees ring-barked for a slow, standing death, a minimum-labour method of clearing land, used throughout Australia before heavy machinery was available. Farmers received long years of visible reproach from the skeletons of their victims.

Humans bathing in the Australian seas were once frequent victims of sharks, a reference to which is in Sam Fullbrook's *Phoenix on Sunday*. John Olsen's *Spring in the You Beaut Country*, despite its bug-eyed snapping-mouthed creatures, is a celebration of insect, animal and plant life's ecstatic seasonal burgeoning in outer-Sydney bush. Lorraine Jenyns's ceramic sculpture is a humorous variant of ancient Egyptian lidded vases, made to contain the entrails of embalmed humans or animal-gods.

Lloyd Rees joins the particular to the universal in *The Timeless Land* where Sydney-region bush evokes not only the steep oracular clefts of ancient Greece but also the art-by-nature's-hand rock-faces so admired by Chinese connoisseurship. Similarly, Fred Williams's gum-tree *Stump* is Chinese in its anthropomorphic hint of a human head. But tree/human metamorphoses are also Aboriginal and also Greek and it is the fusion of timeless Eastern, Western and Aboriginal ways of feeling and thinking which makes such works not only masterpieces of their own time but also portents of a culturally-rich future for Australia.

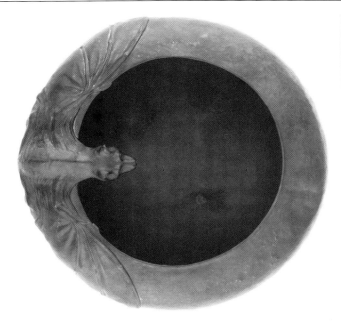

Elizabeth SODERBERG, died 1938. *Flying-fox bowl.* 1912, Sydney. Copper, 7.5 x 22.5 cm. Art Gallery of New South Wales, Sydney. Elizabeth Soderberg Bequest, Gift of the New South Wales Society of Arts and Crafts, 1939

Evan JONES, 1846-1917. *Dessert dish.* Early 20th century, Sydney. Silver-mounted pearl oyster shell (*Pinctada maxima*), 17 cm high. Art Gallery of South Australia, Adelaide. Gift of Mr and Mrs G.H. Michell through the Art Gallery of South Australia Foundation 1980

Robert PRENZEL, 1866-1941. *Fireplace surround,* for a bedroom suite at Glenormiston homestead, near Camperdown, Victoria. c1910, Melbourne. Queensland blackbean, 170 x 188.3 x 34.4 cm. Australian National Gallery, Canberra. Federal Government funds 1980

Merric BOYD, 1888-1959. *Gum-tree bowl.* 1938, Murrumbeena, Melbourne. Earthenware, 14 x 30.5 x 26.7 cm. Arthur & Yvonne Boyd, Bundanon, New South Wales

Gladys REYNELL, 1881-1956. *Emu beaker.* 1917, Camberwell School of Arts & Crafts, London. Earthenware, 10 x 8 cm. Art Gallery of South Australia, Adelaide. State Government funds 1980

Jim KITE (ERLIKILIAKIRRA), born c1873. *Frog.* c1902, Charlotte Waters, Northern Territory. Gypsum, 14 x 11 cm. South Australian Museum, Adelaide. Gift of Mrs C.E. Klotz 1953

J.J. HILDER, 1881-1916. *The dry lagoon.* 1911, Sydney. Watercolour on paper, 64.7 x 95.9 cm. Art Gallery of New South Wales, Sydney. State Government funds 1911

Blamire YOUNG, 1862-1935. *Pastoral symphony.* c1920, Melbourne. Watercolour on paper, 39 x 55.5 cm. Art Gallery of Western Australia, Perth. Great Australian Paintings Appeal 1978

Floy HUBBLE, 1885-1948. *Protea plate*, from a set of six. c1918, Adelaide. Painted decoration on a porcelain blank, 23.4 cm diameter. Art Gallery of South Australia, Adelaide. State Government funds 1983

Lionel LINDSAY, 1874-1961. *Syrian goat and rhododendrons.* 1925, Sydney. Wood-engraving on paper, 17 x 15.3 cm. Art Gallery of South Australia, Adelaide. David Murray Bequest Fund 1973

Klytie PATE, born 1912. *Bottle-brush vase.* c1938, Melbourne. Earthenware, 24.7 cm high. National Gallery of Victoria, Melbourne. State Government funds 1980

Max MELDRUM, 1875-1955. *Four o'clock.* c1910, Pacé, near Rennes, Brittany, France. Oil on canvas, 70.2 x 96.3 cm. Australian National Gallery, Canberra. Federal Government funds 1970

Albert NAMATJIRA, 1902-1959. *Ghost gum, Central Australia.* c1950,
MacDonnell Ranges, Northern Territory. Watercolour on paper, 26 x 36.5 cm.
Art Gallery of South Australia, Adelaide. Gift of the Deutscher Family, 1987, in
commemoration of their arrival in South Australia from Germany in 1848

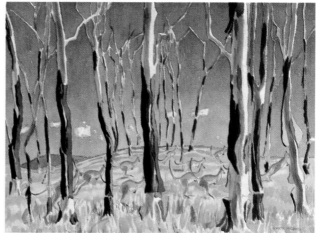

Kenneth MACQUEEN, 1897-1960. *Alarm.* c1940, Millmerran near Toowoomba,
Queensland. Watercolour on paper, 38 x 49 cm. Mrs A.O. Worthington Wilmer

Otto PAREROULTJA, 1914-1973. *Landscape.* c1950, MacDonnell Ranges, Northern Territory. Watercolour
on paper, 68 x 88 cm. Museums & Art Galleries of the Northern Territory, Darwin. Territory Government funds 1974

Weaver HAWKINS, 1893-1977. *Bushscape.* 1949, Sydney. Oil on canvas, 45.4 x 60.8 cm. Alan N. Jennings

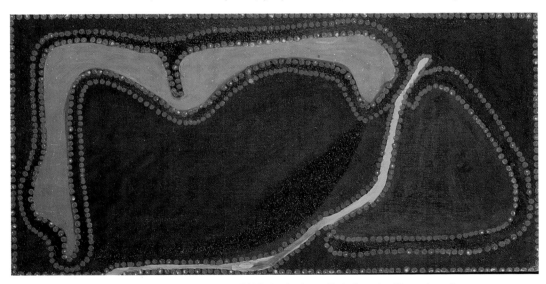

Rover THOMAS, born 1926. *Tjimpulan.* c1984, Turkey Creek, east Kimberley region, Western Australia.
Natural pigment and gum on plywood, 62 x 122 cm. State Library of Western Australia, Perth. Alexander
Library Building Art Collection. State Government funds 1985

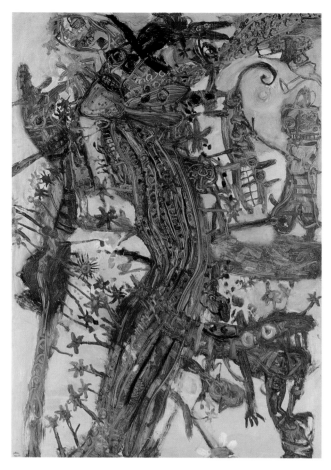

John OLSEN, born 1928. *Spring in the You Beaut Country.* 1961, Sydney. Oil on composition board, 183 x 122 cm. Australian National Gallery, Canberra. Gift of Rudy Komon 1984

Lorraine JENYNS, born 1945. *Baboon with banana.* 1977, Daylesford, Victoria. Earthenware, 36.8 cm high. Art Gallery of South Australia, Adelaide. State Government funds 1978

Sam FULLBROOK, born 1922. *Phoenix on Sunday.* 1968, Buderim, Queensland. Oil on canvas, 98 x 120 cm. Private collection. Courtesy Philip Bacon Galleries, Brisbane

Fred WILLIAMS, 1927-1982. *Stump.* 1976, Melbourne, from a February
1976 sketch at Kyneton, Victoria. Oil on canvas, 123 x 123 cm.
Private collection

Col LEVY, born 1933. *Vase.* 1971, Sydney. Stoneware, 50.3 x 36 cm.
National Gallery of Victoria, Melbourne. State Government funds 1971

Lloyd REES, born 1895. *The Timeless Land.* 1965, Sydney. Oil on canvas, 170 x 132 cm. Private collection
Based on a Kangaroo Valley subject, above the Shoalhaven River, NSW

GUM-TREE IMPERIAL by IAN NORTH

Hans Heysen, *Red Gold*, 1913

Heysen was the first artist to make the ubiquitous "gum-tree" the object of a prolonged artistic embrace and so complete was his conquest of the eucalyptus that it has become an unjustly maligned symbol of his art. The gum-tree as a national symbol, the bush as Arcadia, as Art Nouveau, the bushman as noble peasant: all were well-established in Australian art before Hans Heysen. But by the 1910s, Australian landscape painting had become trivialized by what Heysen called "the art of the colour box",[1] the superficial and the decorative. Even the bright, high-toned Impressionism of Arthur Streeton, Heysen's main rival, had become a formula. Heysen cut through the developing haze of romance through his powers of observation, honed by a delight in drawing and by his love of the natural world. Extolling the virtues of a healthy outdoor life (symbolized by the adoption of knickerbockers and leggings as his uniform dress) he confessed: "The Sun — its light and its warmth — is my religion".[2] Heysen adored "Dame Nature"[3], especially her light and her trees, with a quasi-sensual, quasi-pantheistic fervour, nowhere more clearly expressed than in *Red Gold*.

"I am only trying to paint as truthfully as I can, and that my eyes see and perhaps what I consciously feel. Truth to Nature after all is the goal but truth interpreted through temperament, might interest me as much as ever, but I am seeking it more under the everyday aspect of nature. Rural life under these conditions has always held a great fascination for me and also the animals that 'toil for man' . . . I suppose everything in Nature is much the same wherever you are once the eye has become more or less treated to seize upon the underlying rhythm of nature."[4] So stated Heysen in 1919.

What Heysen's eyes saw, in regarding *Red Gold's* motif, was a view from the Hahndorf-Mount Barker Junction Road, in the Adelaide Hills, rendered in the painting with some artistic licence: Mount Barker, the peak in the left centre background, could not be seen from the artist's vantage-point. The cattle, perhaps a bullock team, were not just *staffage*; they might well have passed down the road, and in any case comprised an essential part of that unity of person, beast and earth which Heysen sought to express. 'Truth' for the artist here centres around the value of rural life (its supposed humanism, honesty and heroic nobility), anchored to an essentialist sense of the "underlying rhythm of nature". Such ideas had force for the artist in their ideological opposition to what he saw as a passing way of life, as Australia began to develop the most urbanized nation on earth (for all of white Australia's fascination for and complex relationship with the bush) on the eve of that ultimate horror of the industrialized West, World War I. By the turn of the century the bush had become the object of regretful nostalgia in Australian culture, just as the countryside was perceived as being under threat in nineteenth-century France. There J.F. Millet, a major influence on Heysen, had sought to assert rural harmony against the express train of civilization, leading, as Heysen saw it, for a "deep dirty morass".[5]

Heysen's values, both personal and artistic, sprang from a life spent mainly on the fringes of rural communities. His father had emigrated to South Australia from Hamburg, Germany, his wife and five surviving children following in 1884. Hans attended five schools before leaving at the age of fourteen to work in a sawmilling and hardware business. Heysen's early talent for painting, fostered by part-time study in Adelaide at James Ashton's Norwood Art School, impressed a quartet of businessmen and they sponsored four years of study in Paris, with travel in Europe including Britain from 1899 to 1903. In 1904, after returning to Adelaide, he sold major oils to public collections, married, and moved to Hahndorf in the Adelaide Hills, a small town originally settled by German immigrants. After further successful exhibitions in Melbourne, Heysen bought The Cedars, a house with some land outside Hahndorf, where he lived for the rest of his life, recording the activities of farm-labourers in oils, watercolours, drawings and (occasionally) etchings.

More than any of his contemporaries, Heysen founded his art deeply and fruitfully on European models. 'Nature's rhythm' in his Hahndorf pastorals is inflected to the lilt of Art Nouveau (*The Coming Home, Mystic Morn*) or, later, the richer sonority of the Baroque (*Red Gold, Droving into the light*). Even Heysen's earliest watercolours were influenced by the English watercolour tradition and his course was modified by the intermingling artistic currents flowing in late-nineteenth-century France, including Academic Realism, Naturalism and Impressionism.

The first, Academic Realism, inculcated through l'Académie Julian and l'École des Beaux-Arts, left Heysen a lingering taste for the classicizing Renaissance tradition in concept and composition, a tendency towards a pictorial marshalling of picturesque subject-matter. This approach was reinforced by a lifelong admiration for Claude Lorrain, and for Camille Corot, the latter's work referring back to Italian art as well as anticipating its antithesis in Naturalism. Naturalism developed in mid-nineteenth-century France along with democratic political aspirations and a middle-class art-market, foreshadowing Heysen's market in Australia. The Barbizon School was the internationally-admired model, and Heysen followed Millet in elevating his subject-matter above the petty details of the present: his rural labourers become Australian equivalents of Fontainebleau peasants. Heysen's debt to the Barbizon School's English precursor, Constable, increased rather than diminished with the passing of time; Constable anticipated Impressionism, which in turn extended for Heysen the directions set by his Adelaide teachers, even if he never fully accepted its pure hedonism and quasi-scientific analysis of light. The Australian *plein air* painters (especially Streeton) and the British crypto-Impressionists George Clausen and E.A. Hornel were greater influences than Monet or Pissarro, and an academic emphasis on tonal, sculptural drawing remained the basis of Heysen's art. Impressionism nonetheless opened Heysen's eyes to the quality of Australian light and enabled him to achieve a greater sense of regional identity.

Heysen, then, sheeted the philosophy of the Barbizon School to a particular Australian location and expounded it with an expressive assurance derived from Claude, Rubens, Constable and Turner. This phase of his art reached its apotheosis in works like *Red Gold*, in which, too, the decorative expansiveness of the then-popular Welsh muralist Frank Brangwyn may be seen, along with the purple drama of children's book-illustrations of the imperial pre-war period.

Hans HEYSEN, 1877-1968. *Red Gold.* 1913, Hahndorf near Adelaide. Oil on canvas, 128.6 x 173 cm. Art Gallery of South Australia, Adelaide. Gift of the Rt Hon. Sir Charles Booth 1913

In works such as *Red Gold*, Heysen had succeeded in giving the Arcadian tradition in Australian painting a dimension at once human and heroic. In no other work of Heysen's do the gums seem so humanoid in their heroic posturing; in few others do the buttery strokes of paint seem to metamorphose into the very stuff of leaves, bark, and soil. At the heart of his triumph was a wedding of humble subject-matter, patiently observed, with grand European stylistic sources. They were fused by the strength of his conviction about the value of a passing way of life. Bernard Smith observed, "Heysen was perhaps the only Australian painter of the Edwardian years to handle the big landscape with success . . . he continued to explore the problem after Streeton and McCubbin had moved on to other interests, and his achievement, all things considered, was more successful than theirs".[6]

Red Gold, titled like a number of Heysen's best-known works by his wife Sallie,[7] epitomized that success on a worldly as well as art-historical level. It was privately purchased from the sixteenth South Australian Society of Arts Federal Exhibition for presentation to the (then National) Art Gallery of South Australia. A popular acquisition from that day to this, it apparently prompted the only letter the artist ever received from his father.[8] Quite as much as Tom Roberts and Arthur Streeton, Heysen, with paintings like *Red Gold*, established white Australia's most persistent vision of the Australian landscape. The values Heysen embodied in his work may be recognized for their social basis without denying their continuing resonance. Like the Barbizon painters before him and increasing numbers of people since, Heysen sensed that modern technology could be environmentally and psychologically disastrous. His ideas and his art may now excite a fresh response from all who echo his question, "What would the world be without horses and trees, skies, and all the other visual things around us . . .?"[9]

ABORIGINAL ORIENTATION by IAN NORTH

Margaret Preston, *Aboriginal landscape*, 1941

Preston's *Aboriginal landscape*, 1941, was part of her war effort. It is one of the smallest, least well resolved and yet the most dynamic of all her 'Aboriginal' paintings. Its very urgency now seems emblematic of the difficult times in which it was painted. None of this seemed to be at the forefront of Preston's mind when she painted the picture. "Australian Aboriginal art is symbolical and hyper-realistic . . . Aboriginal Art represents not the object alone from which it is drawn, but the essential truths which may or may not be visible to the human eye."[1] So stated Preston in 1941, cueing her audience on how she wanted it to read the work.

The paint is laid down baldly with none of the sensuality of Preston's earlier flower-pictures. The forms are firmly described but their treatment is incomplete: cream lines deny the flatness of the shapes they describe at the lower left, the track floats free of the ground, while shadows across it could be fallen trees. All of which only adds to the work's sense of conviction, held together as it is by a taut rhythm of similar shapes over a substructure of intersecting diagonals. The muted earth-colours, the Papunya-style dots, the simplified black lines, all identify the work as 'Aboriginal'. Depth is denied, both formally and metaphorically. The grass is like spears and the trees are like palisades, suggesting the difficulties of penetrating the country and the culture with which it is identified; yet both are affirmed, in the sheer energy with which their fusion is expressed. The painting's title and Preston's statement indicate where she wanted to point the viewer but only partly the path where she had been: as well as incorporating aspects of Aboriginal art, the work also reflects the influence of Oriental art and European Modernism, and in particular the Cubism of 'Purist Paris' in the late 1920s.

Initially, Modernism was the most important of these three factors, because it both legitimated and provided a reference point for her interest in the others. Japanese prints, which helped introduce van Gogh to the notion of composing in flat planes, were a refuge to the young Preston in Paris. Repelled by the (for her) expressionistic, subjective excesses of Lovis Corinth, Gustav Klimt and other members of the German Secession in 1904 she learned from Japanese prints to think in terms of flat planar composition. Chinese painting was also a direct and recent influence on several of Preston's 'Aboriginal Paintings', which she began six years after a trip to China and Japan.

Van Gogh was only the most notable artist of the Post-Impressionist era to be influenced by exotic art. His colleague, the great Post-Impressionist Paul Gauguin, was interested in tribal cultures, another growing focus of fascination at the time. Preston followed his trail, in a sense, around the Pacific. 'Primitivism',[2] via Picasso and the Cubists' search for authenticity by appropriating tribal art, fed not only Preston's 'modernist moment' of 1927-29, but also her interest in Aboriginal art and art which was truly 'national'.

Preston decided in 1924 that the strong black outlines characteristic of her wood-block printing of the time should also be an important ingredient of a national art-style, along with the boomerang shape, concentric circles and the gum-leaf shape, coloured with red, yellow,

ochre and blue. Her immediate justification was "the indigenous art of Australia",[5] her first purpose to promote national forms and colours for the design of domestic items and furnishings. Aboriginal art, she felt, offered a much better basis for developing national design characteristics than simply carrying on the imitation of Australia's flora and fauna which had occurred since settlement and which she herself extended in her popular flower-paintings of the period. Aboriginal as well as Cubist influences appear intermittently in her work of the 1920s and 1930s (the concentric circles of *Aeroplane*, c1925,[6] dot patterns on leaves and blooms, the muted colours and bold outlines of works like *Implement Blue*, 1927).

It was difficult for Preston to be other than a tourist in relation to Aboriginal art, notwithstanding arduous journeys, some taken at an advanced age, to tribal areas in New South Wales, Queensland and the Northern Territory by utility truck and light plane. Even so, her understanding of Aborigines deepened from 1932 to 1939 when she and her husband lived in a house in the Berowra bush, forty kilometres north of Sydney, an area bounded to the east by the Ku-ring-gai Chase National Park. There are found numerous rock-engravings, which Preston undoubtedly discussed with Fred McCarthy, Curator of Anthropology at The Australian Museum, Sydney, a new-found friend, with whom she stayed in touch for twenty years. By 1941, Preston was able to discuss the Australian Aborigine as not just a source of textile designs, but "a true and sensitive artist whose work should be studied and treated with the respect that is due to true art."[7].

Preston's nationalism, too, had been fostered by the Jindyworobaks, a literary group; her friendship since 1934 with Ian Mudie, an organiser of the Australia First Movement; and by the onset of the Second World War. Preston's response to the war eschewed narrow chauvinism: her painting *Japanese Submarine Exhibition*, 1942, showing the display of a midget submarine sunk in Sydney Harbour, was a *cri-de-coeur* expressing her ambivalent feelings about being at war with a country whose culture she revered.[8] In 1940, the artist turned sixty-five. The stage was set for her Aboriginal paintings, seen by some as the pinnacle of her career.

The Aboriginal paintings of 1940-45 show a sophisticated variety of solutions to the problem of producing a national imagery which, widely reproduced, might serve in part as icons of Australia to its worried people.[9] They remained domestic in scale, however, and their very experimentation suggests that Preston was not interested in simplistic propaganda, and that for her the paintings did not necessarily represent an apotheosis of achievement. *Flying over the Shoalhaven River*, 1942, is as calm as *Aboriginal landscape* is dynamic; *Blue Mountains Theme*, 1941, is an amalgam of views, derived not just from Aboriginal but also from northern Chinese influence. *Grey day in the Ranges*, 1942, is an austere concretion of forms. *I lived at Berowra*, 1941, which resembles *Theme* in its sources, is a reassuringly cosy image, in which a view of tranquil waters nestles in the bush.

Aboriginal landscape, in contrast, appears to be more closely based on the landscape than other works of the period, an observation perhaps reinforced by her repetition of the same basic composition in a more

Margaret PRESTON, 1875-1963. *Aboriginal landscape.* 1941, Sydney. Oil on canvas, 40 x 52 cm. Art Gallery of South Australia, Adelaide. D. & J.M. Mortlock Bequest Fund 1982

naturalistic form as *Bush track, N.S.W.*, a monotype of 1946, in which her aim was to render "the rough and tumble of our growth of trees, without design or any other purpose than that of covering space, as the natives do in their well-bred rock paintings."[10] The subject-matter is presumably a track near Berowra. Certainly *Aboriginal landscape* seems less constructed than *Blue Mountains Theme* and has a greater sense of witness than the conventional grandeur of *Burragorang landscape*, 1945.

With the end of the war, Preston's overtly 'Aboriginal' paintings ceased, but Aboriginal motifs and influence appear to a varying degree in her work virtually until the end of her artistic career. Several gouache stencils of 1950-51 represented Aborigines as protagonists in Christian myths, including the Expulsion from the Garden of Eden, a protest at the white treatment of the first Australians.[12] Preston's last major group of work was five *Australian Legend* woodblock prints of c1957, an amalgamation of Western and Aboriginal influences. Some of Preston's gouache-stencil still-lives of the early and mid 1950s show the bold outlines and minimal but vibrant colour schemes she had set as national art desiderata thirty years earlier, and have a freedom and assurance equal to anything she produced.

Preston's involvement with Aboriginal art fed off and into two of the three periods, the 1930s and the 1950s, when Aboriginal culture particularly interested elements of the white community. Her work, therefore, is of especial significance to the third period, the 1980s, when a rapidly growing fascination for Aboriginal culture is spreading beyond cultural and academic ghettoes to encompass the broader society. Several factors may be causing this shift. Economic realities, as the dollar bows to the yen, are underscoring Australia's geographical position in Asia, hence reducing the value of links with Europe and North America. The Christian time-frame which dominates even our predominantly secular society's sense of history, as indicated by the B.C./A.D. divide, is giving way to a much more extended sense of history. A new, respectful realism about Aboriginal culture, away from the complementary poles of contempt and romanticized reverence, is emerging in the white community. White Australians, without seeking to appropriate Aboriginal culture all over again, are beginning to see Aborigines as providing an ancestral cultural base for the entire continent.

Margaret Preston noted in 1942 that by the end of the Second World War, "Australia will find herself at the corner of a triangle: the East, as represented by China, India and Japan, will be at one point, and the other will have the United States of America representing the West."[13] Australia, then, would have little to do with England, and would stand apart from America. Preston was ahead of her time, but she certainly contributed, to use one of her own puns, to this new orientation.[14] In the meantime, her work stands to be admired for its energy and queried for warnings about basing cultural production on that of other cultures.

EXPANDING THE INTERIOR by TIMOTHY MORRELL

Fred Williams, *Silver and grey*, 1969

Although most of Australia is bleached, hot and arid, most of the Australian people live in parts which are least like this. It is only relatively recently (recently even within the brief span of European settlement) that the European culture transplanted to Australia has accepted a popular image of the country as one of withdrawn austerity. Until about the time of the second world war Australian culture was filled with images of fertility and bounty. Until Hans Heysen went to the Flinders Ranges in the 1920s and until the outback and desert paintings of Russell Drysdale and Sidney Nolan in the 1940s and 1950s, among the non-Aboriginal population only intrepid expedition artists painted the kind of country most characteristic of the driest continent.

This is how we think of Australia now, as vast and arid, an image made familiar by photographs. Yet the majority of Australians, who live by the greener coasts, have no thorough experience of their interior landscape. It is glimpsed by some from aircraft, trains and cars, and imagined by most. Few live there. It is not the landscape we intimately know. Fred Williams found a way to paint the landscape we know in terms of the landscape we imagine.

He translated the Australian landscape into a personal calligraphy which is immediately legible to those who know his subject, and this calligraphy is at its most spare and fluent in *Silver and grey*.

Williams said this painting shows the lines of a fence. Perhaps they are roadside fences. Or the two lines could be outlines of rises in the unremarkable open grazing country at Lysterfield, outside Melbourne, between Ferntree Gully and Dandenong, close to where the artist once lived in the suburban eucalyptus forests at Upwey.

In a larger version of this painting, in the Australian National Gallery, we can recognize cattle as well as trees and stumps. It is not the desert. This is the most prosaic and familiar countryside. The artist once remarked that he didn't like the bush. The landscape is not heroically sentimentalized here, the way it has been by most Australian artists who have depicted the vastness and harshness of the country. This stringent image is too insubstantial to support a mythology, and instead of a muscular patriotism there is an aesthetic delicacy. The title evokes the late-nineteenth-century cosmopolitan aestheticism of the Franco-Anglo-American artist James McNeill Whistler, whose work would have become familiar to Fred Williams during the five years he lived in London. Whistler was also familiar as the hero of modern painting for Williams's Melbourne predecessors of the 1880s: Tom Roberts exhibited impressions titled *Cream and Black*, *Rose, Black and Grey*; Arthur Streeton *Pastoral in Yellow and Grey*.

The painting recreates the effect of the brightest shimmering light, which edits the landscape down to indistinct, darker objects, cut out against a sea of glare. In the distance details are reduced to floating specks, like a mirage. This is the antipodean equivalent of Whistler's evocative studies of the indistinct light of evening, and creates poetic effects with bright daylight instead.

Like Whistler, Fred Williams was a master print-maker. His painting and print-making were interdependent. The handwriting of lines and dots in *Silver and grey* evolved from the artist's etching technique. Working in series, he would repeat a motif many times, in prints and paintings, in a long process of refinement. Etchings usually preceded paintings. The landscape which provided the motif for this work would seem to many to be featureless, and at first glance the painting seems to be largely blank, for the vitality of the work is all generated by the powerfully abrupt and abbreviated marks. It is charged like a field of energy by the carefully placed strokes and patches of paint. The dots and dashes printed in ink on blank paper are filled out in paint on the canvas as larger fragments, each one a microcosm of extremely varied colour and detail. Some of his Lysterfield etchings were made not on red copperplates but on silvery zinc and the scratched and pitted surface of a zinc etching-plate is expanded through the greater complexity of paint on canvas to become an analogy of the ancient, light-drenched and eroded surface of the Australian landscape. Within the serene Whistlerian harmony there is rough, hard, mineral-grained brushwork. Despite the monochromatic appearance there are sharp colour confrontations. It is a painting which teaches us to look closer.

Before this picture was painted, Williams worked on a series of bushfire pictures, studying the savage reduction wrought by the recurrent burning of Australia's exceptionally combustible eucalypt vegetation (which has incorporated fire into its regenerative process). The 1968 fire which prompted the bushfire series came extremely close to and nearly destroyed the artist's home at Upwey, an horrific and galvanizing event. The shock of seeing a familiar landscape so ravaged, threatening life, burning undergrowth away, leaving a stark pattern of blackened shapes, is part of the evolutionary history of the drastically purified image *Silver and grey*.

The minimalism of *Silver and grey* is also of course a matter of style. The artist admired contemporary New York colour-field painting, and regarded it as the most significant art of his time. Today however the Chinese and Japanese parallels seem more notable than the American influences. The painting is largely to do with restraint and refinement, and the sparse, rapid, apparently spontaneous but exquisitely modulated brushwork of Oriental masters provides a cultural model for Australians who are expected to think of the Far East as the Near North. Critics noted the Chinese resemblance in Williams's work from 1966. He first visited China in 1976.

Oriental painting is an art of suggestion rather than description, and this is the essential quality of *Silver and grey*. We see it in the arbitrary look of the dragged brushstrokes making a fence, and the irregular blobs making the details of the landscape. There is no attempt at describing topography. The shape of the land is only implied by the objects which rest somewhat temporarily on the surface, arranged by the artist as the components of a pattern.

Unlike traditional Eastern and Western landscape-painting structure, which composes within some sort of framing device of trees, rocks or architecture at the sides, concentrating the viewer's vision inwards, this composition expands outward from the centre. Only the horizon is suggested as a limit to the landscape. This too is one of the ways in which

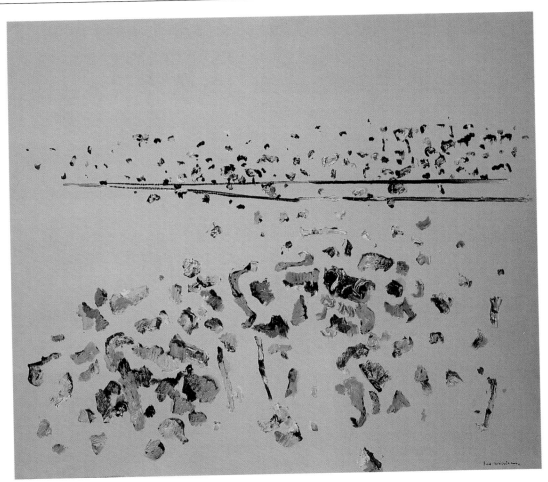

Fred WILLIAMS, 1927-1982. *Silver and grey*. 1969, Melbourne. Oil on canvas, 138 x 153.5 cm. Private collection

we imagine the Australian landscape. When Williams arrived back from England in December 1956 to an Australian summer he was struck by the "unstructured Australian countryside . . . a landscape with no centre of interest — that wasn't naturally composed". That look became his chief interest. In *Silver and grey* we are not looking at a contained view, or a defined unit of countryside. This view expands infinitely. It is conceived largely as an aerial view and reinforces the idea of landscape implanted by air travel, a vast unchanging expanse. In the New South Wales outback in 1967 he became convinced that the landscape "with the skin taken off" was essentially the same throughout Australia, especially from a mile-high aeroplane. He later reflected in his diary, "I suppose the most 'universal' picture is a map? It's worth thinking about".

More than anything *Silver and grey* resembles an artist's palette. It is the ingredients of a painting. In abruptly-combined, not fully mixed, variegated patches, the paint seems raw, not resolved. This stresses the rough nature of the subject, and more importantly, calls on the viewer mentally to complete the picture. The painted shorthand triggers personal memories we have of the landscape, and the painting resolves itself into that remembered landscape, inviting contemplation. We participate in the artist's re-affirmation of our own experience.

It is one of four variants of the subject which the artist had been working up to for some time. In his first year back in Melbourne after moving away from the burnt forests of Upwey he put all four onto canvas in one extraordinary day, 28 May 1969. There would be weeks and months more to finish them but at the end of that day he told his diary, with unusual solemnity, "These are very valuable pictures for me". They were a summing up, a climax of a dozen years.

Like the largest, most ambitious paintings of Arthur Streeton and Tom Roberts, *Silver and grey* is a 'national painting', an attempt at a grand-scale landscape image which becomes nationally emblematic. Inevitably such paintings become emblematic of a time as much as they do of a place. Just as Streeton and Roberts in the late nineteenth century captured the national nostalgia for an heroic pioneering pastoralist era which had already become remote from the lives of most Australians, so *Silver and grey* presents a landscape with which viewers can strongly identify, although it exists primarily in the mind. At a time when the aeroplane and the camera have made Australia's interior country more accessible than ever it has become an imagined place, tantalizingly indeterminate, its endless shimmer encroaching upon the cities of the shore and the minds of their inhabitants.

TWENTIETH-CENTURY ART: CULTURE by DANIEL THOMAS

The new Commonwealth of Australia in 1901 seemed relaxed after the effort of achieving Federation. Painters made sunny impressions of agriculture or else took off to Paris or London. There they supplied the well-off with images of well-being — or, when the 1914-18 Great War came, with images of Australia's first substantial presence in one of these age-old confrontations.

The death of many thousands of young Australian men in France and Turkey in a war with Britain against Germany was accompanied by the rhetoric of public sacrifice. Its reward would be Australia's maturity as a nation in its own (post-colonial) right. The campaigns in the Dardanelles and Palestine were close to the sites of ancient Trojan and Assyrian wars. The soldiers were also perceived as the fulfilment of an evolutionary development, a self-reliant 'national type' formed by the 'harshness' of the Australian bush: a lean physique adaptable to the deserts and mountains of the eastern Mediterranean. (Charles Darwin would have been astonished by so rapid an evolution of a new race.)

The Great War coincided with and was partly the cause of a new push towards Modernism in Australian art. The 1919 exhibition Colour in Art related to Roy de Maistre's interest in the uses of colour for psychiatric treatment of shell-shocked war veterans. The war also boosted manufacturing industry and images of rural production gave way in new art to engineering works, electricity generation, the 'Futurist' excitements of big-city life and leisure. Modernism also serviced a demand for design for industry and commerce, for making and advertising the modern products needed to keep the wheels of the economy turning.

Modernist taste admired the simplicity of folk-craft chairs and basketry. Margaret Preston paid tribute to Aboriginal women's feathercraft in her *Aboriginal flowers*, 1928, and became a promoter of Aboriginal art as a basis for modern design.

Classical simplicity was transferred from Greek statuary to figures on a beach near Wollongong in a 1930 painting by Arthur Murch and from early-Renaissance Italian painting to a Sydney beach in a 1938-40 painting by Charles Meere; the admired Australian type had shifted from the bush worker to the city-based sportsman and surf-rider. The high Renaissance provided the model for Ivor Hele's Michelangelesque Australian soldiers bathing in New Guinea in 1944. Something of early-Renaissance serenity and energy is found in Russell Drysdale's humanist tributes to men and women of the Australian bush, an updating of the spirit of Tom Roberts and Frederick McCubbin.

Dorrit Black's olive grove in the Adelaide Hills is a classicized depiction of fruitful land-use. Disruptive land-use is noted by Horace Trenerry in a rutted road gashing a gentle hill and by Clarice Beckett in an assertive street-pole and the noisy smudge of a motor-cyclist disappearing. Gerald Lewers's *The plough* is a surrealist carving in hard stone of a soft grub powerfully ploughing and cultivating the earth.

The Great Depression and the Second World War forced a change towards more urgent matters of social concern, reflected in both realist and surrealist art: trade-union meetings, food shortages, a cement worker on wartime construction; or the rituals of diplomacy failing to halt the march of Nazi Germany, and indirectly causing an 'invasion' of Melbourne by military personnel, painted by John Perceval and Albert Tucker indulging in a frenzied night-life.

The alliance with the United States in the Japanese Pacific war broke Australia's unquestioning dependence on Britain, but thirty further years of Americanization of Australia was in turn questioned and slowed in the early 1970s after Australia's participation in the American war in Vietnam.

Fuelled by the prosperity that accompanied the Korean War, post-war art kept up with the Modernist styles of, say, 1950s Abstract Expressionism, or 1960s Pop Art and Hard-edge Abstraction but despite the tendency to abstraction it was often also an expression of regional culture: Sydney foreshore fishermen by John Passmore, outer-suburban Melbourne farmers by Ken Whisson. The animation of football crowds by Colin Lanceley and of urban graffiti in a joint work by Mike Brown & Ross Crothall are found in works from their Imitation Realists exhibitions of 1962, a reaffirmation of urban realities and the power of popular culture. Janet Dawson's and Robert Rooney's abstract paintings draw upon the urban landscape encountered in everyday outings to Melbourne supermarkets and stores and Rosalie Gascoigne's relief makes poetic use of Australia's commonest vernacular building material.

Pure, formalist abstraction is found in Ron Robertson-Swann's gravity-release sculptures, but Ralph Balson's paintings are an abstract expression of the twentieth century's greatest intellectual leap, the realization that all matter is a dance of atomic particles and that matter and energy are interchangeable.

Quite suddenly around 1970 the Vietnam experience seems to have caused a major shift in Australian society. Scepticism and questioning replaced acceptance. Art ceased to show its audience a status quo, and began more to question and change the system. Sometimes it was the high-art systems themselves that were questioned, as by Peter Tyndall, or else a frank acknowledgement of their timeless artificiality, as by John Brack, Martin Sharp, Stephen Benwell and recent mannerist, post-modern raiders of the world's visual cultures. However, there was also direct questioning of political and social structures.

Richard Larter's paintings had already employed a sophisticated Pop Art style for such purposes. Craft media as in Margaret Dodd's ceramic motorcar/woman were often used for social statements. It was again a time of prosperity which could subsidize art practice and, beginning in 1970-71 with new artist-run collectives and alternative spaces, and with the first of many poster collectives, a great deal of artistic energy shifted away from production of objects for the art market. Instead, posters, ephemeral sculptures, performance art, photography and video projects helped raise consciousness of environmental pollution, nuclear power's risks, women's disadvantages, non-Anglo-Celtic citizens' needs and, especially, the question of Australian Aboriginal land rights. Urban Aboriginal artist Trevor Nickolls's *Machinetime Dreamtime* expresses bitterness about the loss of nature-based culture. Two years before the Bicentenary, Wendy Dunn's poster proclaimed: "Australia Day = Invasion Day/ 1988/ What's there to celebrate?"

Hugh RAMSAY, 1877-1906. *The artist's studio.* c1901, Paris. Oil on canvas, 60.8 x 50.2 cm. Art Gallery of South Australia, Adelaide. Gift of James Ramsay 1980

Rupert BUNNY, 1864-1947. *Self-portrait.* c1920, France. Oil on canvas, 65 x 50 cm. National Gallery of Victoria, Melbourne. Felton Bequest Fund 1927

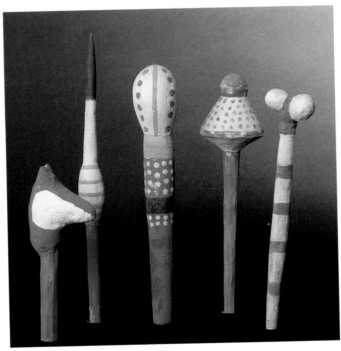

Lake Eyre region, South Australia. *Five Toas* (symbolic place-markers). c1900. (i) Diyari People, *"To the hill where Pintanganina was standing when his dog, Tjakula, ran down to a nearby waterhole to drink"*, 20 x 6.5 cm. (ii) Diyari People, *"To the place where Pintanganina sat preparing some sharp stakes to attach his fishing net"*, 27.5 x 2.5 cm. (iii) Thirrari People, *"To the waterhole where Patjalina noticed that Cooper Creek flowed straight ahead for some distance"*, 30 x 4 cm. (iv) Diyari People, *"To the hill covered with stones where Kujumokuna quarrelled with his uncle over a boundary"*, 29 x 6 cm. (v) Ngamani People, *"To the two round hills which formed from the two waterbags which Pirnawarankana made from the skins of two dingoes which he hunted and killed"*, 28 x 5 cm. Gypsum, ochres on wood. South Australian Museum, Adelaide. State Government funds 1907

E. Phillips FOX, 1865-1915. *A love story.* 1903, London; variant of a 1900 Melbourne painting. Oil on
canvas, 100.7 x 152.2 cm. City of Ballaarat Fine Art Gallery, Ballarat, Victoria. Martha Pinkerton Bequest Fund 1944

Harold CAZNEAUX, 1878-1953. *Children of the Rocks, Argyle Cut.* c1912,
Sydney; 1940s print. Gelatin-silver photograph, 23.6 x 27.7 cm. Australian
National Gallery, Canberra. Federal Government funds 1981

Ruth HOLLICK, 1883-1977. *Quentin Cain.* Late 1930s, Melbourne. Gelatin-silver
photograph, 23.8 x 30 cm. Australian National Gallery, Canberra. Federal
Government funds 1979

George W. LAMBERT, 1873-1930. *Barada Gorge.* 1926-27, Sydney, from sketches in Syria, June 1919, to
re-create the seizure of the Gorge on 30 September 1918 which led to the capture of Damascus. Oil on
canvas, 72 x 92 cm. Australian War Memorial, Canberra. Acquired under Official War Artist commission 1927

Anthony DATTILO-RUBBO, 1870-1955. *The strike's aftermath.* 1913,
Sydney. Oil on canvas, 121.7 x 91.3 cm. Art Gallery of New South
Wales, Sydney. State Government funds 1913

Grace Cossington SMITH, 1892-1984. *Troops marching.* 1917,
Sydney. Oil on paper, 23 x 20.6 cm. Art Gallery of New South
Wales, Sydney. State Government funds 1967.

Frederick McCUBBIN, 1855-1917. *Winter sunlight.* 1908, South Yarra, Melbourne. Oil on canvas, 51 x 76 cm. Art Gallery of South Australia, Adelaide. Gift of T.C. Lothian 1960

Elioth GRUNER, 1882-1939. *Morning light.* 1915, Emu Plains near Sydney. Oil on canvas on plywood, 38.1 x 43.8 cm. Art Gallery of New South Wales, Sydney. State Government funds 1916

Roland WAKELIN, 1887-1971. *Syncromy in Orange Major.* 1919, Sydney. Oil on cardboard, 30 x 40 cm. Art Gallery of New South Wales, Sydney. Bequest of Mervyn Horton 1983
In the colour-music exhibition, Colour in Art, 1919

Roy de MAISTRE, 1894-1968. *The Boatsheds, in Violet Red Key.* 1919, Sydney. Oil on wood, 32.5 x 20.5 cm. Clarice Thomas
In the colour-music exhibition, Colour in Art, 1919

Kathleen O'CONNOR, 1876-1968. *The tea table (L'heure du thé)*. c1928, Paris. Oil, gouache on cardboard, 79.6 x 99.8 cm. Art Gallery of Western Australia, Perth. State Government funds 1949

Anne DANGAR, 1887-1951. *Jug*. c1935, Moly-Sabata near Serrières, Ardêche, France. Earthenware, 23.9 x 13.7 cm. Australian National Gallery, Canberra. Gift of Grace Crowley 1979

Walter Burley GRIFFIN, 1876-1937, designer. *Dining chair*, for Newman College, University of Melbourne. 1917, Melbourne. Oak, leather, 89.5 x 56 x 73.5 cm. Australian National Gallery, Canberra. Federal Government funds 1980

Olive COTTON, born 1911. *Teacup ballet*. 1935, Sydney. Gelatin-silver photograph, 37.5 x 29.5 cm. Australian National Gallery, Canberra. Federal Government funds 1983
For an advertisement for Clarice Cliff's china, David Jones department store, Sydney

Margaret PRESTON, 1875-1963. *Aboriginal flowers.* 1928, Sydney. Oil on canvas, 53.6 x 45.8 cm. Art Gallery of South Australia, Adelaide. Gift of the Art Gallery of South Australia Foundation 1981 Feather flowers made by Aboriginal women

Lake Tyers, Gippsland, Victoria. *Coiled basket.* c1930. Vegetable fibre, 45 x 23 cm. National Museum of Australia, Canberra. Gift of Edmund Milne 1931

Maude BAILLIE, born 1884. *Chiffoniere.* 1904, Wedge Island, Spencer Gulf, South Australia. Blackwood, 142 x 104 x 38 cm. Private collection

Tasmania. *'Jimmy Possum' chair.* c1925, Deloraine, Tasmania. Blackwood, 109 x 62.5 x 47 cm. Australian National Gallery, Canberra. Gift of Diana Cameron 1981

Harold CAZNEAUX, 1878-1953. *The Wheel of Youth.* 1929, Dee Why, Sydney; 1940s print. Gelatin-silver photograph, 27.3 x 21.4 cm. Australian National Gallery, Canberra. Federal Government funds 1976

Ivor FRANCIS, born 1906, designer. *Speed!* 1931, Printers Trade School, Adelaide. Colour process block print on paper, 19.6 x 27.2 cm, from a gouache by Francis. Art Gallery of South Australia, Adelaide. State Government funds 1986

Jessie TRAILL, 1881-1967. *Sydney Bridge IV: The ant's progress, November 1929.* 1929, Melbourne. Etching on paper, 40.4 x 24.8 cm. Art Gallery of South Australia, Adelaide. David Murray Bequest Fund 1932

John KAUFFMANN, 1864-1942. *Jazz.* c1930, Melbourne. Carbon photograph, 22 x 31.2 cm. Art Gallery of South Australia, Adelaide. State Government funds 1988

Arthur MURCH, born 1902. *Beach idyll.* 1930, Thirroul, NSW; Sydney. Tempera on canvas on plywood, 35.5 x 59.1 cm. Art Gallery of New South Wales, Sydney. Visual Arts Board of the Australia Council contemporary art purchase grant 1975

Grace CROWLEY, 1890-1979. *Girl with goats.* 1928, Mirmande, Rhône, France. Oil on canvas, 54 x 72.7 cm. National Gallery of Victoria, Melbourne. Gift of the National Gallery Society of Victoria 1967

Ivor HELE, born 1912. *2/10th Australian Commando Squadron: Wash and clean up.* 1949, Aldinga near Adelaide, from sketches on the north coast of New Guinea 1944. Oil on canvas, 50.8 x 61.4 cm. Australian War Memorial, Canberra. Acquired under Official War Artist commission 1949

Dorrit BLACK, 1891-1951. *The olive plantation.* 1946, Adelaide. Oil on canvas, 63.5 x 86.5 cm. Art Gallery
of South Australia, Adelaide. Bequest of the artist 1951

Horace TRENERRY, 1889-1958. *The road to Maslins.* c1940, Aldinga near
Adelaide. Oil on cardboard, 48.5 x 57 cm. Private collection

Clarice BECKETT, 1887-1935. *Morning shadows.* 1933, Beaumaris, Melbourne.
Oil on canvas, 49.5 x 60 cm. Art Gallery of South Australia, Adelaide. State
Government funds 1980

Peter PURVES SMITH, 1912-1949. *The diplomats.* 1939-40, London. Oil on canvas, 40.5 x 50.5 cm. Australian National Gallery, Canberra. Gift of The Lady Casey 1979

Peter PURVES SMITH, 1912-1949. *Nazi Procession.* 1938, Paris. Oil on canvas, 71.4 x 91 cm. Queensland Art Gallery, Brisbane. State Government funds 1961

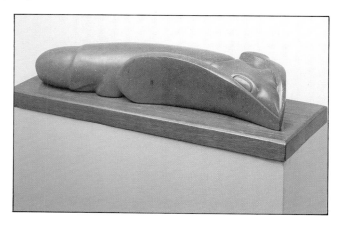

Gerald LEWERS, 1905-1962. *The plough.* 1934, London. Basalt, 14 x 63 x 17 cm. Art Gallery of South Australia, Adelaide. State Government funds 1963

John PERCEVAL, born 1923. *Negroes at night.* 1944, Melbourne. Oil on canvas, 80 x 87 cm. Australian National Gallery, Canberra. Federal Government funds 1976

William DOBELL, 1899-1970. *Cement worker, Sydney Graving Dock.* 1944,
Sydney. Oil on cardboard, 76.2 x 50.8 cm. Australian War Memorial, Canberra.
Gift of the Allied Works Council 1945

Noel COUNIHAN, 1913-1986. *At the meeting 1932.* 1944, Melbourne. Oil on
composition board, 55.5 x 67 cm. State Bank Victoria

Max DUPAIN, born 1911. *The meat queue.* 1946, Sydney. Gelatin-silver
photograph, 27.1 x 37.7 cm. Private collection

Frank HINDER, born 1906. *Subway escalator.* 1953, Sydney. Tempera and oil on canvas on composition board, 92.8 x 72.5 cm. Art Gallery of South Australia, Adelaide. Elder Bequest Fund 1972

Russell DRYSDALE, 1912-1981. *Woman in a landscape.* 1948-49, Sydney, based on a woman at Hill End, NSW. Oil on composition board, 101 x 66.3 cm. Art Gallery of South Australia, Adelaide. State Government funds 1949

Schulim KRIMPER, 1893-1971. *Sideboard.* c1948, Melbourne. Queensland blackbean, 94.3 x 218.2 x 53.5 cm. National Gallery of Victoria, Melbourne. State Government funds 1948

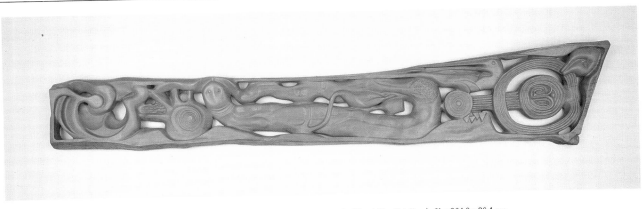

Rosemary MADIGAN, born 1926. *Eingana.* 1968, Adelaide. Wood (English lime), 61 x 364.8 x 30.4 cm.
Australian National Gallery, Canberra. Federal Government funds 1980

Ken WHISSON, born 1927. *Jean's farm.* 1972, Melbourne. Oil on composition
board, 81 x 109.6 cm. Australian National Gallery, Canberra. Gift of the Philip
Morris Arts Grant 1982

John PASSMORE, 1904-1984. *Water's edge no. 4.* 1963, Sydney. Oil on
composition board, 121.9 x 182.9 cm. Art Gallery of South Australia, Adelaide.
A.R. & A.M. Ragless Bequest Fund 1974

Colin LANCELEY, born 1938. *The green footballer playing the field.* 1961, Sydney. Oil, enamel, synthetic
polymer paint, paper, cardboard and other collage on composition board, 85 x 122 cm. Art Gallery of
South Australia, Adelaide. Lisette Kohlhagen Bequest Fund 1981
In the Imitation Realists exhibitions 1962

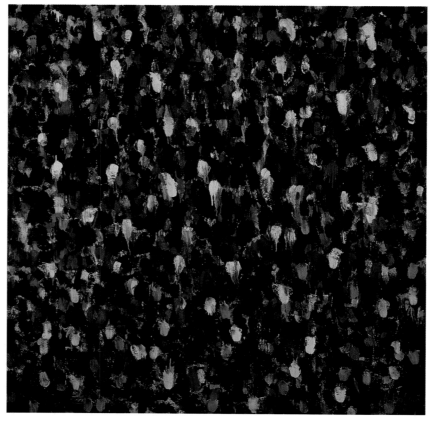

Ralph BALSON, 1890-1964. *Painting.* 1958, Sydney. Synthetic polymer paint on composition board, 137 x
137 cm. Art Gallery of South Australia, Adelaide. State Government funds 1972

Mike BROWN, born 1938, and Ross CROTHALL, born 1934. *Sailing to
Byzantium.* 1961, Sydney. Enamel, pencil, oil crayon on composition board,
91.5 x 122 cm, in 1985 re-creation by Mike Brown of the artists' painted frame.
Australian National Gallery, Canberra. Federal Government funds 1981
In the Imitation Realists exhibitions 1962

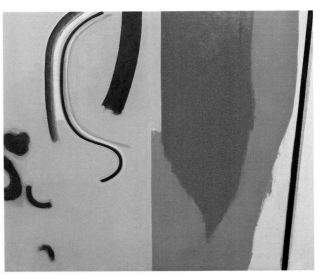

Janet DAWSON, born 1935. *With sauce.* 1963, Melbourne. Oil on
canvas, 25.5 x 20.5 cm. Ann Lewis

Ron ROBERTSON-SWANN, born 1941. *Elvira Madigan.* 1971, Sydney. Rusted steel, 183 x 472 x 203 cm.
Queensland Art Gallery, Brisbane. Gallery funds 1986

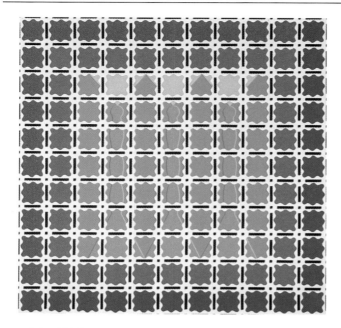

Robert ROONEY, born 1937. *Kind-hearted — kitchen-garden.* 1968, Melbourne. Synthetic polymer paint on canvas, 168 x 168 cm. Australian National Gallery, Canberra. Federal Government funds 1979

Dick WATKINS, born 1937. *Untitled.* 1968, Sydney. Synthetic polymer paint on canvas, 180 x 155 cm. Private collection

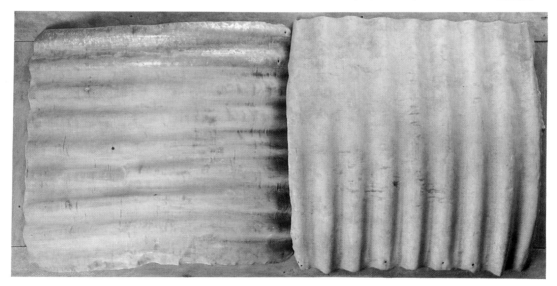

Rosalie GASCOIGNE, born 1917. *Swell.* 1984, Canberra. Corrugated galvanized iron, wood, 77 x 147.7 x 18 cm. Art Gallery of South Australia, Adelaide. D'Auvergne Boxall Bequest Fund 1987

Richard LARTER, born 1929. *Dead Goebbels he say.* 1971, Luddenham, Sydney. Oil on composition board, 122.8 x 60.9 cm. Private collection

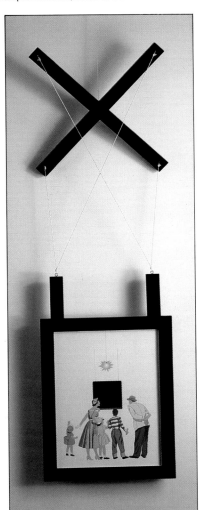

Ivan DURRANT, born 1947. *The Winner.* 1973, Melbourne. Oil on composition board, 122.5 x 105.8 cm. University Art Museum, University of Queensland, Brisbane. Darnell de Gruchy Art Purchase Award 1973

Martin SHARP, born 1942. *Mo.* 1978, Sydney. Colour screenprint on paper, 121 x 65 cm. Art Gallery of South Australia, Adelaide. State Government funds 1987 Nimrod Theatre poster, in Japanese actor-print style, of Garry McDonald's re-creation of Roy Rene's Depression-era character Mo

Peter TYNDALL, born 1951. *detail/ A Person Looks At A Work of Art/ someone looks at something ... with PUPPET CULTURE FRAMING SYSTEM.* 1979, Hepburn Springs, Victoria. Synthetic polymer paint on canvas, wood, suspension wires, 184 x 57 cm (hanging). Artist's preferred media description: CULTURAL CONSUMPTION PRODUCTION. City of Ballaarat Fine Art Gallery, Ballarat, Victoria. Crouch Acquisition 1980

Wendy DUNN, working 1980s. *Australia Day = Invasion Day.* 1986, Sydney. Colour screenprint on paper, 51 x 92 cm. Art Gallery of South Australia, Adelaide. State Government funds 1987

Ann NEWMARCH, born 1945. *Women hold up half the sky!* 1978, Adelaide. Colour screenprint on paper, 80 x 53 cm. Art Gallery of South Australia, Adelaide. State Government funds 1981

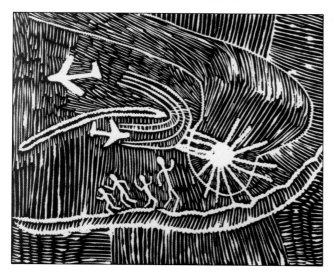

Jimmy PIKE, born c1940. *Jarlujangka Wangki.* 1985, Perth. Photo-screenprint on paper, 50.9 x 67 cm. Art Gallery of South Australia, Adelaide. State Government funds 1987
When hunting with his family as a child, the artist saw a plane appear and bomb the fire lit to drive animals from the scrub

Bob CLUTTERBUCK, born 1951. *Stop the merchants of nuclear death.* 1983, Redletter Press, Melbourne. Colour screenprint on paper, 76.2 x 51 cm. Art Gallery of South Australia, Adelaide. Gift of an anonymous donor 1988

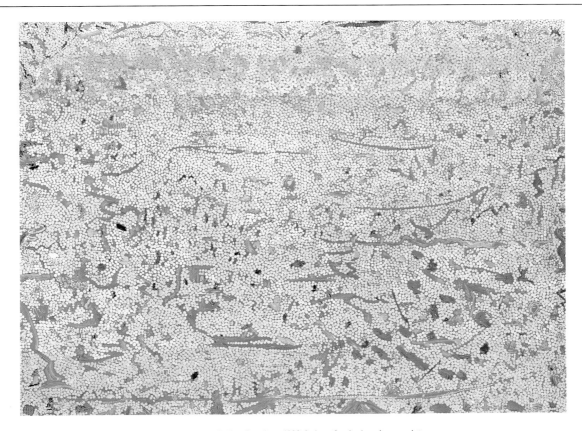

Tim JOHNSON, born 1947. *After Canaletto.* 1986, Sydney. Synthetic polymer paint on canvas,
91 x 122 cm. Private collection

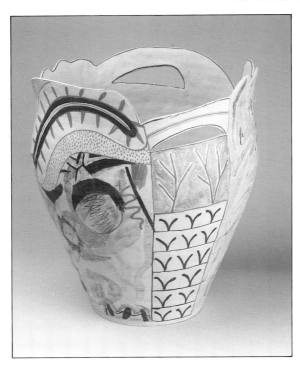

Stephen BENWELL, born 1953. *Tall vase.* 1983, Melbourne.
Stoneware, 42.5 x 37 cm. Art Gallery of South Australia, Adelaide.
State Government funds 1984

Trevor NICKOLLS, born 1949. *Machinetime Dreamtime.* 1981,
Canberra. Oil on canvas, 121.8 x 61.2 cm. Australian National Gallery,
Canberra. Federal Government funds 1982

"NATURE MUST BE THERE" by MARY EAGLE

E. Phillips Fox, *The ferry*, 1910-11

"In art everything must start from the springboard of nature. One may treat nature realistically, decoratively, or as a basis for the expression of ideas, but nature must be there ... Not that I condemn painting in the studio. One must go to nature to learn, as before nature one is objective, a servant. But in the studio one paints to express oneself, and must be a master".

E. Phillips Fox, quoted in the *Argus*, Melbourne, 21 May 1913

The ferry is large enough to become the museum spectator's total, temporary world. Looking is to look down, as in life, at landing-steps, passengers, a red-faced boatman directly below and a boat rocking in unstable water. Standing in imagination above the group, in sunlight, the spectator is confident about the all-roundedness of the steep pictorial space.[1] Fox went so far in re-creating the spontaneous conditions of this peep into a family's ideally happy holiday that the image lower left even includes the onlooker's bulky shadow. Then an almost contrary sensation takes over. A giddy stripiness asserts itself, of bright sunlight, dancing flecks of light, blue and white curving stripes of a woman's dress, red lines on a parasol, diagonal strips of wood in the landing-steps, wooden slats shaping the flat-bottomed boat and, all-pervasive, wherever one looks up and down, the lapping stripes of water.

In a watery scene without horizon the vertical stances of nine people and of a few slim iron stanchions are the gauge of stability. Of these the boatman, whose role in the scene is to balance the ferry boat, is also the one whose steeply foreshortened bulk serves most to stabilize the composition. Fox gave more attention to painting this figure than to any other. More slowly worked, solidly covered with paint, re-worked around the head, the boatman was perhaps the first figure Fox put in.[2] Elsewhere the canvas was loaded swiftly with long strokes of thick paint, and every now and then not touched at all, so that the warm colour and texture of bare canvas eases the tight areas. The gaps characteristically occur at an elbow where an arm bends, in the passage between forms, or simply as a gap between strokes.

Such confident brushwork is rare in a work as large as this. Fox cannot have taken more than a couple of weeks to paint *The ferry*, not as long as he usually took for his bigger Salon pictures.[3] It was at this time that Fox became conscious of how the tempo of his brushing influenced the final effect. If interrupted, he made an effort to return to his canvas in the same state of mind and to paint always at the same swift tempo. The method was demanding, and after painting *The ferry* Fox altered his technique.[4]

A waterside subject of the kind favoured by the Impressionists, and worked mostly in a fast, direct manner, *The ferry* otherwise is not impressionist at all. Instead of being painted outdoors, before the subject, it was worked more than one hundred kilometres away, in Paris, indoors, with the painter relying on earlier outdoor studies and his memory. Further to separate the two occasions of the painting's conception and birth, *The ferry* originated in summer and was painted in winter.

The ferry was begun in an absorbed, indirect way on a summer trip Fox and his wife Ethel Carrick took to Trouville and Deauville in 1909.[5] Fox wanted sunny subjects and they were hard to come by that year. The summer was cold and drab.[6] When the sun did appear Fox painted sketch after sketch. The same motifs recurred — the bird's-eye perspective, the stripes, the clusters of holidaymakers dressed in white, the blue-and-white-striped dress. More particularly the ferry on the river Touques that divides the two resorts provided a study which Fox used as the composition of *The ferry*.[7] The sketch has the same steep perspective and composition as *The ferry* and includes the boatman, ferry-boat (pointing the other way), wooden landing-steps, and a woman dressed in white stepping into the boat. In another sketch the woman in white reappears in the act of stepping off a boardwalk onto soft sand.[8] The two studies project the instant of bodily imbalance in almost perfect shorthand. The woman's weight is on the back leg while the other leg bends, foot already off the ground. Using a model — perhaps his red-haired wife Ethel Carrick — for the central figure in the large canvas Fox finally settled for a slightly less active pose, with both feet firmly on the wooden steps, thereby shifting the indecision from a body in the act of stepping to a woman in the act of making up her mind to step.

The tentative contact between her hand tentatively reaching out and the man's supporting arm, already held firm to take her weight, provides a 'natural' pivot at almost centre image, a visual hiatus which has associations with other ideas of passage, between land and water, 'womanly' trust and 'manly' strength and, of course, there is a visual association with Michelangelo's image of the creation of Adam.

The ferry's central figure appears on a beach in another small painting, *On the sands*.[9] She faces the same way, has a dark blue scarf similarly draped, her hat too is profusely plumed with white feathers and the blue-and-white stripes of her long dress flow with the shape and movement of her body. The dark lace fichu depending from the neck of the figure on the extreme left of *The ferry* occurs in other paintings by Fox.[10]

The costumes are studio props that Fox used more than once, and they remind us that he planned his large images and, it would seem, imagined parts of his small outdoor sketches as well. The girl in *The ferry* may have originated in a study of his niece Louise Fox painted in Melbourne in 1908.[11] Recreating the scene of the Trouville ferry in a Paris studio, Fox used models for at least three of the figures — the central pair and the boatman, climbing a ladder so that he could see them from above.[12] His models were not represented quite as he saw them for, like the artists in du Maurier's popular novel *Trilby*, Fox took bits and pieces from here and there to suit his notion of perfection. Scarcely any women had legs long enough, so we may imagine the woman standing on a box while posing, or else Fox draped the costume over a lay-figure to paint the lower skirt.[13] In some respects Fox went further than most painters in arranging nature to suit a personal ideal. He belonged to the generation that preferred red hair and like most painters had a preference for a certain facial type, in his case slightly flat-boned, wide between the temples and with rounded cheeks, and he shifted many of his sitters towards this ideal.[14]

E. Phillips FOX, 1865-1915. *The ferry.* Winter 1910-11, Paris, from studies at Trouville, summer 1909. Oil on canvas, 114.6 x 152.4 cm.
Art Gallery of New South Wales, Sydney. State Government funds 1949

In *The ferry*, Fox showed the French bourgeoisie of the Belle Epoque: one man in a brown suit, shown as strong, sober, and anonymous — since he is in backview; four women about whom the striking things are that they are as tall as fashion-plates, slim and most beautifully dressed; three children; and a nurse. Life is orderly, holidays are occasions for dressing well, the children smile and stay in place, the sun shines, the plebeian boatman — an outsider — does not rock the boat, and everyone is taken care of. The ideal existence of *The ferry* is that of Fox's other paintings too. "In his paintings of family groups, lunching or dining under the vine-leaved arbours, you feel intensely . . . those spacious days, when there was always a be-capped and be-aproned servant hovering solicitously over the family."[15] Fox was one of many artists to celebrate this charming comfort. Between 1900 and World War One, paintings of this type appeared year after year in Salon and Academy exhibitions. Ritualized, sumptuous comfort was a major theme in the novels of the day; and for that matter, it was a theme of contemporary haute couture.

As well as painting the leisured ideal, many artists managed to live it. If they were poor they made sacrifices. Fox and his painter wife Ethel Carrick remained childless. Without spending much money they lived well. Marrying in May 1905, they lived in Paris, at Montparnasse, in a courtyard apartment, with a handsome garden and a maidservant. Fox sold few paintings, eking out a living mainly through teaching, but he took these students on excursions to the country and seaside (excursions for which the students paid). He had a few students in the summer of 1909 when he visited Trouville.[16] But, while everyone else was on holiday, the artist was not. At Trouville with the summer holidaymakers in 1909 Fox worked. His role — the role of Salon painters of his sort — was that of observer and recorder. Painters of an ideal way of life, soon to be demolished forever by war, they were connoisseurs of pleasure.

LONG-LIMBED, LEAN, RESERVED by ANNE GRAY

George W. Lambert, *A Sergeant of Light Horse in Palestine*, 1920

Next to art George Lambert loved horses and country life. After busy years at work in his Sydney studio on major commissions for the Australian War Memorial and for monumental sculptures, Lambert spent his last days riding in the country. His painting *A Sergeant of Light Horse in Palestine*, 1920, is a tribute to a type of Australian, generally a product of a rural background, who became part of the national mythology during the first world war, the light horseman.

The painting shows a serviceman, seated in the open air before a ridge of dry scrubby hills and a blue sky. He is portrayed in his flannel shirt, sleeves rolled up and forearms bare, nursing his much-prized plumed hat, the symbol of the Australian light horseman. His jacket, with its sergeant's stripes, is placed on the chair behind him.[1]

Lambert has posed his subject in a meditative position, with eyes glancing downwards. Unlike the mass of be-hatted men in the history of portraiture this light horseman holds his hat to his chest — as if he has removed it in respect for his dead comrades, about whom his lowered eyes suggest he may be thinking.

The work is painted in the high-key palette which Lambert adopted as a result of his appreciation of Sandro Botticelli's paintings from fifteenth-century Florence and of his desire to create a picture which would look good under any light. Botticelli's influence can also be found in the downward look, the elegant slender neck, the long-fingered hands with clearly delineated nails and the sculptured features of the face.

This work demonstrates Lambert's observance of a balanced structure: the oval head is counterpoised against the circular form of the plumed hat. The head is silhouetted against a brilliant blue, cloud-dotted sky and separated from and lifted above the lower portion of the picture by the V-shaped outline of the hills, which is mirrored in reverse in the shoulders, and followed through with a repetitive echo in the stripes on the jacket and the angle of the elbow, and again in the pointed curl of the hair and the angular chin.

This work has a sensuousness which is derived, in part, from Lambert's sculptural sense of form, his sharp-focus rendering of flesh and musculature, and from the taut neck and the wiry arms. The intense physical presence of the figure and the manner in which the landscape impinges itself into the foreground as if it were a stage-set combine to give the painting an unusually intimate confrontation with the viewer.

When the first world war began, Lambert was forty, resident in Britain, and unable to enlist in the Australian Imperial Force (A.I.F.). It was not until December 1917, after service with the British Home Forces in Wales, that he was appointed an Australian official war artist. Because of his skill in depicting horses and men he was chosen as the only Australian artist to go to Palestine, where the Australian Light Horse Brigade was engaged in fighting the Turks. He spent the first half of 1918 working in Syria and Palestine making vivid small paintings of the terrain and perceptive pencil portraits of the men. Early in 1919 he accompanied Australia's official war correspondent (later official war historian), C.E.W. Bean on the post-war Historical Mission to the British-Turkish campaign site of Anzac Cove, Gallipoli. Lambert then re-visited Palestine and visited

Syria. Bean described "Lambert with the golden beard, the hat, the cloak, the spurs, the gait, the laugh and the conviviality of a cavalier"[2] and noted that Lambert was "more sensitive than the rest of us to the tragedy — or at any rate the horror — of Anzac".[3]

Lambert was accepted easily by men of all ranks, who recognized his ability as a raconteur and his "abounding spirits, his uncommon gift of mimicry, his shouting love of jest and, above all, his overflowing generosity".[4] He worked hard, enthusiastically painting scenes about him day after day, at all hours, and in steaming heat and choking dust. The light horsemen he mixed with appreciated his considerable mastery and knowledge of horses as well as his skill and dedication as an artist.

Lambert's 1920 image of a light horseman matches H.S. Gullett's account in *The Official History of Australia in the War of 1914-18*, volume VII, 1936, *Sinai and Palestine*: "So far as a distinctive type has been evolved it is . . . young men long of limb and feature, spare of flesh, easy and almost tired in bearing".[5]

The long-limbed, lean and languid figure that Lambert portrays fits easily with such a description. So too does this soldier's rather sensitive glance for, as Gullett observed, the light horseman, "for all his unconventional ways . . . was at least distinguished by shyness and reserve. The young Australian countryman leads a simple and peaceful life. He bears himself modestly . . . A felt slouch hat, a shirt with the sleeves rolled to the elbows, long trousers . . ."[6]

Lambert had much in common with these men: he had spent a good part of his youth living and working on family sheep-stations in New South Wales and whenever the opportunity arose he welcomed the chance to play at being a bushman. He is said never to have been so happy as during the months he spent as an artist with the light horse in Palestine. To this extent this subject is as much a portrait of Lambert's inner self as of a particular individual or of a newly-defined Australian stereotype.

The model for this light horseman is reputed to be Thomas Herbert Ivers (1881-1940), a Sergeant with the 1st Signal Squadron who was employed colouring contour maps for the War Records Section in Palestine. He met Lambert during the latter's visit to Damascus in mid 1919.[7]

A Sergeant of Light Horse in Palestine was painted in 1920, at a time when Lambert was working in a large studio in Kensington, London. Among the other subjects he worked on in that year was his self-portrait, *Souvenir of the Light Horse*, which was painted in the sitting-room of his home in Chelsea.[8] *A Sergeant of Light Horse in Palestine* was first exhibited at Lambert's exhibition at the Fine Art Society's Gallery, Melbourne, in May 1921, and acquired therefrom for the National Gallery of Victoria.

Lambert's painting is notable among the images of Australian light horsemen produced during the first world war in that the subject is shown in his shirt sleeves and holding his hat. On the other hand the generalized drawings by David Barker, published in *Australian in Palestine* and *Kia-ora Cooee*, and the portraits of General Chauvel and Sergeant Major Greenway by W.B. McInnes in the Australian War Memorial's collection, portray their subjects in full dress and wearing the plumed hat. Lambert's light

George W. LAMBERT, 1873-1930. *A Sergeant of Light Horse in Palestine.* 1920, London. Oil on canvas,
77.8 x 61.2 cm. National Gallery of Victoria, Melbourne. Felton Bequest Fund 1921

horseman is also of more slender build than those of other artists; although they resemble Lambert's subject in their angular features.

The light horseman is shown without his horse. Lambert was well able to draw horses and could certainly have painted a worthy picture of a light horseman with his horse. In his drawings, *Charger and groom*, 1918, and *Trooper Hubbard, Rough rider, Australian Remounts*, 1918, he did create an image of a light horseman in a plumed hat, on his mount, in the tradition of nineteenth-century prints and paintings. That he chose not to do so in this painting was intentional.

This work is about an individual, his relationship to the countryside and his memories of his mates, but he is an individual who reflects an Australian type. Lambert created a new model for a military portrait: instead of the noble, the dashing, and the heroic subjects of previous wars he presented a humble, but not humbled, man; he is shown in all simplicity without the pomp of his full-dress uniform, without the glamour and superior status of a horse, and he is the stronger for this.

More important is Lambert's use, in this painting, of the image which perfectly matched certain powerful ideas current in the then-young Australian Commonwealth. The image met a need for national self-definition. Australians who were formed by bush life, by working with animals and the elements in a blond land under a blue sky, would become the no-nonsense, unceremonious soldiers, who excelled at war in the lands of the ancient Mediterranean but knew its cost, were appalled by it, and would not romanticize it. They are tough, wiry, and tender.

THE PLAYFUL SCIENCE OF PICTURING by MARY EAGLE

Max Meldrum, *Chinoiseries*, 1928

Max Meldrum called himself a scientist, liked to pursue a line of thought and throughout a long life continually provoked controversy. *Chinoiseries,* a lovely, fresh, open-hearted portrait of his eighteen-year-old daughter Elsa, playfully dressed up in Chinese silks, proved a point about colour.

It was painted in Paris in the cold early months of 1928, in a draughty studio among the famous La Ruche conglomerate of studios in the Passage de Dantzig.[1] Meldrum had left Australia in 1926 in a mood of displeasure. He had recently fallen out with some patrons and critics; worse, some artists, former adherents, had turned from his tonal theory to adopt Post-Impressionism. Battle lines were drawn, and Meldrum's paintings were being categorized as part of a conservative opposition. Since colour was the banner of the new modernism, the singing colour used with discrimination by Meldrum and the Meldrumites was slighted: "Meldrum had never in his work shown any possession of a full colour sense. All his works tended to black and white . . . He always seemed to regard colour as an intrusion . . . Perhaps a naturally limited, a subnormal colour sense, accounted for this . . . At all events he himself was in the habit of wearing dark glasses while painting", wrote James MacDonald for *Art in Australia* in December 1926.[2]

Exhibited first at the New Salon in Paris, *Chinoiseries* was reviewed there as "a good work in the impressionist tradition".[3] The critic in the Melbourne *Herald*, however, chose to dwell on the local media's stereotype of Meldrum the controversialist when he wrote about this cheerful painting a few months later: "Mr Meldrum — I tremble when I write the name for fear the renewed controversy may fan into flame — is exhibiting a figure study of a laughing girl in a costume rich with brilliant blues and yellows wearing a purple shawl and red shoes by way of showing how he can handle a medley of different colours successfully".[4]

In *Chinoiseries* he employed a colour scheme, bolder than anything tried by Melbourne's modernists, of brilliant primary hues with complementary colours adjacent to each other and scorching dissonances of secondary and primary hues. The ensemble is vibrant but disciplined by Meldrum's scientific placement of tones which holds the work together, quelling the power of colour.[5] Within this tonal discipline the brilliant colour gamut appears to have been created entirely for its own sake, as colour, and possibly also to excite emotions.

Van Gogh is the colourist evoked by Meldrum's palette. *Chinoiseries's* memorable colours are van Gogh's colours: canary yellow, orange, brilliant blue, red, purple, black, white. Van Gogh had written, almost in Meldrum's theoretical vein, "Fromentin and Gérôme see the soil of the South as colourless, and a lot of people see it like that. My God, yes, if you take some sand in your hand, if you look at it closely and also water, and also air, they are all colourless, looked at in this way. *There is no blue without yellow and without orange*, and if you put in blue, then you must put in yellow, and orange too, mustn't you?"[6] One of his colour exercises at Arles in 1888 was a still life in blues and yellows — "The whole on a blue tablecloth, against a yellow background, and among this crockery two oranges and three lemons. So it is a variation of blues, livened up by a series of yellows that go as far as orange".[7]

Chinoiseries possessed 'modern' features other than its colour in an insistent use of patterned fabrics and a Cézannesque diagonal hatching stroke — both cliches of Melbourne's modern painting style. But these modernisms in Meldrum's work were not recognised by Australian critics of the day.

As a *scientist* Meldrum knew about the mood-inducing qualities of colour and the psychological effect of angled lines. Writing around the time he painted *Chinoiseries* he said, "Contrasting tones, colours, etc. [are used] to produce jollity, febrility, even madness".[8] Jollity in *Chinoiseries* is achieved through contrasting tones, colours and patterns; in other words, by the artist skilfully manufacturing the chemistry of pleasure. Equally, playfulness is an expression of the sitter, Elsa, who appreciated, and still enjoys, the graceful game of dressing up. She says, "It was a habit of that time [the 1920s] for men and women to play at times, dressing up".[9] She borrowed the Chinese pyjamas from the daughter of an American patron, Nancy Bottomley.[10] Perhaps Elsa's laughing pose was also intended to be 'Chinese'. The choice of red shoes and purple shawl to accompany the outfit was an acknowledgement that strong colour was characteristic of Chinese taste, further justifying the title *Chinoiseries* (Chinese-style notions).

Around the time of *Chinoiseries*, Meldrum also painted Elsa in a pink taffeta party dress.[11] It was very difficult to paint the highlights on the slippery taffeta, which slithered into another position at almost every breath Elsa took. Whereas *Chinoiseries* took seven days to paint, with about three sittings a day of twenty minutes to half-an-hour each, *The Taffeta Dress* took much longer — about three weeks Elsa thinks.[12]

Personal pleasure was undoubtedly one aspect of painting for Meldrum; painting the highlights on taffeta was the sort of technical problem he relished; as in a different way he enjoyed throwing down the gauntlet to Melbourne with the modernism of *Chinoiseries*. But he schooled himself to eschew anything emotionally expressive.[13] A psychiatrist's use of colour was possible in Meldrum's science whereas personal expression went against the grain; so in *Chinoiseries* the artist balanced blue and yellow in van Gogh's way but without van Gogh's fervour. According to his daughters "when Meldrum was pleased with his work, 'that's objective', he'd say with pleasure".[14] Liking an objective practice Meldrum argued that if he faithfully copied the visual shapes and tones, the personality of the sitter would automatically show. Sometimes, to test his own objectivity, he turned a canvas upside down, painting the patches of colour-tone as an abstract pattern.[15] He advocated giving equal attention to all parts of a canvas rather than more attention to a sitter's face and hands.

According to Meldrum's theory, painting dealt with only one of the human senses — sight. "The eye is solely concerned with tonal, proportional and chromatic values, and the observation, definition, and translation of these three things constitute the highest and purest form of the depictive art. All others in which other elements have intruded themselves belong to a minor form".[16] In painting a picture he began with

Max MELDRUM, 1875-1955. *Chinoiseries*. 1928, La Ruche studios, Passage de Dantzig, Paris. Oil on canvas, 171.5 x 94.7 cm. National Gallery of Victoria, Melbourne. Felton Bequest Fund 1934

the darkest and lighest tones, then patched in the intermediate tones. Psychological, personal and literary meanings were excluded.

What provoked the painting of *Chinoiseries*? Presumably, the sight of Elsa in her fine clothes; in other words a sight familial, natural and incidental to Meldrum's art. However, the connection between father's art and teenage daughter's play seems too convenient to be coincidental. Elsa's extremely inventive art of costume matched Meldrum's liking for artificiality.[17] He liked to paint calico flowers, liked fancy-dress, made a practice of looking at nature through a dark glass to paint a picture, or painting the back-to-front image of life seen through a mirror. Raw nature did not suit: brilliant sunlight bleached tones, early morning and late afternoon light were too unstable, grey overcast days were best for painting landscape but it was even better to paint indoors with artificial light. It would seem he wasn't really interested in nature at all. Even the image he produced mattered only insofar as it was a convincing representation of space.[18] Meldrum directed his attention not to nature – the subject-matter of his painting – but to his technique. In that sense he must be regarded as a formalist and be placed in the formalist stream of twentieth-century art. "Show how the conscious scientific artist is manipulating his colour, tone

and proportion in such a way that the eye must interest itself in them in a certain order"; "Show how the eye is forced to take up or go to certain places at certain times, according to the contrasts of tone, colour and proportion", he wrote in 1928.[19]

What he liked was scientific dialogue, more and more of it, so that he could pursue an evolving point of view. The dialogue was with his own perceptions, an attempt to exclude everything that wasn't tone. Impossible. One can't help feeling that he was pleased as he grew older to discover that nature or his own psychology would always evade his skill. "Some years ago, about the time I was beginning to be able to affranchise myself from the useless tricks and conventions of modern art school training I painted a portrait which I honestly thought to be an absolutely successful rendering of what I saw. My friends supported this idea. Some time after this, I happened to compare it with a later piece of work, when I discovered that it was far from being the perfect illusion which I had thought it to be when first done. I noted in it the intrusion of other knowledge than that derived through the sense of sight . . . I realised then for the first time how far we are liable to mistake the source organs of our idea".[20]

ELECTRICITY CASTLE by ROGER BUTLER

Ethel Spowers, *The Works, Yallourn*, 1933

The Works, Yallourn, 1933, a colour linocut printed in an edition of fifty, by the Melbourne artist Ethel Spowers, could be seen as a celebration of technology. The potential of the vast brown coal deposits around Moe and Morwell in the Latrobe Valley, Gippsland, about 145 kilometres from Melbourne, was first recognized in 1917 and in 1919 the State Electricity Commission of Victoria was established. Yallourn was built as a model workers' town. Huge open-cut mines were begun, power-stations were designed to utilize the brown coal, and briquettes were manufactured from it, partly for the power-stations, but chiefly to sell as industrial fuel and as fuel for home consumption. Production of electricity began in June 1924.

Spowers's print depicts a functional-shaped factory, elevated conveyor-belts supported by triangulated steel pylons, and the rail tracks which bring coal from the mines. All is conveyed in an energetic sweeping rhythm — the railway line enters the composition from the left and focusses attention on the power-station, while the electricity power-poles complete the circular rhythm, carrying away the generated power. Two columns of smoke stream away from the Works.

Although the reading of the image as a homage to industry is plausible it is in many ways an untypical work. Spowers was one of the many women, invariably of independent means, who dominated Australian art during the 1920s and 1930s. Born into a wealthy family with cultural interests — the Spowerses were part-owners of the Melbourne newspapers *The Argus* and *The Australasian* — the daughters were encouraged to take up pursuits typical of the Arts and Crafts period. One sister became a bookbinder, another specialized in needlework, a third studied the violin and Ethel was encouraged in her artistic pursuits. At the age of fifteen, two of her drawings of fairies were reproduced in the *Australasian*.

Almost all of Spowers's work could be described as illustrative: the text declared as in her illustrations for Furnley Maurice's *Arrows of Longing*, 1921, and in her own published and unpublished cautionary tales, or the text implied as in her many illustrations for nursery rhymes and children's games.

Spowers's first woodcuts were produced in England in 1923, where she continued her studies after having attended the National Gallery of Victoria's art school. Her guide, Morley Fletcher's *Wood-block Printing: A description of the craft of woodcutting and colourprinting, based on Japanese methods*, 1916, may account for the Japanese compositional structures to be found in her early prints. Her work from the mid 1920s is similar to that by pictorialist photographers. For example, *The bamboo blind*, 1926, employs the same devices as Harold Cazneaux's 1912 photograph of the same title, and his *Pergola pattern*, c1931. Her interest in children and their games was also shared by her friend, the photographer Pegg Clarke.

In late 1928 and again in 1931, Spowers studied at the Grosvenor School of Modern Art, London, a private school established by the English artist Iain MacNab. The syllabus included architectural composition and ornament, decorative composition, lectures on modern painting and printmaking (etching, engraving, lithography and block-printing).

Claude Flight, who taught linocutting, is now the most widely remembered of the School's teachers but the many Australians who attended have singled out MacNab's insistence on drawing and rhythmic composition as a major influence. Besides Spowers, the Australians included Gladys Owen, Dorrit Black, Eveline Syme, George Bell and Nutter Buzacott.

Spowers absorbed Flight's technique of printing linoleum blocks and began composing in colour rather than relying on a black key-block. Rhythm, which already played a significant role in her work, became more exaggerated.

The prints Spowers produced after her studies at the Grosvenor School have often been seen in the context of Flight's teaching and his superficial alignment with the Futurist dictums of speed and dynamism. However, this overstates the claims made for Spowers as a modernist. Many artists in this period made prints with industrial subject-matter but without considering any modernist theories.

Jessie Traill (1881-1967), a friend of Spowers, also produced prints which depicted industrial achievements in Australia. *Testing the new turbine, Red Cliffs Pumps, August 1922* and her series *Building the Harbour Bridge*, 1928-29, like Spowers's *The Works, Yallourn*, are based on an Edwardian aesthetic. The industrial structures are used as ready-made compositional elements, to be seen silhouetted, or through a smoky atmosphere.

Nor does *The Works, Yallourn* strive to make any social comment. Spowers is not concerned with the destruction of the environment entailed by open-cut mining, the pollution caused by smoke and dust, or the conditions of the workers in the Depression years during which the print was made.

Spowers exhibited with the Victorian Artists' Society, the Arts and Crafts Society, the Women's Art Club and the Lyceum Club, and as well she held six one-person shows between 1920 and 1936. *The Works, Yallourn* appeared in her 1933 and 1936 exhibitions priced at two guineas. Contemporary reviews of these exhibitions were full of praise for her "joyous but keenly-controlled feeling for colour" and "brilliant capacity for pattern-making, always rich and alive" and her sense of humour.[1] But such descriptions referred only to her figurative works.

Whereas prints like *The Works, Yallourn* did not attract any attention they may nevertheless have been an attempt by Spowers to have her work considered as serious art rather than decorative illustration. This print was made in the same year as Napier Waller's mosaic mural *I'll put a Girdle round about the Earth*, highly conspicuous on the facade of Newspaper House, Collins Street, Melbourne. The mural was a celebration of new technology; radio communication as well as railways and ocean liners. In Paris in 1937 Raoul Dufy would design a huge mural, *The Fairy Electricity*. The benefits of electricity for all, instantaneous, clean energy in every home, were a promise for the good times when the Great Depression was over. Meanwhile it might help cheer things up, in a small way, to make this linocut image of the source from which electricity's modern magic would be supplied to the people of Victoria.

Ethel SPOWERS, 1890-1947. *The Works, Yallourn.* 1933, Melbourne. Colour linocut on paper, 15.2 x 34.5 cm. Australian National Gallery, Canberra. Federal Government funds 1976

COLOUR-WORSHIP by DANIEL THOMAS

Grace Cossington Smith, *The Lacquer Room,* 1936

The Lacquer Room was a tea room, opened in 1932 in Farmer & Company, then the leading department store in Sydney. Its opening accompanied the opening of the Sydney Harbour Bridge.

A day in town for ladies of the respectable middle classes was more of a ritual, and perhaps more frequent, before the 1950s mass-motorization and the dispersal of shopping. One dressed up for town and wore a coat. Today, Sydneysiders don't use coats but they were once essential – for the walk to a suburban station or tram-stop, the railway journey, the transfer to a Harbour ferry (if you came on the North Shore Line, and if it was not yet 1932), the ferry-ride which could be wet or windy, and the tram-ride or the walk from Circular Quay to Farmers, which had a distinct superiority to David Jones. Coats stayed on indoors; heating was not good.

From 1932 there was the extra switchback excitement of rising over the water by a great triumph of engineering, the vast new Harbour Bridge, then diving underground to new railway stations nearer the stores. There was an ascent by lift to the sixth floor of Farmers, to begin the day with tea in The Lacquer Room, another experience of modernity and progress: Art Deco lamps, conical jugs, hygienic waitresses, and the brilliant colour of green-lacquered table-tops and red-lacquered chairs (Windsor chairs, of the kind which were usually a dignified brown oak). A lady-artist customer like Miss Grace Cossington Smith would have appreciated that the interior was designed by her stylish, senior fellow-artist Miss Thea Proctor but most customers simply appreciated the unusually cheerful ambience. It was the pleasantest stop during a big-city day in town, over the rainbow of the Sydney Harbour Bridge from the distant leafy suburb of Turramurra.

It is morning because white cloths for luncheon have not covered the green table-tops and because the room is filled with light from the eastern doors which opened onto a garden roof-terrace.

Grace Cossington Smith always carried a sketchbook with her in order to capture, at the decisive moment, a subject she might be "taken by". She must have visited The Lacquer Room many times over four years before she made the furtive pencil-sketch for this painting but she must have known that the golden carpet and the red chairs would some day fall into place as a picture. There was no need to force things; for alert, receptive eyes moments of vision were frequent enough.

At Anthony Dattilo-Rubbo's painting-classes for young ladies Grace had been enthralled by his accounts of Vincent van Gogh and around 1918 she had made an oil study of an imaginary "Van Gough's room/ the walls – violet/ floor red/ bed cover yellow green/ furniture orange." She already felt the power of colour, in painting and in the rooms we inhabit.

Although she later scarcely remembered the 1919 exhibition *Colour in Art*, its two artists, Roy de Maistre and Roland Wakelin were her friends and fellow-students. In that colour-music exhibition de Maistre exhibited, as "Colour Organisation in Interior Decoration", an *Interior in the Key of Yellow*, an *Interior, showing two rooms in related colour keys – Blue Green Major leading into Yellow Green Minor* and an *Interior, in Orange Red Key*. De Maistre gave a lecture "Colour in relation to Painting", saying that: ". . . man has all through the ages been seeking for some means of self-expression through colour . . ."

"What is colour? . . . a few, I believe, are almost unconscious of its presence – for others it constitutes an aesthetic pleasure or an interesting scientific phenomenon . . . But there are many for whom Colour means far more than this – to them it brings the conscious realization of the deepest underlying principles of nature, and in it they find deep and lasting happiness – for those people it constitutes the very song of life and is, as it were, the spiritual speech of every living thing."

Grace Smith, art student, became Grace Cossington Smith, artist, in 1920 and "Colour in Art" remained for her "the very song of life". In the 1960s and 1970s she would answer questionnaires concisely: "All form . . . has an inarticulate grace and beauty; painting to me is expressing this form in colour, colour vibrant with light." Or: "That which [I] express in my work: 'Form expressed in colour vibrating with light; the relation of forms to each other.'" We smile when computer consultants begin designing software for catalogues of paintings and take it for granted that the colours of a painting will be indexed, but instead we should take heed that the thrill of colour is indeed a simple universal experience, expected in art as in nature. Grace Cossington Smith was a person of profound simplicity.

The Lacquer Room was first exhibited in winter, 20 July 1936, with the Contemporary Group, which for the past few years had held its annual exhibition at Farmers. It was painted in the artist's studio at the bottom of the garden of the house at Turramurra where she lived with her father and two sisters; it would have been carried out steadily and decisively over a week or two, from a pencil-sketch and colour notes. The fur-collared coats and the fashionable hat worn by the woman in the background pinpoint the subject to autumn/winter 1936. It was also the year when things were looking up after the bad years of the Great Depression and the store was selling more of these quite expensive coats.

So what caused the artist one morning to do more than order sandwiches, cakes or scones and a pot of tea or coffee? Perhaps the chaotic pattern of the red chairbacks that day reminded her of van Gogh's *Interior of a restaurant*, 1887. But the sketchbook was called forth by a man. Across her green foreground table-top she noticed opposite her a man with glorious blond hair, a colour to catch the morning sunlight and to be orchestrated with the golden carpet. She sketched as inconspicuously as she could. And then she was caught out. Her blond subject looked up, straight at her – and gave her the colour bonus of his own intense blue eyes.

So it is not only a painting of an exceptionally pleasant gathering-place for the modern middle classes of Sydney in 1936. It is also an Annunciation.

Cossington Smith was a devout Anglican Christian, with rectors, nuns and archbishops in her family; Fra Angelico's purity and strength made him one of her favourite painters (along with Cézanne for vibrant, light-filled brushwork and van Gogh for colour and for love of humankind) and she appreciated and rose to the occasion of high moments in public or private life. A blue-eyed stranger looks momentarily at a fortythree-year-old woman doing something odd at a nearby table. Perhaps she is a little embarrassed but it's a normal occupational hazard in her way of life. It is a

Margaret DODD, born 1941. *Bridal Holden.* 1977, Adelaide. Earthenware, satin, 18 x 52 cm. Private collection

On the other hand, cars signify masculinity in their association with speed, violence (both attributes of phallic power) and social independence. The car is firmly identified with masculinity in a country where, traditionally, the sexes are strictly segregated. Thus we are offered a set of oscillating options: to identify with the car as feminine or as masculine, to assume feminine or masculine roles as the viewer. *Bridal Holden* forces these uncertainties into the open: with Dodd's work we see the ritual images of marriage and car-ownership merged in a nightmare Australian identity-crisis.

A series of questions emerges: are Australian men more infatuated with their cars than with their girlfriends and wives? Do Australian women experience anything remotely like the lavish care bestowed on cars? Is the car the phallus, or rather the fetishized object of the phallus's desiring? These are familiar speculations in Australian cultural life, the particular mark of intellectuals rejecting stereotypical Australian masculinity.[9]

Thus Margaret Dodd's experiments with polymorphous perversity: her *Bridal Holden* is now masculine, now definitely feminine, and plays on the inauthenticity one feels (and often enjoys) impersonating the actions or assuming the attributes of the other sex. It is conceivable that Margaret Dodd's Holden cars are transvestites. But if femininity itself is a masquerade, as several recent theorists have suggested,[10] then the Holden woman is a key Australian identity of the late twentieth century.

Bridal Holden is part of the project of Australian feminism. Margaret

Dodd deals with images of Australian femininity, as well as the possibilities facing Australian women in art practice. Her work is part of a revision of contemporary art undertaken by Australian women artists since the 1960s; and Dodd herself was instrumental in setting up the Women's Art Movement, Adelaide as an alternative support-system for women artists.

Margaret Dodd's film *This Woman is Not a Car* cast the ceramic Holdens, including *Bridal Holden*, as players in a horror film about suburban life, alongside actors and life-size cars. Thus cars were finally acknowledged in Australian art, their uneasy metamorphoses reflecting sourly on the machine-utopianism of the early part of this century. Here we see the end of the 'machine man' of Léger in the disillusioned 'machine woman' of the Great Australian Dream.

Margaret Dodd's recent Holden, *Bridal costume for an FJ Holden Discarded*, 1987,[11] is a full-sized shell whose plastic inhabitant has flown, like last summer's cicada, a ghostly Miss Haversham present in a new moment of national economic downturn. Today Holdens appear on Australian roads in the perfect splendour of glossy vintage examples which are nevertheless imperfect, somehow out of kilter with time, precisely because their present ducoed manifestations do not accord with memories of dusty, battle-weary old black FXs and FJs on the highways and back-roads of the past. In the last analysis, the image of the Holden is more enduring than its physical substance.

TWENTIETH-CENTURY ART: THE INDIVIDUAL by DANIEL THOMAS

Myths are the public expression of private emotions and Rupert Bunny's *Rape of Persephone*, a myth of the seasons in which flowers go to the underworld for one third of the year but return in spring, also implies that human death will be followed by some kind of after-life. In real life in Melbourne in 1904 Hugh Ramsay's sisters know that their artist-brother contracted tuberculosis in his studio in Paris and has come home to die. They fill his time by posing for this intimate portrait of affection and resignation.

Bernard Hall's *Sleep* implies safe dreams in the care of wakeful companions; Web Gilbert's *The Dreamer* transforms symbolically into a lily. *Ariadne*, from Greek myth, is an image of abandonment on an alien shore. Norman Lindsay's *Lady and parrot* offers voyeuristic viewers the fantasy that there is no one to appreciate the nude's beauty except her pet bird; the pet Airedales with Napier Waller's wife Christian complete an image of real love and harmony in the garden of their house at Fairy Hills, Melbourne. Thea Proctor's *The rose* may be a mirrored self-portrait and the flower a hint of self-regard as much as an image of close intimacy between two different women. Ethel Carrick's *On the verandah* must depict a visit to personal friends and Lina Bryans's portrait *The Babe is Wise* is an affectionate tribute by a Jewish artist to a fellow-professional, a novelist of Jewish life in Melbourne. Clive Stephen's stone-carving is a woman whose interior power awaits release and Joy Hester's *The lovers* is a resolution to all these reveries about loss, transformation, recognition or mirroring of individual identity. Love is the state in which another seeks to confirm, by physical and emotional embrace, the value and the existence of the self.

Some male images of the inner life are harder. Ludwig Hirschfeld Mack, a refugee from Hitler's Germany found himself behind Australian barbed wire for his first Christmas, 1941, beneath the Southern Cross and improvised a woodcut self-image of bitter irony. Howard Taylor's *Double Self Portrait*, with torso shirt-wrinkles evoking wood-grain, is chiefly concerned with the rectangular framing that art (sculpture as well as painting) imposes on nature but it is also a reminder that the artist himself is a part of nature. The trauma of war can generate inwardness. Stella Bowen's official commission of deceased airmen implies ascent beyond the bomber's combat level, to heaven. Frank Hinder's *Bomber crash* is an experience of momentary departure from the self in a brush with death. The irresistible demands of authority which have long sent men to war are symbolized in Arthur Boyd's *The King*, James Cant's *The bomb* (the latter as much an Eye of God as the eye of a nuclear explosion over Sydney warehouses) and in James Gleeson's *The sower*.

Albert Tucker's 'war art' is a horrified gaze at its social disruptions, its desperate escapes into loveless primal eroticism in the cinemas and blacked-out streets of Melbourne.

Jon Molvig's *A Twilight of Women*, a witches' sabbath with their familiar cats, expresses a more traditional male fear of the power of enchantment by female eroticism. Brett Whiteley's *Christie and Hectorina McLennan*, at first sight equally ecstatic, is an appalled comment on a notorious necrophiliac murderer. Post-war need for order perhaps meant that as well as Expressionist or Surrealist styles, traditional realism would

also be used as a vehicle for the emotions. Charles Blackman's *Running home* shows a child's fear among the shop-signs of Melbourne; Jeffrey Smart's *Holiday resort* shows potential menace in a cheerless South Australian seaside resort.

There has also been a revival of modern sacred art. Justin O'Brien's beautifully controlled relationships between inner and outer space indicate that we are receiving an invisible Annunciation from the Greek island outside the doors as well as from the Angels depicted on a fresco inside. Grace Cossington Smith's *Door into the garden* from her studio is also a doorway into the heaven of a garden in Sydney, a paradise announced by the God-given sun which enters the door. Margaret Preston's 1952 *The Expulsion* depicts an Aboriginal Adam and Eve driven from their Australian Garden of Eden; in 1962 Mawalan Marika, the leading Arnhem Land artist of the time, painted on eucalyptus bark a cross-cultural *Crucifixion*.

Ian Fairweather also painted Christian subjects but his *Monastery*, 1961, was based on memories of Chinese Buddhists contemplating, each in a simple cell-room at Tai Shan, a crowded solitude. His *Lit Bateau* (Bed boat) shows him asleep at night on a raft as he floats back from Darwin to the Indonesia which he loved; but his curled-up posture beneath the sheltering 'ribs' of the raft's sail implies a return to more than Asian cultures — it is a return to a lost mother's womb.

Robert Klippel's branching, articulated *Metal construction* is an edgy metaphor for the branching vessels and nerves within our own bodies or within any organic life and Tony Tuckson's gestural markings are primal affirmations of human identity and the beginnings of communication by visual symbols. Peter Booth's black 'doors' repel escape and forcibly reflect back the self, whereas his baroque nightmares have achieved a kind of difficult self-liberation into a world of danger but of hope. Ken Unsworth's abstract sculpture and Mike Parr's large upside-down self-portrait drawing are images of disoriented vertigo, questioning the very basis of secure, rational belief.

Robert Hunter's minimal grey painting invites contemplation of tranquility as does Ragnar Hansen's silver tea service, dissolving in its own reflective surfaces. Bea Maddock's *Shadow* etchings are about individual absorption into crowds of thousands during a time of national grief, a leader's funeral. Bill Henson's photographs juxtapose a drug-culture face with the dream of beauty offered by art museums.

A more optimistic inwardness and a greater sense of continuity are found in Brian Campion Yinawanga's sculpture showing death as a bridge between two kinds of life, in Brian Blanchflower's ritualistic communion with a rock near Albany in Western Australia, in Tom Risley's revitalized fragment of an Aboriginal canoe from North Queensland, and in Imants Tillers's image of the powerful creativity available for our continuing project of inventing Australia. Aboriginal artists have always confidently created and re-created Australia. The Dreamings painted by Clifford Possum Tjapaltjarri, Billy Stockman Tjapaltjarri, Yala Yala Gibbs Tjungurrayi, Daisy Nakamarra and Turkey Tolson Tjupurrula assisted by his daughters, all realize a place of love between people and of love for the intimately understood world of nature.

Rupert BUNNY, 1864-1947. *Rape of Persephone.* c1913, Paris. Oil on canvas, 54.4 x 81.1 cm. Australian
National Gallery, Canberra. Federal Government funds 1976

Hugh RAMSAY, 1877-1906. *The sisters.* 1904, Melbourne. Oil on canvas, 125.1 x 144.8 cm. Art Gallery of
New South Wales, Sydney. State Government funds 1921

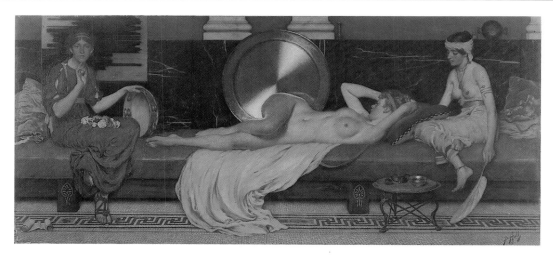

Bernard HALL, 1859-1935. *Sleep.* 1919, Melbourne. Oil on canvas, 64 x 141 cm. National Gallery of
Victoria, Melbourne. Felton Bequest Fund 1919

Web GILBERT, 1869-1925. *The Dreamer.* 1915, London. Bronze, 40 x 47.8 x 36.3
cm. National Gallery of Victoria, Melbourne. Felton Bequest Fund 1922. On
loan to City of Ballaarat Fine Art Gallery, Ballarat, Victoria

Harold PARKER, 1873-1962. *Ariadne.* 1919, London; version of a larger 1908
marble. Marble, 50.2 x 82 x 42.5 cm. National Gallery of Victoria, Melbourne.
Felton Bequest Fund 1921

Norman LINDSAY, 1879-1969. *Lady and parrot.* 1918, Springwood, NSW.
Etching on paper, 11.1 x 11.2 cm. National Trust of Australia (NSW), Norman
Lindsay Museum & Art Gallery, Springwood, New South Wales

Thea PROCTOR, 1879-1966. *The rose.* c1928, Sydney. Hand-coloured
woodcut on paper, 28.5 x 26.6 cm. Art Gallery of South Australia,
Adelaide. State Government funds 1980

M. Napier WALLER, 1893-1972. *Christian Waller with Baldur, Undine and Siren
at Fairy Hills.* 1932, Melbourne. Oil and tempera on canvas, 121.5 x 205.5 cm.
Australian National Gallery, Canberra. Federal Government funds 1984

Clive STEPHEN, 1889-1957. *Garden sculpture*. c1950, Melbourne.
Sandstone, 86.5 cm high. National Gallery of Victoria, Melbourne.
Gift of Dr Val Stephen 1984

Joy HESTER, 1920-1960. *The lovers*. c1956-58, Melbourne. Gouache, ink, oil on
paper, mounted on composition board, 101.5 x 63.4 cm. Art Gallery of South
Australia, Adelaide. State Government funds 1972

Lina BRYANS, born 1909. *The Babe is Wise (Portrait of Jean
Campbell)*. 1940, Melbourne. Oil on cardboard, 94.1 x 73.2 cm.
National Gallery of Victoria, Melbourne. Gift of Miss Jean Campbell 1962
Jean Campbell, author of a novel The Babe is Wise

Ethel CARRICK, 1872-1952. *On the verandah*. 1940s, Melbourne. Oil
on canvas, 111.8 x 86 cm. Private collection

Ludwig HIRSCHFELD MACK, 1893-1984. *"Merry Christmas 1941"*. 1941, Internment Camp, Orange, NSW. Woodcut on paper 9.5 x 7.6 cm. Shepparton Art Gallery, Shepparton, Victoria. Gift of Olive Hirschfeld 1975

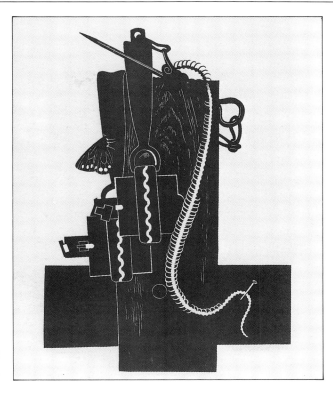

Eric THAKE, 1904-1982. *Crucifixion*. 1936, Melbourne. Linocut on paper, 30.8 x 25.1 cm. Private collection

Rayner HOFF, 1894-1937. *Theseus*. c1932/33, Sydney. Sandstone, bronze, 84.5 x 20 x 27.7 cm. Australian National Gallery, Canberra. Federal Government funds 1985

Howard TAYLOR, born 1918. *Double Self Portrait*. c1949-50, Bickley near Perth. Oil on composition board, 73 x 85.2. Art Gallery of Western Australia, Perth. State Government funds 1985

Stella BOWEN, 1893-1947. *Bomber crew.* 1944, London. Oil on canvas,
86.1 x 63.6 cm. Australian War Memorial, Canberra. Acquired under
Official War Artist commission 1944

James GLEESON, born 1915. *The sower.* 1944, Sydney. Oil on canvas, 76.2 x
50.8 cm. Art Gallery of New South Wales, Sydney. State Government funds 1972
A war-time sower of destruction, paraphrased from J.F. Millet's painting
The sower, 1851

Arthur BOYD, born 1920. *The King.* 1944, Fitzroy, Melbourne. Oil on
canvas on composition board, 87.8 x 111 cm. Australian National
Gallery, Canberra. The Arthur Boyd Gift 1975

James CANT, 1911-1982. *The bomb.* 1945, Sydney. Oil on canvas, 63.6 x 76.4 cm.
Art Gallery of South Australia, Adelaide. Gift of Dora Cant 1985

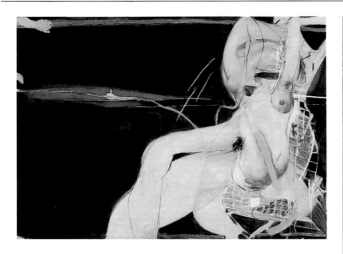

Brett WHITELEY, born 1939. *Christie and Hectorina McLennan.* 1964, London. Oil, wax, charcoal, collage, assemblage on canvas, 162.9 x 214 cm. Australian National Gallery, Canberra. Federal Government funds 1973

Jon MOLVIG, 1923-1970. *A Twilight of Women.* 1957, Brisbane. Oil on composition board, 137.2 x 148.6 cm. Queensland Art Gallery, Brisbane. State Government funds 1984

Albert TUCKER, born 1914. *Image of Modern Evil 9.* 1944, Melbourne. Oil on canvas on composition board, 51.7 x 63 cm. Australian National Gallery, Canberra. Gift of the artist 1981
Based on the interior of the Australia Cinema, Collins Street, Melbourne

Albert TUCKER, born 1914. *Image of Modern Evil 24.* 1945, 47 Robe Street, St Kilda, Melbourne. Oil on composition board, 64 x 53.5 cm. Australian National Gallery, Canberra. Gift of the artist 1981

Jeffrey SMART, born 1921. *Holiday resort.* 1946, Adelaide, from sketches at
Port Elliot, South Australia. Oil on canvas, 50.9 x 60.9 cm. Mr & Mrs Colin Ballantyne

Charles BLACKMAN, born 1928. *Running home.* 1954, Melbourne. Oil
on composition board, 91 x 121.1 cm. Australian National Gallery,
Canberra. Founding Donors' Fund 1985

Justin O'BRIEN, born 1917. *The Annunciation.* 1973-74, Rome, based on
sketches at Skyros, Greece. Oil on three canvases, overall 91 x 127 cm.
Tasmanian Museum & Art Gallery, Hobart. Robb Bequest Fund and Visual
Arts Board of the Australia Council contemporary art purchase grant 1976

Grace Cossington SMITH, 1892-1984. *Door into the garden.* 1959,
43 Kuringai Avenue, Turramurra, Sydney. Oil on composition board, 91.5
x 61 cm. Bendigo Art Gallery, Bendigo, Victoria. Gallery funds 1959

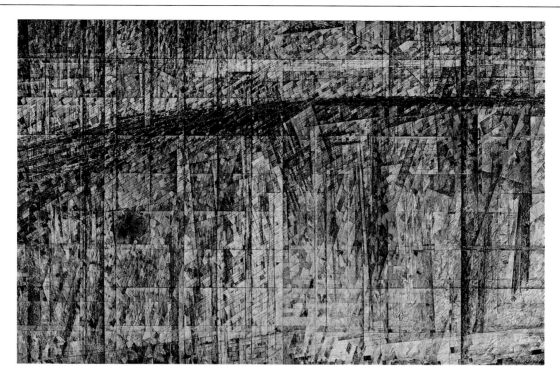

Godfrey MILLER, 1893-1964. *Golgotha.* 1960-64, Sydney. Oil on canvas, 67.3 x 100 cm. Private collection

Ian FAIRWEATHER, 1891-1974. *Lit Bateau.* 1957, Bribie Island near Brisbane, from memories of sleeping at night on a 1952 raft voyage from Darwin to Timor. Gouache on cardboard, 72 x 92.5 cm. Private collection

Roger KEMP, 1908-1987. *The Cross.* c1967, Melbourne. Synthetic polymer paint on composition board, 183 x 137.5 cm. Monash University Collection, Melbourne. University funds 1968

Margaret PRESTON, 1875-1963. *The Expulsion.* 1952, Sydney.
Gouache stencil on black card, 60 x 48 cm. Art Gallery of New South
Wales, Sydney. Gift of W.G. Preston 1967

MAWALAN MARIKA, 1908-1967. *Crucifixion.* 1962, Yirrkala, Northern Territory.
Ochres on eucalyptus bark, 75 x 35 cm. Museums & Art Galleries of the
Northern Territory, Darwin. Territory Government funds 1976

Tony TUCKSON, 1921-1973. *White on black.* 1973, Sydney. Synthetic polymer
paint, paper collage on composition board, 244 x 122 cm. City of Ballaarat
Fine Art Gallery, Ballarat, Victoria. Gallery funds 1974

Tony TUCKSON, 1921-1973. *No. 15; Black on white.* 1960, Sydney. Oil
on composition board, 183 x 122 cm. Michael Tuckson

Peter BOOTH, born 1940. *Painting 1971-72.* 1971-72, Melbourne. Synthetic
polymer paint on canvas, 243.8 x 121.9 cm. Private collection

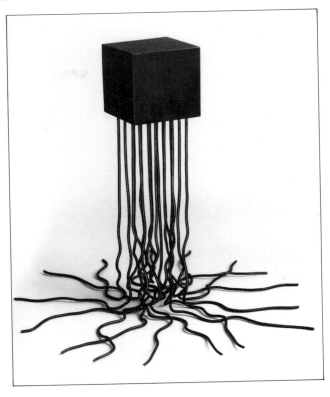

Ken UNSWORTH, born 1931. *Free fall.* 1975, Sydney. Steel, 225 x 200 x 200 cm.
Art Gallery of New South Wales, Sydney. State Government funds 1979

Robert HUNTER, born 1947. *Untitled.* 1977, Melbourne. Synthetic polymer paint, string on canvas, 122.5 x 243.5 cm.
City of Ballaarat Fine Art Gallery, Ballarat, Victoria. Visual Arts Board of the Australia Council
contemporary art purchase grant 1978

Carol JERREMS, 1949-1980. *Vale Street.* 1975, St Kilda, Melbourne. Gelatin-
silver photograph, 20.2 x 30.3 cm. Australian National Gallery, Canberra. Gift
of the Philip Morris Arts Grant 1982

Ragnar HANSEN, born 1945. *Tea service.* 1982, Canberra. Silver,
ebony: teapot 15.1 x 22.9 x 12 cm; jug 10.6 x 17 x 8.8 cm; sugar bowl
6.8 x 11.1 x 10.7 cm; spoon 14.7 cm. Australian National Gallery,
Canberra. Federal Government funds 1982

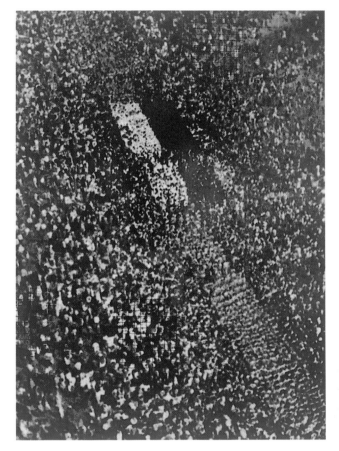

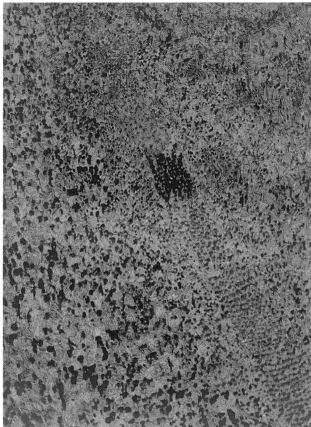

Bea MADDOCK, born 1934. *Cast a shadow.* 1972, Melbourne. Etching on paper, 72 x 49.9 cm. Art Gallery of South Australia, Adelaide. State Government funds 1975

Bea MADDOCK, born 1934. *Shadow.* 1973, Melbourne. Etching on paper, 70.9 x 49.8 cm. Art Gallery of South Australia, Adelaide. d'Auvergne Boxall Bequest Fund 1975

From newspaper photographs of Cairo crowds for President Nasser's funeral

Bill HENSON, born 1955. From the series *Untitled 1983-84.* 1983-84, Louvre Museum, Paris; New York; Melbourne. Type-C colour photographs: triptych, 99.8 x 73.9 cm, 101 x 74.2 cm, 100.3 x 73.5 cm. Art Gallery of South Australia, Adelaide. Gift of Jim Sharman and State Government funds 1986

Sidney NOLAN, born 1917. *Ern Malley.* 1973, London. Oil on composition board, 122 x 122 cm.
Art Gallery of South Australia, Adelaide. Gift of Sidney & Cynthia Nolan 1974
Portrait of the hoax poet launched in *Angry Penguins*, 1944, as having died aged 25 in 1943 of "Grave's
Disease after refusing to be operated upon"; illustrating the line "What would you have me do? Go to the wars?"

Mike PARR, born 1945. *Absterge self portrait, Luridities Series, no. 3: Mengele & Co come back for a
heart transplant.* 1985, Sydney. Charcoal, pastel on paper, 127.5 x 186.7 cm. Art Gallery of South
Australia, Adelaide. State Government funds 1985

Daisy NAKAMARRA, born c1935. *Women's Dreaming.* 1982, Haast's Bluff, Northern Territory. Synthetic polymer paint on canvas, 59 cm diameter. Art Gallery of South Australia, Adelaide. Lisette Kohlhagen Bequest Fund 1982

Fiona HALL, born 1953. *The Seven Deadly Sins: Wrath.* 1985, Sydney. Colour Polaroid photograph, 73.8 x 55.9 cm. Art Gallery of South Australia, Adelaide. State Government funds 1987

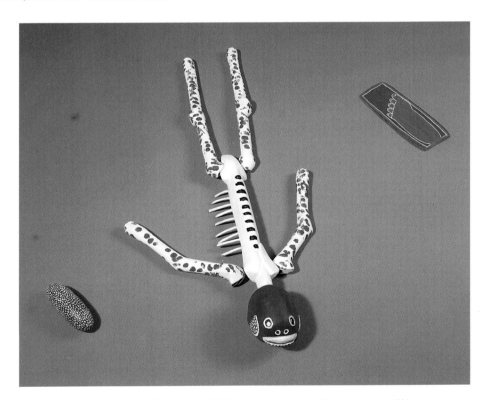

Brian Campion YINAWANGA, born 1937. *Skeleton figure with spirit foot and spirit egg.* 1984, Malyangarnak, Northern Territory. Wood, ochres, eucalyptus bark, three-part installation, 110 x 60 cm (installed); figure armspan 39.3 cm, bark painting 28 x 11.3 cm, wooden egg 5 x 16 x 5 cm. Art Gallery of Western Australia, Perth. State Government funds 1985

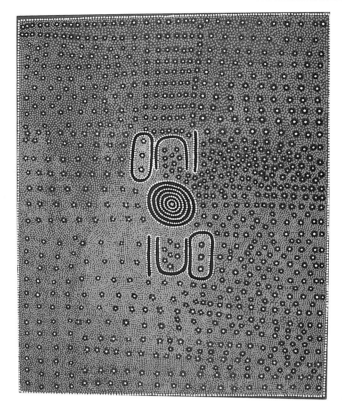

Turkey Tolson TJUPURRULA, born c1945, assisted by his daughters, Pamela NAKAMARRA, born c1967, Kitty NAKAMARRA, born c1970. *Women's Dreaming.* 1981, Papunya, Northern Territory. Synthetic polymer paint on canvas, 160 x 126 cm. Flinders University Art Museum, Adelaide. University funds 1981, accessioned 1985

YALA YALA Gibbs TJUNGURRAYI, born c1928. *Untitled.* c1971-72, Papunya, Northern Territory. Synthetic polymer paint on composition board, 72 x 51 cm. The Australian Museum, Sydney. State Government funds 1983

Brian BLANCHFLOWER, born 1939. *Nocturne 3 (Whale Rock).* 1982, Perth. Oil, bitumen, sand, chalk on canvas, 178 x 254 cm. Art Gallery of South Australia, Adelaide. Elder Bequest Fund 1983
Based on a site near Albany, WA

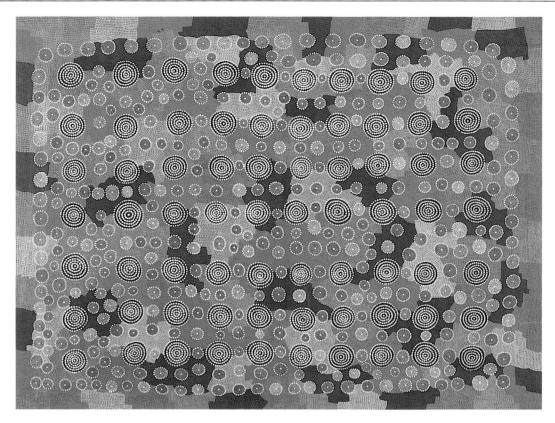

Billy Stockman TJAPALTJARRI, born c1925. *Budgerigar Dreaming.* 1987, Papunya, Northern Territory.
Synthetic polymer paint on canvas, 182 x 232.5 cm. Art Gallery of South Australia, Adelaide. State
Government funds 1987

Tom RISLEY, born 1947. *Cape Direction chair.* 1986, Atherton, Queensland. Wood, 147 x 61 x 75 cm. Art
Gallery of South Australia, Adelaide. State Government funds 1987
Great Barrier Reef flotsam, including a fragment of an Aboriginal dugout canoe, found at Cape
Direction, Cape York Peninsula, North Queensland

SPHINX by GAEL NEWTON

Max Dupain, *Sunbaker*, 1937

When describing this image of a sunbaker — sphinxlike in its monumental impassivity, yet with the tension of a coiled spring — Max Dupain has spoken[1] of it almost as if it had been a kind of found object snapped while on holidays in 1937 at Culburra, on the New South Wales south coast, near the Shoalhaven River.

Like his subject, Dupain was in 1937 a young and athletic man. Since 1934 he had been operating as a professional photographer from his own studio in Sydney, having served an apprenticeship for several years under Cecil W. Bostock, a professional photographer, commercial artist and since before World War I a prominent member of the Pictorial movement in art photography. By 1937, Dupain was well patronized not only in his professional work but also as an art photographer; a suite of his surrealistic nudes and still-life studies had been included in 1935 in Sydney Ure Smith's art journal *Art in Australia*.

Sunbaker was a personal picture yet its style derived from the work of European modern photographers such as Man Ray: its use of an unusual low-angle shot simultaneously monumentalizes the subject and makes it mysterious. The simple shapes of the triangular torso and oval head are located in a shallow space — an unspecific desert environment — and reflect the modern movement's interest in pure forms and the symbolic power of archaic Greek classicism.

Sunbaker was also a nationalistic image, made on the eve of the 1938 celebrations of Australia's Sesquicentenary as a European nation. Whereas earlier generations of artists had depicted settlers playing at being 'at home' in the landscape in picnic scenes, or proudly 'Australian' subject-painters like Tom Roberts had depicted nude men disporting themselves by the water in his *The Sunny South*, 1886/87, Dupain's *Sunbaker* suggests a profound appropriation of the land. This white man lies with his back exposed, fearing no enemies and tanned as nearly dark in skin as the original Aboriginal inhabitants of the continent.

A grand photographic salon was held in 1938 as part of the official Sesquicentenary celebrations. It included work by an older generation of Pictorialist art-photographers, commercial professionals, and even the new modern school of photography. However, the self-congratulatory reviews of that commemorative salon, as it was known, caused Dupain to protest to the newspapers of the day. He believed there was no modern spirit evident in the exhibition, nothing to compare with the work of European and American photographers such as Man Ray and Moholy-Nagy. A spate of letters fuelled a press controversy over modern-versus-pictorial schools of art-photography, mostly defending the judge and reviewer, Harold Cazneaux.

The controversy marks an historical split between two schools of photography. Dupain and others responded by organising a Contemporary Camera Groupe to illustrate their new dynamic approach. It held a brief exhibition in Sydney late in 1938.

The rhetoric of the Contemporary Camera Groupe, which claimed to be "prophetic in its modernity", was perhaps more extreme than the actual exhibits. Harold Cazneaux and Cecil Bostock were also part of the Contemporary Camera Groupe, exhibiting works with the clearer outlines, bolder shapes and sharp lighting of the modern school. Since the late twenties, Cazneaux and other Pictorialists had responded to a new taste by banishing some of the soft-focus atmosphere and quest for gentle harmonies of the Pictorial aesthetic in favour of more dramatic mood and composition. In the same year that Dupain made *Sunbaker*, Cazneaux was in the arid regions of the Flinders Ranges in South Australia, making dramatic, spare landscape studies and his own icon of Australia: *The Spirit of Endurance*. Cazneaux's is a study of a monumental gum-tree also shot from a low angle; its arm-like branches seem to defy the eroding forces of the time and a harsh environment. Other Pictorialists, including F.A. Joyner of Adelaide, made trips to the desert regions, creating in their old age works inspired by the modernist aesthetic as well as by the example of the painter Hans Heysen.

Dupain's *Sunbaker* is a brooding figure. It is different from the usual treatment by 1930s artists of beach scenes and athletic figures as heroic, as popular symbols of progress.

For Cazneaux, the beach was a site for scenes full of human interest, charm and decorative treatment. For Dupain the beach was an arena for dramas of the soul and spirit. It was also an arena for the expression of his interests in the literature which had influenced his own emotional development and philosophy — the works of D.H. Lawrence and the Powys brothers with their interest in vitalism, powerful oppositions of male and female sexuality and intense emotional/physical equivalences.

The Second World War swept away much of the optimism, simple heroicism and high spirits of the thirties. Dupain's *Sunbaker* seems now to anticipate a post-war sobriety and soul-searching. A later image by Dupain, of 1939, shows a girl lying floating almost death-like in the water. In that work, full of despair of the war in Europe, female sensuality has taken over (the sea for Dupain being a metaphor for femaleness and emotions out of control). In *Sunbaker* the ocean's surf is kept at bay on the horizon. Perhaps this dark detached spirit in *Sunbaker* appealed to new audiences in the 1970s; they also favoured photographs of the beach, the bizarre urban landscape of beaches often expressing an angst of a different kind, meanings of their own.

Since the 1970s, Dupain's *Sunbaker*, 1937, has become an icon of Australian photography. It was not often exhibited in preceding decades. It was an important image in the monograph on Dupain published in 1948 by Ure Smith but there it was overlaid with the realist character of the documentary movement in which Dupain had become involved after World War II.

No vintage print of *Sunbaker* has come to light. A print from the 1940s or 1950s would most likely have been much darker, emphasizing Dupain's own reserve in the face of Australia's simple late-1930s optimism, and remaining true to his restless, anxious wrestling with the physical and emotional realities he sees in the Australian environment.

Max DUPAIN, born 1911. *Sunbaker.* 1937, Culburra, NSW. Gelatin-silver photograph, 38 x 43.2 cm. Art Gallery of South Australia, Adelaide. Visual Arts Board of the Australia Council contemporary art purchase grant 1980

"THE CREW ESCAPED AMID FLAMES"[1] by RENÉE FREE

Frank Hinder, *Bomber crash*, 1943-49

At Rabaul, in November 1941, Frank Hinder had his "only real war experience". He had been sent to New Guinea to advise on camouflaging another airstrip near Rabaul and was off on "aerial reconnaissance" when his Lockheed-Hudson aircraft crashed shortly after take-off. It had got as high as the palm-trees, bounced on its nose, bounced again, and fell back on its belly. The petrol-tanks in the wings burst into flames. Back at the camp, soldiers on church parade heard thuds, saw the smoke, and concluded that the volcano, Matupi, across the bay, had had a minor eruption.[2]

Relieved not to be "a box of ashes", Hinder could not reveal what happened to wife and colleagues in Sydney. He translated his experience into drawings and paintings.

First, using one sheet, Hinder made four small watercolours, which capture the experience in a tropical setting.[3] Three show the plane side-on with the volcano, palm-trees and smoke — from the viewpoint of a spectator. Passengers and crew escaped and stood watching. Black smoke mushrooms almost as if from the crater of the volcano in the distance. The fourth shows simply a circle, a cross-section of the fuselage with men huddling inside, flames from the cockpit seen down a tunnel space within the circle. This is from a participant's viewpoint, yet drawn from a detached position. Hinder has described the uncanny experience of being inside and outside at the same time. "All I can remember is when something like that happens, you are completely out of yourself — awareness without knowing anything." Others who have been close to death have felt this mystic departure from the bodily self.

The circle concept embodies the essence of the experience and was developed further in a drawing dated 1941. Further drawings developed from realism to semi-abstraction, and led to the final one, dated 1942, in which the plane is presented tail-first: double rudder at the bottom; fuselage, now elongated, rising vertically from centre foreground; wings spread edge-to-edge horizontally across the middle, dark smoke and flames billowing off-centre to the top.

There are two versions of the painting, both executed in tempera, dated 1943 and 1943-49 (the latter mainly executed in 1948). They differ slightly but derive from the same drawing. The Art Gallery of New South Wales version is smaller, due to the reduction of the composition at top and sides. The inside/outside experience is made vivid by the X-raying of the fuselage; geometric division of light, colour, form suggest the controlled fear of the men moving towards the figure attempting to open the door. Hinder can remember only the odd feeling of unreality. The colours of the New South Wales version perhaps reflect this sensation — pale green and pink with an orchid-like strangeness. The Australian War Memorial's version is more immediate in effect, more violent in colour. (A similarly violent effect was intended in an unfinished painting, *Bayonet drill*, 1945.) Hinder wanted to return to his earlier circle concept by cutting an oval mount to echo the shape of the fuselage and to concentrate attention on the drama inside. After a trial on the New South Wales version, it became clear that the whole composition carried the meaning. Inside and outside are united in one rhythm. The figures are grouped in the shape

of a flame, hardly interrupting the ring of fire which is broken only by the dark uniform of the figure opening the door. The topmost figure merges into the flames, mirroring what happened in reality when the pilot suffered minor burns before escaping from the cockpit into the fuselage.

Unlike most other Australian artists, Hinder chose America for his apprenticeship, 1927-1934. There he met and married Margel Harris, who was to become a major sculptor. In New York, Howard Giles and Emil Bisttram taught him Dynamic Symmetry, as proclaimed by Jay Hambidge. Dynamic Symmetry describes not only a method of establishing proportions but also a philosophy of creativity. Dynamic = movement. Symmetry = relationship. Hinder's special characteristic is to crystallize, through preliminary drawings, the interaction of man and his surroundings in intuitively-shaped compositions which link the particular subject with appropriate rhythms in the world at large. Man doing his job is in tune with himself and in tune with the universe. A final summer school with Bisttram at Taos, New Mexico further gave the Hinders a sense of the union of man, landscape and architecture and a feeling for transcendental and symbolic art.

When Hinder and his wife returned to Australia in the artistically conservative 1930s they helped introduce the modernist credo that art should be of its own time and place. Contemporary artist friends were practising Cubism as taught by André Lhote in France. Hinder was not interested in cubist still-life, but in people in daily activity and in crowds caught up in the tension of urban environments, both symbolic for the modern movement. The theme of people working was perhaps nurtured by experience of the Depression in America and seeing the humanist art of the Mexican muralists, particularly José Orozco.

European art movements that united man with his surroundings were Futurism and the Section d'Or. Hinder came close to being Australia's only futurist but did not share that early-twentieth-century movement's enthusiasm for destroying the past or glorifying war. Hinder brings the classicism of Cubism to futurist subjects with Orphism's division of light and transparent planes. Jacques Villon, Robert Delaunay, Lyonel Feininger and Franz Marc were among the artists he admired.

Flight has been a recurring theme in Hinder's art. *Bomber crash* is not intended to show destroyer destroyed. The plane was not on a bombing mission. Hinder was in that plane and, like the other men, doing his job in defence. In 1945 he painted another real flying experience of a searchlight effect. *Bomber crash* is a depiction of a particular event in which, incidentally, no-one was killed. The semi-abstract style unites particular and universal, the idea of victims sacrificed in war.

Since Hinder was not an official war artist his war subjects reflect a personal testimony. The first two were inspired by stories of refugees — *Little man with a big gun*, 1939, as Mussolini was called, and *Flight (Refugees)*, 1942, which became *Flight into Egypt* in a later version and won the Blake Prize for religious art in Sydney in 1952. Hinder's attitude to war is summed up in lithographs of 1946-47, with ironic titles *Christian Civilization A.D. 27* and *Christ is with us*; self-seeking political leaders and hypocritical church-leaders demanded sacrifice of the people in war to

Frank HINDER, born 1906. *Bomber crash*. 1943-49, Sydney, from sketches at Rabaul, 1941. Tempera, oil glazes on gesso on composition board, 59.6 x 49.1 cm. Australian War Memorial, Canberra. Federal Government funds 1951

gain their ends. Hinder is an agnostic, but with a belief in an overall design, which he symbolizes in his art. However, religious overtones are present in many of his works, though not deliberately intended. The aircraft takes on the form of the Crucifix; the men, sacrificial victims like Christ, seem ennobled by Renaissance robes, haloes; the dark towering conflagration is given a 'halo' of light. The medium, tempera on gesso, is an early Renaissance one.

Fellow-artist Frank Medworth commented that *Bomber crash* reminded him of the work of William Blake. Hinder remembers lectures on Blake by Eleonore Lange, German art-historian and friend. Blake often showed flames on altars, figures in circles surrounded by fire. The forms of the fire and the skewed upward flowing curves are Blakeian. It could be said that *Bomber crash* represents sacrifice and purification. Hinder's work with camouflage was appropriate; seeing and making manifest visual

relationships in different things is an integral aspect of his art. It derives from his philosophic and scientific outlook, formed in the 1920s revival of Greek thought, of the interpenetration of all things, the atoms of matter in a perpetual dance. Hinder has said that the artist's role is to make science and philosophy visible and his 'Bible' of interesting quotations contains Bertrand Russell's "Matter has become as ghostly as anything in a spiritualistic seance." Hinder's accurate observation, confirmed by others with similar experiences, is expressed in division of form, light, colour, the artistic equivalent to the discovery that matter is not solid. He has reconciled the atoms of the event in a perpetual dance, a total design. *Bomber crash* becomes a cipher of Fire, of Flux, of War. It is like a chemical and physical change in a crucible, where matter is transformed to ashes and spirit.

THE CITY OF NIGHT by RICHARD HAESE

Albert Tucker, *Victory girls*, 1943

Born in 1914, old enough and young enough to have vivid memories of Australian soldiers training for the first great war of this century, Albert Tucker painted at twenty-nine one of the indelible images of a second war whose effect was to transform Australian society in fundamental and irrevocable ways. The subject of *Victory girls* is far removed from the battlefields of the war — though the artist had earlier painted symbolic and expressive responses to what he imagined to be that reality. The image that *Victory girls* presents, however, seems every bit as nightmarish. Tucker's theme is how modern war strikes at and corrodes the very heart of the societies it touches, disrupts and often destroys all that once seemed so fixed and enduring.

At a time of crisis and mobilization for total war, Albert Tucker had been conscripted into the army in Melbourne in April 1942, eventually working as an artist producing drawings of patients with war-wounds at the Heidelberg Military Hospital. He was discharged in October 1942.[1] This first-hand experience of the horrific consequences of what happened to men at war both physically and psychologically affected the artist deeply and was documented in his art. Increasingly, however, his concerns centred on the question of how this war bore upon his central preoccupation, the relationship between the individual and society. It was a preoccupation that had its origins in bitter memories of the effect on Australian society and upon the artist's own family of the consequences of the Great Depression. An early interest in Marxist ideas concerning this relationship had given way by 1942, under the influence of such writers as George Orwell, W.B. Yeats and, above all, T.S. Eliot, to a deep concern for the fate of individual sensibilities and culture in the face of violent social forces and change — a theme that underpinned Tucker's art throughout and immediately following the war years. Between 1940 and 1943 the first explorations of this theme take place against a specific backdrop of war in a series of apocalyptic images, with the artist exploring a range of styles and visual modes: Surrealism, Social Realism, Expressionism, New Objectivity, Cubism. With *Victory girls*, painted in August 1943, Tucker achieves a new and personal symbolic expressionism, and if the painting summarizes the preoccupations of the previous three years, it already contains in its style and its theme the essential character of his major achievement, the *Images of Modern Evil*, painted from 1943 to 1947.

No earlier painting in Australian art prepares us for the confrontation of *Victory girls*. Its capacity to shock has scarcely diminished with the years in terms of either its subject or its raw directness of attack. Two young women, stripped to the waist and adorned only with make-up and short red-white-and-blue skirts occupy the space within a circle formed by the groping embraces of three soldiers. The large clumsy hand of the soldier on the right clutches at a breast, while the hand of his companion on the left seems to have disappeared beneath the folds of the skirt. The dance of the two women, a grotesque parody of courtship-ritual and fertility-rite, had been suggested by a newspaper report of girls performing a strip-tease at this time for a group of soldiers in a city alleyway. These are Melbourne's notorious wartime "victory girls", so named because of their 'patriotic' display — young girls, many teenagers, who flocked into the city in search of the money and good time offered by the presence of thousands of American and Australian soldiers.

During 1942-43 Melbourne was a city transformed. The introduction of conscription and the withdrawal home of the Australian divisions from the Middle East to face the Japanese threat, made the presence of men in uniform ubiquitous. American troops, too, had appeared in such numbers that Australians felt in the grip of an invading army, an invasion that peaked in January 1943 when 18,000 American troops of the First Marine Division disembarked at Melbourne fresh from the battle of Guadalcanal. They would remain for six months. By 1943 any honeymoon period was over as the full sexual and social consequences of this presence were inescapable, and memories still fresh of the strangling of three women in May 1942 by the American soldier Edward Leonski, on leave in Melbourne.[2] Tucker had painted the subject of Leonski early in 1943,[3] seeing in Leonski's pathological killings merely the most dramatic evidence of what he was increasingly driven to see as the dissolution and collapse of his world and its values — a condition mirrored in the sinister appearance of this blacked-out city. During the day the familiar urban enclosure seemed dominated by drinking, gambling schools and an ever-present threat of violence. During a night-time deepened by the blackout the sense of menace was attended by an unbridled sexuality in which prostitution was practised openly in the gardens and along the streets between the city and St Kilda. In Tucker's words: "Not only was Cain abroad, but also the Great Whore of Babylon. This gave an atmosphere that was primal and violent".[4]

Victory girls is a direct response to this wartime atmosphere but it was not the artist's first depiction of the subject of graceless sexuality. Two years earlier, in 1941, Tucker had painted *Pick up* in which two men trail a pair of women into an alleyway. Discarded beer bottles litter the street. The men in this case are civilians, all flash suits and slicked hair; the women, equally dressed to kill, walk arm-in-arm, their transparent dresses disguising nothing. *Pick up*, with its debts to the German artists George Grosz and Otto Dix, lacks the power of the later painting, although we recognize that these four ugly figures illuminated by a pool of garish green light are the same four central figures within *Victory girls*. The 1943 sisters have the same features, but these — eyeballs, snout-like nose, enormous vermilion V-shaped lips filled with teeth — are no longer merely features; they are now assembled like rudimentary organs forming a head given over completely to sensory and masticatory functions. Similarly the upper torso is a stick to which are attached breasts and a ribcage — the entire apparatus surrounded by a shock of blonde or red hair. These armless puppets are as human as the grinning heads of clowns that Tucker saw at St Kilda's Luna Park and their laugh is the same mechanical screech of inane laughter. The image is less misogynist than misanthropic since the companions of these puppet-whores are every bit as ugly and dehumanized. The men of 1943 have now been put into uniforms of slouch hats, boots and gaiters, and huge ill-fitting khaki great-coats. The characters of their faces are the same as in the earlier painting only more extreme: on the left a jutting jaw with teeth, on the right the porcine leering face now almost completely bestial.

Albert TUCKER, born 1914. *Victory girls.* 1943, St Kilda, Melbourne. Oil on composition board, 64.6 x 58.7 cm. Australian National Gallery, Canberra. Federal Government funds 1971

Victory girls represents a dramatic turning point in Tucker's art with its fusing of primitivistic forms within a new spatial frame. The deeper coherent space of *Pick up* is now abandoned for the non-illusionistic and expressive space of analytic cubist painting, a consequence of a systematic investigation into Cubism by the artist over the previous two years. Tucker's *Self-portrait*[5] of 1941 and the psychological heads of 1942 demonstrate the artist's grasp of a new visual language, fractured forms and frontal space, evolved by Picasso and Braque early in the century. Sidney Nolan, too, had been exploring Cubism at this time but whereas Nolan linked the new language with naive representation Tucker, like the German painter Ernst Ludwig Kirchner, found in Picasso's dismemberment and reassemblage of the human form a means by which expressionism could be given even more extreme social and emotional loadings. Thus the insistent frontal character of *Victory girls* with its flattened frieze of figures fills the picture space and allows no escape from what the artist demands that we acknowledge. In *Pick up* the women tottered on high heels; now their skirts and tapering legs, together with the boots of the men, conjoin in a dynamic swirl of form, angles and curves all jumbled together. The energy and directness of the brush-strokes imparts a strident and insistent rhythm to the entire composition. Tucker's emphasis on the primitivist side of Cubism is apparent in the mask-like heads of *Victory girls*, just as the rudimentary assemblages of the female figures have their origins in the artist's interest in African and Melanesian sculpture. The female figures manifest the primal power of the fertility fetish; whatever interest in Aboriginal art Australian artists may have shown before this painting, with *Victory girls* 'primitivism' makes its first full-blooded appearance in Australian art. Tucker had produced in August 1943 at least one sketch, entitled

Victory girl,[6] but depicting only the two figures on the right of the final painting. Preparation for the painting was thus minimal and the vigour of its attack makes it one of Tucker's most unpremeditated works, reflecting in its ferocity all the anger of biblical prophecy and revelation. From 1940 onwards Tucker's art sprang from a passionate concern to see what was happening to his world and to state what he saw without compromise. Like his admired German models, Otto Dix and Max Beckmann, Tucker has refused to avert his gaze and does not allow the viewer to do so either. Tucker had grown up in the decades between the wars, years that in spite of stresses and crises, left the fabric of an isolated Australian world and its Edwardian sense of values and beliefs largely intact. By 1943, that pre-war order and stability seemed in danger of disappearing entirely in the chaotic wake of radical change. The new order with its ration books and state control over all aspects of social activity had its reverse side for the artist in a vision of a city in moral ruin and decay. Tucker had painted Melbourne in 1940 as the setting for T.S. Eliot's moral wasteland.[7] Three years later in *Victory girls* we hear more loudly still that "rattle of the bones and chuckle spread from ear to ear"[8] which echoes through Eliot's poem *The Waste Land.*

After *Victory girls* the past seems beyond recovery, and the subsequent series *Images of Modern Evil* deals with the world after the fall. But *Victory girls* is more than a prologue to that tour de force. It is a painting that registers with seismographic precision and immediacy the very moment of the collapse of a culture.

CONVULSION AND CALM: DEATH IN THE AFTERNOON by JANE CLARK

Sidney Nolan, *Death of Constable Scanlon*, 1946

As a sixth-generation Australian of Irish ancestry, Sidney Nolan has always identified closely with the infamous Irish-Australian bushranger Ned Kelly, hanged in Melbourne in 1880.[1] As a young child he heard first-hand accounts of the 'Kelly wars' from his grandfather who had been stationed as a policeman in north-eastern Victoria at the time; however, all Australians know that during Kelly's last stand, at Glenrowan, he wore home-made armour, including an iron helmet-mask. On more than one recent occasion Nolan has commented that his 1946-47 narrative series of Ned Kelly paintings, of which *Death of Constable Scanlon* is the best known, was really at least as much about himself as the nineteenth-century outlaw.

"You would be surprised if I told you", says Nolan. "From 1945 to 1947 there were emotional and complicated events in my own life. It's an inner history of my own emotions but I am not going to tell you about them . . . It seems strange, but when I painted the Kellys I thought of them as very angry, violent pictures, and so did everybody else. Today [1984] they look quite tranquil", he adds, "but still on target".[2] When he left the army in mid 1944 he was "more than interested in violence", he says; "We had been taught about arms and the use of the utmost violence".[3] However, as he said in 1961, the key ingredients of these paintings were "Kelly's own words, and Rousseau and sunlight".[4]

For all their apparent naivety and spontaneity — swiftly worked *alla prima* in bright Ripolin enamel colours on Masonite composition board — they remain perhaps the most considered and resolved works of his oeuvre to date: the result of his determination to paint the Australian landscape, of his exhaustive historical research and of what fellow-artist Albert Tucker called "his long immersion in radical modernism".[5] He spent hours in the Public Record Office and the Public Library, poring over contemporary newspaper reports, primary historical documents, the Royal Commission Report of 1881 and, especially, J.J. Kenneally's *Complete Inner History of the Kelly Gang and their Pursuers,* 1929. As an army deserter, an 'outlaw' with the false name "Robin Murray", Nolan would have had some fellow-feeling for the bushrangers. He produced an unrecorded number of sketches, drawings and smaller paintings before embarking in 1946 on a uniformly-sized series of larger works from which he eventually selected a 'core' group of twenty-seven for exhibition.[6]

Hitchhiking with the Adelaide poet Max Harris in 1945 through the Kelly country around Glenrowan, Nolan had felt that the bush was "the most real aspect of life, because of the smell and the light and everything else."[7] As he explained when the paintings were first exhibited, "I feel that a desire to paint the landscape involves a wish to hear more of the stories which take place within the landscape".[8] He was looking for something to put *in front* of the landscape, he says. And his solution was the unforgettable, stark geometric black silhouette of Ned Kelly's home-made armour. Abstract black squares had been "floating around in modern art for some time", as Nolan himself later pointed out.[9] "All I did was put a neck on the square", he says. But this powerful iconic shape made an inspired combination of narrative and symbol unparalleled in Australian art: ranked by London art critic Robert Melville in that company of twentieth-century

personages which includes Picasso's minotaur, Giorgio De Chirico's mannequins, Max Ernst's birdman, Francis Bacon's pope and Alberto Giacometti's walking men. The menacing rigidity of that iron mask provides just the schema that a painter needs to tell his story with the minimum of anecdotic invention.[10]

Whimsical, capricious, idiosyncratic in the technicque and choice of media and often supremely poetic, Nolan achieved an extraordinary range of mood and visual effects in his Kelly paintings of the 1940s. Humour unexpectedly gives way to pathos, irony to tragedy; violence in one episode to tranquil domesticity in the next. Here in *Death of Constable Scanlon,* the brutality of murder is somehow mitigated by the lyricism of the wonderful, loosely-scribbled, yellow sunlit setting, its spatial clarity established by the horizontal shadows cast by vertical fence-posts, tree-trunks and stumps. Michael Scanlon was the second policeman to die at Kelly's hands on that fateful afternoon at Stringybark Creek in October 1878. From then on, all four members of the gang were outlawed and could be shot on sight. "In a sudden violent action time seems to stand still", Nolan has explained; "I have exaggerated; the bridle must have been long, but that and the levitated horse and constable increase the unreality of violent events. Kelly seems to be present only as a force of destiny".[11] In contrast to the comic, gravity-defying figure of the unfortunate police officer, catapulted from his horse, the larger-than-life bushranger posed in the foreground, eyes modestly downcast, seems ironically calm, sardonically detached — perhaps even slightly apologetic for the explosive violence apparently due to his presence. In the instant of this murder at Stringybark Creek, Kelly is transformed from bushranger to outlaw and already wears the armour which he will invent two years later at Glenrowan.

Kelly did not know Constable Scanlon, nor the gang's next victim Sergeant Michael Kennedy. He "had nothing against them", but he objected strenuously to the "brutal and cowardly conduct of a parcel of big ugly fat-necked wombat-headed big-bellied magpie-legged narrow-hipped splay-footed sons of Irish Bailiffs or English landlords which is better known as officers of Justice or Victorian Police". And he added belligerently: "Those men came into the bush with the intention of scattering pieces of me and my brother all over the bush and yet they know and acknowledge I have been wronged . . . Scanlon who carried the rifle slewed his horse around to gallop away but the horse would not go and quick as a thought fired at me with the rifle without unslinging it and was in the act of firing again when I had to shoot and he fell from his horse".[12]

By citing the French naive painter Henri Rousseau as one of his 'ingredients', Nolan acknowledged stylistic inspiration from a range of unsophisticated traditions of imagery including works by *le douanier* himself, children's or primitive people's painting and folk art.[13] By citing "Kelly's own words" as another ingredient Nolan further acknowledged the power of naive, direct, untutored expression; he counts Ned Kelly and Ern Malley as Australia's best literary artists and he titled a 1954 painting of Kelly's plaster death-mask *Death of a Poet*. When the Ned Kelly paintings were first exhibited in April 1948 James MacDonald, *The Age* art critic and former director of the National Gallery of Victoria, declared: "Nolan has a

Sidney NOLAN, born 1917. *Death of Constable Scanlon*. 1946, Heidelberg, Melbourne. Ripolin enamel on composition board, 90.5 x 121.5 cm. Australian National Gallery, Canberra. Gift of Sunday Reed 1977

second-rate halloween or boogie-woogie notion of depiction — particularly in these Kelly daubs". A year later, however, they were hailed in Paris as "a revelation . . . the work of a true poet and true painter" and a strikingly original "contribution to modern art".[14] Bernard Smith later summed them up as ". . . bright and colourful, with that light and dexterous grace so characteristic of Nolan . . . The wit is eager, the spacing delightful and the mock-heroic sentiment disarmingly charming. . .".[15]

As Nolan explained when the paintings were first exhibited, the Kelly saga "can perhaps be called one of our Australian myths. It is a story arising out of the bush and ending in the bush."[16] During the mid 1950s,

after settling in Europe, he again painted many of the same episodes in a new series — including a death of Constable Scanlon.[17] And he has returned repeatedly to the Kelly theme in later years: portraying Kelly as the iron-masked outsider, as an Irish larrikin, prankster, romantic folk-antihero, victim of historic circumstance. Sometimes he is a watchful 'spirit of the place' — as here; sometimes the pursuer, sometimes the pursued. Ned Kelly was a legend even in his own lifetime. Nolan's square black Kelly silhouette has become an enduring icon in the visual vocabulary of Australian identity. It is an image of the teasing erotic calm which can call forth chaotic violence.

MORALITY AND MATERIALISM by GRAZIA GUNN

Arthur Boyd, *Interior with black rabbit,* 1973

Arthur Boyd was born in 1920 at Murrumbeena, an outer suburb of Melbourne. The family lived in a house built in 1908 by his father Merric Boyd, an artist-potter. Arthur started to paint and to model in clay at an early age. Initially, in the 1930s, he painted landscapes and portraits.

It is, however, the images of the 1940s which define the essence of Boyd's artistic consciousness and remain the source material for his paintings to date. Images from this early period are dislodged from one composition and incorporated into another, linking the past and extending the narrative into the present. Boyd paints stories in the best metaphysical manner. The paintings refer to opposite forces of vice and virtue, compassion and cruelty, tenderness and hate, despair and hope, the spiritual and the material.

"I'd like to feel that through my work there is a possibility of making a contribution to a social progression or enlightenment. It would be nice if the creative effort or impulse was connected with a conscious contribution to society, a sort of duty or service. I think you have to be able to make something which does involve concepts and ideas."

Boyd achieves this and goes beyond it. The themes in his paintings are charged with moral implications.

Interior with black rabbit was painted in Highgate where Arthur Boyd lives when in London. The picture is dated 1973 and it is one of a group of works painted in the early 1970s. In most of these works Boyd quotes images from other paintings while introducing new ones, thus extending his visual vocabulary. The images which have made up Arthur Boyd's pictorial compositions since the 1940s have remained constant throughout his work. The now familiar images in each composition make up a continuous narrative of the artist's field of vision.

Interior with black rabbit with its iconographical links and cross-references is no exception. The painting is one of a pair, the other being *Woman injecting a rabbit.* Both works refer to cruelty, hedonism and material greed. The rabbit is the new element in the two paintings. This image was introduced following a visit to an animal-research laboratory in London. Since everything in Boyd's work has meaning beyond the visual image itself, he recounts what he saw at the laboratory. "I went to see this chap, a research scientist who sticks electrodes into rabbits' brains and he finds the pleasure zone of the brain, and every time the rabbit presses the electrode it gets a surge of pleasure, so the more it presses the more·

shocks it gets and eventually it just goes batty."

In the painting *Woman injecting a rabbit,* gold coins are represented. These had previously been introduced in the Nebuchadnezzar paintings of the 1960s. Coins are Boyd's symbol of materialism and greed, the implication being that money is the modern source of evil which affects everybody; even the artist who, in *Interior with black rabbit,* is represented as a clown holding paint-brushes, a substitute for the deadly syringe the woman is holding in the other painting. The moral implications are similar in both works; varying degrees of greed directing the hand of both artist and scientist.

The image of the artist with a clown's ruff appears in further works and is a reference to Boyd's attempt to join the theatre. The white paint-rag the rabbit is sitting on first appeared as a handkerchief and kite in the 1940s South Melbourne paintings. The overall composition is divided down the middle, the dark tones on one side represent a closed internal space, the brightness on the other represents open space — the gloomy tones of the interior add mysticism to the strange action of the clown-artist aiming his paint-brushes at the black rabbit with the red eye. The high-key landscape visible through the window on the right implies sunny, harmonious order. The landscape parallels the Garden of Eden, reflecting the story of original sin and redemption. The Garden seen through a window offers a glimpse of the ideal but, with a typical Boydian twist, wire is placed in front of the window, making it inaccessible and metaphorically suggesting a Paradise Lost.

Boyd is a master at counterpointing opposite forces both thematically and technically. *Interior with black rabbit* exemplifies Boyd's technical mastery in modulating colour and in applying paint. The two-part composition shows two different ways of painting. On one side leaden brush-strokes create a dense, gloomy backdrop for the rabbit and clown, while on the other light and subtle brush-strokes, twisting and turning, capture the properties of light peculiar to Australia. The landscape is saturated by light of such intensity that it emphasizes the impenetrable opacity of the interior.

Although this work was painted in London, it is the Australian landscape which is represented. It is the artist's homeland that holds the images of his visual code and these in turn have made up a personal system of reference which dominates his style of expression.

Arthur BOYD, born 1920. *Interior with black rabbit.* 1973, Highgate, London. Oil on canvas, 152.4 x 122 cm. Australian National Gallery, Canberra. The Arthur Boyd Gift 1975

Arthur BOYD. *Woman injecting a rabbit.* 1973. Oil on canvas, 152.4 x 122 cm. Australian National Gallery, Canberra. The Arthur Boyd Gift 1975

FORCE OF NATURE by FELICITY ST JOHN MOORE

Danila Vassilieff, *Stenka Razin*, 1953

This bust-length figure of Stenka Razin with arms raised and clasped in a gesture of triumph is Vassilieff's masterpiece in sculpture. It is one of approximately thirty major carvings in a total output of just over a hundred sculptures, many of them quite small, made by the painter-sculptor during the eight years (1947-54) he devoted to sculpture. To his friend and patron, John Reed, who had asked the price of *Stenka Razin* and misspelt the name, he wrote "By the way, the name of it is Stenka Razin, a Russian bandit", concluding his letter with the wishful thought "I hope somebody will be able to buy my Stenka Razin".[1]

Stenka Razin, peasant rebel and ataman (leader) of the Don Cossacks, and executed in Red Square in 1672, was celebrated in legend and song for his daring feats, such as his capture of a Persian princess whom he later tossed into the Volga. Like Razin, Vassilieff was a Cossack, having been born in a village near Rostov-on-Don in South Russia, but his fate was exile from his homeland as a result of siding with the Counter-Revolutionaries (White Russians) in the aftermath of the Russian Revolution.

In the mid 1930s, shortly after his arrival in Australia, Vassilieff used to sing the song of Stenka Razin in his rich bass voice, once threatening to throw his girlfriend into Sydney Harbour. Later, around the time of his second marriage when he tended to revert to the Russian sources of his art, he painted a 'fresco' of Stenka Razin on the fireplace wall of the house he built himself and named Stonygrad at Warrandyte, outside Melbourne.

Besides being a link with his Russian culture, *Stenka Razin* represented for Vassilieff a kind of *alter ego*. Both were men of action with a reputation for cavalier behaviour towards women.

Stenka Razin, 1953, developed from double-sided, half-male and half-female reclining figures of the previous year. These divided figures were conceived as metaphors for change, an idea that is personified in *Dionysus*, a small carving in the same sequence, whose beard is similar to that of *Stenka Razin*.

The sculpture's creation coincides with the return of Vassilieff's wife Elizabeth, in February 1953, from a brief visit to the Soviet Union, suggesting that these two events were connected and that her return, and most likely the books she brought back, precipitated the carving. There was a revival of interest in Stenka Razin in contemporary writings of Russian history. In them he was classed as a seventeenth-century prototype of the twentieth-century revolutionaries.

Indeed, there is a distinct resemblance between the upright rectangular shape of the carving and the wooden frame around Razin in a frequently-reproduced illustration of his execution.[2] Moreover, Vassilieff's adoption of a double-sided image, with frontal and profile views linked by a single eye-hole, mirrors the saying of Razin's followers, often quoted in Soviet histories, "At the head of them stands only one head, but Razin has two". Given Vassilieff's then current preoccupation with divided images, that saying may well have provided the catalyst for his use of opposing viewpoints to portray the conflicting aspects — leader and libertine — of Razin's character.

On one side, the relatively formal, abstract treatment of the profile head would appear to signify leadership and discipline. Two concave planes are arranged one on top of the other suggesting an eye-socket and a hollow cheek; a flat plane incised with parallel lines denotes the back of the head and hair.

On the other side, the libidinous or dionysiac aspect of Razin's character is represented by means of mismatched eyes, which combine to produce a wicked wink; a warlike broken nose; and a barbed beard formed by a double row of tooled serrations. The liveliness of Razin's expression is heightened by the asymmetry of the features, the avoidance of horizontals and verticals, the interplay of positive and negative forms, and the contrasting shapes of the voids — circular eye-hole, elongated gash in the upper arm and pincer or letter shape[3] around the head.

By carving out spaces inside the marble, in particular by undercutting the arms so that they move in space in defiance of gravity, Vassilieff stresses and challenges the tensile strength of the marble. This testing of the material increases the dynamic thrust of the raised-arms pose and drives the eye towards the climax of the gesture — the mechanically grooved fingers of the crossed, clenched hands.

Vassilieff's cut and thrust with the marble depended on his expertise with tools and instinctive grasp of the structure of Lilydale marble; in turn, perhaps, on his original training as an engineer. A man of almost superhuman physical strength, he carved directly into the hard stone with an electric drill attached by a cable to a half-horsepower motor, and a range of fittings such as grinding wheels. His control of the method is evident in the clean-cut edges, the curvilinear rhythms defining the meeting-points of the planes and the constantly varied cross-sections of the arms. Of particular importance to his sculpture was the flexibility of his technique, which, together with his natural resourcefulness, allowed him to respond in kind to the metamorphic character of his chosen material, Lilydale marble.

This marble, from the Thomas Mitchell Quarry, Lilydale, a short distance from Warrandyte, has a wide variety of textures and colours but had been little used by sculptors when Vassilieff began to carve it in 1947. His attachment to Lilydale marble, a marine deposit, was founded principally on its mottling, that is, on the smooth, hard, circular corals which spotted the texture of the stone. These corals provided the perfect foil for Vassilieff's method and his response, first to their shape, and second to their unpredictability, underlies the rare integrity of his sculpture.

Responding to the random distribution of the corals, whose size and shape remained uncertain until the final cutting back and polishing, Vassilieff fully utilized the chance coincidence of flaw and feature. Thus, Razin's bulbous winking eye corresponds with a grey coral discovered and nurtured during the carving process; similarly, his open mouth is formed by a second happy 'accident' in the area between nose and beard.

This dialogue with the grain depended on polishing the surface to reveal the pattern of mottles and intricate veining of the marble. Achieved with the help of machine-tools and various abrasives, the smooth glossy finish unifies the carving and at the same time, through the qualities of transparency and reflection, adds to the effect of movement.

Danila VASSILIEFF, 1897-1958. *Stenka Razin*. 1953, Stonygrad, Warrandyte near Melbourne. Lilydale limestone, 51.2 x 39.5 x 15 cm.
Australian National Gallery, Canberra. Federal Government funds 1973

There is a deeper significance to Vassilieff's affection for the boldly patterned surfaces achievable with Lilydale marble, and that is their resemblance to the brightly painted surfaces of the wooden folk-carvings of his childhood. In addition to being unpredictable and thus a counterpart of his 'spontaneous' carving technique, the marble patterns found in nature were a visual equivalent to folk-art decoration.

The originality of Vassilieff's sculpture lies in his successful marriage of two traditions: the expressive figurative tradition of Russian folk art on the one hand, and the formal language of European modernist art on the other. Indeed *Stenka Razin* is at once primitive and sophisticated: primitive in its simple block-like shape, human scale, vitality and tactility, its combination of organic and mechanical forms and also in its subject matter, since the representatation of popular heroes is common in folk art;

sophisticated in its structural tensions, dramatic changes of plane, unity of form and content, and most of all its individualism – the result, in part, of Vassilieff's identification with his subject.

In retrospect, *Stenka Razin* appears as the embodiment of Vassilieff's expression through the figurative image of his individual, emotional and imaginative experience.[4] The same approach was presented more directly in his paintings, which were the main source of his influence on his younger Melbourne contemporaries, notably Arthur Boyd, John Perceval and Sidney Nolan. The persistence of figurative expressionism in the paintings of those artists gives continued relevance to *Stenka Razin*, which can be seen as the encapsulation of Vassilieff's contribution to Australian art.

FORMS AND LANGUAGES by BETTINA & DESMOND MacAULAY

Robert Klippel, *Opus 247 Metal construction*, 1965, 1968

To announce a truth, as Barthes pointed out, is to stipulate the existence of an enigma.[1]

The truth that Robert Klippel has laboured for decades to announce through his sculptures and drawings is an inner reality predicated on a dominant 'language of forms'. His is a project of late modernism, its aesthetics deriving from tensions between formal logic, chance, inevitability, and closure, and between notions of shape and discrimination, vitality and stillness, and transparency and hiddenness. After a period of apathy its critical reception, which tended (as it still does) to be moral, organicist or zoomorphic, became enthusiastic, Klippel being widely accepted as an independent spirit and one of Australia's greatest artists.[2]

On the assumption that 1988 is indeed a year amenable to re-codings, this essay concerns itself with exploring some contradictions that surround Klippel's truths and enigmas, especially as they relate to *Opus 247 Metal construction*, 1965, 1968. This mid-career sculpture is central to the oeuvre of one of the very few Australian artists whose work is intimately connected with industrial civilization.

Although born in Sydney in 1920, and resident there for most of his life, Robert Klippel chose to locate his significant art studies and experiences beyond Australia. After naval service (1939-45) he studied in England and worked and exhibited in London (1947-48) and Paris (1949-50). In the United States (1957-63) Klippel worked and exhibited in New York and taught sculpture and exhibited in Minneapolis, returning briefly to the latter city as a visiting professor of sculpture (1966-67) after remarriage in London. Of the hundreds of works produced through those experiences, *Opus 247* is a major and pivotal work of a sculptor whose artistic solitariness and early, instinctively internationalist sympathies separated him from the mainstream.

Klippel's project has been explained in modernist terms by his friend, monographer and sometime collaborator and co-exhibitor James Gleeson. Klippel wishes, writes Gleeson, to achieve an aesthetically fruitful union of mechanical and organic forms, and to endow each conformation with an inner logic, so that "the apprehended form is to the hidden form as the skin is to the body, taking its contours and particularities from the forms and functions it contains".[3] Klippel is concerned, that is, with revelation, with making invisible forms visible through a visual 'language of forms'.

Klippel devised the alphabet of his 'language of forms' methodically, studying the underlying shapes employed by others — Picasso, Gaudier-Brzeska, Henry Moore — until he believed his own language to be fully internalized. With this language Klippel cannibalized industry's 'offal', as he had earlier cannibalized art shapes, to make his junk sculptures, metal constructions and assemblages.

The idea of form as essential shaping principle, as inherent and determining, carries an implication of metaform or something like ideal form. Rather than mimesis Klippel, remarkably, pursues a language parallel to nature's. Although he has not made a special study of Plato, Klippel was exposed to some Platonic ideas through the writings of the Indian art-philosopher Ananda Coomaraswamy.[4] The Socratic contradiction in Klippel, striving for a series of small perfections on the way to consummation, is that the imagistic nature of any language denies the possibility of perfection which, if attained, would negate the image.[5] It is a profoundly modernist idea that serial small 'truths' may ultimately disclose an Absolute. And yet at the beginning of Klippel's search for an inner reality there is another paradox. *Opus 48 "Entities Suspended from a Detector"*, the 1948 sculpture displayed the following year at the Galerie Nina Dausset in Paris,[6] could be said to have disjunctively reached an ontological channel, one that accommodates abstract entities, rather than the expected epistemological channel of modernism. Klippel, who believes there is conscious or unconscious direction of the abstract, is uncomfortable with the idea of too large a role for the irrational. One is reminded of cybernetic entropy, where a closed system tends to move from a less to a more probable state. In Klippel's later career, chance is seen (epistemologically) as a contrived release of knowledge.[7]

The rationality of Klippel's project, which has followed this route obsessively to reach *Opus 247*, may yet be linked with a psychology of detachment and retrieved order. The discontinuous linkages of Klippel's life may disclose not a truth or absolute, but a possibility of multiple meanings from new insights into the work of this artist, who has often expressed his belief that art and life are one.[8]

His American experiences aside, Klippel is a first-generation Eurocentric Australian whose early life seems susceptible to a formalist outcome. Klippel's childhood, spanning the 1920s and earlier 1930s, included some years at boarding-school. His Polish-born father operated a thriving textile business and, at seventeen, Robert followed family interests by studying wool-classing. In the young Klippel, dutifulness and industry went with model-making (ships in childhood, aircraft in wartime), and the painstaking manipulation of pre-determined miniature shapes in precise configurations. The track of Klippel's life — then as later, in his American years — seems analogous to the tunneller's obsession with following a true path (and perhaps, eventually, finding the light).

The critical 'American' decade leading to *Opus 247*, which many critics read as a culmination with two-way reference to various chronologically earlier works, is one of significant psychological complexity. There is a cluster of emotional events from 1956 to the sculpture's beginning in 1965. It takes in the physical upheavals of moving from continent to continent, city to city, and retracing the path; two ulcer operations; a marriage breakdown, separation and new friendships; new teaching-posts and workshops; severe financial problems — and their unexpected alleviation; and exhibitions in four cities in two countries.

In the process, Klippel discovered he could incorporate found objects and machine parts in his sculptures, a realisation that opened a material path to *Opus 247*. This work has become increasingly ambiguous in the production of meaning, for example in the 'epistemic break' that discloses the IBM-NCR *materiel* now referring visually both to history and to a changed industrial referent (the technologies of computerization), despite Klippel's self-alienation as an artist from the social process.[9] The modernist organic view — as much alive to decay as growth — which

Robert KLIPPEL, born 1920. *Opus 247 Metal construction.* 1965, 1968, Sydney. Steel, computer parts, wood, 198 x 145 x 126 cm, on
steel stand, 71 x 101.3 x 77.2 cm. Queensland Art Gallery, Brisbane. Gift of the Queensland Art Gallery Foundation 1983

incorporates a residual *memento mori* in the work can also be read as a
postmodern irony.[10]

Opus 247 is a welded and brazed steel sculpture of found objects
(IBM and NCR machine parts) and wood on a steel stand. It was exhibited
in Sydney's Bonython Gallery (in 1969) and Opera House (in 1973), and
was bought in 1983 by the Queensland Art Gallery.

Klippel acknowledged it as "a whole exhibition in one work" and, as
Gleeson observed, it is also a "city of forms" that demands the projected
kineticism of walking around it. Like human cities it is intricately subdi-
vided and its architectures contain and reflect sites of varying formal
power, but its rusting modernist surfaces paradoxically deflect and question meaning.

To Klippel, *Opus 247* is the apotheosis of the 1960s assemblages
which fully engaged him by 1963, a complex reconciliation of concepts
and themes from earlier drawings and metal constructions, that was

followed by a period of simpler works.[11] Gleeson, who reads *Opus 247*
partly through musical images (it is not a lyric, it is orchestrated, it has
scale and movement),[12] gained the consent of Klippel, who defers to
Gleeson's facility with titles, to use the word 'opus' to preface the sculptor's
works. It neatly emphasizes the serial compositional nature of Klippel's
project, in which all works in progress are carefully recorded in notebooks
and given chronological numbers. (In January 1988 Klippel was working
on Opus Numbers 715-720.) It also calls up the Pateresque idea that all art
aspires to the condition of music, without making any concession to
revolutionaries against the extremes of rationalist order like John Cage.

In a world where modernist reality is now at an advanced stage of
deconstruction, Robert Klippel's *Opus 247* has the integrity to provide for
the avenues of meaning through which it may be approached in a
postmodernist future.

SHARED SOLITUDE by MURRAY BAIL

Ian Fairweather, *Monastery*, 1961

In the winter of 1933, as Shanghai was being bombed by the Japanese, Ian Fairweather left the city by train for Peking. On the way north he stopped off at the sacred mountain Tai Shan, in Shantung province. By the time he climbed to the monastery at the summit it was snowing. Fairweather stayed the night. The silence in the monastery was broken only by monks shuffling past and pulling on prayer ropes. And the walls flickered with hundreds of wicks floating in golden bowls. Fairweather left the next day and went on to Peking. Almost thirty years later, in 1961, at his annual exhibition in Sydney, Fairweather showed a painting, large by his standards, titled *Monastery*. Alongside his monogrammed signature he had written in Chinese, almost to himself, "auspicious" or "lucky day".

So the bald chronology of a painting that remains somewhere at the summit of Australian art.

In those intervening years — between the night spent in a monastery and the completion of a painting called "monastery" — Fairweather wandered in a wilderness of misunderstandings with strangers, solitude, poverty, wars, near-death on a raft voyage (see *Lit Bateau* in this anthology), to name just a few of the tribulations; he lived in Bali, in Peking, the Philippines, India, parts of Australia, mostly in the tropics, until he settled for Bribie Island, to the north of Brisbane, in a hut made of thatch and bits of tin: a life devoted to study and meditations on his life and the rendering of it into art. Among its qualities it may be said of *Monastery* that it could hardly have been composed by a person of narrow experience. It is also the product of a reclusive, aloof mind. This can be felt by anyone approaching *Monastery* without knowing the title or anything of the artist.

Fairweather's paintings are meditations on his experiences. Essentially these began in the Philippines in 1936 when he re-composed the Peking he had left only a few months before, and continued through the 1940s in Calcutta and Melbourne with small exquisite remembrances of China — an extreme form of what might be called Post-Impressionism. India in turn was recalled almost as doodles in ink years later, in Cairns.

As Fairweather grew older and settled on his island in Australia he looked back further in time and distance. It took him five years to make something of his perilous raft voyage from Darwin to East Timor (*Lit Bateau*, 1957, has the artist lying on the raft at night, looking distinctly apprehensive). Later still, in the 1960s, his distillation of what he saw as the essence of a group of women bathing in a pool in Bali, or a great temple and its gong, or the jumble of Shanghai are rendered twenty, twenty-five and more years after the event. The images became generalized and more subjective. In the process he developed his own distinctive calligraphy.

In painting *Monastery* the artist's brush-hand and mind wander together over a moment thirty years back in an eventful life, tracing at the same time something of the journey back from that moment, and in doing so the experience is re-experienced. A distant place and a region of the mind overlap. On one level *Monastery* can be read as a map on the difficulty of memory. At a higher, deeper level *Monastery* evokes the privacy and inner harmony of all spiritual experiences. It represents all monasteries, all contemplative silences. "Painting is a personal thing", he said, soon after painting *Monastery*. "It gives me the same kind of satisfaction that religion, I imagine, gives to some people."

Within *Monastery* is also something of the history of modern European art. Except for Surrealism most of the established -isms had made their appearance in Fairweather's work by 1961, but always from a great distance in time and place, and mostly through the sighting of reproductions. And then his interpretations — or what he borrowed for his purposes — have been so individual that some observers who look for a literal transference of, say, Cézanne's short brush-strokes, or an exact treatment of Cubism (with mangoes replacing apples), have experienced difficulties in accepting any such influences at all. Good artists of course don't work in such a plain way. But it does point in Fairweather's case to the inadequacy of descriptions.

Monastery has an unmistakable modern stamp. Cubism and Chinese calligraphy inform its presence; and yet it is far from being a cubist work, much less an example of pure calligraphy.

From 1929 to 1932 Fairweather lived in Shanghai, and Peking through 1935. He became absorbed in all things Chinese. He learned to speak and write the language; he often signed and dated his paintings in Chinese. (Late in life his idea of recreation was to read a Chinese dictionary or practise translations.) He had stood for hours in front of the great calligraphies, and visited a master calligrapher outside Peking and watched as he painted. "There was about them a serenity, a chaste beauty . . .". Similarly he has explained, "I don't like bright colours. The Chinese managed to do their finest paintings with no colour at all . . . To me there's something vulgar about coloured things." In a very real sense Fairweather was a pioneer in mixing with the cultures of the region (including Aboriginal art), while maintaining his European traditions.

Line perhaps not surprisingly entered his oil paintings in 1935, though it was basically an outlining of European concerns. From the late 1940s it wandered virtually non-stop in gouache and ink, delineating figure-groups, or revisiting landscapes increasingly distant in memory. As in much Eastern art, tone had been discarded. His line continued an investigative course until around 1956 when Fairweather evidently realised the danger of producing little more than decorative patterns. He understood too that appearances were more complex.

He began overlapping his line, and when that gave the necessary depth, but threatened congestion, he improvised volume from Cubism, not through a turning of surfaces, but by twisting of line — and here and there opening holes as pictorial windows, ventilation, supplying further illusion of depth with deliberately exposed over-painting. The picture surface was broken up but held together by line. This also seemed to match his view of the world: it consists of many fleeting, inter-related impressions.

It is from 1956 that Fairweather's paintings grow impressive in their depth and complexity; and Fairweather responded in scale.

Then with little warning, towards the end of 1959, he produced twenty paintings, mostly all grey, and entirely abstract. Fairweather called them 'soliloquies'. These memory-blurs, and a larger, slightly more colourful group that followed, lasted little more than six months. By mid-

Ian FAIRWEATHER, 1891-1974. *Monastery*. 1961, Bribie Island near Brisbane. Synthetic polymer paint on four cardboard sheets, overall 144 x 185.5 cm. Australian National Gallery, Canberra. Federal Government funds 1976

1960 Fairweather complained, "After my little dip into abstraction I find I can't get back again and am quite bushed."

To many observers even today this remarkable group represents an aberration, a branching off into nothingness. But aside from their quality — and they are among the finest abstract paintings in Australian art — the most individual and complete in resonance — it can be seen now that they laid the foundations for *Monastery*. It was in the first group to emerge from his foray into 'soliloquies', his brush dipping into the same tin of grey paint. Indeed, without its title, which extends the painting, *Monastery* would be more 'abstract'.

Monastery is shaped by a discursive, light calligraphy. The formation of various cells parallel to the plane, deepened by over-lapping and interlacing, and the many small suggestive brush-touches — and the black hole just above the centre — which imply all kinds of privacies, prevent the work solidifying into stone. Dribbles are left along the bottom to remind again of the original picture surface, and so encourage an entering.

'Shadows' almost slashed on, notice those angled in the bottom corners, also encourage the viewer's entry; and the painted borders on the sides owe something to Aboriginal painting. There is a suggestion of a pink glow, a single blob of turquoise. Otherwise, it is almost entirely grey.

No amount of formal description though can suggest the painting's presence. Fairweather has attempted to reach and understand some deep equilibrium of the senses, based upon his experiences. And so its formal features, its passing references to Europe and the East, cancel each other out to this end, or rather, combine to produce a peculiar knowledgeable calm.

Fairweather occupies a solitary eminence in Australian art. Always admired by artists he was almost seventy when he painted *Monastery* in 1961, and went on to produce further work of outstanding quality, until his death in 1974. In this he has defied the local trajectory: producing his finest work in old age, instead of decline.

LOVE AND THE WIND by TIM JOHNSON

Clifford Possum Tjapaltjarri, *Man's love story*, 1978

This painting can be placed on the ground with the tracks of the mythological ancestors in the same plane as the painted tracks, thus demonstrating its direct relationship to the land it depicts and to the paintings done on the ground, from which it derives. Western Desert paintings like *Man's love story* were first made in 1971, at Papunya in the Northern Territory; Geoff Bardon, the art teacher at that Aboriginal community's school, introduced the use of acrylic paint on portable supports.

Three mythologies are depicted. The principal mythology tells of two men of the Tjungurrayi subsection group. One of the men came west from Yulima to Yinyalyingi where he found the white sugary substance Lurrka on leaves at the foot of some mulga trees. Lurrka indicates the presence of Tjula or honey-ants, for which the man was searching. The predominant iconograph on the left indicates this action. The white u-shape is the seated man, the concentric circles are the hole dug by the man and also the honey-ants' underground chamber. The straight white line is the man's journey-line into the painting from the west. The thin white hooked shape on the man's right is the digging-stick and the Lurrka are the small white shapes above.

The iconograph on the right symbolizes the activities of the other Tjungurrayi man, at Ngalu, a site close by but geographically distinct from Yinyalyingi. Tjungurrayi came to this site, sat down as is shown by the footprints coming in from the top and the brown u-shape, and proceeded to spin hairstring on a simple cross-spindle known as Wurrakurru. The spindle is shown leaning to the upper right from the concentric circles that represent the site Ngalu. The Tjungurrayi sent a bush telegram ("thoughts on the wind") to the Napanati woman with whom he was in love but who belonged to the kinship subsection that he was not entitled to marry. He was so distressed by her approach that he lost concentration on his spinning and his hairstring was blown away by the wind. This is shown in the brown flecks behind him, that is below the brown u-shape.

During the night four Nangala women approached and sat in the darkness around the camps of the two men. Nangala is the correct marriage partner for Tjungurrayi. They are depicted as the dotted u-shapes at the right and left of the painting and are accompanied by their digging-sticks. The large oval area of black dots at the centre symbolizes Kanala, the area in which post-initiatory young men are taught this mythology and the associated law in ceremonies known as Mallierra.

The long bars at the top and bottom of the Kanala are Mirrawarri or mirages but their part and the part of the fawn-coloured wriggly shapes in the left of the painting which represent Kupatadi, an edible green cater-pillar in the narrative, was not described. The white footprints traversing the bottom left of the painting show the path of Arrumai the goanna-man who passed through the area in mythological times, chasing a Kungka or woman. Arrumai himself is represented by the concentric circles halfway along his path. The path of another small goanna-ancestor Kulluntjirri, who eventually went to the lake site Mutjuku, is depicted in the long wavy brown line at the top right of the picture. The coloured background dots symbolize mulga and witchetty seed which was traditionally collected, ground and used in the preparation of a nutritious damper.[1]

Man's love story can clearly be identified as one of Clifford Possum's masterpieces. He painted other larger more complex pictures in the late 1970s and a number of large canvases in the 1980s. But in the 1980s his style has tended towards either enlarged details of more elaborate Dream-ings, symmetrical repetitions of simpler designs or new unusual stories. These more recent developments do not in any way limit his work since its iconographic qualities and its conceptual layerings are its strengths.

Aspects that combine to make this painting unique apart from its beautiful story and extraordinary technique include the relationship of the rectangular shape of the canvas to the formal qualities of the design. The design is still unrestricted, so that although the symbols are roughly centred the aerial view of sites and tracks takes on a topographical character adjusted to its internal meanings which are revealed by the story. Although rarely so complex, a topographical look is a characteristic of the work of artists from the Anmatjera tribe to which Clifford Possum belongs. The complexity of the artist's mind and in particular his ability to depict observations of nature with the equivalent of a bi-lingual fluency, interprets and conveys the poetry that lies at the heart of Aboriginal culture.

Large canvases were produced at Papunya from about 1975 onwards. But whereas the earlier paintings on board utilized brushwork that is often painstakingly delicate and labour-intensive it took some years to develop this on a larger scale closer to that of the original ground-paintings. Part of the reason for the successful scaling-up from the earlier paintings is that in the mid 1970s dots were being painted with brushes instead of sticks. Today Clifford Possum uses a stick for dotting: "slowly use em, not brush, stick, that's like old people . . ."[2] But *Man's love story* is all done with a brush. Hence the subtle variations in the colour, size and shape of the dots and the more spontaneous look to the picture that comes from the faster painting-method. Aboriginal artists always work however with extreme care and concentration. "Every dot slowly and carefully."[3]

To understand the picture apart from its story one needs to consider two points of view. One would suggest that the viewer is outside the frame of reference for comprehending much of the Aboriginal significance. But this belongs to Clifford Possum and his culture and since it is produced for the West the painting gives deep insights into his world. It presents the allegorical characteristics of ancestral figures, the narrative of their exploits, the continuity of the design that records these exploits and the way in which the artist's own personality and style interface with the conceptualized geography to create a contemporary painting style. What might look like flagged or jigsaw-puzzle shapes in subtle tertiary colours are easily identified as desert imagery to the observant. Further, circles, lines and u-shapes forming a vaguely coat-of-arms effect when seen in elevation can be read as illusionistic space, vast since the story pervades space and time, but detailed once the three-dimensional attention-rivetting aspect of the spindle, the tracks and other figurative elements are observed.

From another point of view the viewer is taken into the picture by knowledge of the culture it depicts. In this way it becomes more than just

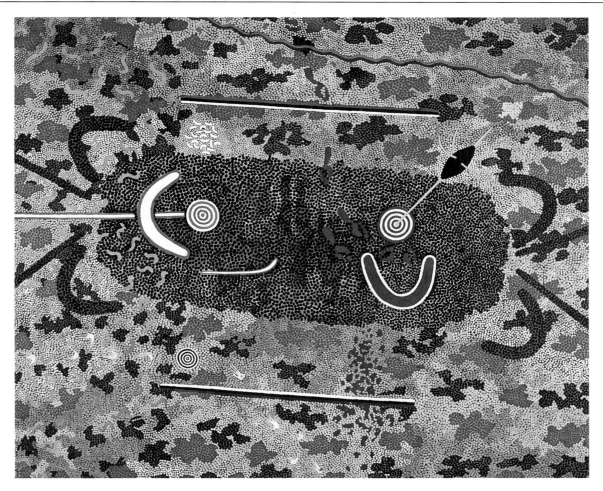

Clifford Possum TJAPALTJARRI, born 1934. *Man's love story.* 1978, Papunya, Northern Territory.
Synthetic polymer paint on canvas, 214.5 x 257 cm. Art Gallery of South Australia, Adelaide. Visual Arts
Board of the Australia Council contemporary art purchase grant 1980

another great painting. It becomes extraordinary that it even exists and stands alongside Western art-history with so much presence and familiarity. Clifford Possum may well have seen some examples of Western art, but his first visit to a major city wasn't till 1984. A more likely explanation is that the materials of acrylic on canvas have a family of stylistic characteristics and specific design-possibilities that develop from the kind of 'truth to materials' philosophy that is common to both Aboriginal art and Abstract Expressionism. In tribal contexts of course the sacred qualities of materials used are of vital importance as is the 'zen' approach to painting that influenced Abstract Expressionism.

Tribal Aboriginal culture indicates a new way of looking at Western art. It still uses symbols that pre-date most European art-history. A complex of orally-transmitted secret information (which brings to mind Tibetan Buddhism) and a set of symbols and teachings combine with a belief in spirit in all matter. This meets a Western technology well versed in destructive powers. But the effects of power and its ability to destroy are exactly what Aboriginal art deals with. For example, many stories are about the destruction of ancestors during or after mythological events and their rebirth and influence on future events. As one Papunya artist recently said: "The money belongs to the ancestors", illustrating just this point, that the ancestors will enable the culture to survive.

In discussing a 1973 version of *Man's love story*, Geoff Bardon recalls

"somehow the men got the idea that I was soon to be married. This misunderstanding brought about many love stories".[6] The story is still painted and a recent Petunia and Budgerigar Dreaming painted by Hilda and Ruth Napaltjarri at Yuendumu contains exactly the same story with the same site Yinyalingi and some details of the women's activities. There are other love stories for example a 'loverboy' possum story and the amorous adventures of a goanna-ancestor and a promiscuous mother-in-law.

Finally a brief description of the painting-method is helpful in explaining the links between the story, the artist and the culture he represents. Over a monochrome background the artist paints all the design elements, working from the concentric circles outwards, recording the symbolic 'traces' of ancestral heritage. Treatment of scale and narrative elements has a verisimilitude related to meaning within the story and geographic space is conceptualized. Hence human footprints could be larger than say geographic features. After the design and its details are recorded the artist begins to fill the picture with dots, varying colour to represent different aspects of the story or landscape. Sometimes the dots cover shapes painted during the design stage, creating strong illusions of three-dimensional space within a generalized flatness. Artists work with the canvas flat on the ground, sitting on it to reach the central areas, using paint-jar lids with the colours carefully mixed to exactly the right consistency for dotting.

PARADISE LOST: PARADISE REGAINED by FRANCES LINDSAY

Peter Booth, *Painting 1982*, 1982

This macabre scene is one of the most disturbing images in Australian art. Peter Booth says that *Painting 1982* is about man's brutality,[1] and certainly this horrific depiction of men devouring each other's flesh in a dark nightmare world is a grim judgement on society and man's violence and inhumanity to man. Here we are confronted with a shocking representation of destruction and carnage, a charnel-house where the living and the dead are massed together, the former feasting on the latter and on the maimed and dying. This is a twilight zone inhabited solely by male creatures, where the victims of one ruined civilization are being consumed by the survivors and mutants of a second, such as the figure with the blazing red eyes who has two sets of hands emerging from the folds of his cocoon-like cape. The human figures are likened to the animal world's scavengers, the crow and the eel, preying on the carrion which surrounds them, while the ominous, gloating six-armed and crab-clawed figure of Beelzebub[2] oversees this sordid banquet. In the background, hovering in a darkened sky above a blazing horizon, is a group of hybrid winged creatures which are half-man, half-insect. They have the power of flight even though they are weighed down by the oversized penile appendages which betray their mortal origins.

If salvation or redemption are to be found in this satanic setting it is with these flying figures who have undergone a transmogrification from human to insect life. They represent man's metamorphosis and transcendence from bestiality to a higher spiritual existence in which man, beasts, insects and organic life co-exist. They might also represent a strategy for survival: escape from danger by metamorphosis into animals or plants is a commonplace in ancient Greek mythology; insects have an important place in Australian Aboriginal stories of creation and regeneration.

Here then is not a depiction of insurmountable horror and despair, but a story of hope and renewal, re-birth and re-incarnation. This is the essence of Peter Booth's art. From darkness and ignorance man can emerge with enlightenment and spiritual knowledge to a new life. The journey from darkness to light, from ignorance to knowledge, from a cataclysmic world to an arcadian realm of peace and beatitude, is the most consistent and overriding theme in Booth's art. This visionary quality places him amongst those great late-eighteenth-century and early-nineteenth-century artists whose work he admires, such as Francisco Goya, William Blake and Samuel Palmer. Booth's art has the double-edged aspect of Goya's work in particular, where violence is counterbalanced with comedy and pessimism with optimism. In *Painting 1982*, the heaped dead bodies call to mind Goya's series of etchings *Disasters of War*, c1808-1815; the image of cannibalism evokes Goya's *Saturn devouring one of his children*, c1820-23; and the theme of man's violence to his fellow man suggests Goya's *Fight with clubs*, where two men batter each other in a merciless exchange. Goya's concern, like Booth's today, was for humanity and the threat which it brings to its own existence through ignorance and brutality.

The genesis and evolution of Booth's images are to be found in an impressive body of works on paper which he has produced since the early 1960s. The theme of cannibalism first appears in a drawing dated June 1979,[3] and continues in subsequent drawings and paintings until 1983; the image of metamorphosis appears around 1980, in a drawing of a two-headed cocoon-shaped man,[4] and recurs in several guises in later works where we see hybrid creatures with human heads and insect or animal bodies. The cocoon image is repeated often — as an anonymous swaddled sheath, as human figures wrapped from head to foot in bandages, and as thick folds of fabric enveloping figures. It is the chrysalis through which man will be transformed into an imago (the perfect form of an insect). In the history of art, there are numerous images of man and beast united in form. Often these are symbolic representations of man's transgression as a result of his primitive and instinctual nature. In Booth's art this transmutation is double-edged. It occurs because of man's retreat to sub-human behaviour, but it also represents his ultimate salvation.

Painting 1982 gives expression to our deepest psychological fears and anxieties, warns us of the dangers lurking within man's heart and reminds us of the unimaginable catastrophes which are possible in an age of nuclear threat. Many of the images in Peter Booth's work come from his dreams or subconscious mind, others are drawn from his direct experience and observation of nature. In *Painting 1982* the large eel or snake, an age-old symbolic representation of Satan, is in fact derived from Booth's observation of large eels in the Hastings River, on the north coast of New South Wales, which he frequently visited around that time; the carcass bones come from the sight of uncovered butchers' refuse trucks; and the dramatic torso and head in the right-hand corner, though reminiscent of foreshortened figures in seventeenth-century Italian paintings by Caravaggio, is a painter colleague who posed for Booth.

Booth's art has always welcomed a psychological reading. From the late 1960s until 1974 he produced a series of large over-lifesized paintings, often referred to as 'Doorway paintings', which were vertical black rectangles with a thin framing border of colour on three sides. Superficially within the Minimal aesthetic, these paintings reflected the viewer in their shiny expressive surfaces and so mirrored personal thoughts and fantasies. Booth was born in wartime England and lived in Sheffield until he was seventeen: these black rectangles had associations with the industrial skyline of Booth's native city, remembered as seen through a window at night by a child; they also relate to drawings of factories and landscapes done in Melbourne at the same time as the abstract paintings. The nocturnal landscape seen through a window and the image of man journeying down a darkened road towards lights were the key elements in a large group of gestural drawings produced in 1976[5] which culminated in 1977 in Booth's first large figurative painting.[6] In these drawings we find the image of man travelling through a landscape, blinded sometimes by explosions and cities in flames, but moving always towards light. This is the epic story of Booth's art. Man must make his journey through darkness and descend through the holocaust to Hell, before being reborn into a new world of peace and harmony. Paradise may be lost, but it can also be regained.

Peter BOOTH, born 1940. *Painting 1982.* 1982, Melbourne. Oil on canvas, 197.7 x 274 cm. Art Gallery of South Australia, Adelaide.
A.M. Ragless Bequest Fund 1983

WHERE TRUTH IS NO STRANGER TO FICTION
by NICHOLAS BAUME

Imants Tillers, *Kangaroo blank,* 1988

In 1770, with Captain Cook in what is now north Queensland, Joseph Banks first spotted "an animal as large as a greyhound, of a mouse colour and very swift".[1] He asked an Aborigine its name. Legend now has it that in his native tongue the Aborigine replied, "I don't understand" — an expression Banks misunderstood as the name of this strange creature, the "kanguru".[2] Banks took back to England from his voyage on the Endeavour countless botanical and other specimens, including a kangaroo skin. To preserve the image of this extraordinary animal, Banks commissioned "the greatest of English animal painters",[3] George Stubbs, to depict it using as a model the skin collected in Australia; perhaps the skin was stuffed or inflated for its portrait session. Stubbs also had access to drawings by a shipboard artist, Sydney Parkinson.

Imants Tillers learned of Stubbs's painting through its reproduction with the title *Kangaroo* as a frontispiece in the 1962 publication of Banks's *Endeavour Journal*.[4] The painting was first shown, in London in 1773, with the title *A Portrait of the Kongouro from New Holland, 1770*.[5] Tillers was intrigued by this picture of a kangaroo standing in its native habitat — or rather, by this reconstruction, without any first-hand observation, of a hitherto unknown animal in an equally unfamiliar landscape. Stubbs never set foot in Australia, nor ever laid eyes on a kangaroo. The master of accurate animal portraiture had made use of the evidence available, but his picture is nevertheless of a partly imaginary animal in a wholly imaginary Australian landscape.[6]

Imants Tillers is an art-world fossicker, hunting for images to be 'melted down' and re-cast in a mould of his own creation. On several levels *Kangaroo* was suited to this process of transformation. Stubbs's painting is sweetly ironic for Tillers, an artist preoccupied with working from images he has seen only in reproduction. In *Kangaroo* the usual relation is inverted; instead of the Australian artist being frustrated by his isolation from the original overseas, in this instance the European artist was handicapped by his distance from Australia.

Stubbs's image — adhering to the conventions of its genre — is presented as a descriptively objective rendering of a kangaroo *in situ*. There are, as might be expected, obvious errors (obvious over two hundred years later). Nevertheless, to see Tillers's use of *Kangaroo* as a send-up of its 'mistakes' would be to miss his point entirely. Tillers's work repeatedly celebrates the mistaken and rejoices in the inauthentic — not simply to abandon 'truth', but to recognize the productivity of error.

Insofar as it convinced its contemporary audience, Stubbs's image turned fantasy into truth. Not an eternal truth — as our present scepticism suggests — but a provisional one. Tillers's fascination with mistakes is not sheer perversity, it is appreciation of the genealogy behind truths. Mistakes, the German philosopher Nietzsche argued, invariably end up as truths; "That which we now call the world is the result of a number of errors and fantasies".[7] So it is with our understanding of the term 'kangaroo', founded apparently upon nothing other than misunderstanding.

In *Kangaroo blank*, Tillers's reworking of Stubbs's painting, the notorious animal has disappeared, leaving only a background of 'Australian' landscape. The unlikely kangaroo was posed on a rocky outcrop which now lies bare and uninhabited. The image begins to look like a stage that has been left blank, and that may be what Tillers refers to in his title.[8] Stubbs's image is, however, only half the story.

Tillers does not simply copy images he finds in the work of other artists. Whereas in *Kangaroo blank* the kangaroo has been subtracted, another image has been added. To the right of the kangaroo's former standpoint the diagramatic outline of a cylindrical column has appeared, with perspectival lines radiating across the picture from its vertical axis. This column is used in the art of a Japanese-American painter, Arakawa, working in New York.

An exploration of the "mechanism of meaning"[9] is Arakawa's stated purpose, attempting to picture the mind's unconscious thought-processes. Lending a different meaning to the word 'blank', Arakawa asks, "What is emitted point-blank at a moment of thought, anyway?"[10] Tillers's layering of two contrasting images from utterly different contexts is something of a point-blank confrontation, a new thought emerging from a collision of types. Both Stubbs's and Arakawa's images are faintly absurd, the first because it suggests accuracy without first-hand observation, the second as it purports to visualize the immaterial — a moment of thought. The contrast of these images is, however, only the beginning of Tillers's transformation. From Georges Braque to Andy Warhol, from Piet Mondrian to Sol LeWitt, the grid is a recurrent form in twentieth-century art. Tillers reinvents the grid in a way that makes light of its pretensions (as pure form without connotation, as flat surface without illusion), while exploiting it as a pictorial device. In *Kangaroo blank* Tillers plays with the flatness of the grid (formed by a series of individual canvasboards fitted together) by superimposing another, differently gridded layer of canvasboards on which the radiating column is painted. Radial lines create an illusion of space and depth, in contrast to the typically flat and literal lines of the modernist grid. The superimposed layer, only partially painted with the background landscape, also looks like a half-open window onto this strange scene. Tillers takes delight in combining elements that, in modernist terms, seem incompatible; objective flatness and illusionistic depth.[11]

For all its intellectual sophistication, *Kangaroo blank* is richly sensuous as painting. Through his technique of layering various media — including acrylic and metallic paints, gouache, oilstick — Tillers achieves an extraordinary range of surfaces and textures. The diagramatic column, for example, is painted in metallic gold, its radiating arms taking on a more symbolic than scientific value. Combined with a now empty, rather brooding landscape, the image relates to nineteenth-century romantic and symbolic landscapes of northern European derivation. Tillers's parents were displaced by war to Sydney from Latvia, a northern extension of the German-Baltic culture which produced the intense sparsity of Caspar David Friedrich's paintings. As the forms of the painting emerge from a densely-painted black background, a study takes shape in the symbolism of light and dark. A window — that which allows light (or spirit) into a darkened space — permits us to glimpse the column's golden beams distributing their ethereal light.[12]

It is the questioning of identity that links the themes of Tillers's work.

Imants TILLERS, born 1950. *Kangaroo blank*. 1988, Mosman, Sydney. Synthetic polymer paint, gouache, oilstick, oil on 78 canvasboards, overall 213 x 196 cm. Yuill/Crowley

Frontispiece, J.C.Beaglehole, The Endeavour
Journal of Joseph Banks, 1962

In *Kangaroo blank* Tillers refers to our past reliance, whether we be Aboriginal or Euro-Australian, on outsiders' representations of who we are, even when their perspective — like Stubbs's — is well-intentioned but ill-informed. The more we look at his paintings, the more pervasive Tillers's own presence becomes, not only through his very particular method of painting but also through constant references to the artist's role and his shifting identity. Tillers's own name may appear in his works and their titles, or be somehow suggested by forms he depicts.[13] In *Kangaroo blank* the letter "I" is suggested by Arakawa's column and by the area just to its left, not painted over with landscape. "I", the first-person–singular pronoun, may also function as a noun (as in "The I"), referring to the metaphysical subject or ego, as well as to the initial of Tillers's first name.

In this context, Tillers's work is perfectly encapsulated by the words of Arakawa, who refers to art as "A condition of suspended confusion through which 'I' may shift under observation".[14]

Each of the canvasboards that comprise one of Tillers's paintings is individually numbered in a continuous sequence. The artist considers the totality of his canvasboards to be one monumental, ongoing work. The realization of such an all-inclusive work (there were at the beginning of 1988 well over 16,000 components) would be preposterous, its installation an impossible confusion. Drawn, however, from that huge work — like the three hundred works in the present anthology drawn from two hundred years of Australian art history — the panels comprising *Kangaroo blank* suspend, for a moment, the unending confusion.

NOTES TO ESSAYS

Mawalan Marika, *The Wawelag Sisters and Yulungurr the Rainbow Serpent*, 1959, by Michael A. O'Ferrall, Curator of Aboriginal and Asian Art, Art Gallery of Western Australia, Perth

1   J.A. Tuckson, R.M. Berndt, in R.M.Berndt (ed), *Australian Aboriginal Art*, Sydney: Ure Smith, 1964.
2   N. Williams, in N. Craburn, *Ethnic and tourist arts: Cultural expressions from the fourth world*, Berkeley: University of California Press, 1976.

Charlie Numblar, *Wandjina spirit*, c1973, by John E Stanton, Curator, Anthropology Museum, The University of Western Australia, Perth

1   I.M. Crawford, "Wandjina paintings", in R.M. Berndt & E.S. Phillips (eds), *The Australian Aboriginal heritage: An introduction through the arts*, Sydney: Australian Society for Education through Art, in association with Ure Smith, 1973, pp. 108-117.
2   R.M. & C.H. Berndt, with J.E. Stanton, *Aboriginal Australian art: A visual perspective*, Sydney: Methuen Australia, 1982, pp. 149-50.
3   George Grey, *Journals of two expenditions of discovery in Northwest and Western Australia*, 2 vols, London: Her Majesty's Government, 1841.
4   J.R.B. Love, "Rock paintings of the Worora and their mythological interpretation", *Journal of the Royal Society of Western Australia*, 16, Perth, 1920/30, pp. 1-24.
5   H. Petri, *Sterbende Welt in Nordwestaustralien*, Braunschweig: Limbach, 1954, pl. 20c.
6   I.M. Crawford, *The art of the Wandjina*, Melbourne: Oxford University Press, 1968, pp. 79-80.

Declan Apuatimi, *Male figure*, c1973, by Margaret K.C. West, Curator of Aboriginal Art & Material Culture, Museums & Art Galleries of the Northern Territory, Darwin

The principal monograph on the work of Declan Apuatimi is Margaret K.C. West, *Declan, a Tiwi Artist*, Perth: Australian City Properties Limited, 1987.

Peter Marralwanga, *Ngalyod the Rainbow Serpent*, 1983, by Luke Taylor, Visiting Research Fellow, Australian Institute of Aboriginal Studies, Canberra

1   He died there in 1987. Readers should refrain from mentioning Marralwanga's name to people from this region, for it may cause distress to his close relatives.
2   Western Arnhem Land Aborigines recognise a hierarchy of creator Beings. The first Creator was an androgynous Rainbow Serpent called Yingarna. The son of this Being is Ngalyod, and the daughter is Ngalkunburrlyaymi, a female water-spirit often painted as a woman with a fish's tail. It is generally agreed that it was Ngalyod who travelled under the earth and created sacred places, Ngalyod is also occasionally attributed with androgynous characteristics, although in this essay I identify the figure as a male.
3   See P. Cooke, *An exhibition of paintings by*

Djakku (Peter Marralwanga), Maningrida: Maningrida Arts and Crafts, 1981.
4   See P. Cooke, *op. cit.*
5   See full discussion of Marralwanga's repertoire in Luke Taylor, *"The same but different": Social reproduction and innovation in the art of the Kunwinjku of Western Arnhem Land*, unpublished Ph.D. thesis, Australian National University, Canberra, 1987.

John Lewin, *Kangaroos*, 1819, by Elizabeth Imashev. Pictures Research Librarian, Mitchell Library, State Library of New South Wales, Sydney

1   Now in the Mitchell Library, Sydney, the Bowman Flag, made by members of the Bowman family, is of cream silk, painted with flowers and a kangaroo and emu bearing a coat of arms.
2   The definitive discussion on *The Kangaroo in the Decorative Arts* is the catalogue of an exhibition of that title prepared by Terence Lane, National Gallery of Victoria, Melbourne, 1979.
3   *Historical Records of Australia*, series I, vol. X, pp. 136-138. Despatch with enclosures marked "no. 23 of 1819," dated 25 March 1819 from Governor Macquarie to Earl Bathurst. Original now in the Public Record Office, London.
4   The engraving faces p. 236 of Oxley's *Journals …*, London, 1820. The watercolour, held by the Mitchell Library, Sydney (ML ref. SVIB/ARB/1) is dated "May 5, 1824", probably added later. It is similar to three other watercolours thought to be by Taylor, also in the Mitchell Library: "Erskine Park New South Wales", "Treachery Head N.S.W.", "Port Macquarie New South Wales."
5   *Balier's New South Wales Gazetteer and Road Guide …*, Sydney, 1866, pp. 10, 587.
6   The 1819 date on this elaborated watercolour suggests that Lewin was working directly from Evans's sketch, or possibly from Taylor's monochrome watercolour, at the same time as he was working from Evans's other sketches for the Government Despatch of 25 March 1819.
7   During his first years in the colony he collected specimens, drew and engraved the plates for his only two published works: *Prodromus Entomology …*, London, 1805, and *The Birds of New Holland …*, London, 1808; a second edition of *The Birds* was published in Sydney by Lewin himself in 1813.
8   Koalas and Platypus, Mitchell Library, Variegated lizard, private collection; Opossum, Art Gallery of South Australia.
9   See H. J. Frith & J. H. Calaby, *Kangaroos*, Melbourne: Cheshire, 1969, p. 27.
10. One, in oils by an unknown artist, is now in the Mitchell Library. It was formerly in the possession of the family of J.T. Bigge, the Royal Commissioner who came from London in 1819-20 to investigate Macquarie's administration. A mid-nineteenth-century watercolour copy appeared for sale at a Christie's auction, Melbourne, 14 April 1986.

William Strutt, *Black Thursday, February 6th, 1851*, 1864, by Christine Downer, Picture Librarian, State Library of Victoria, Melbourne

1   *Herald*, Melbourne, 6 February 1883, pp. 4-5; *Herald*, 7 February 1883, p. 3, col. 4-5; a letter, signed "One who always read Garryowen", appeared next to Garryowen on 7 February, recommending Strutt's *Black Thursday* and the autotypes after it.
2   William Strutt, *The Australian Journal of William Strutt 1850-1862*, edited by George Mackaness, Parts I and II, Sydney, 1958. A typescript of the journal is held in the Rex Nan Kivell Collection, National Library of Australia, Canberra, NK 4367, no. 1862/33.
3   The *Herald* and the *Argus* carry reports of the fires from 7 February 1851 onwards.
4   Heather Curnow, *The life and art of William Strutt*, Martinborough, New Zealand: Alister Taylor, 1980. This monograph provides an exhaustive account of Strutt's life and work.
5   Heather Curnow, *William Strutt*, catalogue of an exhibition presented by the Australian Gallery Directors Council, Sydney, 1980, p. 14.
6   Barbara Scott, "Louis-Philippe's Musée historique in the Chateau of Versailles", *Apollo*, London, November 1987, pp. 358-361; *All the banners wave: Art and War in the Romantic Era 1792-1851*, catalogue of an exhibition at Brown University, Providence, Rhode Island, 1982, pp. 21-26.
7   *Art Journal*, London, 1864, p. 251.
8   Letter of Sir Redmond Barry to Augustus Tulk, 21 January 1865, in Public Library Records, Public Record Office of Victoria.
9   *Argus*, Melbourne, 23 November 1868, p. 5, col. 6. Smith mentions that £60 had been subscribed in London for the purchase.
10 Letter from Strutt to the Editor of the *South Australian Register*, Adelaide, dated 13 July 1883, reprinted in Wivell's *Catalogue of a Grand Fine Art Exhibition of William Strutt's Great Historical Picture Black Thursday*, [1883].
11 Wivell, *op. cit.*
12 *Argus*, 16 March 1883, reprinted in the Wivell catalogue, no pagination.
13 Victorians' Jubilee Exhibition, Catalogue, Melbourne, 1884. *Black Thursday* was no. 420.
14 Victorian Gold Jubilee Exhibition 1851-1901, Art catalogue, Bendigo, 1901, no. 156.
15 William Gilbee (1825-1885) bequeathed £1,000 to the National Gallery of Victoria to send an artist to England to paint a picture of historical interest. E. Phillips Fox's *Landing of Captain Cook at Botany Bay, 1770* (1902) and John Longstaff's *Arrival of Burke, Wills and King at the deserted camp at Cooper's Creek, Sunday evening, 21st April, 1861* (1907) were the result.
16 Letter of Thomas Gill to the President of the Public Library Board of South Australia, 17 December 1902, Picture Collection, La Trobe Library, Melbourne.
17 The painting has been on display since the La Trobe Library building opened in 1965. Studies

for the painting include: *"Black Thursday. A rush for life through Cape Otway Forest... 1851"*, watercolour of 1851 in Strutt's *Victoria the Golden* in the Victorian Parliamentary Library; *The actors' cart, Black Thursday, February 6th 1851*, oil on paper, c1863, illustrated in Deutscher Fine Art catalogue, Melbourne, November 1987; *Black Thursday* (compositional drawing), pencil and wash, Rex Nan Kivell Collection, National Library of Australia, Canberra; 2 pencil studies, *Boy on cart*, and *Man on horse*, City of Ballaarat Fine Art Gallery; *Black Thursday, Melbourne, Victoria*, pencil and watercolour, c1863, Australian National Gallery, Canberra.

18 Robert Hughes, *The Art of Australia*, Penguin, revised ed., 1970, pp. 49-50.

19 Curnow, *ops. cit.* These two works contain the most comprehensive published research on Strutt and have been largely responsible for major changes in public and official taste in the acquisition policies of Australian art museums.

Eugene von Guérard, *North-east view from the northern top of Mount Kosciusko*, 1863, by Tim Bonyhady, art historian and lawyer, Canberra

BIBLIOGRAPHY: *Eugene von Guérard's Australian Landscapes*, Melbourne: Hamel & Ferguson, 1866-68; Georg Neumayer, *Results of the Magnetic Survey of the Colony of Victoria executed during the Years 1858-1864*, Mannheim, Germany: Schneider, 1869; Candice Bruce, *Eugen von Guérard*, Canberra: Australian National Gallery/ Sydney: Australian Gallery Directors Council, 1980; Candice Bruce, Edward Comstock & Frank McDonald, *Eugene von Guérard: A German Romantic in the Antipodes*, Martinborough, New Zealand: Alister Taylor, 1982; Tim Bonyhady, *Images in Opposition: Australian landscape painting 1801-1890*, Melbourne: Oxford University Press, 1985; Tim Bonyhady, *Australian Colonial Paintings in the Australian National Gallery*, Canberra: Australian National Gallery/ Melbourne: Oxford University Press, 198[7].

Louis Buvelot, *Winter morning near Heidelberg*, 1866, by Jocelyn Gray, Art historian, Melbourne

1 First exhibited as *Summer afternoon, Templestowe*, by 1888 its title had shifted to *Summer evening near Templestowe*, a better pair to *Winter morning near Heidelberg*.

2 *In lit.* Abram-Louis Buvelot to Eugène Girardet, 27 December 1875.

3 From a letter of Mrs Charles Perry, in R. Perry, *Contributions to an Amateur Magazine*, quoted James Grant & Geoffrey Serle, *The Melbourne Scene 1803-1956*, Carlton, Victoria: Melbourne University Press, p. 59.

4 National Gallery of Victoria, Melbourne.

5 Calder, Parker & Seddon, *Ruffey Creek Reviewed*, Centre for Environmental Studies, University of Melbourne, 1974, Table 5.

6 *Ibid.*, pp. 17-18.

7 Australian National Gallery, Canberra.

8 Jocelyn Gray, "A New Vision: Louis Buvelot's press in the 1870s", *Studies in Australian Art*, Department of Fine Arts, University of Melbourne, 1978, pp. 15-26.

9 *Argus*, Melbourne, 11 September 1879.

10 Margaret Kiddle, *Men of Yesterday*, Carlton, Victoria: Melbourne University Press, 1961, pp. 478-9 &

ch. 19, "The End of the Beginning".

Major James Taylor, *A Panoramic View of Sydney*, 1823, by Robert Dixon, Lecturer, Department of English, James Cook University of North Queensland, Townsville

1 Richard D. Altick, *The Shows of London*, Cambridge, Massachusetts: Harvard University Press, 1978, chapters 10 and 13. The painted walls did not move.

2 For biographical details see Rex & Thea Rienits, *Early Artists of Australia*, Sydney: Angus & Robertson, 1963, pp. 194-195.

3 See Bernard Smith, *European Vision and the South Pacific*, revised edition, Sydney: Harper & Row, [1985], pp. 200-1 and 234-5.

4 For reproductions of the watercolours, notes on their provenance, and discussion of the problems of dating and attribution, see Tim McCormick (ed.), *First Views of Australia, 1788-1825*, Sydney: David Ell Press, 1987.

5 See John Ritchie, *Punishment and Profit: The Reports of Commissioner John Bigge on the Colonies of New South Wales and Van Diemen's Land*, Melbourne: Heinemann, 1970.

6 See Jeanette Hoorn, "Joseph Lycett: The Pastoral Landscape in Early Colonial Australia", *Art Bulletin of Victoria*, Melbourne: National Gallery of Victoria, no. 26, 1986, pp. 4-14.

7 See J.B. Hirst, *Convict Society and its Enemies*, Sydney: George Allen & Unwin, 1986, p. 41.

8 See Howard Tanner, *Converting the Wilderness: The Art of Gardening in Colonial Australia*, Sydney: Australian Gallery Directors Council, 1979, ch. 1.

9 Hirst, *Convict Society and its Enemies*, pp. 37-8.

10 Ritchie, *Punishment and Profit*, pp. 199-200.

11 See Rollo Gillespie, *Viceregal Quarters*, Sydney: Angus & Robertson, 1975.

12 Morton Herman observes that "this drawing . . . is, architecturally, just about as unreliable as such a thing could be." *The Early Australian Architects and their Work*, Sydney: Angus & Robertson, revised edition, 1970, pp. 87-8.

13 Peter Cunningham, *Two Years in New South Wales* (1827), cited in Suzanne Mourot, *This Was Sydney: A pictorial history*, Sydney: Ure Smith, 1969, p.30.

14 Ritchie, *Punishment and Profit*, pp. 149, 158.

15 See Robert Dixon, *The Course of Empire*, Melbourne: Oxford University Press, 1986, pp. 57-8.

16 Macquarie to Bathurst, 8 October 1814, *Historical Records of Australia*, I, 8, p. 368.

Augustus Earle, *Mrs John Piper, with Thomas, Eliza, Anne and William Piper*, 1826, by Joan Kerr, Associate Professor, Department of Fine Arts, University of Sydney

1 The painting is not signed or dated. Either about April or August 1826 would be the most likely dates, the former because Captain Piper held a "magnificent fete" at Henrietta Villa in late April which appears to have marked re-entry into society after mourning the death of a son Hugh in July 1825, as well as celebrating a temporary reprieve from insolvency. But Ann was then very pregnant; hence a couple of months after the birth of Frederick in June 1826 would be a more

likely time for Piper to have commissioned the work. The fact that he had taken out a massive mortgage on his property in March and in April had been almost forced to sell up did not, characteristically, curtail his extravagances.

2 The dates of the children's births etc. have been compiled from various sources, particularly the Mutch Index (Mitchell Library) and K.A. Johnson & M.R. Sainty's edited *Census of New South Wales November, 1828*, Sydney, 1985. Elizabeth Imashev at the Mitchell Library also gave genealogical assistance. Mrs Piper's name was entered as "Ann" in the 1828 census and various other places, although "Mary Ann" on her tombstone in the Presbyterian section of the Bathurst General Cemetery. The sketch in the National Library of Australia which may be John Piper junior is illustrated in Eve Buscombe, *Artists in Early Australia and their Portraits*, Sydney: Eureka Research, 1978, ill. 6/46, p. 199.1. That no final oil painting is known to have eventuated may well have been due to the catastrophic collapse of the family fortunes (although portraits by Earle are still being discovered).

3 I would like to thank Frank McDonald, Sydney for informing me that the child I am suggesting is Alexander Septimus Piper is in mourning. His dress was identified by Marion Fletcher, Melbourne, and confirmed by the Victoria & Albert Museum, London. Mr McDonald made many helpful suggestions about this painting, and the other Piper portraits, which helped shape this essay.

4 Cedric Flower, *Clothes in Australia: A pictorial history 1788-1980s*, Kenthurst, New South Wales: Kangaroo Press, 1984, p. 26.

5 Dr Lang's Scots Church in Sydney did not open until 1826. (Piper was president of the committee for its erection.) Until then the family's regular place of worship was St Philip's Church of England. In Bathurst, Piper also helped found a Presbyterian church, again as chairman of the building committee. The first minister married the Pipers' governess.

6 See "Henry Kitchen" and "James Wyatt" in Howard Colvin, *A Biographical Dictionary of British Architects 1600-1840*, London: John Murray, 1978.

7 For the story of the erection of Henrietta Villa see Helen Proudfoot, "Captain Piper and Henrietta Villa", *JRAHS*, Sydney, vol. 59, no. 3, 1973, and Philip Cox & Clive Lucas, *Australian Colonial Architecture*, Melbourne: Lansdowne, 1978, p. 149. Both Henrietta Villa and Government House, Sydney, had the ubiquitous colonial verandah added to their original designs.

8 For Governor Brisbane's portrait see Tim Bonyhady, *The Colonial Image*, Sydney: Ellsyd Press, 1987, p. 16, and Harold Spencer, "The Brisbane Portraits", *JRAHS*, vol. 52, pp. 1-8.

9 *The Tasmanian*, Hobart, called Piper "the Tax-gatherer adorned with a pair of Admiral's epaulettes" after his fall from grace in April 1827. It is quoted in M. Barnard Eldershaw [Marjorie Barnard and Flora Eldershaw], *The Life and Times of Captain John Piper*, Sydney: Ure Smith, 1939, reprinted Ure Smith 1973, p. 144, a book I have relied on for much biographical information.

10 Peter Chapman (ed.), *The Diaries and Letters of G.T.W.B. Boyes: volume I 1820-1832*, Melbourne:

Oxford University Press, 1985, pp. 189-90, letter to Mary Boyes dated Sydney, 6 May 1824.

11 J.H. Donohoe, *Norfolk Island 1788-1813: The people and their families*, Sydney: privately published, 1986. The class consciousness of the Sydney 'exclusives' is discussed more fully in Joan Kerr, "Views, Visages, Invisibility: Themes in the art of colonial New South Wales" in Barry Pearce & Patricia R. McDonald (eds), *The Artist and the Patron*, Sydney: Art Gallery of New South Wales, 1988.

12 The wedding was celebrated very quietly by private license at St Philip's, Sydney; John and Eliza Harris were the witnesses and Rev. William Cowper the celebrant. The family was apparently not aware of its date until it was revealed (from the St Philip's Church Register and the Bigge Report: Appendix, ML A 2130, p. 1) in Marjorie Barnard's entry on John Piper for the *Australian Dictionary of Biography*, vol. 2, 1967.

13 Elizabeth Garling called Piper "The Prince of Australia", according to M. Barnard Eldershaw, *op. cit.*, p. 178.

14 Early in 1826, the new governor, Ralph Darling, abolished the lucrative post of Naval Officer and past muddle and mismanagement soon overtook Piper. In April 1827, Piper tried to drown himself. At the auction sale at Henrietta Villa on 4 June 1827 neither Daniel Cooper, the mortgagee and new owner of the house, nor any other emancipist bidder, was invited to luncheon, a gesture which caused much ill-feeling and lost Piper money. His fair-weather exclusive friends did not prove generous. (See M. Barnard Eldershaw, *op. cit.*, pp. 146-47.)

15 Tim Bonyhady, *Australian Colonial Paintings in the Australian National Gallery*, Canberra: Australian National Gallery, 198[7], pp. 90-95.

16 Garling senior lent the Captain's portrait by "Earl" to the "Exhibition of the Society for the Promotion of the Fine Arts in Australia: the First", held in Sydney in 1847 (no. 123), although it is not known whether this was the full-length painting. The two large paintings were presented to the Mitchell Library in 1921 by R.H. Cox Esq. and Mrs Bertha Dale (nee Cox) — connections of both the Piper and Garling families through William Cox's son Edgar who married Mary Andrewina Piper in 1843, William Cox himself being Piper's cousin. See L.M. Mowle, *A Genealogical History of Pioneer Families of Australia*, Adelaide: Rigby, fifth edition 1978, pp. 109-129 (under Cox).

17 A critic in *The South East Asian Register*, Sydney, part 1, no. 1, October 1827, considered Earle a better view than portrait painter; cited Eve Buscombe, *op. cit.*, p. 68.

18 Few personal details are known about Ann. She possibly played the violoncello since Elizabeth Macquarie sent her one as a farewell gift, mentioned in a letter of 9 February 1822 (Piper Papers, Mitchell Library). Surviving fragments of Anne Piper's journal for 1841 (Mitchell Library) give some indication of her mother's sociable, easygoing and apparently conventional character. Ann's mother, Mary Smith, died on Norfolk Island in 1792. A James Sheers (presumably her father) was employed as an assistant in the Sydney Hospital dispensary on 28 April 1814 at the low, unskilled, salary of £25 per annum, no connection

with the Pipers being acknowledged then. In 1838, however, James Sheers died on Piper's property at Bathurst, aged 103 (M. Barnard Eldershaw, *op. cit.*, p. 31 and Bathurst District Historial Society). Yet when Edgar Cox provided information for his mother-in-law's death certificate in 1872, he gave Ann's maiden name as "Shires"; her father's name and occupation unknown; mother unknown; and date and place of her marriage to Captain Piper unknown. She obviously remained reticent about her past. How James Sheers fitted into the Piper household at Alloway Bank, Bathurst, is therefore unclear, although it has been suggested he lived there as 'old retainer' rather than relative.

Richard Read, *Miss Julia Johnston*, 1824, by John Jones, Associate Director, Deutscher Fine Art, Melbourne

1 Eve Buscombe, *Artists in early Australia and their portraits*, Sydney: Eureka Research, 1978, pp. 32-39.

2 Known as Richard Read junior, he was an estranged son.

3 Jocelyn Gray, "Richard Read", *Australian Dictionary of Biography*, vol. 2, 1966.

4 A.T. Yarwood, "George Johnston", *Australian Dictionary of Biography*, vol. 2, 1966.

5 Anita Schorsh, "Mourning Art: A Neoclassical Reflection in America", *The American Art Journal*, vol. VIII, no. 1, May 1976, pp. 4-15.

6 Specifically "The Laureat Bard", the fellow former convict, Michael Robinson.

7 George F.J. Bergman, "Esther Johnston", *Australian Dictionary of Biography*, vol. 2, 1966.

Augustus Earle, *Trajan inconsolable after the Battle of Ctesiphon*, c1827, by Ron Radford, Curator of Paintings and Sculptures, Art Gallery of South Australia, Adelaide

1 Classical figure decorations of Apollo (based on the Apollo Belvedere), Minerva, goddess of wisdom, and Melpomene, muse of tragedy, were painted for a concert of the Sydney Amateur Concert Society of which Earle was one of the committee members and one of the four "Directors of the Evening". The concert took place, with the blessing of Governor Darling, in the room immediately over the courthouse in Castlereagh Street. Earle's three classical figures were painted on three panels which were used to board up the front windows to improve the acoustics and the room was illuminated by specially made Grecian lamps. See *The Australian*, Sydney, 22 July 1826. (I am grateful to Anita Callaway who drew my attention to this description of the concert.)

2 This recently-discovered painting by Earle, like a number of the artist's other smaller Australian oils, is painted on a thin linen canvas and had never been removed from its original Australian cedar stretcher until recent restoration (1987) when it was temporarily removed from the stretcher to strengthen the fraying edges of the canvas. The Sydney-made frame, recently restored, if not original is probably from the 1840s and certainly not later than the 1850s.

est being formed by Trajan's outstretched leg and arm overlapping the vertical figure of the soldier. Other works by Augustus Earle, especially *Boy with a sulphur-crested cockatoo* (M.J.M Carter Collection, Art Gallery of South Australia), are made up of similar compositional triangles. Also typical of Earle's compositions are the slightly clumsy proportions, the stiffness of the figures, the deliberate gestures of the arms and hands, the touch of red (of the soldier's cloak) to enliven the composition, and the treatment of the jewellery and uniforms. The cliffs which form a backdrop are generalized in a very similar manner to the rocky cliffs in his oil painting *Bougainville Falls, Prince Regent's Glen, Blue Mountains, New South Wales*, c1827 (National Library of Australia), a painting of similar size and proportions.

3 Robert Dixon has elaborated this theme in his excellent *The Course of Empire: Neo-classical culture in New South Wales 1788-1860*, Melbourne: Oxford University Press, 1986.

4 These aspirations of the young colony were more vividly allegorized in Earle's concert-theatre decorations. Between the panel on which he painted Melpomene and the central panel of Apollo he painted the British Royal coat of arms. Between Apollo and Minerva he painted the "assumed" coat of arms of Australia, ". . . as if upborne by wisdom and the liberal arts", wrote *The Australian* on 22 July 1826. The writer went on to describe Earle's Australian coat of arms: "A Kangaroo and Emu appeared to sustain the rising sun of Australia, which darting its rays elliptically upward, whilst yet half sunk beneath the blue expanse of ocean, gave a promise of future brilliancy./ Hope, reclining on her anchor, with a benignant smile, secured to rise up on the sunbeams . . . Beneath the rising sun was the following appropriate motto 'E parvis magna' (from small beginnings, great results proceed)".

5 John McGarvie's diary (late 1820s), Mitchell Library, State Library of New South Wales, Sydney, (A1332), p. 235. Also *Sydney Gazette*, 28 and 30 July 1826, p. 3, in which "A.B. Marramatta" (McGarvie's pseudonym according to Jocelyn Hackforth-Jones) mentions Earle's "fine engraving" of Trajan. The principal monograph is Jocelyn Hackforth-Jones, *Augustus Earle: Travel Artist: Paintings and drawings in the Rex Nan Kivell Collection, National Library of Australia*, Canberra: National Library of Australia, 1980.

6 The composition of Earle's *Trajan Inconsolable after the Battle of Cresiphon* has some similarities to the composition of Washington Allston's *Saul and the Witch of Endor* (Mead Art Museum, Amherst College, Massachusetts) which Allston commenced in America in 1820 possibly before Earle had left America. The composition of Earle's painting is also related to *Marius at Minturnae*, 1786, by Jean-Germain Drouais (Louvre, Paris).

7 To supplement his income Earle sold books and engravings in Sydney, as well as art materials. He advertised prints after old masters. *Sydney Gazette*, 27 December 1826, p. 1, "Mr Earle . . . has now at his Disposal, a small, yet interesting collection of Books, Engravings, and Prints (Proofs) . . . [It includes] A Collection of Engravings, from Paintings and Drawings, by the most

celebrated Masters, containing a Series of fine Specimens after Vandyke, Annibal Caracci, Murillo, Carlo Dolce, Salvator Rosa, Teniers, Rembrandt, Vandervelde, Brauwer, Netcher, Titian, &c. &c. engraved and etched in the best manner, by the most eminent Artists — in 2 vols. . . . . [also] A Collection of fifty Parts, from antique Gems, engraved by Mr John Spilsbury." (I am grateful to Anita Calloway who drew my attention to this notice.)

Benjamin Duterrau, *The Conciliation*, 1840, by Tim Bonyhady

BIBLIOGRAPHY: *Hobart Town Courier*, 18 September 1835, 23 June 1837; Petition and Memoranda, May-June 1837, C.S.O. 5/42/896, State Library of Tasmania, Hobart; letter G. Whitcomb to George Augustus Robinson, 13 October 1851, A7088, Mitchell Library, Sydney; Tim Bonyhady, "Benjamin Duterrau's Paintings of the Conciliation of the Tasmanian Aborigines", *Bowyang*, Adelaide, no. 3, 1980; Tim Bonyhady, *Australian Colonial Paintings in the Australian National Gallery*, Canberra: Australian National Gallery/ Melbourne: Oxford University Press, 198[7].

John Glover, *A View of the Artist's House and Garden, in Mills Plains, Van Diemen's Land*, 1835, by Ron Radford

1   Arcadia, still the name of an agricultural province in Greece, has also been a continuing theme in poetry and art since ancient Greek and Roman times. In art it was an ideal region of agricultural and pastoral simplicity and happiness, inhabited by shepherds and nymphs; its whereabouts was vague. *Et in Arcadia Ego* was a phrase coined in seventeenth-century Italy expressing the humanistic sentiment, "Even in Arcadia death is to be found". The inscription appears in paintings from that time onwards, on skulls or masonry, particularly tombs. By Glover's time the phrase had generally come to mean "I too once lived in Arcady" or expressed merely nostalgia for a golden age or for the passing of youthful love.

2   The island of Tasmania was named Van Diemen's Land by the seventeenth-century Dutch navigator Abel Tasman and retained that name officially until 1855, after Glover's death. The name Tasmania was in unofficial local use by the early 1820s but Van Diemen's Land remained the more familiar name for European consumption.

3   This is contrary to what has been formerly written about the painting: John McPhee, *The Art of John Glover*, Melbourne: Macmillan, 1980, p. 35; Howard Tanner, *Converting the Wilderness: The Art of Gardening in Colonial Australia*, Sydney: Australian Gallery Directors Council, 1979, p. 36; Tim Bonyhady, *Images in Opposition*, Melbourne: Oxford University Press, 1985, p. 49. See Ron Radford, *John Glover's house and garden*, Adelaide: Art Gallery of South Australia, 1985.

4   Claude Lorrain (1600-1682), who painted idealized classical landscapes around Rome, was the most influential of all European landscape painters and the most important single influence on Glover's art. In his day John Glover was called an English Claude. Glover owned two paintings by Claude and a Claudean-style painting by Richard Wilson (1714-1782) which he was fond of exhibiting with his own work for favourable comparison.

In his 1835 London exhibition of Tasmanian works, for instance, he included the two by Claude. In the sale of his paintings on 18 and 19 May 1830 immediately before his departure for Tasmania, Glover included direct copies he had made from Claude Lorrain, Gaspard Poussin (1625-1675, also known as Gaspard Dughet) and Aelbert Cuyp (1620-1691). Although the very naturalistic approach in the house-and-garden picture has more in common with the domestic approach of Dutch landscape painting, the radiant sun is a direct reference to Claude who was the first artist effectively to use the glowing sun in his landscapes.

5   John Murdoch, *The Discovery of the Lake District*, London: Victoria & Albert Museum, 1984, p. 65. The Tasmanian Museum & Art Gallery, Hobart, owns a very Claudean view by Glover of Blowick Farm.

6   If Wordsworth epitomized the cult of nature and English rural landscape in poetry, then his friend John Constable (who also painted Lake District subjects at the beginning of the nineteenth century) did the same in painting. Constable was an envious rival of Glover, as the latter initially received the popular success denied the more original artist. It is interesting that two of Constable's most naturalistic and assured works from the first half of his career are the two paintings of his family's farm, *Golding Constable's kitchen garden*, 1815, and *Golding Constable's flower garden*, 1815 (both owned by Ipswich Borough Council, Suffolk), which, like Glover's house-and-garden picture, had personal significance for the artist.

7   See James Backhouse's Journal, 9 May 1833, part 6, p. 41, MS B730, Mitchell Library, State Library of New South Wales, Sydney.

8   Much of the present bushland surrounding Patterdale farm is denser than in Glover's day. Aborigines had regularly burnt off the undergrowth.

9   Sketchbook, National Library of Australia, Canberra. Shipping records Hobart 1835, Archive Office of Tasmania, Hobart.

10   For further information on the artist, the painting and its provenance see Ron Radford, *John Glover's house and garden*, Adelaide: Art Gallery of South Australia, 1985, a pamphlet published to accompany a small exhibition which in January 1985 celebrated the 150th anniversary of the painting.

Eugene von Guérard, *Stony Rises, Lake Corangamite*, 1857, by Ron Radford

1   James Bonwick, *Western Victoria: Its Geography, Geology and Social Condition: The Narrative of an Education Tour in 1857*, Melbourne: Heinemann, 1970, pp. 16-17.

2   Marjorie Tipping (ed.), *An Artist on the Goldfields, The Diary of Eugène von Guérard*, South Yarra, Melbourne: John Currey, O'Neil, 1982, p. 72. Other monographs are Candice Bruce, *Eugen von Guérard*, Sydney: Australian Gallery Directors Council/ Canberra: Australian National Gallery, 1980; Candice Bruce, Edward Comstock & Frank McDonald, *Eugene von Guérard: A German Romantic in the Antipodes*, Martinborough, New Zealand: Alister Taylor, 1982.

3   The symbolic invasion of the European black-

berry into native pastures can also be seen in von Guérard's *Mount William from Mount Dryden*, 1857, Art Gallery of Western Australia, Perth.

4   The theme of the displacement of the Aborigines is present in the artist's pair of Gippsland homestead paintings, *Bushy Park*, 1861, National Library of Australia, Canberra. One of these paintings features an Aboriginal family and a young tree symbolically growing behind a dead one. In the other painting there are no Aborigines present but there is a symbolic combat between a white bull and a dark bull. By contrast von Guérard had earlier, in 1854, painted *Warrenheip Hills near Ballarat*, National Gallery of Victoria, Melbourne, which is an unspoilt Aboriginal Arcadia with no hint of a threat of European invasion. He presented them more heroically and less vulnerably in *Aborigines in pursuit of their enemies*, 1854, National Library of Australia.

5   G.A. Robinson, *Journals, March-May 1841*, cited by Paul Carter, *The Road to Botany Bay*, London: Faber & Faber, 1987, p. 340. Von Guérard the following year painted a pair of paintings for the Manifolds: a view from the verandah of their homestead Purrumbete (Australian National Gallery, Canberra) and one of the homestead seen from across Lake Purrumbete (private collection, Melbourne).

6   Geologically, the Stony Rises was formed when the solid crust of the basaltic flow from nearby Mount Porndon collapsed as the molten basalt from beneath withdrew due to ruptures of the temporary solidifying front of the basaltic flow. This was combined with the individual narrow flows of lava emerging from the base of the broad lava crust. (I am grateful to Bernie Joyce of the Department of Geology, University of Melbourne for this information.)

7   James Bonwick, *op. cit.*, pp. 19-20. Over ten years later, E. Laird in his *Ramble of a Globetrotter*, London: Chapman & Hall, 1875, p. 57, also emphasized the strange atmosphere of the Stony Rises when he wrote: "We passed by a lake 90 miles in circumference; it is very salt. We then went through what is termed The Stony Rises — they are huge blocks of stone lying in all shapes and forms, and covered with moss. At twilight, or on a moon-light night they must have a weird look, and a fertile imagination could easily conjure up hob-goblins, ghosts, &c. Generally, there are a number of kangaroos about here; . . . "

8   It is unlikely that grass-trees ever grew in the Stony Rises as these plants usually grow in much poorer sandy soil. In the early and mid nineteenth century, grass-trees (sometimes called 'black boys') were generally perceived as characteristically Australian plants.

9   Mitchell Library, State Library of New South Wales, Sydney, sketchbook, pp. 47-49.

10   Frederick Dalgety originally owned the Ferntree Gully painting (now Australian National Gallery, Canberra) as well as *Stony Rises, Lake Corangamite*. He lent them both to the Commissioners for the colony of Victoria's industrial exhibit at the International Exhibition, South Kensington, London, 1862.

Conrad Martens, *View from the crags above Neutral Bay*, 1857/58, by Jocelyn Gray

1   Martens's account book lists a *View of Sydney from Neutral Bay*, for "[. . ...] Fanning Esq" in 1857 and a *View from the crags above Neutral Bay*, for "Alf Denison Esq." in June 1858. In the absence of full provenance for the two versions of the same view now owned by the Australian National Gallery and the Alan Bond Collection respectively, it is not possible securely to assign them to 1857 or 1858. However, the Alan Bond version has a greater emphasis on Sir William Denison's associations, and is here assumed to be the one completed in 1858.

2   C.H. Currey, "Sir William Thomas Denison", *Australian Dictionary of Biography*, vol. 4, 1972.

Julius Schomburgk, The *John Ridley Testimonial candelabrum*, 1860, by Judith Thompson, Curator of Australian Decorative Arts, Art Gallery of South Australia, Adelaide

1   In 1855 Smith & Nicholson of London made a centrepiece for presentation to the Colonial Secretary of New South Wales which was one of, if not the first embellished with "the zoology and vegetation of Australia prominently characterized; around the stem are representatives of the aboriginal and colonial population". See *The Illustrated London News*, vol. 27, p. 685. It was, however, only one of a number of pieces of silver made by this and other British firms to feature Australian vegetation and animals; silver not specifically intended for Australia also featured these motives.

2   The style was also emulated by Australian silversmiths, an excellent example being the cricket match depicted in the centrepiece made in Sydney in the late 1870s by William Kerr (Museum of Applied Arts & Sciences, Sydney).

3   As typified by William Edwards and Ernest Leviny in Melbourne, William Kerr in Sydney, J.M. Wendt and Henry Steiner in Adelaide.

4   Julius Schomburgk was selected to be the maker of the testimonial but the reason for selecting him is not known. However, he had previously made a silver mount for a medal awarded to South Australians for wheat at the Great Exhibition of 1851 (now in the collection of the Art Gallery of South Australia, Adelaide), possibly a precedent and deciding factor in the choice. Julius Schomburgk's elder brother Otto had participated in the organisation and emigration from Prussia (with financial assistance from Humboldt, amongst others) of a large group of well-educated Germans who in 1849 formed the "Büchsfelde" community forty kilometres north of Adelaide. Following the 1848 revolution and in Germany's ensuing unsettled conditions, a Berlin Migration Society was formed by a party of intellectuals and idealists. They sailed from Hamburg in March 1849, arriving at Port Adelaide on 7 August 1849. The name Büchsfelde was chosen for their settlement in honour of Leopold von Büch, the scientist who with Alexander von Humboldt had provided funds to assist the establishment of these Germans in South Australia. Among the intellectuals in this group were also Julius's elder brother Richard, the botanist, as well as Carl Linger, a

composer, and Alexander Schramm, a painter. Linger composed the "Song of Australia", conducted the first Philharmonic Orchestra in Adelaide and founded a famed Liedertafel. Schramm observed and depicted the South Australian Aborigines in his paintings. Richard Schomburgk did valuable work in economic botany and allied fields and became Director of the Botanic Gardens of Adelaide. Julius and his sister Caroline departed Germany and joined their brothers at Büchsfelde in 1850. He was then in his thirty-eighth year and was trained as a goldsmith. Schomburgk's arrival in South Australia was preceded by that of another German gold-and-silversmith, Charles Firnhaber who had arrived in early 1847 and had established his business by 1851. Julius Schomburgk worked with Charles Firnhaber on *The Hanson Cup* in 1861/2; see John Hawkins, *Australian Silver 1800-1900*, Sydney: National Trust of Australia (N.S.W.) Women's Committee, 1973, pp. 60, 62, 63. Germans in South Australia prior to the group of 1849 were mostly rural workers and artisans who preferred to live in isolated communities but were accepted and respected in the British colony as hard-working and honest people. On the other hand, the well-educated Germans entered public life in the colony easily and quickly; the British Royal Family was closely related to German courts and German scientists, composers, artists and philosophers were highly influential and highly regarded in Britain.

5   The Danish/German Jochim Wendt arrived in Adelaide in 1854, Henry Steiner in 1858, others in the 1870s.

6   South Australia, proclaimed as a colony of Britain in 1836 and being a non-penal colony, was intended to be financially self-supporting but land speculation was rife in the first years and culminated in near ruin by 1841-42.

7   29 September 1860.

8   Silver-lead was mined in the suburbs of Adelaide at Glen Osmond from 1841; gold had been discovered in the Mount Lofty Ranges in 1846 and successfully mined there at Echunga from 1852; malachite was mined at the very wealthy copper mines at Burra from 1845.

Charles Summers, *Maquette for the Burke and Wills Monument*, 1862, by Christine Downer, Pictures Librarian, State Library of Victoria, Melbourne

1   Royal Society of Victoria, Melbourne, *Exploration Committee records, 1857-1873*, La Trobe Manuscripts Collection, State Library of Victoria, Melbourne. The records include those of The Exploration Committee; Victorian Exploring Expedition; Victorian Relief Expedition (Howitt); Queensland Relief Expedition (3, incomplete records); and other material including the collection of watercolours and drawings by the expedition's artist, Ludwig Becker. Becker died at Bulloo, eight miles south of Cooper's Creek on 28 April 1861.

2   *Argus*, Melbourne, 5 November 1861, p. 4, col. 3.

3   *Ibid.*, 6 November 1861, p. 4, col. 6-7. "There remains for us now only the 'sweet sorrow' of publicly recording our sense of the noble doings and heroic sufferings of Burke and his party".

4   Royal Society of Victoria, *loc. cit.* The relief expedition under Howitt left Melbourne on 4 July 1861

to search for Burke.

5   Victorian Exhibition of Fine Arts, held at 105 Collins Street East, Melbourne, 1861, nos. 133, 134.

6   *Argus*, 22 November 1861, p. 4, col. 7.

7   *Ibid.*, 29 November 1861, p. 4, col. 7. Christine Downer, "Charles Summers and the Australian Aborigines", *Art and Australia*, Sydney, vol. 25, no. 2, summer [December] 1987, pp. 206-212.

8   Mimi Colligan, *Canvas and wax*, unpublished Ph. D. thesis, Monash University, Melbourne, 1987; *Argus*, 13 January 1863, p. 5, col. 3.

9   Victoria, *Chief Secretary's records*, Public Record Office of Victoria. VPRS 1189, box 757.

10 The Board consisted of Professor W. P. Wilson, Frederick Wilkinson, Dr William Gilbee, Alexander Fisher, James Smith and W. H. Archer. Another member, C. J. Griffith died during the life of the Board.

11 Board of Design, *Report of the Chairman*, Chief Secretary's Records, Public Record Office of Victoria, VPRS 3991, box 212.

12 *Examiner & Melbourne Weekly News*, 5 September 1863 and *Australasian*, Melbourne, 22 October 1866, p. 790, both list Summers dressed as Michelangelo at fancy-dress balls.

13 *Argus*, 22 April 1865, p. 5.

14 The sculpture now stands on a much smaller plinth, which has a postbox-like horizontal slit through which water flows in place of the *Preparing to start relief*. The back of the plinth now houses two of the four bas-reliefs, while a bronze coping-wreath, decorated with a pattern of nardoo plants in flower, has been removed altogether and lies damaged in a yard in West Melbourne. The highly chlorinated water has caused discolouration and possible damage to the two bronze figures, and the relief panels have been the subject of occasional vandalism.

15 *Australasian*, 20 January 1866, p. 8, col. 6-7.

Benjamin Law, *Woureddy . . .*, 1835, *Trucaninny . . .*, 1836, by Tim Bonyhady

BIBLIOGRAPHY: *Morning Star*, Hobart, 7 July 1835, p. 2; James Ross, *Ross's Hobart Town Almanack and Van Diemen's Land Annual for 1836*, Hobart: Ross, 1836; Graeme Sturgeon, *The Development of Australian Sculpture 1788-1975*, London: Thames & Hudson, 1978; Mary Mackay, "Early Tasmanian Sculptures; A reassessment", *Bowyang*, Sydney, no. 5, April/May 1981; N.J.B. Plomley, "Pictures of the Tasmanian Aborigines", *Art Bulletin of Tasmania*, Tasmanian Museum & Art Gallery, Hobart, 1983; Margaret Glover, "Benjamin Law (1807-90)", *Art Bulletin of Tasmania*, 1985.

Thomas Bock, *Mathinna*, 1842, by Hendrik Kolenberg, Curator of Art, Tasmanian Museum & Art Gallery, Hobart

1   The principal source of information on Mathinna is N.J.B. Plomley, an authority on the history of the Tasmanian Aborigine. In his "Notes on some of the Tasmanian Aborigines, and on portraits of them", *Papers and Proceedings of the Royal Society of Tasmania*, Hobart, vol. 102, part II, pp. 47-54, he properly warns that since Mathinna ". . . has passed into romantic legend. Before this legend acquires the patina of acceptance it will be well to outline the little known about her." Plomley's main sources are G.A. Robinson's jour-

nals and papers, and the Franklin papers (both Lady Franklin's and Sir John Franklin's), and the records of the Chief Secretary's Office in the State Archives, Hobart. Refer also to: N.J.B. Plomley, "Thomas Bock's portraits of the Tasmanian Aborigines", *Records of the Queen Victoria Museum, Launceston*, new series, no. 18; *Friendly Mission: The Tasmanian journals and papers of George Augustus Robinson 1829-1834*, Hobart: Tasmanian Historical Research Association, 1966; and *Weep in Silence*, Hobart: Blubber Head Press, 1987. Mathinna has been the subject of numerous studies and books apart from N.J.B. Plomley's work. Best known is Nan Chauncy, *Mathinna's People*, Melbourne: Oxford University Press, 1967; the most recent, produced for school children, is Heather Felton, *The Lowreenne People and Mathinna: On being Aboriginal — Book 3*, Hobart: Education Department of Tasmania, 1984.

2   There are at least two other portraits of Mathinna, by John Skinner Prout (1805-76) and Francis Simpkinson De Wesselow (1819-1906), both drawn from life in 1845 following a visit to Wybalenna, Flinders Island. See Tony Brown & Hendrik Kolenberg, *Skinner Prout in Australia 1840-48*, Hobart: Tasmanian Museum & Art Gallery, 1987, no. 48; and Max Angus, *Simpkinson De Wesselow: Landscape Painter in Van Diemen's Land and the Port Phillip District 1844-1848*, Hobart: Blubber Head Press, 1983, no. 23.

3   There is a portrait of Towterer by W.B. Gould in the Mitchell Library, State Library of New South Wales, Sydney. It was used as an illustration to N.J.B. Plomley, "Pictures of the Tasmanian Aborigines", *Art Bulletin of Tasmania*, Hobart: Tasmanian Museum & Art Gallery, 1983, p. 45.

4   It is believed that Mathinna was the Aminia referred to in the Coroner's Inquest in September 1856 which stated: "Aminia on the first day of September in the year aforesaid in the County aforesaid, being intoxicated with liquor, and laying herself down on her face in mud and water on the road near The Snug, it so happened that the said Aminia was there and then choked, suffocated and stifled of which said choking suffocation and stifling the said Aminia there and then died."

5   For biographical details on Thomas Bock see N.J.B. Plomley in Joan Kerr (ed.), *Dictionary of Australian Artists; Working Paper I: Painters, Photographers and Engravers 1770-1870, A — H*, Sydney: Power Institute of Fine Arts, University of Sydney, 1984; and Hendrik & Julianna Kolenberg, *Tasmanian Vision: The art of nineteenth century Tasmania: Paintings, drawings and sculpture from European exploration and settlement to 1900*, Hobart: Tasmanian Museum & Art Gallery, 1988.

6   According to Sir John Franklin's correspondence a copy may have been made of Bock's portrait of Mathinna. See Eve Buscombe, *Artists in early Australia and their portraits*, Sydney: Eureka Research, 1978, pp. 300-301. Bock, like many artists before and after him, made copies of his own work.

7   Frances J. Woodward, "Lady (Jane) Franklin", *Australian Dictionary of Biography*, vol. 1, 1966.

8   Tim Bonyhady, *Australian Colonial Painting in*

the *Australian National Gallery*, Canberra: Australian National Gallery/ Melbourne: Oxford University Press, 198[7], pp. 208-10.

9   Quoted in a museum display of Tasmanian Aboriginal life, Tasmanian Museum & Art Gallery, Hobart, current in January 1988.

10 Quoted from W.F. Rawnsley, *The Life, Diaries and Correspondence of Jane, Lady Franklin, 1792-1875*, 1923, by Joan Kerr in her lecture "Aborigines in Australian colonial art", given throughout Australia in the 1980s.

11 Max Angus, *Simpkinson De Wesselow*, *op. cit.*, p. 177.

J.M. Crossland, *Nannultera, a young cricketer of the Natives' Training Institution, Poonindie*, 1854, by John Jones

1   Mathew Blagden Hale, 1811-1895: Archdeacon of Adelaide 1847-1857; Bishop of Perth 1857-1875; Bishop of Brisbane 1875-1885.

2   John Tregenza, "Two notable portraits of South Australian Aborigines", *Journal of the Historical Society of South Australia*, Adelaide, no. 12, 1984, pp. 22-31. This supersedes the previous literature, which describes the sitters as "Natives of Western Australia", probably meaning the western part of South Australia.

3   John Michael Crossland was born probably in 1800, probably in London. He appears to have studied at the Royal Academy Schools. He exhibited portraits and subject-paintings, principally Italian banditti and peasants, at the Royal Academy intermittently from 1832 and at the Society of British Artists from 1845 (see Algernon Graves, *The Royal Academy of Arts Exhibitors 1769-1904*, London, 1905-06, vol. 1, p. 210; Jane Johnson, *Works Exhibited at the Royal Society of British Artists 1824-1893 and the New English Art Club 1888-1917*, London: Antique Collectors Club, 1975, p. 113). He had painted portraits of the Secretary and Chaplain to the St Ann's Society. In Adelaide he set up a studio, first in Waymouth Street and then at Apollo Place, King William Street (see Andrew Garran, *Royal South Australian Almanac and General Directory*, Adelaide, 1854 and 1855). Crossland, like Alexander Schramm, regularly exhibited paintings at Barnard's Exchange in Hindley Street and, up till his death at Encounter Bay in late January 1858, seemed to make a fair living. Crossland's fee for a full-length commissioned portrait of James Hurtle Fisher was 70 guineas. Its elaborate gilt frame cost 50 guineas (*The South Australian Register*, Adelaide, 28 December 1854, p. 3, col. c). Crossland charged Archdeacon Hale only six pounds and five shillings for the portrait of Samuel Conwillan.
It is unlikely that Crossland visited the Bendigo goldfields as has been suggested (Ron Radford, "Australian's Forgotten Painters: South Australian Colonial Painting 1836-1880: Part Two 1850-1880", *Art and Australia*, Sydney, vol. 25, no. 1, spring 1987, p. 94). I am indebted to Necia Gilbert of Adelaide for her research in these matters.

4   There are three versions of this subject. One of the 1853 portraits is in the National Portrait Gallery, London. Another portrait of Sturt is in the collection of the Art Gallery of South Australia, Adelaide.

5   Conwillan (who died in 1860) was one of the

eleven foundation members of the Institution. See John Tregenza, *loc. cit.*

6   A. de Quincey Robin, "Mathew Hale and the Poonindie Experiment", *University Studies in History*, Perth: University of Western Australia Press, vol. V, no. 2, 1968, pp. 34-49; Graham Jenkin, *Conquest of Ngarrindjeri*, Adelaide: Rigby, 1979, p. 64.

7   Mathew Hale, *The Aborigines of Australia being an Account of the Institution for their Education at Poonindie in South Australia*, London: S.P.C.K., 1889, p. 50.

8   Augustus Short, *The Poonindie [sic] Mission Described in a Letter from the Lord Bishop of Adelaide to the Society for the Propagation of the Gospel*, London: S.P.C.K., 1853, pp. 17-20.

9   *Early Days at St Peter's College, Adelaide, 1854-1878: A Biographical Sketch of George Henry and Julia Warren Farr by Members of Their Family*, Adelaide, 1936, p. 53.

10 A. de Quincey Robin, *loc. cit.*, p. 47.

11 *Ibid.*, p. 48.

Frederick McCubbin, *Lost*, 1886, by Jane Clark, Curator, National Gallery of Victoria, Melbourne

1   Ann Galbally (ed.), "Notes by Frederick McCubbin", *La Trobe Library Journal*, 6, Melbourne, 24 October 1979, pp. 69 ff. (original in McCubbin Papers, State Library of Victoria, Melbourne). For further biographical details, see Ann Galbally, *Frederick McCubbin*, Melbourne: Hutchinson, 1981 and Jane Clark & Bridget Whitelaw, *Golden Summers: Heidelberg and beyond*, Sydney: I.C.C.A., 1985, pp. 22-3.

2   One of his earliest surviving paintings is a *Sketch from Antony and Cleopatra*, 1880 (private collection). His coach-painting apprenticeship was bearable "as long as I could think that some day I might paint pictures like I saw engravings of Titian and Turner and Raphael".

3   "Notes by Frederick McCubbin", *loc. cit.*, p. 75. Julian Ashton claimed to have taken McCubbin "out to Heidelberg and help[ed] him paint landscapes"; McCubbin himself stated, "I painted I think the first picture that was ever painted in this part of the world entirely out-of-doors" *(ibid.)*.

4   This was the first (1885) of the famous semi-permanent artists' camps to be established in the outer-suburban bush around Melbourne. It is depicted by Tom Roberts in *The artists' camp*, 1886 (National Gallery of Victoria, Melbourne). Later sites were bayside Mentone (1887) and, up the Yarra Valley, the Eaglemont estate at Heidelberg (1888) which gave rise to the term 'the Heidelberg School' as a popular art-historical label for the group of new artists working in Melbourne (and Sydney) from 1885 to the 1890s. These camps were a focus for artistic camaraderie as well as for *plein-air* paintings inspired by European example. See Clark & Whitelaw, *op. cit.*, pp. 54 ff.

5   *The Australasian Supplement*, Melbourne, 19 March 1887.

6   27 April 1888, p. 2. Streeton called it "the fresh air, true-tone in values idea" — encouraged by Roberts following his return from Europe in 1885.

7   See Clark & Whitelaw, pp. 54 ff., 142 f., 173; and Leigh Astbury, *City Bushmen: The Heidelberg School and the rural mythology*, Melbourne: Ox-

ford University Press, 1985. The emphasis on characteristic local figures or activities set in a specific landscape, the shallow space and high horizon, and the decorative foreground details are all typical of this international late-nineteenth-century 'Naturalist' style. Bastien-Lepage (1848-1884) was at the height of his fame in the early 1880s.

8   In 1892 McCubbin exhibited a sequel entitled *Found* (known from photographs), which shows a bearded man cradling an exhausted child in his arms. He returned to the theme in 1907 with another *Lost* (National Gallery of Victoria): a little boy sitting alone in a sun-dappled bush clearing. David Thomas has suggested that McCubbin's *Childhood Fancies*, 1905 — two children watching fairies in a woodland glade — may owe something to Henry Lawson's sentimental tale of "The Babies in the Bush", in *Joe Wilson and His Mates*, 1901, where the tormented mother tells of her lost children being cared for by bush fairies ("Frederick McCubbin", *Art and Australia*, Sydney, June 1969, p. 72).

9   David Thomas, *loc. cit.*, p. 67.

10 Galbally, *Frederick McCubbin*, illus. 20.

11 *Australasian Art Review*, 1 December 1899, p. 25. An earlier essay on the 'pioneer' theme was his student prize-winning *Home Again*, 1884 (National Gallery of Victoria). *Lost* was followed by *Winter evening, Hawthorn*, 1886 (Castlemaine Art Gallery & Historical Museum, Castlemaine, Victoria), *Down on his luck*, 1889 (Art Gallery of Western Australia, Perth), *A bush burial*, 1890 (Geelong Art Gallery, Geelong, Victoria); and several more major canvases culminating in the triptych *The Pioneer*, 1904 (National Gallery of Victoria).

12 To a journalist in The Age, Melbourne, 10 February 1894, p. 15.

Arthur Streeton, *Golden Summer, Eaglemont*, 1889, by Terry Smith, Head, Department of Fine Arts, University of Sydney

1   Undated letter, probably 1890, in R.H. Croll (ed.), *Smike to Bulldog: Letters from Sir Arthur Streeton to Tom Roberts*, Sydney: Ure Smith, 1946, p. 14.

2   Helen Topliss suggests that this panel may be *Impressionists' camp*, no. 47 in The 9 by 5 Impression Exhibition *(The Artists' Camps: Plein air painting in Melbourne 1885-1898*, Clayton, Melbourne: Monash University Art Gallery, 1984, p. 26).

3   Letter, 1890, Conder to Roberts, in R.H. Croll (ed.), *From Smike to Bulldog*.

4   *The 9 by 5 Impression Exhibition*, Buxton's Rooms, Melbourne, August 1889, catalogue printed by Fergusson & Mitchell. See Ann Galbally, "Aestheticism in Australia", in Anthony Bradley & Terry Smith (eds), *Australian Art and Architecture: Essays presented to Bernard Smith*, Melbourne: Oxford University Press, 1980.

5   Arthur Streeton, "Eaglemont in the Eighties", *Argus*, Melbourne, 16 October 1934, p. 49.

6   Topliss, *op. cit.*, gives an account of Heidelberg's earlier popularity. Also see D.S. Garden, *Heidelberg: The land and its people 1838-1900*, Melbourne University Press, 1972, pp. 18-21.

7   Charles Rosen & Henri Zerner, *Romanticism and Realism: The mythology of nineteenth-century*

art, London: Faber & Faber, 1984, p. 67. Streeton's vista landscapes also exemplify another of the authors' contentions, that it was in landscape that "the two extreme tendencies of Romantic style — realism and art for art's sake — could be reconciled" (p. 35). I have argued elsewhere that Australian contemporary history painting, such as Roberts's shearing paintings, also effected this conjunction (see my essay on *Shearing the rams* in *Australian Art and Architecture: Essays presented to Bernard Smith, op. cit.*).

8   Letter of 2 July 1890 to the Editor, *Argus*, published 14 July 1890, p. 10.

9   Undated letter, probably summer 1888-89, in Croll, *op. cit.*, p. 6.

10 Debate about the nature of the Heidelberg School artists' "impressionism" has raged since the first review of The 9 by 5 Impression Exhibition. A recent example occurred in *The Age Monthly Review*, Melbourne, December 1985/ January 1986 (Bernard Smith), February, July and August 1986 (Terry Smith).

11 Jane Clark & Bridget Whitelaw, *Golden Summers: Heidelberg and Beyond*, Sydney: I.C.C.A., 1985. The painting won a *mention honorable* at the Paris Salon in 1892. There it was bought by an English artist. Streeton subsequently re-purchased it for £60 and cleaned and retouched it for exhibition in Melbourne and Sydney 1920-24. A private collector in Victoria bought it for 1,000 guineas and it disappeared into the limbo of dull reproduction until it was sold in May 1985 for $1 million. Cleaned and with the retouching removed, it became the centrepiece of the touring exhibition *Golden Summers: Heidelberg and Beyond*, 1985-86. For further information on the artist see *Art in Australia*, Sydney, special numbers 1919, 1931; Ann Galbally, *Arthur Streeton*, Melbourne: Lansdowne, 1979; Patrick McCaughey & Jack Manton, *Australian Painters of the Heidelberg School: The Jack Manton Collection*, Melbourne: Oxford University Press, 1979; William Splatt & Susan Bruce, *Australian Impressionist Painters: A pictorial history of the Heidelberg School*, Melbourne: Currey, O'Neil, 1981.

Arthur Streeton, *"Fire's on"*, 1891, by Barry Pearce, Curator of Australian Art, Art Gallery of New South Wales, Sydney

1   There is an interesting discussion by Tim Bonyhady about the "glare aesthetic", the painting of bright sunlight through tonal contrast as practised by late-nineteenth-century European and American artists, in his *Images in Opposition*, Melbourne: Oxford University Press, 1985, pp. 148-153.

2   Extract from Streeton's letter to McCubbin, probably October 1891, as published in R.H. Croll, *Smike to Bulldog*, Sydney: Ure Smith, 1946, pp. 20-23.

3   Extract from Streeton's letter to Roberts dated 17 December 1891, as published in R.H. Croll, *Tom Roberts*, Melbourne: Robertson & Mullens, 1935, pp. 187-189.

4   *The Age*, Melbourne, 27 May 1892.

5   The biblical quote comes from Daniel, Ch. 3, v. 6. Cited by Leigh Astbury in "Poetic impulses in Australian landscape painting: The Heidelberg School reconsidered", *Meridian: The La Trobe*

University English Review, Bundoora, Melbourne, vol. 4, no. 2, October 1985, p. 137, n. 79. There is a valuable discussion in this article concerning the equilibrium in *"Fire's on"* between Streeton's realism and his romantic idealism.

6   *Shearing the rams*, 1890, National Gallery of Victoria, acquired 1932; *A break away!* 1891, Art Gallery of South Australia, acquired 1899.

7   For example, in the Art Gallery of New South Wales, *Villers-Bretonneux*, and *Boulogne*, both acquired 1920.

8   *Golden summer, Eaglemont*, 1889, private collection, Perth; see Jane Clark & Bridget Whitelaw, *Golden Summers*, Sydney: I.C.C.A., 1985. *"Still glides the stream and shall forever glide"*, 1890, Art Gallery of New South Wales, acquired 1890. *Cremorne Pastoral*, 1895, Art Gallery of New South Wales, acquired 1895.

9   For a general biography of Streeton refer to Ann Galbally, *Arthur Streeton*, Melbourne: Lansdowne, 1979.

10 Published in Croll, *Tom Roberts, op. cit.*, p. 186.

11 *Cutting the tunnel*, Art Gallery of New South Wales, Sydney, gift of Howard Hinton 1937.

W.C. Piguenit, *The Flood in the Darling 1890*, 1895, by Barry Pearce

1   Glover 1767-1849, arrived 1831; Martens 1801-78, arrived 1835; von Guérard 1811-1901, arrived 1852; Chevalier 1828-1902, arrived 1855; Buvelot 1814-1888, arrived 1865.

2   According to Piguenit's friend W.V. Legge, who in 1914 published an appreciation of the artist shortly after his death, Piguenit made his first trip abroad when he went to England in 1898, then aged 62. McCubbin first travelled in 1906, at the age of 51.

3   Clifford Craig, *The Engravers of Van Diemen's Land*, 1961, cited by Daniel Thomas, *Australian Art in the 1870s*, Sydney: Art Gallery of New South Wales, 1976, p. 41.

4   *Sydney Morning Herald*, 4 October 1889, p. 5, col. 2. Cited in Tim Bonyhady, *Images in Opposition*, Melbourne: Oxford University Press, 1985. Bonyhady here expands on the comparison of Piguenit's work with the Scottish school, pp. 81-82.

5   Legge, *op. cit.*, p. 8, cites Piguenit's expression of admiration for "English" work hanging in the Art Gallery of New South Wales, and if Piguenit visited Melbourne he would have also seen examples of new British landscape painting; in 1869 the National Gallery of Victoria bought a painting by Peter Graham which proved to be one of Melbourne's most popular paintings of the 1870s; see Bonyhady, *op. cit.*, p. 82.

6   Piguenit's strongest supporter in Sydney was Eccleston du Faur, one of the founders of the Art Gallery of New South Wales. In 1875 du Faur organized an artists' and photographers' camp in the Grose Valley of the Blue Mountains, which Piguenit attended in his first recorded trip to New South Wales. Du Faur was involved in the subscription towards donating Piguenit's *Mount Olympus, Lake St Clair, Tasmania* to the "proposed" Art Gallery in the same year. Under du Faur's guidance as honorary Director until 1892 then as President of Trustees until his death in 1915 (one year after Piguenit's), no less than five

purchases and one gift (from Sir James Fairfax) of the artist's paintings came to the Art Gallery of New South Wales. Tim Bonyhady's discussion of the relationship between Piguenit and du Faur in *Images in opposition*, *op. cit.*, pp. 82-86, sheds an important light on the context of Piguenit and the wilderness theme in nineteenth-century Australian art.

7 *The Town and Country Journal*, 26 April 1890, p. 32.

8 Aby Altson, 1867-c1949, won Victoria's second triennial travelling scholarship for his painting, which is in the National Gallery of Victoria's collection. See Jane Clark & Bridget Whitelaw, *Golden Summers*, Sydney: I.C.C.A., 1985, illus. col. p. 48.

9 State Library of New South Wales, Sydney, Dixson Galleries, DG D6 F.27.

10 The artist's diary is in the State Library of New South Wales, Mitchell Library, ML MSS 2896.

11 *Launceston Examiner*, 15 September 1877, p. 5, col. 3. Cited by Bonyhady, *op. cit.*, p. 82. See also Legge, *op. cit.*, p. 4. Note also Piguenit's lecture *Among the Western Highlands of Tasmania*, given in Hobart in 1893 to the Australasian Association for the Advancement of Science.

12 *Sydney Morning Herald*, 21 April 1890.

13 Art Society of New South Wales, Sydney, spring exhibition, 1890, nos. 181 and 217 respectively.

14 Artist's biographical files, Art Gallery of New South Wales.

15 Streeton moved from Melbourne to Sydney in the year of Piguenit's visit to the floods. Roberts followed the year after.

16 The secession of this group was primarily instigated by Tom Roberts, who became its first President 1895-97.

———————————

David Davies, *Moonrise*, 1894, by Ron Radford

1 Quoted in Jane Clark & Bridget Whitelaw, *Golden Summers: Heidelberg and Beyond*, Sydney: I.C.C.A., revised edition 1986, p. 185. Although *Moonrise*, 1894, was generally favourably received by the critics and professional artists its minimal qualities irritated many visitors to the National Gallery of Victoria when it was first put on display. It has never been especially popular with the general public.

2 Notably *A hot day*, 1888 (National Gallery of Victoria) and *Under the Burden and Heat of the Day* (City of Ballaarat Fine Art Gallery).

3 James MacDonald, *The Art and Life of David Davies*, Melbourne: Alexander McCubbin, c1920, p. 8.

4 Davies is believed to have had, besides Price, other occasional teachers in the first half of the 1880s; they included J.F. Martell, James Oldham and John Mather.

5 Davies would have almost certainly come in contact with John Mather and his tight, realistic work through his early patron James Oddie, the principal founder (and benefactor) of the Ballarat Fine Art Gallery. The younger artist is believed to have taken occasional lessons from Mather. James Oddie gave three major landscapes by Mather (dated 1883, 1884 and 1886) to the Gallery in mid 1886 and at the same time he gave five early landscapes by Davies. In 1890 Oddie gave *Under the Burden and Heat of the Day*, 1890, to

the Gallery, having paid Davies £100 for it. This sum was twice the artist's asking price and enabled Davies to study and travel to Europe. Davies from 1886 was one of the few financial members of the Ballarat Fine Art Gallery Association and was asked to be an overseas advisor to the Gallery while in France and Britain. No other Australian artist has been so closely associated with a public gallery during his or her formative years.

6 James MacDonald, *The Art of Frederick McCubbin*, Melbourne: Lothian, 1916, pp. 82-95.

7 What he saw and studied in Europe would have generally confirmed what he had already been aware of in Australia. He certainly would have known of Whistler before he left. Furthermore, the Ballarat Fine Art Gallery, with which he had been so closely associated, had by 1890 numerous conservative contemporary European landscapes by artists whose work he would have seen later at the Royal Academy, London, or in the Paris Salon where he had also exhibited. The 1894 illustrated publication of the Royal Academy illustrates a painting by Fred Hall entitled *Moonrise*. Many of the Ballarat Gallery's European landscapes were sunsets or grey days. One of these pictures, a landscape, by French artist Louis Brémond, was acquired in 1889 and is worthy of special mention here. It is a simple composition of a crest of a broad hillside illuminated by the grey light of a finishing day. The distant peasant woman and her child are only incidental to the almost barren grassy slope. J.A. Powell, the professional secretary of the Ballarat Fine Art Gallery and known to Davies, was author of the Gallery's descriptive catalogue first published in March 1891; in it he wrote of Brémond's painting, "... clever in the manipulation of subdued colours and striking atmospheric effects, this broadly treated ... landscape painting – almost barren of incident, but by no means devoid of poetic feeling – appeals to the mind rather than to the eye ... the indefinable charm that lurks beneath the peaceful aspect of nature at rest ...". Powell could have been describing one of David Davies' later nocturnes of the mid 1890s and Davies would certainly have owned and read a copy of this catalogue that recorded and described so many of his own early paintings. But there are other precedents for Davies's moonrise paintings that are Australian, namely a small group of works by Roberts and Streeton of the late 1880s. If one, for instance, removes the 'Asian' sapling from Tom Roberts's *Evening, when the quiet east flushes faintly at the sun's last look*, c1887 (National Gallery of Victoria), one can observe the basis for a moonrise subject by Davies (although Davies's works are more tonal). Davies would surely have seen this painting which was exhibited in Melbourne in 1888 and 1893. However, even more closely related is a small moonrise subject by Roberts in a private collection in Ballarat which depicts merely tufts of grass and a bare horizon and a centrally-placed moon. So close in apperance is Roberts's work to the work of Davies that it was attributed to Davies until only recently. (It is illustrated on p. 7 [cat. No. 9] in the catalogue of the Exhibition

of Nocturnes and Twilights entitled *Moonrise*, Ballarat Fine Art Gallery, 1973.) These nocturnal paintings by Roberts would have inspired young Streeton at the beginning of 1888 to paint his *Box Hill evening* (M.J.M. Carter collection, Art Gallery of South Australia), a dark and minimal composition evenly divided between land and sky, illuminated by a white moon.

8 James MacDonald, *The Art of Frederick McCubbin*, p. 88.

———————————

Charles Conder, *A holiday at Mentone*, 1888, by Ron Radford

1 *Winter morning after rain, the old bridge, Gardiner's Creek*, 1885, oil on canvas, 44.3 x 65 cm, M.J.M. Carter Collection, Art Gallery of South Australia, Adelaide.

2 Jane Clark & Bridget Whitelaw, *Golden Summers: Heidelberg and Beyond*, Sydney: I.C.C.A., 1985, p. 101.

3 *Coogee Bay*, 1888, oil on board, 26.6 x 40.7 cm, National Gallery of Victoria, Melbourne.

4 *All on a Summer's Day*, 1888, oil on canvas, 40.6 x 28.8 cm, M.J.M. Carter Collection, Art Gallery of South Australia, Adelaide.

5 Just as Conder's *A Holiday at Mentone* was his major effort for the Victorian Artists' Society exhibition of November 1888, so Streeton's *Early summer – Gorse in bloom*, 1888, was Streeton's major contribution to the same exhibition. Streeton displays the mastery in handling, aerial perspective and light that had such an effect on his friend Conder. But possibly the placement of the paling fence by the culvert and almost certainly the decorative placement of the little girl followed by the lamb, and the bonneted girl by the fence, show Conder's influence. Perhaps also the aesthetic calligraphic foreground arrangement of the dying gorse is a reference to Conder.

6 *Table Talk*, Melbourne, 23 November 1888, p. 6.

7 *The Yarra, Heidelberg*, 1890, oil on canvas, 49.9 x 90.2 cm, private collection, Sydney, is Conder's only Australian painting larger than *A holiday at Mentone*.

———————————

Frederick McCubbin, *Down on his luck*, 1889, by Leigh Astbury, art historian, Melbourne

1 Helen Topliss, *The Artists' Camps: Plein air painting in Melbourne 1885-1898*, Monash University Gallery, 1984, pp. 20-1; cf. Jane Clark & Bridget Whitelaw, *Golden Summers: Heidelberg and Beyond*, Sydney: I.C.C.A., 1985, p. 131.

2 *Table Talk*, Melbourne, 26 April 1889, p. 5.

3 See Leigh Astbury, *City Bushmen: The Heidelberg School and the rural mythology*, Melbourne: Oxford University Press, 1985, chapter 4.

4 Graeme Davison, "People Moving" in Graeme Davison, J. W. McCarty & Ailsa McLeary (eds), *Australians 1888*, Sydney: Fairfax, Syme & Weldon, 1987, p. 251.

5 See Geoffrey Blainey, *The Rush that never Ended*, Melbourne: Melbourne University Press, 2nd ed. 1969, esp. pp. 299-300.

6 Cf. Leigh Astbury, *City Bushmen*, pp. 87-8.

7 S. T. Gill, *Gold Digging in Australia, 'Bad Results'*, 1852, watercolour, 20.1 x 26.5 cm, National Library of Australia, Canberra.

8 Alexander Sutherland (ed.), *Victoria and its Metropolis: Past and Present*, Melbourne, 1888, vol. 1, p. 346, and vol. 2, p. 708.

Tom Roberts, *A break away!* 1891, by Leigh Astbury

1 Francis Adams, "The Labour Movement in Australia", *The Fortnightly Review*, London, August 1891, reprinted in Ian Turner (ed.), *The Australian Dream*, Melbourne; Sun Books, 1968, p. 196.

2 See Leigh Astbury, *City Bushmen: The Heidelberg School and the rural mythology*, Melbourne: Oxford University Press, 1985, pp. 107-13.

3 R.L. Heathcote, "Land", in Graeme Davison, J.W. McCarty & Ailsa McLeary (eds), *Australians 1888*, Sydney: Fairfax, Syme & Weldon, 1987, p. 61.

4 G.L. Buxton, *The Riverina, 1861-1891*, Melbourne: Melbourne University Press, 1967, pp. 247-8; Geoffrey Bolton, *Spoils and Spoilers: Australians make their environment 1788-1980*, Sydney: George Allen & Unwin, 1981, p. 85; for a brief discussion of Brocklesby station, see Terry Smith, "The Divided Meaning of Shearing the Rams: Artists and Nationalism 1888-1891", in Anthony Bradley & Terry Smith (eds), *Australian Art and Architecture*, Melbourne: Oxford University Press, 1980, p. 111.

5 R.H. Croll, *Tom Roberts: Father of Australian landscape painting*, Melbourne: Robertson & Mullens, 1935, p. 36.

6 See Buxton, *The Riverina*, *op. cit.*, ch. 8; cf. Ursula Hoff, "Reflections on the Heidelberg School, 1885-1900", *Meanjin*, Melbourne, vol. 10, no. 2, 1951, pp. 129-30.

7 *Argus*, Melbourne, 31 October 1891.

8 Frank Mahony, *Rounding up a straggler*, 1889, oil on canvas, 91.5 x 127.6 cm, Art Gallery of New South Wales, Sydney, purchased 1889.

9 Croll, *Tom Roberts*, *op. cit.*, p. 36.

10 *Argus*, 4 July 1890.

11 Croll, *op. cit.*, p. 36.

12 Cf. Tom Roberts, compositional sketch for *A break away!* c1890-1, pencil on paper, 9 x 12 cm. Reproduced Astbury, *City Bushmen*, p. 120, fig. 166.

13 *Argus*, 31 October 1891.

14 Croll, *op. cit.*, p. 37.

15 Croll, *op. cit.*, pp. 56-7.

Tom Roberts, *Shearing the rams*, 1888-90, by Virginia Spate, Power Professor of Fine Art, University of Sydney, Sydney

1 This essay is heavily indebted to Terry Smith's "The Divided Meaning of Shearing the Rams: Artists and Nationalism, 1888-1891" in Anthony Bradley & Terry Smith (eds), *Australian Art and Architecture: Essays presented to Bernard Smith*, Melbourne: Oxford University Press, 1980.

2 *Argus*, Melbourne, 26 June 1890, cited in full in R.H. Croll, *Tom Roberts: Father of Australian landscape painting*, Melbourne: Robertson & Mullens, 1935, p. 33.

3 *Argus*, Melbourne, 28 June 1890; Tom Roberts's letter, *Argus*, 4 July 1890.

4 *Table Talk*, Melbourne, 30 August 1889.

5 *End to a career — an old scrub cutter* (1888) is lost; illustrated from the catalogue of the Victorian Artists' Society, May 1888, in Leigh Astbury, *City Bushmen: The Heidelberg School and the rural mythology*, Melbourne: Oxford University Press, 1985, p. 106.

6 See Terry Smith, "The Divided Meaning . . .", pp. 110-22; Astbury, *City Bushmen*, p. 111.

7 Terry Smith, "The Divided Meaning . . .", pp. 114-119; Nigel Lendon, "Ashton, Roberts & Bayliss: Some relationships between illustration, painting and photography in the late nineteenth century" in Bradley & Smith, *Australian Art and Architecture*, pp. 77-80.

8 Flora Shaw, *Letters from Queensland*, London, 1893, quoted in Terry Smith, "The Divided Meaning . . .", p. 113.

9 As Terry Smith points out, a strike broke out at Brookong in August 1888, and its leaders were still in prison when the work was exhibited. The purchaser was Edward Trenchard of Edward Trenchard & Co., Melbourne; *Table Talk*, 18 July 1890. Roberts's most important politician friend was Dr William Maloney; Smith, "The Divided Meaning . . .", p. 243, n. 36.

10 See David Jaffe, "Cutting the dags from Shearing the Rams", *Bowyang*, University of Sydney, vol. 7, March 1982, pp. 31-33, for Roberts's knowledge of still photographs of animal and human locomotion.

11 *Argus*, 26 June 1890. For reproductions and information on studies, see Helen Topliss, *Tom Roberts 1856-1931: A catalogue raisonné*, Melbourne: Oxford University Press, vol. 1, nos. 149-149b; illustrated in vol. 2.

12 *Argus*, 4 July 1890.

13 William Hatherell, "Shearing", 1888 in E.E. Morris (ed.), *Cassell's Picturesque Australia*, Melbourne, 1887-89, vol. 2, p. 221; illustrated Astbury, *City Bushmen*, p. 109; *Gubbie Wellington*, Topliss, no. 156.

Bertram Mackennal, *Circe*, 1892, by Noel Hutchison, Principal Lecturer in Fine Art, Faculty of Art and Design, Victoria College, Prahran, Melbourne

1 Ludovic Baschet (ed.), *Catalogue illustré de Peinture et Sculpture, Salon de 1893*, Paris, 1893. Mackennal's work was listed as no. 3125 in the catalogue and illustrated p. 269. The bronze cast made in c1902 is inscribed 1893 but the plaster was completed in 1892; see Jane Clark, *Golden Summers*, Sydney: I.C.C.A., 1985, pp. 180-181.

2 Noel S. Hutchison, "Sir Edgar Bertram Mackennal (1863 — 1931)", *Australian Dictionary of Biography*, vol. 10, 1986.

3 *Ibid*.

4 *Argus*, Melbourne, 10 July 1891, 11 July 1891.

5 Quoted in Leonard B. Cox, *The National Gallery of Victoria 1861-1968: A search for a collection*, Melbourne: National Gallery of Victoria, 1970, p. 425, n. 31.

6 Circe appears in the lost *Telegonia* as the mother of Telegonus the son of Odysseus. He kills Odysseus and she marries Telemachus her former lover's son. See "Odysseus" in the *Oxford Classical Dictionary*, 2nd ed., Oxford, 1970.

7 See Apollonius of Rhodes, *The Voyage of the Argo* (Penguin Classics), Harmondsworth, 1959.

8 Homer, *The Odyssey* (Penguin Classics), Harmondsworth, 1946.

9 See Ad de Vries, *Dictionary of Symbols and Imagery*, Amsterdam, 1974, for thorough explanations of the imagery used. The relationship of the headpiece to either Medea's or Medusa's hair of snakes should not be overlooked. All three women had the powers of sorcery and witchcraft.

10 See Isabel McAllister, *Alfred Gilbert*, London, 1929 for an illustrated account of Alfred Gilbert. Gilbert's work is currently undergoing a well merited re-discovery and re-evaluation by art historians.

11 The term 'The New Sculpture' was coined by the British art critic Edmund Gosse. See Edmund Gosse, "The New Sculpture, 1879 — 1894", *Art Journal*, London, 1894, in three parts. Both Gosse and the other leading English critic of sculpture, M.H. Spielmann, believed that Mackennal was too 'French' for English taste in works like *Circe*.

12 Quoted in Jeremy Cooper, *Nineteenth Century Romantic Sculpture*, London, 1975, p. 91.

13 Quoted in Leonard B. Cox, *op. cit.*, p. 50.

14 *Argus*, 29 March 1901. Mackennal brought the full-size bronze-painted plaster cast with him to Melbourne and exhibited it with some other of his works at the National Gallery of Victoria, February 1901. The Trustees wished Mackennal to produce and pay for a life-size bronze cast out of the payment of £800 and they also wished to have copyright. For the public controversy following the artist's rejection of the offer see *Argus*, 1 April 1901, and Edmund Fisher, "Mackennal the Australian", *Bulletin*, Sydney, 13 April 1901, p. 15. Mackennal's toughness is indicated by Fisher, who writes "Mackennal has the strong artistic brain in the hard business head". The terms agreed with Pinschof were that Mackennal would cast the full-size version in bronze at his own expense (about £200) and ship the completed bronze back to Pinschof in Melbourne. Copyright was to be held by the artist. This meant that Mackennal could have the statuette edition of Circe cast.

15 A completed bronze statuette was first shown at the Royal Glasgow Institute of Fine Arts exhibition in 1905. Statuettes of Circe were later shown as part of the official British art sections in the huge Franco-British exhibition at Shepherd's Bush, London, 1908, and the International Fine Arts Exhibition, Rome, 1911; and at the Victorian Artists' Society, Melbourne, October 1910, for sale at £100.

16 See Noel Hutchison, *Bertram Mackennal* (Great Australians), Melbourne: Oxford University Press, 1973, for further information.

Sydney Long, *The Spirit of the Plains*, 1897, by Joanna Mendelssohn, art historian, critic and curator, Sydney

1 *Sydney Mail*, 9 October 1897; *Daily Telegraph*, Sydney, 2 October 1897.

2 "The Trend of Australian Art Considered and Discussed", *Art and Architecture*, Sydney, January 1905. The principal monograph is Joanna Mendelssohn, *The Life and Work of Sydney Long* (Copperfield Art Collection), Sydney: McGraw-Hill, 1979.

3 *Bulletin*, Sydney, 23 October 1897.

4 "Eccleston du Faur", *Australian Dictionary of Biography*, vol. 4, 1972.

5 First published in London, 1899, frequently reissued. Pedley died in 1898.

Hans Heysen, *Red Gold*, 1913, by Ian North, Head, South Australian School of Art, Adelaide

This essay is a reworking of the author's "The Originality of Hans Heysen", in Ian North (ed.), *Hans Heysen Centenary Retrospective*, Adelaide: Art Gallery Board of South Australia, 1977 (reprinted as *Heysen*, Melbourne: Macmillan, 1979).

1 Hans Heysen, letter to Lionel Lindsay, August 1920, La Trobe Collection, State Library of Victoria, Melbourne, MS9104.
2 Hans Heysen, letter to Lionel Lindsay, 20 March 1912, La Trobe Collection, *loc. cit.* Discussions with Dr John Tregenza were valuable in identifying the significance of this quotation.
3 Colin Thiele, *Heysen of Hahndorf*, Adelaide: Rigby, revised ed. 1974, p. 34.
4 Hans Heysen, letter to Lionel Lindsay, 7 February 1919, La Trobe Collection, *loc. cit.*
5 Hans Heysen, letter to Sydney Ure Smith, 18 March [1940?], Mitchell Library, State Library of NSW, Sydney, MS31/4/2363.
6 Bernard Smith, *Australian Painting, 1788-1970*, Melbourne: Oxford University Press, 1971, p. 113.
7 Colin Thiele, *op.cit*, second ed., 1969, p. 151.
8 *Ibid.*, p. 15.
9 Hans Heysen, letter to Lionel Lindsay, 5 February 1961, La Trobe Collection, *loc. cit.*

Margaret Preston, *Aboriginal landscape*, 1941, by Ian North

This essay draws mainly on research published in Ian North (ed.), *The Art of Margaret Preston* (co-authored with Humphrey McQueen and Isobel Seivl), Adelaide: Art Gallery Board of South Australia, 1980, and in Roger Butler, *The Prints of Margaret Preston*, Canberra: Australian National Gallery/ Melbourne: Oxford University Press, 1987.

1 Statement in *Australia National Journal*, Sydney, vol. 2, no. 6, May 1941, p. 12, printed beneath a colour illustration of *Aboriginal landscape* in association with an article by Preston, "New Developments in Australian Art".
2 The definition and pejorative aspects of the word 'primitivism', and the suitability of its frequently used substitute 'tribal', is discussed in William Rubin, *"Primitivism" in 20th Century Art: Affinity of the Tribal and the Modern*, New York: Museum of Modern Art, 1984, vol. I, pp. 1-7 and under note 1 on p. 74.
3 See Humphrey McQueen, *The Black Swan of Trespass*, Sydney: Alternative Publishing Co-operative Ltd, 1979, pp. 151-152, for a discussion of the role of craft in Preston's work.
4 Margaret Preston, "Woodblocking as a Craft", *Art in Australia*, Sydney, 3rd series, no. 34, October 1930, p. 27.
5 Margaret Preston, "The Indigenous Art of Australia", *Art in Australia*, 3rd series, no. 11, March 1925, p. 34.
6 Reworked 1936 (Roger Butler, *op.cit.*, p. 183).
7 Margaret Preston, "Aboriginal Art", *Art in Australia*, 4th series, no. 2, June 1941, p. 46.
8 See Humphrey McQueen, *op. cit.*, pp. 158-9 for a wider analysis of this work.
9 *Aboriginal landscape* was reproduced in *Australia National Journal*, vol. 2, no. 6, May 1941, p. 12 (colour); *Studio*, London, vol. CXXIV, no. 595, 1941, cover (black and white), and p. 123 (col-

our); *Australian Present-Day Art*, Sydney: Ure Smith, 1943, p. 61 (colour); *AFIA WORLD*, American Foreign Insurance Association, summer 1963, p. 5. See also Ann Stephen, "Margaret Preston's Second Coming", *Art Network*, Sydney, no. 2, spring 1980, p. 15, for discussion of Preston's wartime work.
10 Margaret Preston, statement printed under a reproduction of *Bush Track*, N.S.W., in S. Ure Smith (ed.), *Margaret Preston's Monotypes*, Sydney: Ure Smith, 1949, opp. pl. 8.
11 Lloyd Rees, interview with Ian North and Isobel Seivl, Sydney, 29 August 1979.
12 See also Humphrey McQueen, *op. cit.*, pp. 161-2, and Ian North, "Model of an Era", in *The Art of Margaret Preston*, *op. cit.*, pp. 11-12.
13 Margaret Preston, "The Orientation of Art in the Post-war Pacific", *Society of Artists Book*, Sydney, 1942, p. 7.
14 See the title of the article given under note 13 above, as pointed out by Roger Butler, *op. cit.*, note 78, p. 49.

Fred Williams, *Silver and grey*, 1969, by Timothy Morrell, writer, curator, Adelaide

BIBLIOGRAPHY: James Mollison, *Fred Williams etchings*, Sydney: Rudy Komon Gallery, 1968. James Mollison, *Fred Williams: A souvenir book of the artist's work in the Australian National Gallery*, Canberra: Australian National Gallery, 1987. Patrick McCaughey, *Fred Williams 1927-1982*, Sydney: Bay Books, revised ed. 1987. The artist's papers, Mrs Fred Williams, Melbourne.

E. Phillips Fox, *The ferry*, 1910-11, by Mary Eagle, Curator, Department of Australian Art, Australian National Gallery, Canberra

1 Fox was often praised for his ability to give the impression of an enveloping space, for example *Temps*, Paris, 14 April 1912. Dr Ruth Zubans has written a monograph on Fox for publication by Oxford University Press and also wrote the text for the Australian Eye Series film about *The ferry*. A fine, small book about Fox in print is Len Fox's *E. Phillips Fox and his family*, 10 Little Surrey Street, Potts Point, Sydney: Len Fox, 1985.
2 The author is grateful for the advice of Ann Gaulton, conservator in the Conservation Department of the Art Gallery of New South Wales, Sydney, and to Alan Lloyd who examined the painting with her. Fox painted the figures before painting the watery background and used the bare canvas as his 'drawing'. That is, he did not paint right to the edges of forms but left some unpainted canvas to read as an unobtrusive passage between, for instance, water and body or neck and shoulder. He gave the centre of his canvas greater liveliness of texture and colour, working with thicker paint in brighter colours with the strongest tonal contrasts, whereas the quieter outer figures are more thinly and smoothly painted. There are very few fumbles or changes of mind. Bright stripes that had run the length of the boat in his preparatory sketch were first put in, then painted over (bits are still visible along the boat's rim) and another stripe employed, under the seat of the boat and running in the opposite direction. Fox's reason for making the change was aesthetic. The new, short stripes

are a firm counter-rhythm to the flow of strokes in the water. Towards the end Fox added a small patch of mauve and white colour in the shady lower left. Once again its purpose was most probably aesthetic, since without the patch of colour the image falls away in that corner; however, the patch has been read as a handkerchief dropped either by the little girl or the woman on the edge of the group.
3 In the winter of 1910-11 when *The ferry* was painted, Fox's time allowed for painting two or three large canvases was all of four winter months, approximately October to mid-February, when he sent paintings for Royal Academy and Salon exhibitions. *The ferry* and *Lamplight* (University of Melbourne) and *Déjeuner* (possibly an earlier work) were sent across the Channel for the Royal Academy exhibition in London. *Lamplight* almost certainly was painted after *The ferry*, and marks the beginning of a new technique for his larger paintings. It was painted much more slowly on a ground that prohibited fast and facile brushwork. In a letter to Hans Heysen written 13 September 1911 Fox explained "I have also lately taken a fancy for absorbent canvases, as I find my work is less slick & not so clever. I prepare them myself with special size and plaster of Paris"; photocopy of letter in Heysen papers, National Library of Australia, Canberra.
4 The reason Fox altered his brush technique between painting *The ferry* and *Lamplight* almost certainly relates directly to the difficulty he experienced in coming back to a large canvas day after day and painting with a consistent brushstroke. He wrote to Heysen in the letter of 13 September 1911 (*loc. cit.*) that he and Ethel Carrick were painting nudes in their garden, "very interesting work but mighty difficult. I try to complete a 25 [small size] canvas at one go – for better or worse – I find I get better results – coming back when one is not in the same attitude generally busts up the show".
5 The date 1909 for the trip to Trouville is from Ethel Carrick's chronological outline of Fox's career written for the Art Gallery of New South Wales in the 1940s. I have followed the Foxes' close friend Violet Teague in locating the ferry at Trouville-Deauville, see *Herald*, Melbourne, 21 June 1913. There are good supporting reasons for this. The ferry in Fox's picture is a small flat-bottomed boat ("le bac" in French — and *Le bac* was *The ferry*'s title when exhibited at the Société Nationale des Beaux Arts in 1912). These ferries were used for river crossings, not sea travel, which rules out Dieppe as a site for Fox's ferry. There is a river ferry across the mouth of the river Touques between Trouville and Deauville. *The ferry* shows not a flat landing-stage but a flight of steps with iron stanchions up and down the steps — appropriate for the continuous changes of level in a tidal river. Finally one of the studies for *The ferry* is *Promenade* (Australian National Gallery, Canberra), the location of which is identifiable by the boardwalk and wooden railing as Trouville.
6 "We have had a wretched summer, no sunlight, most dissapointing [*sic*] especially when one has sunny motives on hand", wrote Fox to Norman Carter on 10 September 1909; Carter papers, Mitchell Library, Sydney.

7   *Study for The ferry*, private collection, Melbourne.
8   *Promenade*, c1909, Australian National Gallery. There are stylistic correspondences with *The ferry* in *Promenade*, namely the high viewpoint and use of stripes — tents, boards, sand and sea — to provide an allover patterning.
9   Private collection, Perth. The striped dress was used by Ethel Carrick in *Beach scene*, c1909 (Australian National Gallery), and by Fox in *The arbour* (National Gallery of Victoria) and *The terrace* (University of Melbourne). The artist's niece Louise Porker (née Fox) thought her mother Irene had been given the dress eventually; interview with author, 1985.
10 The fichu also appears in *The muslin dress* (National Gallery of Victoria) and *Portrait of a lady* (Art Gallery of South Australia).
11 A portrait of Louise clinging to the side of her mother appears in *Motherhood* (Art Gallery of New South Wales), though of this girl the family explained "The head is Louise's, the body is Cousin Dorothy's, and the feet Cousin Rosie's." Fox painted a type rather than individualized his figures. Louise seems to have been the source for the girls in *The arbour*, *The ferry*, and *The terrace*.
12 The perch or ladder is supposition, based on the fact that Fox used models and viewed them from above. Models were used for the central man and woman and the boatman. The others are probably lay-figures.
13 The tale of standing on a box, and Fox painting the lower part of the skirt from a lay-figure is told by the artist's sister-in-law Irene Fox who posed for the mother in *Motherhood*; see Len Fox, *E. Phillips Fox and his family*, *op. cit.*, p. 66. Irene Fox was not tall but many of Fox's women are taller than any real woman, and he was probably in the habit of using lay-figures for the drapery.
14 "Mrs Alma Tadema . . . has copper-coloured hair. She has set the new fashion in the colour of coiffures. The favourite tint is at present just one shade lighter than bronze", gossiped the *Mirror*, Melbourne, 21 December 1888, p. 232. From the 1880s Fox painted many of his women red-haired. Three women who modelled for him around the time of *The ferry* were his wife Ethel Carrick, his cousin Etta Phillips, and Edith Anderson — who married Penleigh Boyd. They were all painters. Fox sometimes portrayed them with dark brown hair and more often with red hair. He changed Irene's brown hair to red in *Motherhood*. Because Fox painted a type it has proved very difficult to identify the women in his pictures.
15 Radio talk by the Director, (National) Art Gallery of New South Wales, "News Review", A.B.C. National network, 23 March 1949.
16 See letter to Norman Carter, 10 September 1909, Carter papers, Mitchell Library.

George, W. Lambert, *A Sergeant of Light Horse in Palestine*, 1920, by Anne Gray, Senior Curator of Art, Australian War Memorial, Canberra

1   The jacket shows what appear to be four stripes on the sleeve, rather than the three appropriate to a Sergeant serving in Palestine. The four stripes would indicate the coat belongs to a Staff Sergeant Major, who would have remained in Australia, and thus is incorrect for this subject.

2   C.E.W. Bean, *Gallipoli Mission*, Canberra: Australian War Memorial, 1948, pp. 15-16.
3   *Ibid.*, p. 108.
4   H.S. Gullett, "Lambert and the Light Horse", *Art in Australia*, Sydney, series 3, no. 33, August-September 1930.
5   H.S. Gullett, *The Official History of Australia in the War of 1914-18*, vol. VII, *Sinai and Palestine*, Sydney, 1936, pp. 35-6.
6   *Ibid.*, pp. 34-5.
7   AWM file 895/3/55.
8   Amy Lambert, *Thirty years of an artist's life*, Sydney: Society of Artists, 1938, pp. 134-8.

Max Meldrum, *Chinoiseries*, 1928, by Mary Eagle

1   "La Ruche", named for the beehive shape of the central structure, was a conglomerate of nearly 140 studios built out of material left over from the Paris Exposition of 1900. Meldrum stayed there at times in the years between 1900 and 1911, and occasionally on his second stay in France between 1926 and 1931. Accommodation was cheap and the studios buzzed with life. The list of famous inhabitants in the years before 1928 is formidable: Soutine, Léger, Archipenko, the Delaunays, Chagall, Jacques Lipchitz, Henri Laurens, Blaise Cendrars, Max Jacob, Pierre Reverdy, Foujita. Most were immigrants from central Europe, though there were also Japanese, Americans, Australians. A good many were communists, and Meldrum's politics were socialist. He probably first encountered La Ruche through his sculptor friends, Jean and Alfred Boucher and on his second stay became friendly with Madame le Plat, who had a studio upstairs.
2   J.S. MacDonald, "Some Victorian Landscape Painters", *Art in Australia*, Sydney, December 1926, pp. 62-64. Meldrum's early paintings had been dark, but after 1916 brilliant colour effects were included in a number of still-lives, portraits and interiors. In the Victorian Artists' Society, Melbourne, May 1917, Meldrum exhibited *Poland*, a portrait of Madame de Tarczynska in a red-white-and-blue Polish national dress, which he had painted to offset criticism that his palette was too dark. Meldrum and his adherents used dark glasses to reduce glare, their reason being that the reduction in light aided them in distinguishing tones. Brilliant sunshine, sunrise and sunset light and other ephemeral light-effects were avoided by Meldrumites, because they did not allow sufficient time for the exact recording of tones.
3   Société Nationale des Beaux Arts, opening 23 April 1928, no. 1323, Chinoiseries; *Paris Times*, "Salon 1928" [late April 1928], newsclipping in Meldrum family papers. Five paintings by Meldrum had been exhibited in the 1927 Salon, a signal success following which he had been elected "Associé" of the Société Nationale des Beaux Arts. He may have painted *Chinoiseries* to mark his triumph.
4   *Herald*, Melbourne, 25 July 1928, newsclipping in Meldrum family papers.
5   "Colour is the third and least important factor in depictive art", wrote Meldrum. "Like the instruments in an orchestra it introduces variety on a tonal scheme . . . colour by itself suggests nothing to our intellects and would only appeal to uncon-

trolled sensuality . . . Periods of national decadence have always been marked by . . . an increasing admiration for mere colour". Max Meldrum, "The Invariable Truths of Depictive Art", 1917, in Colin Colahan, *Max Meldrum his art and views*, Melbourne: Alexander McCubbin, [1919], pp. 43-44, and see p. 58.
6   Vincent van Gogh letter to Émile Bernard [Arles, 2nd half June 1888], in *The Complete Letters of Vincent van Gogh*, 3 vols, Greenwich, Connecticut: New York Graphic Society, 2nd ed. 1959, vol. 3, p. 491.
7   Vincent van Gogh letter to Emile Bernard [Arles, May 1888], in *The Complete Letters of Vincent van Gogh, op. cit.*, p. 485.
8   Quoted from Meldrum's untitled handwritten manuscript, [c1928], a small book with Max Meldrum's address "Hotel Messidor, rue de Vaugirard (Metro Convention)", Wallach papers, National Library of Australia, Canberra, p. 37. He instanced a practical example of colour-psychology: "A room could be consciously built and decorated in order to produce on the inmates certain moods".
9   Elsa Thomson to the author, 1982.
10 Elsa Thomson to the author, 1982, and to Audrey Mulder subsequently. Meldrum exhibited a portrait of Nancy Bottomley in 1929.
11 According to Elsa Thomson they were both painted in the early weeks of 1928 before Meldrum left for the United States in late March.
12 Elsa Thomson to the author.
13 The self-portrait in *Family group*, c1910-11, Australian National Gallery, is a rare instance, and early.
14 Ida Meldrum and Elsa Thomson to the author, 1982.
15 Mary Mansfield who visited Meldrum in his studio "years ago", saw a picture he was working on "upside down on the easel". *Sunday Telegraph Magazine*, Sydney, 28 January 1940, p. 4. Elsa Thomson to the author.
16 Max Meldrum, "The Invariable Truths of Depictive Art", 1917, in Colin Colahan (ed.), *Max Meldrum his art and views*, 1920, p. 75. Meldrum formulated the basic elements of his theory between 1912 and 1917, but didn't stop there, elaborating and refining upon his tonal theory for the rest of his life. A second theoretical text, *The Science of Appearances as formulated and taught by Max Meldrum, arranged and edited by Russell Foreman*, was published by the Shepherd Press, Sydney in 1950. His daughters say that he began to write this second text in France in 1927-28, before making a lecture tour of the southern states of America. The first lecture was delivered mid April 1928: he wrote the actual lecture on Depictive Art in Chicago in the first two weeks of April 1928.
17 For example *Poland*, 1917, Australian National Gallery. Meldrum liked to paint artificial flowers, too. They didn't wilt, so were more stable than fresh flowers but part of the attraction may have been their detachment from real life. Detachment is an aspect of almost all his paintings. Dark glasses separated his outdoor subjects from real life. Indoors, Meldrum looked into a mirror to paint. The mirror had the effect of doubling the distance between himself and his subject but it also detached him from the first-hand reality of his subject. Sometimes the mirror reversal of left

and right makes nonsense of the image – the piano in *Rehearsal*, 1942, Australian National Gallery, for instance. Psychologists have argued that western paintings are read from left to right, because westerners write and read from left to right. If this is so Meldrum's paintings confuse our expectations.

18 A scientist of depictive art, Meldrum's aim was "to acquire the necessary science by which the impression of something seen can be conveyed spontaneously to the observer"; Max Meldrum, "A Century of Australian Painting", *Pandemonium*, Melbourne, October 1934, p. 11. Meldrum disliked connoisseurs. While the production of a successful picture was "an extremely difficult thing" the spectator need not (should not?) possess any special connoisseurship. He was aware of the contrast between the passive role of the spectator and the wizardry of the artist. "For as the art of depiction becomes more and more complex and spontaneously intelligible so the mental control of the methods employed becomes more imperative and exacting. Progress without mental control is impossible". *The Science of Appearances as formulated and taught by Max Meldrum*, op. cit., p. 30.

19 Quoted from Meldrum's manuscript, cited above, note 8, pp. 3,4.

20 Sidney Wallach typescript of a manuscript by Max Meldrum "Random Reflections and Experiences of a Painter", [c1928], Wallach papers, National Library of Australia, p. 16.

Ethel Spowers, *The Works, Yallourn*, 1933, by Roger Butler, Curator, Australian Prints, Posters and Illustrated Books, Australian National Gallery, Canberra

1 *Sydney Morning Herald*, 10 July 1936, p. 5.

Grace Cossington Smith, *The Lacquer Room*, 1936, by Daniel Thomas Director, Art Gallery of South Australia, Adelaide.

The pencil-sketch for the painting is in an undated sketchbook which includes sketches for paintings exhibited in 1935 and 1936; all Cossington Smith's sketchbooks are in the Australian National Gallery, Canberra. The principal source for the artist is Daniel Thomas, *Grace Cossington Smith*, Sydney: Art Gallery of New South Wales, 1973. Joyce Duerre who worked at Farmers in the 1930s and her sister Vesta Davies who was a frequent visitor, in January 1988 gave valuable information about the store and The Lacquer Room; Jane de Teliga researched fashion in Sydney of the mid 1930s; Alan Lloyd, Conservator, Art Gallery of New South Wales, examined the unfinished figure. Grace Cossington Smith herself, for a ten-minute film on *The Lacquer Room* made in 1979 by David Muir in Film Australia's series *The Australian Eye*, spoke of the blue eyes of the man who became aware of being sketched. She also in that film spoke of The Lacquer Room as being in David Jones, an understandable slip in old age for by then David Jones had long been Sydney's leading store. Farmer & Co. merged with Myer in January 1961 and the store changed its name from Farmers to Myers in 1976 and then to Grace Bros when it took over in 1983; in 1988 the site of the former Lacquer Room is occupied by the store's Blaxland Gallery. The painting inspired the decoration of the New Edition Tea Rooms, opened in 1980 at the New Edition Bookshop, Oxford Street, Paddington, Sydney; Robert Gray provided information about William de Winton's New Edition.

Charles Meere, *Australian Beach Pattern*, 1938-40, by Linda Slutzkin, Senior Education Officer, Art Gallery of New South Wales, Sydney

1 *Poster: Empire Games, Feb. 5 1938: Sydney calls you ... Australia's 150th Anniversary Celebrations*, colour photo-lithograph, Deutscher Fine Art, Melbourne; ill. *Australia and Australia-Related Art: 1830s-1970s*, 25 November 1987, no. 89.

2 See Bruce Stannard, *The Face on the Bar Room Wall: Australian pub posters 1929-1950*, Sydney: Angus & Robertson, 1982.

3 Commonwealth Department of Health, quoted in Richard White, *Inventing Australia*, Sydney: George Allen & Unwin, 1981.

4 See Linda Slutzkin, *On the Beach*, Sydney: Art Gallery of New South Wales, 1982.

5 Sir Baldwin Spencer, quoted in Geoffrey Caban, *A Fine Line: A history of Australian commercial art*, Sydney: Hale & Iremonger, 1983.

6 *The Beach*, dated 1939, working cartoon, pencil on paper, 92 x 112 cm. Art Gallery of New South Wales, Sydney.

7 Quoted in Linda Slutzkin, *Charles Meere, 1890-1960*, Sydney: S.H. Ervin Gallery, 1987.

8 *The Sun*, Sydney, 22 August 1952.

David Moore, *European migrants arriving in Sydney*, 1966, by Helen Ennis, Curator of Photography, Australian National Gallery, Canberra

The author gives special thanks to David Moore who kindly provided her with information on this photograph.

1 Howell Walker, "New South Wales: The State that Cradled Australia", *National Geographic*, Washington, November 1967, p. 592.

2 David Moore in Ian McKenzie (ed.), *David Moore: Photographer*, Richmond, Melbourne: Richmond Hill Press, 1980.

3 For immigration to Australia see Geoffrey Sherington, *Australia's Immigrants: 1788-1978*, North Sydney: George Allen & Unwin, 1980.

4 Max Dupain in *David Moore: Photographer*, op. cit.

5 David Moore, op. cit.

6 *Ibid.*

Russell Drysdale, *Man feeding his dogs*, 1941, by Christopher Saines, Manager, Curatorial Services, Queensland Art Gallery, Brisbane

1 Commentary by Russell Drysdale, in the 10-minute film *Man feeding his dogs*, The Australian Eye, Series 3, number 15, Film Australia in collaboration with the Queensland Art Gallery and the Queensland Film Corporation, 1980.

2 Quoted in Geoffrey Dutton, *Russell Drysdale*, London: Thames & Hudson, 1964, p. 11.

3 Russell Drysdale, in the film *Man feeding his dogs*, The Australian Eye, op. cit.

4 *Ibid.*

5 Russell Drysdale, "A self-portrait", in Geoffrey Dutton, *Russell Drysdale*, op. cit., p. 96.

6 See *Russell Drysdale Drawings 1935-1980*, Melbourne: Joseph Brown Gallery, plates 16, 23, 24, 27.

7 Patrick McCaughey, "Foreword", in *Russell Drys-dale Drawings 1935-1980*, op. cit., no pagination.

8 See Christopher Saines, *Russell Drysdale, 'Man feeding his dogs', 1941*, Brisbane: Queensland Art Gallery, 1985, Diagram 1.

9 *Ibid.*, plate 2. Assuming that the seated dog would have been positioned in a similar relationship to the lower right edge, the format of the canvas would have closely approximated one often used by Drysdale from the late 1930s to early 1940s. See for example, *The rabbiter and his family*, 1938, 61.5 x 76.7 cm and *The crow trap*, 1941, 40.7 x 60.8 cm. The nearer to square format of *Man feeding his dogs*, 1941, 51.2 x 61.1 cm, closely accords with other works of that year. See for example *Moody's pub*, 1941, 50.8 x 61.4 cm and *Man reading a newspaper*, 1941, 61 x 76.2 cm.

10 James Gleeson, "Russell Drysdale", *Art Gallery of New South Wales Quarterly*, Sydney, 2, 1, October 1960, p. 42.

11 George Johnston, "Introduction", in *Russell Drysdale*, Brisbane: The Johnstone Gallery, August 1967, p. 2.

12 Patrick McCaughey, op. cit.

John Brack, *The car*, 1955, by Ian Burn, artist and writer, working in the labour movement, Sydney

1 This essay is excerpted (with amendments) from Ian Burn, "Is art history any use to artists?", *Art Network*, Sydney, autumn 1985. Additional information was provided in December 1987 by the Birdwood Mill motor museum, Birdwood, South Australia, and by the artist. Further information on the artist and the picture is in Ronald Millar, *John Brack*, Melbourne: Lansdowne, 1971 and in Robert Lindsay, *John Brack: A retrospective exhibition*, Melbourne: National Gallery of Victoria, 1987.

John Brack, *Barry Humphries in the character of Mrs Everage*, 1969, by Robert Lindsay, Senior Curator of Contemporary Art, National Gallery of Victoria, Melbourne

1 Barry Humphries, *A Nice Night's Entertainment: Sketches and monologues 1956-1981*, Sydney: Currency Press, 1981.

2 Patrick McCaughey, "The Complexity of John Brack", in *John Brack: A retrospective exhibition*, Melbourne: National Gallery of Victoria, 1987, p. 9.

3 Robert Lindsay, "The Figure in the Carpet: Some literary and visual sources in the works of John Brack", in *John Brack: A retrospective exhibition*, op.cit., p. 17.

4 J.A.D. Ingres, *Comtesse d'Haussonville*, 1845, oil on canvas, 131.8 x 92 cm, The Frick Collection, New York.

Margaret Dodd, *Bridal Holden*, 1977, by Julie Ewington, Senior Lecturer, Art History and Theory, Canberra School of Art, Canberra.

1 Richard White, *Inventing Australia: Images and Identity 1688-1980*, Sydney: George Allen & Unwin, 1981, ch. 10, "Everyman and His Holden".

2 S.A. Cheney, *From Horse to Horsepower*, Adelaide: Rigby, 1965, p. 258.

3 *The Holden Story*, [Melbourne?]: General Motors-Holden, Corporate Relations Department, 1977, is a useful guide to the history of the early Holdens.

4 Richard White, op. cit., p. 164.

5 M. Dunn, Australia and Empire: 1788 to the present, Sydney: Fontana, 1984, esp. pp. 164 ff.

6 Funk ceramics were discovered by Dodd while a student at the University of California, Davis, working with Robert Arneson; she graduated in 1968. Funk challenged the modern Japanese-derived ceramic aesthetic of personal response to a refined tradition, and engages directly with contemporary social icons. Only a quarter of the artists in Peter Selz's exhibition Funk, University Art Museum, Berkeley, 1967, were ceramists. See Judith Thompson, Skangaroovian Funk: Peculiar Adelaide Ceramics 1968-78, Adelaide: Art Gallery of South Australia, 1986.

7 See Penelope Scott, "Psychological consequences of inequalities in transport", in M. Bevege, M. James & C. Shute (eds), Worth her Salt: Woman at work in Australia, Sydney: Hale & Iremonger, 1982, pp. 187-193.

8 The importance of the Bride is attested by specialist publications devoted to her cult. Australian Bride was published continuously in Sydney from 1954 to 1979, when it changed its title to Australian Bride and Setting Up Home. After 1981 Mode for Brides took over the magazine's functions.

9 Two splendid examples: Allan Ashbolt, "Godzone: 3) Myth and Reality", Meanjin, Melbourne, 24(4), December 1966, "what more does he want to sustain him, [the Australian man of today] except a Holden to polish, a beer with the boys, marital sex on Saturday nights, a few furtive adulteries . . .", quoted in White, p. 167; and Ian Moffitt, "Let's Go Riding in the Car, Car", in The U-Jack Society, Sydney: Ure Smith, 1972, ch. 7.

10 Mary Ann Doane, "Film and the Masquerade — Theorising the Female Spectator", Screen, London, vol. 23, no. 3/4, September-October 1982, pp. 74-88.

11 Pictured in Good Weekend: The Sydney Morning Herald Magazine, 2 January 1988, p. 7, under the heading "Bride of the Week", and accompanied by the question, "Is it a veiled threat to all those in love with their cars?" Collection of the artist. The work was completed in December 1987 and exhibited at Gallery 460, Avoca, NSW, during 1988. This new Holden bride differs from the 1977 ceramic in several important respects, despite the special family resemblance. The 1987 Holden is definitely a discarded costume rather than a costumed persona, the bonnet mascot is now a sphinx accompanied by a 'registration sticker' defining the sphinx and, most obviously, it is a real-size cast of an FJ Holden with a distinct presence, rather than a Lilliputian modelled from the past.

The author has donated her writer's fee to the Art Gallery of South Australia to be used for the purchase of work by Aboriginal women artists.

Max Dupain, Sunbaker, 1937, by Gael Newton, Exhibition Curator, Shades of Light: Photography and Australia 1839-1988, Australian National Gallery, Canberra

1 1988 Interview with Gael Newton, Australian National Gallery artists' files. See also Gael Newton, Max Dupain, Sydney: David Ell, 1980.

Frank Hinder, Bomber crash, 1943-49, by Renée Free, Senior Curator and Curator of European Art, Art Gallery of New South Wales, Sydney

1 This quotation is from the findings of two Boards of Inquiry.

2 Hinder has recently put together his account of the crash in loose-leaf diaries on his experiences with camouflage. In them he has pasted news-cuttings, photographs, drawings and written account. They have been given to the Australian War Memorial, Canberra.

3 This sheet and another watercolour are in the collection of the Art Gallery of New South Wales.

Albert Tucker, Victory girls, 1943, by Richard Haese, Department of Art History, La Trobe University, Melbourne

1 Christopher Uhl, Albert Tucker, Melbourne: Lansdowne, 1969, pp. 22, 89. Tucker was drafted into the army 14 April 1942 and discharged 26 October 1942.

2 John Hammond Moore, Over-Sexed Over-Paid & Over Here: Americans in Australia 1941-1945, St Lucia, Brisbane: University of Queensland Press, 1981, pp. 147-8. Leonski was hanged 9 November 1942 at Pentridge Gaol in Melbourne.

3 Memory of Leonski, February 1943, oil on composition board 61 x 78 cm; ill: Uhl, Albert Tucker, pl. 4B.

4 Interview with the artist, 6 November 1987.

5 Self-portrait, 1941, oil on composition board, 44.8 x 32.3 cm, Australian National Gallery, Canberra.

6 Victory girl, August 1943, watercolour, gouache, brush and ink, 24 x 39.6 cm, Australian National Gallery, Canberra.

7 The Futile City, 1940, oil on cardboard on composition board, 44.4 x 54.6 cm, Heide Park & Art Gallery, Bulleen, Melbourne.

8 T.S. Eliot, Collected Poems 1909-1962, London, 1974, p. 70.

Sidney Nolan, Death of Constable Scanlon, 1946, by Jane Clark

1 For biographical and art-historical details, see Colin MacInnes et al., Sidney Nolan, London: Thames & Hudson, 1961; Elwyn Lynn, Sidney Nolan: Myth and imagery, London: Macmillan, 1967; Brian Adams, Sidney Nolan: Such is life, a biography, Melbourne: Hutchinson, 1987; Jane Clark, Sidney Nolan: Landscapes and legends, Sydney: I.C.C.A., 1987, rev. edn. Cambridge University Press 1988.

2 6 September 1984, interview quoted in Elwyn Lynn & Bruce Semler, Sidney Nolan's Ned Kelly, Canberra: Australian National Gallery, 1985, p. 9; he made similar statements to Maggie Gilchrist, quoted in Nolan at Lanyon, Canberra: A.G.P.S., 3rd edition, 1985, p. 5.

3 Lynn & Semler, op. cit.

4 Quoted by MacInnes, op. cit., p. 30.

5 Angry Penguins, Melbourne, no. 5, 1943. He chose the very fluid and fast-drying Ripolin brand of enamel partly because Picasso had called it "healthy paint".

6 The group, dated 1 March 1946 to 18 May 1947, was exhibited at the Velasquez Gallery, Melbourne in April 1948. Nolan had already sold one of them to Clive Turnbull and he gave the remaining twenty-six to Sunday Reed, having lived with the Reeds at Heide, Heidelberg, Melbourne, dur-

ing the time he painted them. All except First-class marksman are now in the Australian National Gallery, Canberra, those from Sunday Reed given "with love", along with numerous drawings. Other Kelly paintings of the same period, but not included in the Velasquez Gallery exhibition, are now in the Nolan Gallery, Lanyon, Canberra, together with an earlier 1945-46 series, of smaller size; one is in the Art Gallery of New South Wales and others in private collections.

7 Nolan quoted in Noel Barber, Conversations with Painters, London: Collins, 1964, p. 90.

8 Quoted in The Australian Artist, Melbourne: Victorian Artists' Society, vol. I, no. 4, July 1948. 9Lynn, 1985, p. 10.

10 Quentin Bell, "Sidney Nolan: An Australian painter", The Listener, London, 18 May 1961, p. 867.

11 Lynn, op. cit., p. 26.

12 Ned Kelly's "Jerilderie letter", written some time between the bank robbery at Euroa, 10 December 1878 and the hold-up at Jerilderie, 8-10 February 1879.

13 Henri Rousseau (1844-1910) was called le douanier because he was a French customs officer as well as an amateur Sunday painter; in the twentieth century he became the symbol of sophisticated modernist interest in the Primitive and pseudo-Primitive. John Reed had given Nolan "a little book with Rousseau's Tiger Hunt in it" — which he very much admired. The library at Heide contained several books on American and European naif art. In addition, a recent sojourn at fellow-artist Danila Vassilieff's nearby house, Stonygrad, had rekindled Nolan's interest in naive art traditions (and, no doubt, in incredible stories of escape and adventure).

14 Daily Telegraph, Sydney, 15-19 December 1949, quoting Jean Cassou, head of the Musée nationale d'art moderne, Paris.

15 Australian Painting 1788-1960, Melbourne: Oxford University Press, 1962, p. 282.

16 The Australian Artist, July 1948, loc. cit.

17 Death of Constable Scanlon, 1955, was no. 38 in Nolan's exhibition at the Redfern Gallery, London, May 1955; present whereabouts unknown. For other examples from this second series, painted in matt enamels and oils in comparatively subdued colours, see Jane Clark, Sidney Nolan: Landscapes and legends, pp. 115 ff.

Arthur Boyd, Interior with black rabbit, 1973, by Grazia Gunn, Curator, Contemporary Art, Australian National Gallery, Canberra

BIBLIOGRAPHY: Grazia Gunn, Arthur Boyd: seven persistent images, Canberra: Australian National Gallery, 1985; Ursula Hoff, The Art of Arthur Boyd, London: André Deutsch, 1986

Danila Vassilieff, Stenka Razina, 1953, by Felicity St John Moore, Principal Lecturer, Education, Australian National Gallery, Canberra

1 Vassilieff to John and Sunday Reed, letter from Swan Hill 23 July 1956.

2 Reproduced in Felicity St John Moore, Vassilieff and his art, Melbourne: Oxford University Press, 1982.

3 The shape of the void around the head resembles closely the Hebrew letter "het", while the elon-

gated gash in the arm looks like the Hebrew letter "yude". In combination these letters mean "hayee" – alive. The letters are worn by modern Jewish men around their necks. The dot could represent the "e" in "hayee".

4   *Stenka Razin* was exhibited officially for the first time in October 1957 in a retrospective exhibition of 39 sculptures at the Gallery of Contemporary Art, Melbourne, where it carried the top price of 275 guineas. That price was 75 guineas above the price of *Mechanical Man*, the second most expensive sculpture, now also in the Australian National Gallery collection. Neither sculpture was among the only six pieces sold in his lifetime. By contrast, Vassilieff's sculptures are highly prized today and a number are on permanent display in public collections.

Robert Klippel, *Opus 247 Metal construction*, 1965, 1968, by Bettina MacAulay, Curator of Australian Art, Queensland Art Gallery, Brisbane, and Desmond MacAulay, writer, Brisbane

1   Roland Barthes, "Textual analysis of a Tale of Poe", in Marshall Blonsky (ed.), *On Signs: A semiotics reader*, London: Basil Blackwell, 1985, p. 87.

2   Early supporters of Klippel's work included James Gleeson, Ralph Balson, John Olsen, and a few other painters. Critical acclaim by Daniel Thomas, Robert Hughes, Donald Brook, Laurie Thomas, and others enhanced his reputation. For a selection of reviews, see Ken Scarlett, *Australian Sculptors*, Melbourne: Nelson, 1980. See also Gary Catalano, *The Years of Hope: Australian art and criticism 1959-1968*, Melbourne: Oxford University Press, 1981.

3   James Gleeson, *Robert Klippel*, Sydney: Bay Books, 1983, p. 12.

4   Robert Klippel, conversations with Bettina Mac-Aulay, 10 August 1984 and 15 January 1988.

5   See Plato, "Cratylus" 431-33, *The Dialogues of Plato*, transl. B. Jowett, New York: Random House, repr. 1937, p. 221 ff. See also "Cratylus" 389, p. 179 ff.

6   The exhibition was arranged at the persuasion of the surrealist apologist André Breton. See Graeme Sturgeon, *The Development of Australian Sculpture 1788-1975*, London: Thames & Hudson, 1978, p. 144.

7   See Gleeson, pp. 37, 306.

8   For a discussion of this refer to Hazel de Berg, recorded interview with Robert Klippel, 1965, National Library of Australia, Canberra.

9   See Jon Bird, "On Newness, Art and History: Reviewing *Block*, 1979-85", in A.L. Rees & F. Borzello (eds.), *The New Art History*, London: Camden, 1986, p. 37.

10   In that postmodernism, being itself a position on modernism, writes its own commentary on critical life and death. See "The End of Art Theory", in Victor Burgin, *The End of Art Theory: Criticism and Postmodernity*, London: Macmillan, 1986.

11   See Gleeson, and Klippel's conversation (15 January 1988) with Bettina MacAulay.

12   Gleeson, pp. 306, 310.

Ian Fairweather, *Monastery*, 1961, by Murray Bail, novelist, Sydney

The principal monograph on the work of Ian

Fairweather is Murray Bail's *Ian Fairweather*, Sydney: Bay Books, 1981.

Clifford Possum Tjapaltiarri, *Man's love story*, 1978, by Tim Johnson, artist, Sydney

1   This and the first four paragraphs are based on the 1978 story for the painting written by John Kean, the then art adviser at Papunya.

2   From an interview with Clifford Possum conducted by Tim Johnson at Papunya in 1983.

3   Michael Nelson Tjakamarra, from a film made by the ABC in 1984.

4   And more recently Yuendumu.

5   See Andrew Crocker, *Charlie Tjaruru Tjungurrayi*, Orange City Council, Orange, NSW, 1987, p. 12.

6   Geoff Bardon, *Aboriginal Art of the Western Desert*, Adelaide: Rigby, 1979.

BIBLIOGRAPHY: Geoff Bardon, *Aboriginal Art of the Western Desert*, Adelaide: Rigby, 1979. Andrew Crocker, *Mr Sandman Bring me a Dream*, Sydney: Aboriginal Artists' Agency/ Alice Springs: Papunya Tula Artists, 1981. Anne Marie Brodie, *The Face of the Centre*, Melbourne: National Gallery of Victoria, 1985.

Peter Booth, *Painting 1982*, 1982, by Frances Lindsay, Director, University Gallery, The University of Melbourne

1   Conversation with the artist, November 1987.

2   Lord of the Flies: the Devil, in Milton's *Paradise Lost*.

3   *Drawing June 1979* (Large cannibal), brush and ink, silver casein, 65 x 102.5 cm, National Gallery of Victoria, Melbourne, purchased through the Art Foundation of Victoria with the assistance of Rudy Komon Fund 1985.

4   *Drawing 1983* (Two-headed cocoon man), charcoal and pastel, 20 x 24.8 cm, National Gallery of Victoria, Melbourne, purchased through the Art Foundation of Victoria with the assistance of Rudy Komon Fund 1985.

5   A group of 19 gestural landscape drawings by Peter Booth, all entitled *Drawing 1976*. Gouache, compressed charcoal and acrylic (various sizes). National Gallery of Victoria, Melbourne, presented by the artist in memory of Les Hawkins.

6   *Painting 1977*, Oil on Canvas, 182.5 x 504.5 cm, National Gallery of Victoria, Melbourne, presented by the artist in memory of Les Hawkins.

Imants Tillers, *Kangaroo blank*, 1988, by Nicholas Baume, art historian and critic, Sydney

1   J.C. Beaglehole (ed.), *The Endeavour Journal of Joseph Banks 1768-1771*, Sydney: The Trustees of the Public Library of New South Wales in association with Angus & Robertson, vol. II, 1962, p. 84.

2   *Ibid.*, p. 94, n.1.

3   *Ibid.*, p. vii.

4   *Ibid.*, p. ii.

5   It was painted in 1771 or 1772, and shown at the annual exhibition of the Society of Artists, London, in 1773. The work is oil on wood panel, 59 x 70 cm (*The Endeavour Journal*, p. vii). It is currently in the collection of Parham Park, West Sussex.

6   Banks's commission to paint an unobservable subject must have been a challenge to Stubbs, noted for his "passionate concern for anatomical

accuracy" (*Tate Gallery – an illustrated companion*, London: Tate Gallery Publications, 1987, p. 87).

7   Friedrich Nietzsche, *Human, All Too Human* (trans. M. Faber with S. Lehmann), Lincoln, Nebraska & London: University of Nebraska Press, 1984, #16.

8   It is also tempting to speculate that whereas a combination of evidence and imagination enabled Stubbs to paint his version of a kangaroo, Tillers, even with the benefit of first-hand observation, has simply drawn a blank.

9   Arakawa & Madeline H. Gins, *The Mechanism of Meaning*, New York: Harry N. Abrams, 1979.

10   *Ibid.*, p. 4.

11   Tillers has treated this theme on a monumental scale in his paintings *Lost, Lost, Lost*, 1985, and *Heart of the Wood*, 1985.

12   Grid-symbolism is a theme of Rosalind Krauss's essay "Grids", in which she argues, "behind every twentieth-century grid lies – like a trauma that must be repressed – a symbolist window parading in the guise of a treatise on optics". *The Originality of the Avant-Garde and other Modernist Myths*, Cambridge, Massachusetts: MIT Press, 1985, p. 17.

13   Examples of this include *The Unnamable*, 1985, and *Hiatus*, 1987.

14   *The Mechanism of Meaning*, *op. cit.*, p. 90.

FURTHER READING

Selected general texts on Australian art

Ronald M. Berndt, Catherine H. Berndt & John E. Stanton, *Aboriginal Australian Art: A visual perspective*, Sydney: Methuen Australia, 1982

Jennifer Isaacs, *Australia's Living Heritage: Arts of the Dreaming*, Sydney: Lansdowne Press, 1984

Peter Sutton (ed.), *Dreamings: The art of Aboriginal Australia*, New York: The Asia Society Galleries & George Braziller/Melbourne: Viking O'Neil/London: Viking Penguin, forthcoming 1988

Wally Caruana (ed.), *Windows on the Dreaming: Aboriginal paintings from the collection of the Australian National Gallery*, Canberra: Australian National Gallery, forthcoming 1989

William Moore, *The Story of Australian Art: From the earliest known art of the continent to the art of today*, Sydney: Angus & Robertson, 1934, 2 vols. Reprinted

Daniel Thomas, *Outlines of Australian Art: The Joseph Brown Collection*, South Melbourne: Macmillan, 1980 (Expanded edition)

Bernard Smith, *European Vision and the South Pacific 1768-1850: A study in the history of art and ideas*, Sydney: Harper & Row [1985] (Second edition)

Robert Dixon, *The Course of Empire: Neo-classical culture in New South Wales 1788-1860*, Melbourne: Oxford University Press, 1986

Tim Bonyhady, *Images in Opposition: Australian landscape painting 1801-1890*, Melbourne: Oxford University Press, 1985

Leigh Astbury, *City Bushmen: The Heidelberg School and the rural mythology*, Melbourne: Oxford University Press, 1985

Jane Clark & Bridget Whitelaw, *Golden Summers: Heidelberg and Beyond*, Sydney: I.C.C.A., 1985

Richard Haese, *Rebels and Precursors: The revolutionary years of Australian art* [1930s-1940s], Ringwood, Victoria: Allen Lane, 1981

Bernard Smith, *Australian Painting 1788-1970*, Melbourne: Oxford University Press, 1971 (Second edition)

Graeme Sturgeon, *The Development of Australian Sculpture 1788-1975*, London: Thames & Hudson, 1978

Gael Newton, *Shades of Light: Photography and Australia 1839-1988*, Canberra: Australian National Gallery/ Sydney: Collins Australia, 1988

Roger Butler, *Australian Prints in the Australian National Gallery*, Canberra: Australian National Gallery, 1985

Andrew Sayers, *Drawing in Australia: Drawings, watercolours, pastels and collages from the 1770s to the 1980s*, Canberra: Australian National Gallery, forthcoming 1988

John McPhee, *Australian Decorative Arts in the Australian National Gallery*, Canberra: Australian National Gallery, 1982

Peter Timms, *Australian Studio Pottery & China Painting*, Melbourne: Oxford University Press, 1986

ACKNOWLEDGEMENTS

Assistance to the Exhibition and Book

ALEXANDER LIBRARY David Pike, Assistant State Librarian

ALLPORT LIBRARY & MUSEUM OF FINE ARTS, STATE LIBRARY OF TASMANIA Geoffrey Stilwell, Special Collections Librarian

ANTHROPOLOGY MUSEUM, UNIVERSITY OF QUEENSLAND Lindy Allen, Curator

ART GALLERY OF NEW SOUTH WALES Edmund Capon, Director; Barry Pearce, Curator of Australian Art; Nicholas Draffin, Curator of Prints and Drawings; Ljubo Marun, Registrar; Alan Lloyd, Conservator; Avenel Mitchell, Curatorial Assistant.

ART GALLERY OF WESTERN AUSTRALIA Elizabeth Churcher, Director; Michael A. O'Ferrall, Curator of Asian and Aboriginal Art; Erica Persak, Registrar; John Olive, Conservator; Helen Topliss, Curator of Paintings; Bruce Adams, former Curator of Paintings

THE AUSTRALIAN MUSEUM Des Griffin, Director; Ronald Lampert, Curator of Aboriginal Art; Kate Khan, Project Officer

AUSTRALIAN NATIONAL GALLERY James Mollison, Director; John McPhee, Senior Curator of Australian Art; Roger Butler, Curator of Australian Prints, Posters and Illustrated Books; Wally Caruana, Curator of Aboriginal Art; Mary Eagle, Curator, Australian Art; Helen Ennis, Curator of Photography; Andrew Sayers, Curator of Australian Drawings; Christopher Menz, Assistant Curator of Australian Decorative Arts; Tim Fisher, Curatorial Assistant, Australian Paintings & Sculptures; Andrew Durham, Conservator; Jane Hyden, Publications; Warwick Reeder, Registrar.

AUSTRALIAN WAR MEMORIAL Anne Gray, Senior Curator of Art

BENDIGO ART GALLERY David Thomas, Director; Gabrielle Nestor, Centenary Exhibition Coordinator

CITY OF BALLAARAT FINE ART GALLERY Margaret Rich, Director; Judith Rushford, Administrative Officer

CITY OF PORTLAND Mr P.K. Shanahan, Chief Executive; Ray Jones, Publicity & Promotions Officer

THE FLINDERS UNIVERSITY OF SOUTH AUSTRALIA Flinders University Art Museum, Amzad Mian, Director; Carol Cheshire, Acting Curator; Vincent Megaw, Associate Professor, Department of Visual Arts

LA TROBE COLLECTION, STATE LIBRARY OF VICTORIA Jane La Scala, State Librarian; Christine Downer, Picture Librarian

MACLEAY MUSEUM, UNIVERSITY OF SYDNEY Peter Stanbury, Director; Lydia Bushell, Curator of Anthropology

MITCHELL LIBRARY, STATE LIBRARY OF NEW SOUTH WALES Alison Crook, State Librarian; Margaret Calder, former Pictures Librarian; Elizabeth Imashev, Acting Pictures Librarian; Cheryl Evans, Rosemary Crooks, Pictures Section

MONASH UNIVERSITY GALLERY Jenepher Duncan, Director

MUSEUM OF APPLIED ARTS & SCIENCES Anne Watson, Curator of Furniture, Woodwork, Architectural & Interior Decoration

MUSEUM OF VICTORIA Robert Edwards, Director; Gael Ramsay, Curator of Donald Thomson Collection; Gaye Sculthorpe, Curator, Aboriginal Studies

MUSEUMS & ART GALLERIES OF THE NORTHERN TERRITORY Colin Jack-Hinton, Director; Margaret K.C. West, Curator of Aboriginal Art & Material Culture

NATIONAL GALLERY OF VICTORIA Rodney Wilson, Director; Patrick McCaughey, former Director; Nancy Staub, Deputy Director Programmes; Kenneth Hood, Deputy Director Collections; Geoffrey Edwards, Curator of Glass and Sculpture; Robert Lindsay, Senior Curator of Contemporary Art; Jan Minchin, Curator of Twentieth Century Australian Art; Bridget Whitelaw, Curator of Nineteenth Century Australian Art; Terry Lane, Senior Curator of Decorative Arts; Gordon Morrison, Registrar; Philip Jago, Publications Officer

NATIONAL LIBRARY OF AUSTRALIA John Thompson, Director, Australian Collections and Services; Corinne Collins, Acting Pictorial Librarian, Australian Collections and Services; Barbara Perry, Pictorial Librarian; Harry McCarthy.

NATIONAL MARITIME MUSEUM, GREENWICH Richard Ormond, Director; David Cordingly, Head, Department of Pictures; Claire Venner, Loans Officer

NATIONAL MUSEUM OF AUSTRALIA Don McMichael, Director; David Kaus, Assistant Curator

NATIONAL TRUST OF AUSTRALIA (NEW SOUTH WALES) Dinah Dysart, Director S.H. Ervin Gallery

NATIONAL TRUST OF AUSTRALIA (WESTERN AUSTRALIA) John Pickworth, Administrator

QUEENSLAND ART GALLERY Doug Hall, Director; Joe Devilee, Senior Exhibitions Officer; Bettina MacAulay, Curator of Australian Art Pre-1950; Andrew Dudley, Registrar.

ROBERT HOLMES à COURT COLLECTION Roderick Anderson, former Curator of Art; Anne Marie Brody, Curator of Art

ROYAL GEOGRAPHICAL SOCIETY, LONDON Brigadier G.R. Gathercole, Deputy Director

ROYAL SOCIETY OF VICTORIA Dr T.P. O'Brien, President; Douglas Black, Executive Officer

SHEPPARTON ART GALLERY Victoria Hammond, Director; Donald Coventry, Tim Rollason, Curators

SOUTH AUSTRALIAN MUSEUM Lester Russell, Director; Peter Sutton, Head of Anthropology; Philip Clarke, Curatorial Officer; Philip Jones, Curator of Aboriginal History; Christopher Anderson, Curator of Social Anthropology; Steve Hemming, Curator, Aboriginal History

STATE BANK VICTORIA John Gunn, Manager Special Duties

TASMANIAN MUSEUM & ART GALLERY Don Gregg, Director; Hendrik Kolenberg, Curator of Art; Julia Clark, Curator of Anthropology; Romek Pachuki, Conservator; Simon Cuthbert, Photographic Services

UNIVERSITY OF ADELAIDE Mr F.J. O'Neill, Registrar; Pamela Runge, Curator

UNIVERSITY ART MUSEUM, UNIVERSITY OF QUEENSLAND Nancy Underhill, Director; Kate Ravenswood, Curatorial Assistant

VARIOUS Candice Bruce, Bluestocking Research, Sydney; Deutscher Fine Art, Melbourne; Diane Dunbar, Curator of Art, Queen Victoria Museum & Art Gallery, Launceston, Tasmania; Kevin Fahy; J.B. Hawkins Antiques, Sydney; Horden House, Sydney; Ray Hughes Gallery, Brisbane & Sydney; Frances Lindsay, Director, Melbourne University Gallery; Rod Lucas, Bibliographer, Australian Institute for Aboriginal Studies, Canberra; Tim McCormick Australian Arts, Sydney; Joyce McGrath, Art Librarian, State Library of Victoria, Melbourne; Nevill Keating Pictures Limited, London; Stephen Rainbird; Terry Smith; Professor Virginia Spate, Power Department of Fine Art, University of Sydney; Martin Terry, Curator of Art, Australian National Maritime Museum; Father Uren, Rector, Newman College, Melbourne; Lyn Williams; Ruth Zubans, University of Melbourne; Watters Gallery, Sydney; Yuill/Crowley, Sydney

ART GALLERY OF SOUTH AUSTRALIA James Schoff, former Administrator; Christopher Johnstone, former Manager Public Programmes; Judith Hamilton-Shephard, Registrar; Jane Hylton, Associate Curator of Paintings and Sculptures; Barbara Fargher, Photographic Services; Judith Thompson, Curator of Australian Decorative Arts; Ellaine Rankin, Secretary; Eric Graves, Ian Trenerry, Installation Crew

STATE CONSERVATION CENTRE OF SOUTH AUSTRALIA Ian Cook, Director; Robert Wilmot, Senior Conservator, Paintings; Alan Phenix, Conservator, Paintings; Fred Francisco, Conservator, Art on Paper; Anne-Marie Dineen, Conservation Assistant, Art on Paper; Sarah Slade, Objects Conservator

PHOTOGRAPHIC CREDITS

Photographs of works from public institutions were supplied by the photographic departments of those institutions.

Additional photographic work was done by:

Terence Bogue, John Burgess, John Delacour, Fenn Hinchcliffe, Henry Jolles, Matt Kelso, McKenzie Gray, Clayton McWhinney, Brian Stevenson, Richard Stringer, Greg Weight, Ray Woodbury.

INDEX